INVISIBLE INK

Also by the Author

Rebellion in the Ranks: Mutinies of the American Revolution

INVISIBLE INK

SPYCRAFT OF THE
AMERICAN REVOLUTION

JOHN A. NAGY

WESTHOLME
Yardley

Westholme Publishing, LLC
Eight Harvey Avenue
Yardley, Pennsylvania 19067

Visit our Web site at www.westholmepublishing.com

First Printing November 2009
10 9 8 7 6 5 4 3 2 1

ISBN: 978-1-59416-097-4

Printed in United States of America

On the book jacket: A rebus letter "America to her Mistaken Mother," published by Mary Darly, London, May 11, 1778. In a rebus, small pictures replace letters in words making a puzzle for the reader to solve. It was a popular form of entertainment in the eighteenth century. This letter was written in response to another rebus letter entitled "Britannia to America," a plea from Great Britain to America to reconsider its alliance with France and to accept the terms of peace that Britain sent to America with the Carlisle Commission. An Indian princess was commonly used in eighteenth-century prints to represent America. She is holding the new American flag and a fleur-de-lis which symbolizes France. The five children in the letter is a reference to the Carlisle Commissioners. The rebus reads:

(America) (toe) her (miss)taken (moth)er.

(Yew) s(eye)lly (old woman) t(hat) (yew) have sent a (lure) (toe) us is very (plain) (toe) draw our at(ten)t(eye)[attention] on from our re(awl) (eye)ntrests (butt) we are determ(eye)n'd (toe) ab(eye)de by our own ways of the th(eye)nk(eye)ng [thinking]. (Ewer) (five) (child)ren (yew) have sent (toe) us sh(awl) (bee) treated as V(eye)s(eye)tors, & safely sent home aga(eye)n. (Yew) may (console)t them & adm(eye)re them, (butt) (yew) must (knot) (x)pect (one) of (ewer)(puppet)s w(eye)ll (comb) home (toe) (yew) as sweet as (yew) sent h(eye)m twas cruel (toe) send so pretty a (man) so many 1000 miles & (toe) have the fat(eye)gue of re(urn)ing (back) after (spike)(eye)ng h(eye)s (coat) & d(eye)rt(eye)ng [dirtying] t(hose) red (heel) (shoes). (Eye)f (yew) are w(eye)(eye) [wise] follow (ewer) own ad(vice) (yew) gave (toe) me take home (ewer) (ships) sold(eye)(ears) [soldiers] guard (well) (ewer) own tr(eye)fl(eye)(ling) [trifling] & leave me (toe) my self as (eye) am at age (toe) know my own (eye)ntrests. W(eye)thout (ewer) (fool)(eye)sh ad(vice) & know t(hat) (eye) sh(awl) (awl)ways regard (yew) & my Brothers as relat(eye)ons (butt) (knot) as fr(eye)ends.

(Eye) am (ever) (great)ly (eye)njured.

Daughter Amer(eye)k.

To Ida Marie Nagy, Jennifer Ann Nagy, and Lisa Marie Nagy, with thanks for your encouragement, help, and patience

To the memory of my sister Linda Susan Joan Nagy-Chizmarik

CONTENTS

List of Illustrations

INTRODUCTION

*Knowledge of the spirit world is to be obtained by divination; information
in natural science may be sought by inductive reasoning; the laws of the
universe can be verified by mathematical calculation: but the dispositions
of an enemy are ascertainable through spies and spies alone.* —Mei Yao-
ch'en, Chinese poet and military commentator, c. 1050 A.D.

The need to cultivate the use of spies and the information they
acquire has been known throughout the ages. Sun Tzu, a great
Chinese military general, wrote in the 6th century B.C. that "to
remain in ignorance of the enemy's condition simply because one
grudges the outlay of a hundred ounces of silver in honors and emol-
uments [for spies], is the height of inhumanity. One who acts thus is
no leader of men, no present help to his sovereign, [and] no master of
victory."[1] He believed that a successful general needs the knowledge
of the enemy's dispositions and what he intends to do. Sun Tzu
believed that this knowledge "can only be obtained from other men."[2]
Chia Lin says that an army without spies is like a man without ears or
eyes.[3]

General Sun Tzu classified spies into five classes: (1) local spies;
(2) inward spies; (3) converted spies; (4) doomed spies; and (5) surviving spies. He defined "local spies" as using the services of the local residents. His "inward spies" are the "officials of the enemy." These
inward spies are clearly explained by Tu Mu, a Chinese military
expert of the Tang dynasty. Tu Mu recommends finding "worthy men
who have been degraded from office, criminals who have undergone
punishment; also, favorite concubines who are greedy for gold, men
who are aggrieved at being in subordinate positions, or who have been
passed over in the distribution of posts... Officials of these several
kinds, should be secretly approached and bound to one's interests by
means of rich presents. In this way you will be able to find out the
state of affairs in the enemy's country, ascertain the plans that are
being formed against you, and moreover disturb the harmony and cre-

ate a breach between the sovereign and his ministers."[4] However, one must always be cautious of the information acquired by inward spies, as the spy's information may be a deception. British General and Governor of Quebec Guy Carleton was having a problem separating the intelligence wheat from the chaff. He sent a report to British Colonial Secretary Lord George Germain that acknowledged the best accounts are mixed with lies.[5] Even in the eighteenth century, this was not the way to impress your boss.

Sun Tzu's category of "converted spies" is for the double agents who are really working for you. Both Sun Tzu and George Washington believed that a spy could be turned to the side that pays more. Henri de La Tour d'Auvergne, Viscount de Turenne, whom Napoleon called the greatest military leader in history, gives an insight on the treatment of spies.[6] He said, "Spies are attached to those who give them [the] most, he who pays them ill is never served. They should never be known to anybody; nor should they know one another. When they propose anything very material, secure their persons, or have in your possession their wives and children as hostages for their fidelity. Never communicate anything to them but what is absolutely necessary that they should know."[7]

The nature of the American Revolution provided ample motivation for both inner and converted spies. Besides attempting to secure independence from Great Britain, the American Revolution also became a civil war between the patriots and the loyalists. It was a war between brothers as well as fathers and sons. We are all familiar with stories of how patriots tarred and feathered some rascally loyalist, but we forget that the loyalists also threatened the rebels. Charles Pettit writing to Joseph Reed in July 1775 mentioned that in Perth Amboy, New Jersey, which had a large number of loyalists, "a Whig [nonloyalist] was the object of abuse wherever he went."[8] People were forced to take sides. A civil war certainly added to the motivation for individuals to spy on their enemy and help their own cause.

However, the deception game can be played by discovering the spy and feeding him or her false reports which they bring back and swear as being accurate. A "doomed spy" is a person doing things in the open for the purposes of deception. Tu Yu gives a good exposition of the meaning: "We ostentatiously do thing[s] calculated to deceive our own spies, who must be led to believe that they have been unwittingly disclosed. Then, when these spies are captured in the enemy's lines, they will make an entirely false report, and the enemy will take measures accordingly, only to find that we do something quite different. The spies will thereupon be put to death." In some cases in China when the enemy realized he was deceived, the unfortunate envoy was boiled alive.[9]

"Surviving spies" are those who bring back information from inside the enemy's camp. Tu Mu described the qualifications needed for the job. "Your surviving spy must be a man of keen intellect, though in outward appearance a fool; of shabby exterior, but with a will of iron. He must be active, robust, endowed with physical strength and courage; thoroughly accustomed to all sorts of dirty work, able to endure hunger and cold, and to put up with shame and ignominy."

The word "spy" encompassed several different situations during the American Revolution. It definitely included the person who in nonmilitary clothing went secretly behind enemy lines to bring back intelligence. But it was also used to describe activities conducted by persons in front of the enemy's lines rather than behind. In North Carolina, for example, individuals, who may or may not have been in uniform, who were sent to destroy bridges that were in the path of the British army were called spies.[10] On the Western frontier and in upstate New York the word "spy" also included people whose job we would think of as a scout or part of an advance patrol. Colonel Daniel Brodhead of the 8th Pennsylvania Regiment defined a frontier spy as someone who "must act with great caution by covering or otherwise defacing their footsteps and keeping off frequented paths in daytime and only use the path at night."[11] For example Colonel John Floyd wrote to Colonel William Preston on December 8, 1780, from Beargrass about their scouts: "Our spies returned a few days ago from the Miamia but made no discovery of a number of Indians who it was said were on their march to attack the fort at the Falls [Louisville, Kentucky]."[12] Francis Allison, Jr., writing from Sunbury, Pennsylvania, to Governor Reed on July 28, 1779, discusses spies. Three of the garrison of Freeland's Fort were killed and scalped within sixty yards of the fort and two others taken prisoners. Allison says the spies saw a large number of Indians with some redcoated British regulars. They never went into the Indian camp but observed it from a distance.[13] George Washington and Major Henry Lee wrote to each other concerning lookouts along New York's Hudson River and referred to them as spies.[14] Lookouts on the frontier were also called "Indian Spies" or "Spy Guards."[15] This book will not concern itself with military personnel, scouts, gathering reconnaissance information.

In the eighteenth century, military intelligence was often obtained from deserters, captured mail, agents sent on specific spying missions, loyalists, runaway slaves, and revolutionaries who were willing to help the cause by providing what they knew. Information was collected from wherever it could be obtained, although there are examples where the source cannot be verified, as with Murphy Steel of the Black Pioneers who claimed to have received his information from the highest source; that is, directly from God.[16] Information from deserters if obtained quickly would provide a quick insight into the enemy's position. It did not take very long for deserters to cross over to the other side as they were highly motivated to vacate the area. For example, George James was an African American servant of Captain Elijah Wadsworth, regimental quartermaster of Colonel Elisha Sheldon's 2nd Regiment of Continental Light Dragoons. At 9 a.m. on July 13, 1781, James left the American camp and on the 14th was providing the British with information.[17]

Intelligence could be obtained by soldiers who were released on parole. A parole was a promise given by a prisoner of war that when he was unconstrained he would not bear arms or participate in the war until he was exchanged.[18] Not all soldiers kept their word of honor. Captain Hankes had traveled on his parole in February 1779 from Elizabeth Town, New Jersey, to Staten Island, New York, under a flag of truce and picked up information along the way on American General William Maxwell's troops.[19] This was not an isolated occurrence as both sides played this game of ignoring the full extent of the parole. Alexander Phillips complained to Sir Henry Clinton on October 3, 1781, that "others . . . are sent from here [New York City] on parole make an excuse to return here to answer their paroles and get what intelligence they can of your Excellency from us and then return to the rebels."[20]

Additionally intelligence was collected by the Commissary of Prisoners. Both sides had individuals assigned to provide for their soldiers and sailors that were being held captive by the other side. Loyalist Brigadier General Cortland Skinner advised that "the rebel

Commissary [General of Prisoners Abraham] Skinner has given every information and will as often as admitted to come to N[ew] York and that Colonel [Matthais] Ogden [of the 1st New Jersey Regiment] now on parole, brought every intelligence and still collects it, notwithstanding his word is given to the contrary."[21]

Flags of truce were used on many occasions to obtain information by both American and British interests. Vice Admiral Richard Howe on the ship *Eagle* off Sandy Hook wrote to General Sir Henry Clinton forwarding instructions which he had received as a circular from Lord George Germain dated at Whitehall on February 19, 1778. It stated the King wanted Clinton to print two legislative bills from the House of Commons and "to embrace every opportunity of circulating them by Flags of Truce or private persons among the rebel troops."[22] Because of American Flags of Truce arriving on frivolous reasons from Connecticut, British Major General Robert Pigot, Commandant of New York City issued an order on June 7, 1777 that "no Flags of Truce are permitted to land anybody, have any intercourse with the troops or inhabitants but be obliged to return from whence they came."[23] The situation had gotten so bad that both sides restricted the locations where they would accept flags of truce. The British would only accept flags at Staten Island, Paulus Hook, Kingsbridge, Morrisania, and those places on Long Island that were designated by Oliver De Lancey.[24]

The world of a spy is as mysterious as the tricks of a magician. A magician performs his or her illusions before the view of an audience but must not give away the means by which the trick is performed. Spies must be able to accomplish their missions while hiding in both the shadows and bright sunlight and they dare not reveal their true identity for to do so could be fatal.

Those who had not performed their craft successfully usually met their demise. During the eighteenth century under normal circumstances, execution by firing squad was for a gentleman who had committed a crime, but a gentleman would never be a spy. For spies it was either death by hanging like a common thief or death by disease and deprivation in the hold of a prison ship.

In order to keep things secret, spies were given access to the latest technology of their day and they used it. Generals used deception to aid and to deceive both spies and the enemy. The 2004 movie

National Treasure displayed several of the secret methods available in the eighteenth century such as the message written on the back of the Declaration of Independence in invisible ink.[25] Another method used in the movie involved selecting the upper case letters of a passage in the Silence Dogood letters (written by Benjamin Franklin using an alias) to form a message.

Within these pages the tricks accomplished by those magicians known as spies who performed during the American Revolution will be revealed. This book will be concerned with clandestine operations conducted by spies and the craft they used to accomplish their missions. It will give cursory insight into the large number of codes and ciphers used for diplomatic correspondence. A few individuals were involved in both spy activities and diplomatic correspondence. In those cases, such as James Lovell, some diplomatic ciphers show the depth of his knowledge of the subject.[26]

I have included examples of what was known and available for use during the American Revolution. I have also included different usages of spy technology from Benedict Arnold's correspondence with British headquarters and the messages of the American Culper spy ring. These examples were chosen because they are the most documented. Spies who operated over short distances and traveled between the lines did not need to consistently record their reports as they could provide verbal depositions. Because both were conducted over long distances and required the use of intermediaries to deliver the messages, the correspondence had to be accomplished in writing, leaving us a rich record. Both American and British forces used spycraft to gain an advantage over the other. George Washington's better military application of the intelligence gathered and disinformation dispensed proved key to the eventual American victory.

Chapter 1

EARLY SPYCRAFT: CODES, CIPHERS, AND STEGANOGRAPHY

Spies have been around forever and have always used the latest tools to aid their mission. Codes and ciphers are among their earliest tools. In a code, a number or character represents entire words and requires that both the sender and the receiver have identical numerical listings, such as a codebook. A familiar code is the United States Postal Service's Zip Code system. A cipher uses a letter to represent another letter. Ciphers can be traced back to the substitutions made for proper names in the cuneiform writing of the Sumerians, the hieroglyphics of ancient Egypt, and the Mayan civilization. The oldest codebook, from Susa in present-day Iran, is a cuneiform tablet with a list of numbers in one column and its cuneiform signs in an adjacent column. Hebrew scribes writing down the book of Jeremiah used a reversed alphabet simple substitution cipher known as the Atbash cipher. It splits the alphabet into two equal halves and substitutes the first letter of the alphabet for the last and the second letter for the second to last, etc. Many names of people and places are believed to have been deliberately obscured in the Hebrew Bible using the Atbash cipher.

The Spartans of early Greece were the first to use cryptography in military operations in the fifth century B.C. using two cylinders of equal size. One cylinder was retained by the headquarters and the other given to the general going into battle. A slip of parchment, inscribed by being wrapped around the cylinder, is then sent to the

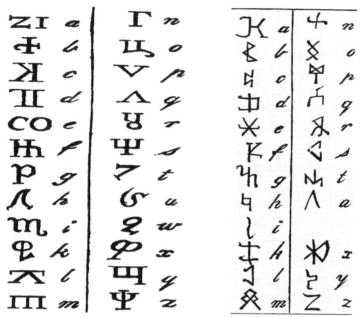

The cipher charts of Charlemagne (left) and King Alfred the Great (right). Neither contain the letters J and V, while Alfred's also lacks W. (*From Henfrey, English Mechanic and World of Science, January 13, 1871*)

general in the field. The commander takes the parchment, wraps it around the cylinder, and sees the message by reading down the cylinder.[1] This method was still being used in seventeenth-century England.[2]

Both Charlemagne and Alfred the Great of Wessex used substitution ciphers for secret communications. In the ninth century Rabanus Maurus, Abbot of Fulda and Archbishop of Mayence, used a cipher that replaced the vowels with dots. It used one dot for "i," two dots for "a," three dots for "e," four dots for "o," and five dots for "u."[3] One of the weaknesses of a single or mono-alphabetic substitution, however, is that every letter in the plaintext message is represented by another letter, and always the same letter. A cipher used in Venice in 1411 improved upon earlier substitution ciphers by employing arbitrary symbols, multiple equivalents for vowels, and nulls.[4]

Leon Battista Alberti, whom many people consider the quintessential Renaissance man, invented the cipher disk and cryptographic key

in 1466. Alberti's cipher disk was polyalpha-
betic, meaning that a new alphabet could be
created each time by turning the disk. It consisted of a fixed outer disk containing the
plain text and a movable inner disk with the
corresponding cipher text. To encipher a message you have to decide on the starting position of the inner disc; this forms part of the
key. The other part of the key is a rule for the
movement of the inner disk; for example, it
could be moved nine positions counterclock-
wise every fourth letter. Alberti's disc had
twenty-four positions containing twenty letters and four numbers in the outer disk. The
numbers could represent anything decided
between the users—letters or words. His system thus allowed the use of codes.[5]

Statue of Leon Battista
Alberti (1404–72) in
the Uffizi Gallery,
Florence, Italy.

The first printed book on cryptology, the
science of analyzing and deciphering codes
and ciphers, was *Polygraphiae* written by
Abbott Johannes Trithemius at the Abbey of Saint Jacob in Würzburg
and published in 1518. The second book, *Opus Novum*, followed in
1526. It was written by Jacopo Silvestri, who may have been a cipher
clerk at the Vatican. These were followed by *Subtilitas de Subtilitate
Rerum* (The Subtlety of Matter) in 1554 by Girolamo Cardano, the
first cryptologist to propose the autokey method of encipherment. He
also became famous for the Cardano grille, a sheet of stiff material
with irregularly spaced rectangular holes which was placed over the
writing paper. The secret message was then written in the holes, the
grille or mask was removed from the writing paper, and a harmless
message was filled in around the secret message to camouflage its
being there. To read the message, an identical grille or mask was
placed over the writing. A major fault in the system was the awkward-
ness in phrasing the surrounding message often led to suspicions of a
secret message within. Cardano grilles or masks are in the General Sir
Henry Clinton Papers from the American Revolution.[6]

John Wilkins in his book *Mercury, or the Secret and Swift
Messenger* published in 1641 reminds us that the letters of the alpha-

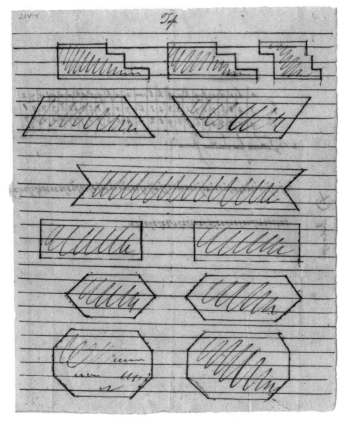

One of several Cardano grilles or masks from the General Sir Henry Clinton Papers at the William L. Clements Library at the University of Michigan. (*CP 234:4 William L. Clements Library*)

bet we use for a word really represent an idea. By the use of a different language the same idea is represented by a different combination of letters. The use of ciphers is just a different language used to represent the same idea.[7] Wilkins told of many of the uses of secret writing at this early period. In this first English-language book on cryptography, he tells about the use of codes and ciphers that used double alphabets, hieroglyphics, musical notes, the Bible, and the transposition of letters and words. Also in use at the time were abbreviations, dropping letters, adding extra letters, and invisible inks.[8]

Antoine Rossignol and his son Bonaventure developed the "Great Cipher" after 1626 to encrypt Louis XIV's most secret documents. In the Great Cipher each of 587 numbers stood for a French syllable rather than a single letter. It also used codes to instruct the decoder to ignore the previous section. It was not broken until around 1893 when Commandant Etienne Bazeries, who worked at the French Ministry of Foreign Affairs Sales Office, realized that each number stood for a French syllable. He broke the code when he realized a particular sequence of numbers 124, 22, 125, 46, and 345 stood for *les ennemis,* that is, the enemies.

The British House of Lords was sufficiently familiar with ciphers that it allowed the introduction of deciphered writings in the 1723 trial of Bishop Francis Atterbury.[9]

Shorthand is another cipher that had been around for quite some time. The first work in shorthand written in English was by Dr. Timothy Bright in 1586 when he wrote the Book of Titus in what was called "charactery." In 1588 he published *Characterie: An Arte of Shorte, Swifte, and Secrete Writing by Character.*[10] Many books, such as *La Plume Volante: The Flying Pen-Man or the Art of Short Writing* by William Hopkins in 1674, were in common use in England a long time before the American Revolution. The Marquis of Worcester's book *A Century of the Names and Scantlings of Such Inventions* with its sections on ciphers had been printed five times before the American Revolution and twice during the war.[11] *A Century of the Names* and other shorthand writing books would have been readily available to anyone interested. British General Sir Henry Clinton used his own version of shorthand for his personal notes to keep them from inquisitive eyes. He even devised a different shorthand system for filing his documents.[12] Shorthand has progressed from the nonletter forms to text messages as LOL (laugh out loud) and CU (see you).

John Wilkins stated the obvious, that any writing to remain a secret must be devoid of suspicion and difficult to interpret.[13] Once detected, a message may be interpreted, but if it can remain hidden, it cannot be deciphered. Under Queen Elizabeth I, Sir Francis Walsingham set up an elaborate intelligence system. In 1586, his operatives intercepted a coded correspondence between Mary Queen of Scots and Anthony Babington. The correspondence when deciphered by Thomas Phelippes exposed her involvement in Anthony Babington's plot to murder Elizabeth. What made the discovery special was not the coded correspondence itself but the fact that the messages were hidden inside a beer barrel bung to make their detection even harder. Indeed, the beer barrels were allowed to pass into Mary's prison. The art of hiding a message in such a way that no one but the sender and the intended receiver knows of its existence is called steganography. Today the term would include the hiding of messages in digital computer files and images.

Steganography is an important feature of secret communications, because while a cipher or code hides the meaning of a message, it does not conceal the fact that a message exists. Steganography does not necessarily have to involve a code or cipher, however. For instance, Histiaeus while at the Persian court wanted to send a message to Aristagoras, who was in Greece to instigate a revolt. Histiaeus shaved the head of his most trusted slave and tattooed a message there. When the slave's hair grew back, he was sent to deliver the message. When the messenger arrived, Aristagoras was to shave his head and reveal the message.[14]

Another example occurred during the English Civil War. Royalist Sir John Trevanion was being held in Colchester Castle awaiting his execution. He was saved by a letter from a friend. It read:

> Worthie Sir John—Hope, that is ye beste comfort of ye afflictyd, cannot much, I fear me, help you now. That I wolde saye to you, is this only: if ever I may be able to requite that I do owe you, stand not upon asking of me. 'Tis not much I can do: but what I can do, bee you verie sure I wille. I knowe that, if dethe comes, if ordinary men fear it, it frights not you, accounting it for a high honour, to have such a rewarde of your loyalty. Pray yet that you may be spared this soe bitter, cup. I fear not that you will grudge any sufferings: only if bie submission you can turn them away, 'tis the part of a wise man. Tell me, an if you can, to do for you any thinge that you wolde have done. The general goes back Wednesday. Restinge your servant to command.
>
> R.T.

The letter contained a secret message. By taking the third letter after each punctuation mark, a message is revealed. It reads, "Panel at east end of chapel slides." After his petition to his jailers to pray in the chapel was granted, he made his escape through the moveable panel.[15]

In the fifteenth century Italian scientist Giovanni Porta described how to conceal a message in a hard-boiled egg. An ink is made with an ounce of alum and a pint of vinegar. This special penetrating ink is then used to write on the hard boiled egg shell. The solution penetrates the shell leaving no visible trace and is deposited on the surfaced of the hardened egg. When the shell is removed, the message can be read.

The use of invisible ink between the lines of visible writing is another example of steganography. As far back as the first century AD, Pliny the Elder explained how the "milk" of the thithymallus plant could be used as an invisible ink. Although transparent after drying, the ink turns brown upon gentle heating. Many organic fluids behave in a similar way, because they are rich in carbon and therefore char easily. Indeed, it was not unknown for twentieth-century spies who ran out of manufactured invisible ink to improvise using their own urine.

Steganography, hiding a message in such a way that it is apparent to no one but the sender and the intended receiver, has a distinct advantage over cryptography, which hides the meaning of a message but does not conceal that a message exists. Truly secret messages do not attract attention to themselves, to the messengers, or to the recipients. A visible coded message will arouse suspicion and may in itself be incriminating.

The Spanish at San Roque, a high point near Gibraltar, used a system of fire lights to convey messages of the number of warships anchored in the Bay of Gibraltar and the number that sailed away to the Governor of Cádiz. "The lights they did show, and the distance of time between each light or lights" represented the alphabet. They also used the lights to signify numbers. When the entire fleet was involved, one constant fire was maintained.[16]

In the eighteenth century each general ran his own intelligence service. Any military officer on a general's staff or someone intent on moving up the ranks needed to know at least the basics of cryptography and steganography. Codes and ciphers were not an unknown subject. Businessmen needed to converse secretly with each other and their agents. Affairs of the heart also needed some privacy as letters passed through the hands of travelers who carried them to their destinations. John and Mary Winthrop of Massachusetts, for instance, corresponded before 1700 in a private cipher regarding intimate matters.[17] A young Thomas Jefferson kept his courting of Rebecca Burwell veiled in his correspondence with John Page.[18] Secret writing was not just a man's practice. Catherine W. Livingston writing to Sarah Livingston Jay used a cipher in parts of her letter of July 10, 1780, to keep it from prying eyes.[19]

But the effectiveness of each intelligence operation varied greatly due to the skill of the spies and the general running the operation. Prior to George Washington taking command of the assembled troops at Boston, the American intelligence system was, as expected, a decentralized operation. Various self-appointed groups would gather what information they thought might be useful. Each group had its own leader but no central keystone to direct its operations. It was intelligence by committee. The closest person to a central clearinghouse for the collected information in Boston at the time was Dr. Joseph Warren.

As with higher commanders of the period, General George Washington personally established and then controlled his own military intelligence service.[20] He did use case agents to control groups of spies in the field. Although he knew of operators in the field he did not always know the names of the individual spies working for his case agents. He knew the importance of secrecy and scolded his case agents when they became careless. Going back to his early career, twenty-three-year-old George Washington had served in the French and Indian War under British Major General Edward Braddock, who had use of a cipher, but it is not known if Washington had any experience with it.[21] Washington's expense account for military service during the American Revolution recorded expenditures for military intelligence of $7,617 (dollars) and $55,145 lawful money (originally paid in state or foreign currency but converted to United States dollars).[22]

Washington's adept selection of spy methods and ability to exploit British vulnerabilities to deception would be crucial in the Revolutionary War.

Chapter 2

SECRET COMMUNICATION

All generals need to know the plans of the enemy. They want to know the quantity and types of supplies available and distributed, which will tell them if the troops assembling and embarking are real or a deception. The need for secrecy in transmitting this intelligence is of the utmost importance. As a result, in a variety of ways— on paper, as artwork, through the air itself, and in person—messages are conveyed in complete confidence.

Many spies during the American Revolution used code names to hide their real identity when sending in their reports in case their correspondence went astray. Some just used their initials or their initials in reverse order. Using one's initials was not ideal, but it was better than having one's full name on treasonous documents. Andrew Fürstner, for example, was a farmer from Lancaster County, Pennsylvania, who used his initials A.F. as a courier between his brother-in-law William Rankin and British headquarters in New York City. He also carried at least one of Benedict Arnold's letters to New York City for Joseph Stansbury. Daniel Martin, a British spy, used the code letters M.D. when he wrote from Chatham, New Jersey, on June 17, 1780 to Hessian General Baron Wilhelm von Knyphausen,[1] and while writing from his hometown of Paramus, New Jersey, on July 3, 1780, to British General Sir Henry Clinton, he used the code letters D.M.[2]

Instead of using initials, some spies who wanted more secrecy about their activities used a fictitious name. Abraham Bancker, an American spy operating on Staten Island and in New York City, used the code name "Amicus Republicae."[3] Irish-born Dr. George Smith, who was the main British spy in Albany, New York, used the cover names of Hudibras, "B," and "Captain B." His son, Terance Smith, naturally was Little Hudibras. Benedict Arnold used the name of Monk (a reference to Scottish General George Monk who was Oliver Cromwell's loyal deputy in Scotland).[4] Arnold's accomplice Joseph Stansbury used Paliwoledash as well as Jonathan Stevens as his code names. Lieutenant Colonel Nisbet Balfour of the 23rd Regiment of Foot called himself "Mr. Turner" when he wrote on April 22, 1780, to General Sir Henry Clinton, whom he addressed as "Uncle."[5]

Even with code names or using initials to conceal their identities, spies and those who wished to transfer secret information had to figure out effective methods. One of the most unusual methods of transferring information was employed by Margaret Moncrieffe, a teenager.[6]

Captain James Moncrieffe, twice widowed, had been sent to Staten Island to be with the British army, which was consolidating its forces there and preparing to attack the Americans on Long Island. His thirteen-year-old daughter, Margaret, wrote to General Putnam in New York City asking to go to Staten Island to be with her father. (She had taken refuge in the household of New Jersey Governor William Livingston, her first stepmother's brother.)[7] Putnam had Colonel Webb, his aide-de-camp, fetch Margaret from Elizabeth Town and bring her to New York City to stay with his family at 1 Broadway, which was also his headquarters, until arrangements could be made.[8] Margaret enjoyed going to the gallery on top of the house where she viewed Upper New York Harbor and its surrounds with a telescope.[9] A flag of truce arrived from now Major Moncrieffe requesting his daughter. Margaret wrote that General George Washington refused to allow her to leave and he stated that she should remain a hostage for her father's good behavior.[10]

Major Aaron Burr had noticed "as he was looking over her shoulder one day at General Putnam's headquarters," that, "[w]hile she was painting a bouquet, the suspicion darted into his mind that she was using the 'language of the flowers' for the purpose of conveying intelligence to the enemy."[11] The "Language of Flowers" is mentioned in the fable "The Rose and Butterfly" published in 1732.[12] Jean Baptiste de Boyer Argens wrote in 1765 that a "nosegay made in a certain manner contains as many...ideas, as could be thrown into a letter of eight pages in length."[13] Burr informed General Washington, who had

Margaret removed to the quarters of General Thomas Mifflin at King's Bridge at the northern end of York Island (now Manhattan).[14]

The Americans also used some unusual means to relay messages. During the British occupation of Boston the Americans needed a way to communicate with the outside world. The city in the eighteenth century was a peninsula with a very narrow land connection, where British troops were stationed, restricting traffic and messages going in and out. The most famous message sent from Boston was by means of lanthorns (lanterns) hung in the North Church steeple. Second Lieutenant Colonel William Conant of the 1st Middlesex County Militia, Paul Revere, and some other gentleman on April 16, 1775, devised the system that if the British went out of Boston by water, two lanthorns would show on the steeple, and if by land over Boston Neck, then one lanthorn was the signal.[15] Captain John Pulling and Robert Newman, sexton of Christ Church, reportedly hung the lanthorns that started Paul Revere and others on their famous rides through the Massachusetts countryside warning of the British approach.[16]

A letter from Boston reported in a London newspaper that American spies in Boston were sending information out of the city by "making signals by night with gunpowder, and at day, out of church steeples." The letter stated that three people were arrested, and they admitted they had been sending signals for the previous seven days.[17] At this time, it was common to kill flies using gunpowder, and the evidence suggests that the conspirators were exploding gunpowder, ostensibly to kill flies, in such a pattern as to send signals to the American army.[18]

Another type of secret correspondence was the use of masks. This method had been around since at least 1556 when Dr. Girolamo Cardano published a cipher system that employed masks to reveal hidden letters.[19] The secret message would be revealed when the correct mask was placed over the letter, blocking out unwanted words or letters.

There are several dumbbell masks (the eighteenth-century term, which today we call an hourglass) among the Clinton papers at the William Clements Library.[20] General Clinton also used a mask with a rectangle cut in different sections of the page. Masks were used by the British but apparently not by Americans during the Revolution. Sir Henry Clinton used this method in his personal correspondence.

William Phillips wrote to Clinton from Bath, England, in January 1776 that he had received Clinton's letter. Phillips who was a close personal friend advised that he is "in the country and without the Cypher Paper. I hast much difficulty in making it out, and still more you have combined the secret part so very well with the letter that I was some time, and not till several readings, ere I found there was a secret centre."[21]

General Clinton sent a message to Major General John Burgoyne hidden in a dumbbell mask on August 10, 1777, detailing General Howe's movements toward Philadelphia. The letter read as follows: "Sir W. Howe is gone to the Chesapeake bay with the greatest part of the army. I hear he is landed but I am not certain. I am left to command here with too small a force to make an effectual diversion in your favor. I shall try something at any rate. It may be of use to you. I owe to you I think Sr. Ws [Sir William Howe's] move just at this time the worst he could take."[22]

General John Burgoyne wanted the British army in New York City to make a move in his direction and get to Albany as was planned. Burgoyne used a masked letter when he wrote to General Sir Henry Clinton on September 21, 1777, and on the 23rd asked Clinton to attack Fort Montgomery.[23] Burgoyne sent Daniel Taylor on a return trip to General Clinton in New York City. Burgoyne followed Taylor by sending Captain Thomas Scott of the 53rd Regiment of Foot and Captain Alexander Campbell of the 62nd Regiment of Foot the following night, September 27. Taylor was the first to arrive. The messages encouraged Clinton to attack Fort Montgomery: "Have lost the old cipher, but being sure from the tenor of your letter you ment it so to be read, I have made it out—An attack, or even the menace of an attack, upon Fort Montgomery, must be of great use, as it will draw away a part of their force, and I will follow them close. Do it my dear friend directly."[24]

Among Clinton's papers was a letter cut in five shapes as a puzzle. There is no information as to how the document was sent. Unfortunately only four pieces survive; the recipient would need all the pieces to complete the letter.[25]

Secret writing was not always necessary. Because of the proximity of New Jersey to New York City and Staten Island, spies were able to move freely between the lines. Major General James Pattison,

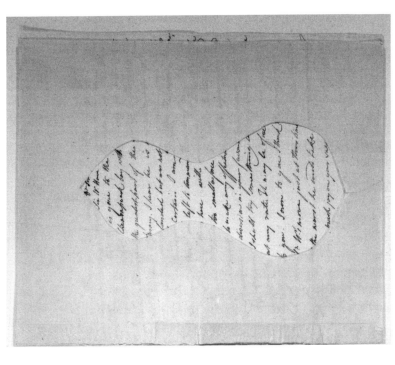

Another of the masks from the General Sir Henry Clinton Papers. This letter contains the secret message of August 10, 1777, right, from General Clinton to General John Burgoyne that General Sir William Howe went to the Chesapeake. (*William L. Clements Library*)

Commandant of the City and Garrison of New York, advised Brigadier General James Patterson, commanding on Staten Island, that "Communication between this City [New York City] and the Jerseys to a certain degree I apprehend to be unavoidable." He says that "every precaution used to prevent improper persons from obtaining passports, by granting none but on the application or recommendations of known or supposed friends of government" must be observed. His secretary maintained a register book which contained the passes granted. Major General Pattison found that people were having a hard time making their way from Elizabeth Town to Staten Island to New York. Mrs. Asseley and her daughter, Mrs. McGillop, who had an old pass, took fifteen months to make the journey and finally came across in a canoe to Staten Island without their pass. Patterson was of the opinion that allowing people to pass and return "to and from Staten Island opens a channel for intelligence from your post." His solution was to establish a flag of truce vessel to go weekly from New York City to Elizabeth Town, "for the purpose of carrying such persons to and from that place as may be though expedient to give permission."[26] However, it did little to slow the movement of spies onto and through Staten Island.

Spies would pass the lines disguised as smugglers to hide their true purpose. Because of this ease of movement, many of their reports would have been delivered verbally in person. Their access is demonstrated by the amount of smuggling as reported by Lieutenant Lewis J. Costigan of the 1st New Jersey Regiment, who was agent "Z" in New York City, to General George Washington dated December 7, 1778.[27] "The species of provisions especially fresh in great plenty except bread." He advised as to the extent of illegal trade that was carried out by just the citizens of the Shrewsbury area of Monmouth County, New Jersey. They supplied New York City that year with "not less than one thousand sheep, five hundred hogs, and eight hundred quarters or up-wards of good beef, a large parcel of cheese besides poultry."[28]

The punishment for going across the lines into New York was in many cases just a fine. For example, in a special session of Oyer and Terminer court that was held at Monmouth Court House (Freehold), New Jersey, on July 27, 1779, Jacob Burge of Middletown, New Jersey, was charged with going to New York on June 10, 1778, without a pass. He admitted the offense and was fined £150.[29] Also at a session of court for Monmouth County in July 1779, James Cook, yeoman of Shrewsbury, New Jersey, was charged with going over to New York City on March 10, 1778. He pled guilty and received a fine of £30.[30]

This all happened despite or even possibly with the cooperation of Major Richard Howell of the 2nd New Jersey Regiment and a small patrol who from August to October 1778 were stationed at Black Point to stop this illegal trade.[31] Washington had become concerned about the conduct of Howell and his men; he wrote to Lord Stirling on October 21, that "some instances of commerce between the inhabitants and the enemy . . . may have been tolerated." Washington further instructed Lord Stirling to investigate the situation and told him, "if you discover any improper connivance, or concurrence on the part of the officers at Shrewsbury, that you will take proper measures not only to prevent it in future, but to punish the past."[32]

Washington and the continental army were never able to stop the smuggling between New Jersey and New York, and the problem escalated as the war continued. When General Sir Guy Carleton in 1782 took over command from General Sir Henry Clinton, the British navy blockaded the Delaware River. This resulted in an increase in the illegal trade with New York. The New Jersey areas that bordered New York from Bergen County south through Monmouth County were not well guarded and it was very easy to bypass the military patrols. General Washington attempted to ban people with passes from crossing beyond the lines except at Dobbs Ferry, New York, by the issuance of an order on May 10, 1782, that all communications with the British were to be made through Dobbs Ferry. However, the ban was not successful. Neither side really wanted to end the practice of smuggling as it provided a cover story for spies who crossed the lines. Loyalist Brigadier General Cortland Skinner mentioned that Captain Thomas Ward in the King's Militia Volunteers was carrying cloth between the lines.[33]

Farther north, smuggling was a constant source of problems for both Connecticut and Rhode Island where there was a significant amount of British clandestine traffic across Long Island Sound. Walter Bates of Stamford, Connecticut, relates that in 1778 his brother and "hundreds of others" passed by night over to Lloyd's Neck, north of Huntington, Long Island, New York.[34] Pilots like John Ketchum of Norwalk and John Gable of Glastonbury directed transportation across Long Island Sound. Azariah Pritchard of Derby claimed to have landed at least 160 persons on the opposite shore on Long Island from Milford Bay in 1776 and 1777.[35]

Caleb Brewster from Fairfield wrote to George Washington on February 14, 1781, "there is a constant communication kept up for trade and intelligence by the enemy boats, bringing over goods and taking provisions in return." Brewster had just captured such a boat and was sending the following prisoners: "Joseph Easton Trowbridge, Capt. of the Boat, Henry Gibbs, Benjamin Prescott: These three are from New Haven and have been condemned to the mines for illicit trade but broke gaol [jail]. James Smith, Capt. of the King's Militia Volunteers. From the Block House on Tredwells Banks are Thomas Davis, Thomas Wilson, Christopher Young, and Job Mosier."[36]

The British in Newport were also having their problems with illegal contraband getting into the city. General William Howe on February 5, 1778 while at Philadelphia wrote to Major General Robert Pigot concerning the clandestine trade in flaxseed and advised that the trade should "be prevented by every precaution in your power, and punished when detected."[37]

In Charles Town (Charleston), South Carolina, despite British efforts to stop it, the illicit trade with the enemy continued. One method was to bring the goods to Georgetown, South Carolina, and then ship them as British goods into Charles Town. British supplies were going out of Charles Town through Georgetown to the American army.[38] It appears that the British looked the other way for the trade in nonessential goods. Aedanus Burke wrote in January 1782 to Arthur Middleton that "the Commandant [General Alexander Leslie] winks at a little traffick carried on by our people, but 'tis in such paltry articles w[hi]ch they know can be of little use to us."[39]

The reason for concern by the British with bringing items into their lines, even when needed, was that it could result in dire consequences. Pompey Lamb, a slave of Captain Lamb, under the disguise of selling vegetables to the British at the fort at Stony Point, New York, collected information on the fortifications and provided them to American General Anthony Wayne.[40]

Abraham Clark while in Congress in Philadelphia on May 22, 1782, further described the situation of communication across the lines, "Money is going from hence to New York to amounts almost incredible and if not prevented will soon drain the continent of all hard cash; we are with hasty strides ruining ourselves by this destructive commerce."[41] The practice got so great that Chevalier De La Luzerne the French Minister lodged a protest concerning the illegal trade with the Continental Congress. As Congresses do, they referred it to a committee which issued its report on October 30, 1782, stating, "a continuance of the flagitious clandestine commerce therein set forth between some of the citizens of the state of New Jersey and the enemy cannot but be attended with the most destructive consequences to the operations of the allied powers by invigorating those of the common enemy, and therefore call for every exertion to suppress it in the most speedy and effectual manor possible." Congress instructed New Jersey to heed the problem and a copy of the report was sent to General George Washington.[42]

Washington responded to Major General Benjamin Lincoln, the Secretary of War, on November 6, 1782, from army headquarters at Newburgh, New York: "The allotment of the whole continental army to that duty would not prevent the practice . . . I shall however continue, as I have ever done, to discountenance it by every means in my power, especially between the Sound [Raritan Bay] and the North River, where the parties which attend to the motions of the enemy, prevent intercourse; but to guard the extensive frontier of New Jersey is out of my power."[43] He also wrote to New Jersey Governor William Livingston: "The evil complained of has been long growing, and has at length arisen to a height truly alarming."[44] Washington in his letter to the Benjamin Lincoln, Secretary of State, even explained why he could not use small groups of guards to patrol the New Jersey coast. "Small Guards are not only subject to be cut off, but the Sentinels are liable to be bribed by individuals concerned in the traffic, as I have too much reason to believe has sometimes been the case."[45]

Samuel Culper, Jr. (Robert Townsend), writing on December 27, 1779, from Setauket, Suffolk County, Long Island, New York, reported that "The markets [in New York City] are well supplied with fresh provisions of every kind, and will continue so while there is any cattle in Connecticut and New Jersey. A considerable number of cattle and other provisions is daily brought over from Connecticut to the East end of Long Island, and from thence conveyed to New York; and there has ever been regular supplied from Shrewsbury, Middletown, and every other part of East Jersey. It is almost needless to mention King's Bridge, for it has been, and ever will be practice to get supplies that way."[46] This movement of goods resulted in lots of contact and, by extension, opportunity to pass along intelligence of military importance.

Smuggling to a degree was tolerated because the practitioners were sometimes very useful to provide information in more important concerns. William Clarke was a case officer for the British Secret Service who ran a watchdog operation in London. In September 1782, Clark had a mission to find a Mr. Pelivé before he could convey intelligence to France. After failing to locate him on his own, he paid Captain Killick, commander of a smuggling cutter, £27,14,6 for his information on Mr. Pelivé and as compensation for the hire of his vessel that had been waiting for Pelivé for the purpose of taking Pelivé to France.[47]

The Earl of Shelburne sent instructions for obtaining intelligence over and above the information coming from Jamaica. His proposal was to send neutrals from Saint Croix and Saint Thomas to Havana, Cuba, and Hispaniola "(under the pretext of perhaps trading, and that with very small and swift vessels) you may establish a natural and authentic basis for intelligence. From this center, accurate and constant information under the shape of mercantile news, I should hope may circulate down to Jamaica and round to yourselves, and in a mode that will be pointed out to you may even reach Sir Guy Carlton through the revolting provinces." Shelburne sent two letters from important merchants to persons in the Danish islands (Saint Croix and Saint Thomas) who could possibly assist in setting up the operation. He wanted information on the arrivals and departures of vessels, victories and defeats, and troop movements. The information was to be sent in a mercantile form to either of Messrs. Manning or Baille in London.

Shelburne advised that the most dangerous part of the operation was the sending of the information to Jamaica and that the proper person needed to be picked for the job. The efforts expended on this task were to be made known to the commanding officers at Jamaica and New York so that they could coordinate their efforts. He further advised that "if you get mercantile letters of credit in your islands for the expenses incurred on this occasion, bills drawn upon Mr.

Manning or Mr. Baille of London, if properly advised of, will be taken up by his majesty's servants here which seems the most natural of covered mode of settlement that can be devised from hence."

Shelburne sent a draft of the letter that either Baille or Manning would send. It read:

> London, April 22, 1782
>
> Dear Sir:
>
> Though I do not know the party by whom this letter may be delivered to you, yet I have so much confidence and respect for the channels through which it is to pafs, that I must beg your utmost attention to every matter which the bearer may have to propose or request. Humanity, and the nature of the subject which is too delicate for explanation upon paper will require the most perfect secrecy and address on all sides; and I am sure that I can not only depend on your performing your part in the transaction most scrupulously, but on your pardoning the liberty which I am reduced to take upon this occasion in which we are all deeply interested.[48]

A most ingenious way of forwarding intelligence about an individual was used by Charles Gravier, Count de Vergennes.[49] Before the American Revolution he served in diplomatic posts at Constantinople and Stockholm. After the ascension of twenty-year-old Louis XVI as King of France on May 10, 1774, Vergennes became the Minister for Foreign Affairs. It was a position he held until his death in 1787. He provided cards of introduction or recommendation to individuals who were entering or leaving France to communicate with the diplomatic agents of France. The bearer would present the card to the government agent expecting to get preferential treatment because of the influence of the Count de Vergennes. The card would not only identify the individual but provide great detail about them. The bearer would be the one providing the secret correspondence. The color of the card indicated the country of origin of the bearer. A yellow card indicated the person was English, red indicated Spanish, white was Portuguese, green was Dutch, red and white was Italian, red and green was Swiss, and green and white was Russian. The shape of the card indicated the person's age: under twenty-five was a circular card, between twenty-five and thirty was oval, between thirty and forty-five was octagonal, between forty-five and fifty was hexagonal, between fifty and sixty was square, and over sixty was an oblong card.

The bearer of the card most likely believed that the Count was obtaining special attention for them, which he was; however, it was not precisely the attention they were led to believe. By placing two lines below the name to underscore it would give the bearer's physical appearance. Wavy and parallel lines indicated the bearer was tall and lean. If the underscore converged, the bearer was tall and stout. A flower on the border indicated the countenance of the individual. A tulip indicated a person who was aristocratic and pensive while a rose indicated an open and amiable person. A period after a person's name on the card indicated that he was a Catholic, a semi-colon was a Lutheran, a comma was a Calvinist, a dash indicated a Jew, and no stop was an atheist. A narrow decorated line around the border would by its length tell if the person was a bachelor, married, or widowed. Other marks told the individual's profession, the purpose of visit, and, most important, if the person needed surveillance.[50]

Chapter 3

BLACK CHAMBERS

As part of secret service operations in Europe, governments set up a "black chamber" operation in their postal system. The "black chamber" staff was to intercept the mail, read it for pertinent information, reseal it, and send it to its destination without anyone realizing the intercept had taken place. The French had been running their *cabinet noir* or "black chamber" since 1590. Both the English and French employed specialists who restored the broken wax seals on letters. In the eighteenth century there was no expectation of privacy when the postal system was used.

The British secret service included an office within the Post Office Department. Beginning in 1765, warrants were issued by each Secretary of State ordering the opening of all diplomatic mail going though London. Mail was normally opened on suspicion or in search of designated letters. Letters going through the Inland Office were opened in the Secretary's Office by his clerk. Foreign mail was opened in a special office usually called the "Secret Office" that was funded and directed by the Secretary of State. By 1772, the Deciphering Branch was transferred to it.[1] The Secret Office was paid out of the secret service money allocated to the Secretary of the Post Office at the Exchequer from the Civil List revenue. The Secret Office also would prepare sham letters and send them to unsuspecting recipients.

A Mr. Bode, who was from Hanover, was brought to England specifically to run the secret service office, which he did for over fifty years from 1732 to 1784. Mr. Bode's assistant was Anthony Todd from around 1751 to 1792. The most-secret intercepts were restricted to the King, Lord North, and the two Secretaries of State. The British Secret

Service in 1780 was run by William Eden, Undersecretary of State. Eden's reports would be sent to Lord North, who would decide what information was to be provided to King George III.

Gilbert Barkly was a spy for British Prime Minister Lord Frederick North in Philadelphia from 1775 to December 12, 1777. Barkly's reports were sent to William Strahan, member of Parliament, publisher of the *London Chronicle*, and printer to the King. The Scottish-born Strahan was to forward Barkly's letters to Gray Cooper, Under Secretary of the Treasury.[2] Barkly's letter of September 5, 1775, to Strahan was intercepted by the Post Office. Anthony Todd reported to William Eden that the Post Office was often handling twenty letter intercepts a day.[3] In October 1777 Todd complained about all the work in copying seals and handwriting in creating fake mail. He told Eden, "The seals I think you will find to be very well imitated, as you will tolerably I hope the writing, if it is not a particular hand, or a great deal of it, for if there should be a great deal there is more room for faults, and besides too as it must be imitated like to drawing much time will be required to a long letter." Todd went on to say that what Eden told him will not be sent to the Whitehaven newspaper.[4] It appears that Todd sent his fake letters to the *Cumberland Chronicle* or *Whitehaven Public Advertiser* published in London.[5]

Sometimes the agents at the Post Office were unable to keep their work a secret. William Donaldson suspected that since red sealing wax appeared over the black wafer on his letter, that his letter of June 23 had been opened in the post office.[6]

In North America, Hugh Earl Percy suspected in September 1774 that letters sent through the American postal system were opened and stopped.[7] After the Battles of Concord and Lexington in April 1775, the local American militia laid siege to Boston. Hordes of armed men were responding to the Lexington Alarm and were marching to Cambridge to aid the oppressed peoples of Massachusetts.[8] By April 25, all secure land communication between the cities of Boston and New York had ceased. The city of Boston and the British army were now effectively under a siege. Its only open access was through its harbor. Royal Lieutenant Governor Cadwallader Colden of New York and John Foxcroft, deputy postmaster at New York City, wrote to General Thomas Gage in Boston that all mail was being sent by boat as the previous mails had been opened at Hartford and New Haven.[9]

John Stuart, British Superintendent of Indian Affairs for the Southern District, was having the same mail security problem a few months later. The seventy-five-year-old Stuart wrote on July 9, 1775, to Gage in Boston advising him that mail addressed to him was being intercepted in Charles Town, South Carolina. Stuart believed that some of General Gage's instructions to him had fallen into rebel hands.[10]

The Continental Congress on November 20, 1775, received some intercepted letters from Cork, Ireland, which were brought by Captain Robbins in the captured schooner *Two Sisters*. Washington forwarded the missives with his letter of November 11 to Congress. Upon receipt the Continental Congress appointed a committee of seven made up of John Adams, Benjamin Franklin, Thomas Johnson, Robert Livingston, Edward Rutledge, James Wilson, and George Wythe "to select such parts of them as may be proper to publish."[11] The committee brought in their report on the 24th and Congress ordered a thousand copies of the portions selected by the Committee to be printed and distributed.[12] These events confirmed that there was no expectation of privacy in the mail.

Rebels would routinely search the letters of suspected loyalists. Having your mail read could have dire consequences. Attorney General of New Jersey Cortland Skinner wrote a letter in December 1775 to his brother Lieutenant Colonel William Skinner in the British army. It indicated Skinner's hope that the British military would get things right and support the people who backed the British government.[13] The letter was intercepted by the militia and forwarded to Congress. On January 9, 1776, Congress ordered a certified copy of the letter sent to the New Jersey Committee of Safety and instructed Colonel William Alexander also known as Lord Stirling to arrest Cortland Skinner.[14] As soon as Cortland Skinner heard of the intercept he fled Perth Amboy, leaving behind his wife and thirteen children as well as his 482-volume library. He took refuge on board the British warship *Asia* in New York harbor.[15]

The Continental Congress received a letter dated April 14, 1776, from the Committee of Baltimore, which enclosed intercepted letters from the British Secretary of State to Governor Robert Eden of Maryland. It indicated that the governor had "carried on a correspondence with the British ministry, highly dangerous to the liberties of

America." Congress called for the seizure of Eden and his papers by the Council of Safety of Maryland.[16]

By April 1776, the practice of opening the mail by a multitude of committees and individuals to search for correspondence threatening to the United Colonies was causing much inconvenience for the public. Congress resolved that "no committee but the council or committee of safety in each colony, or such person as they shall, on extraordinary occasions, authorize, should stop the constitutional post, open the mail, or detain any letters." The Congressional resolution reduced the number of people intercepting the mail but legalized the committee of safety in each colony to intercept, delay, open, and read the mail.

Elias Nexsen was a New York City merchant who was caught up in mail interception as a private citizen.[17] When the British landed at Staten Island, New York, in early July 1776, a gentlemen's agreement permitted the merchants' market boats to supply both the American and British without any harassment. This allowed the merchants to get in touch with the British on Staten Island, the Americans in New York City, and the British on ships in New York City harbor.

The story says that the commander of the British forces on Staten Island New York asked Nexsen to deliver a letter to Royal Governor William Tryon, who was on board a ship in the harbor. As he was putting the letter in his vest, Nexsen slipped his finger under the flap in order to loosen the sealing wafer, which was still moist. When he reached New York City he went to General Washington's headquarters and provided the letter to General Washington. Washington read and resealed the letter, which told of the forthcoming attack on Long Island. He had Nexsen deliver the letter to Royal Governor Tryon as requested.[18]

David Gray was a native of Lenox, Berkshire County, Massachusetts. He joined up with Ethan Allen at the age of nineteen and served at the Battle of Ticonderoga. After serving in 1776 under Captain David Nobles in Colonel Patterson's Regiment, he enlisted in Colonel Vose's 1st Massachusetts Regiment in 1777 and served with it until 1780. During the last half of 1779, he was used as a courier at Lake George and resided in Hinsdale, New Hampshire. During this time he showed an aptitude for obtaining information on secret loyalist activities. He was brought to the attention of General George

Washington, who subsequently employed him as a spy. Gray mentioned to the Tories in Hinsdale that the Continental money was no good and that he wanted to go to New York City. They bankrolled him and recommended him to Captain Becket at Rope Ferry, Connecticut. Becket got him across to Long Island and supplied him with some more money. He went to Brooklyn to see a Colonel Crane whom he knew from his hometown and who ran a store on the side. Crane introduced him to Colonel Beverly Robinson, who employed him as one of two couriers from New York City to Colonel Samuel Wells in Brattleboro, Vermont. The other courier was Samuel Wells's son-in-law Micah Townsend. Wells was a resident British spy feeding information both to Canada and to New York City.

Gray would travel from Long Island over to the Rope Ferry and Black Point, Connecticut, and pass through Hartford on his way to Colonel Wells.[19] He would return to New York City through Westchester County, New York, the Rope Ferry, or Black Point. However, he would detour and bring the messages to General Washington, in the Hudson highlands. Washington was able to read the messages prior to Gray making his scheduled deliveries.

Gray worked as a double agent for about a year. On one of his trips back to New York City, Captain Becket had an associate take Gray to Oyster Pond Point, where he was to pick up a message in the top drawer in Tuttle's back room and deliver it to Colonel Beverly Robinson.[20] It was a letter from Sir Guy Carleton, Governor of Canada. Robinson was unavailable, so Oliver De Lancey took Gray directly to General Sir Henry Clinton to deliver Carleton's message. Clinton decided to employ Gray as a courier to Carleton and paid him 20 guineas and promised him 70 more when he returned.[21] General Sir Henry Clinton stated on June 28, 1781, that he thought he could depend on Gray. In 1781 Gray assisted a Lieutenant Lyman in making his escape from Long Island to Connecticut; however, this blew his cover and ended his career as a spy. In the spring of 1782, he rejoined his former company under General William Heath at West Point.

The Continental army had its own intrigues with postal messages. George Washington wrote to Governor George Clinton of New York that Mr. Fish of the Saratoga district came to him on April 15, 1781. Fish advised that a Moses Harris was to meet Ensign Smith and his party coming from Canada on April 20, Harris was to receive a parcel of letters and take it to Albany and bring another parcel back to Ensign Smith. Harris had proposed to Fish that Fish should intercept him and take the parcel. Washington had an alternative plan. He suggested that Harris take the letters to General Philip Schuyler, "who might contrive means of opening them without breaking the seals, take copies of the contents, and then let them go on. By these means we should become masters of the whole plot; whereas, were we to seize Harris upon his first tour, we should break up the chain of communication, which seems so providentially thrown into our hands."[22] Governor Clinton wrote to General Schuyler and included the letter he had received from General Washington. Clinton stated that he had some reason to believe Fish and Harris.[23] George Washington was trying to set up a "black chamber" in upstate New York to intercept, read, and forward the British mail. Opening letters was a game both sides could play.

Chapter 4

INVISIBLE INK

Many of us as children wrote with lemon juice or milk on a white piece of paper. We watched as the liquid disappeared. When heat was applied to the paper, the writing magically reappeared and we were amazed. Although this was a new experience for us as children, the practice has been around for a very long time. In the Edgar Allan Poe story *The Gold Bug*, when one of the characters was visiting William Legrand, he was distracted by a Newfoundland dog named Wolf and accidentally held a piece of parchment near the fire. The image of a skull appeared on the parchment, and as Legrand applied more heat, the symbol for Captain William Kidd and a message in cipher appeared.[1] In Poe's time several chemical compounds were used for invisible writing.[2]

Poe evokes the mists of alchemy when describing invisible inks, but several common liquids—lemon juice, grapefruit juice, and vinegar—also serve the purpose. As they are mildly acidic, when they are used as a writing medium, they weaken the fibers of the paper. When heat is applied to the paper, the treated portion that is weaker part burns and turns brown more rapidly than the untreated portion of paper. Sir Hugh Plat published a method of invisible writing in 1653. He told of writing a secret message in milk on the reverse or blank side of a normally written document. The normal side of the document is held toward a fire and the milk writing will then become visible. His other way was to write a normal letter but to write between the lines in gall water. To make gall water he said the [oak] galls needed to be infused for a short time otherwise some color can be seen. To bring this secret message to light, "you must dissolve some coppress in fair water [clear and pure water] and with a fine caliber pencil, first dipt in the coppress water, you must artly moist the interlining of your letter, and thereby, you shall make it sufficiently legible."[3]

J. Falconer in a 1692 book describes several ways of accomplishing invisible writing. Letters written with dissolved alum are not discernible until the paper is dipped in water. Letters written with goat fat are not visible till dust is feathered upon them. Falconer also advised that the yolk of a raw egg when dissolved in fountain water produces invisible writing on paper. The entire paper is blackened with ink. It is then dried but the ink over the writing is not absorbed. By scraping the page gently with a knife the writing becomes visible. Another method was mixing "a little common ink with so much water that little or nothing of the blackness appear[s] in it; with this write your secret intentions upon clean paper. When it is thoroughly dryed, write an ordinary epistle with another ink, (made of gunpowder beat and mix with rain water) upon the very letters you scribed before. The last ink will wash off with a sponge dipt in water boiled with [oak] galls which will also blacken the first." He also states that another way to make the first writing appear is to wet the document with the juice of unripe white grapes.

Another method for invisible writing uses dissolved tragacanth and white lead.[4] The writing will not be visible until held between a bright light and the eye. In the eighteenth century one could also use a more risky method—one where there is the possibility of destroying the document if you are not careful. Mix wine vinegar, egg white, and quicksilver or white lead. "Writing therewith, or with gum of any kind of salt, or with such liquor, as renders the letters described incombustible. . . . The letters shall not be legible until the papers be burnt black and the written parts of it do still remain white."[5]

There are examples of invisible writing by both the Americans and the British during the American Revolution. On the American side, letters in the George Washington papers contain invisible writing by Samuel Culper and Bezaleel Kerr.[6] Silas Deane and Dr. Boyer Pillon also used invisible ink. On the British side Governor General of Canada Frederick Haldimand, Edward Bancroft, William Smith, and Benjamin Thompson used invisible ink. George Washington said Royal Governor William Tryon of New York used an invisible ink of the same kind or similar to his.[7]

The first documented instance of invisible ink being used during
the American Revolution was by Benjamin Thompson, later known as
Count Rumford. Thompson wrote a letter at Woburn, Massachusetts,
on May 6, 1775, to someone in Boston with an invisible part that provided information on the situation in that part of the country. The
invisible part stated: "Sir If you will be so kind as to deliver to Mr.
____ of Boston, the papers which I left in your care, and take his
receipt for the same. You will much oblige. Your Humble Servant
[erased] Saturday May 6th 1775."[8] Benjamin Thompson was a suspected British loyalist. He had been run out of his hometown in
Rumford (now Concord), New Hampshire, for assisting British deserters on their way to headquarters in Boston.[9] At the time Thompson
wrote the letter, he may have also been an accomplice of the British
spy Dr. Benjamin Church.[10] It has been proposed by some historians
that Thompson destroyed incriminating documents that had
belonged to his friend Church. Thompson prior to his marriage in
1772 had studied medicine and conducted scientific experiments. He
and Dr. Church most assuredly were acquainted. Dr. Church had
been arrested by the Americans as a British spy at the end of
September 1775.[11] The following month Thompson sold his real
estate in Woburn and Wilmington, Massachusetts for £750.[12] On the
day he left Woburn, October 13, 1775, he advised people that he was
going to the West Indies.[13] He was driven by his stepbrother, Josiah
Pierce, in a country vehicle to Providence, Rhode Island. He then
traveled by boat to Newport, where he boarded the British warship
Scarborough. From Newport, Thompson went to Boston instead of
the West Indies. He stayed there till Boston was evacuated by the
British on March 24, 1776.[14]

There were three types of sympathetic ink formulas that were in use
during the American Revolution. The ink used solutions of bismuth,
gallo-tannic acid, or lead. The bismuth solution was the acetate developed by ammonia water. The gallo-tannic acid was produced by soak-
ing powdered nutgalls in water and developed by an iron or ferrous
sulphate solution also known as copperas ($FeSO_4$). By the application
of ferrous sulphate as the counteragent over the area written with the

diluted gallo-tannic acid, the chemical reaction of the ferrous sulphate being changed to ferrous gallo-tannate would make the writing visible. The lead ink which was a lead acetate also known as sugar of lead was developed by hydrogen sulphide. The chemical reaction changes the lead acetate to black lead sulphide (PbS). By using X-rays and ultra-violet light, it was discovered that Thompson's invisible letter was written with gallo-tannic acid while the visible part of the letter was written with carbon ink.[15] Benjamin Thompson studied medicine under Dr. Jay of Woburn and was friends with Dr. Church. He had the technical knowledge and access to the ingredients to make the sympathetic ink.

Sometimes things do not go as well as one hoped. John Jay commented about a letter with invisible parts he received from Silas Deane in Paris. Deane, a thirty-seven-year-old Connecticut attorney from Yale, did a poor job in constructing the letter. There were visible sections that stood out as being blank, which would draw attention from prying eyes. Also "there are many blots in one of the letters and in one or two instances the lines cross and run into one another."[16]

Silas Deane in order to disguise all the blank space in a letter where he had written with invisible ink included his information in two letters. One was addressed to John Jay and the other to Robert Morris, but both were sent to John Jay. Jay sent the Morris letter to him before he read his letter. Realizing his mistake, he had to get the Robert Morris letter back.[17] A few days later Morris expressed the documents back to Jay. Morris in his reply advised Jay that Deane "had communicated so much of this secret to me before his departure, as to let me know he had fixed with you a mode of writing that would be invisible to the rest of the world; he also promised to ask you to make a full communication to me, but in this use your pleasure; the secret, so far as I do or shall know it, will remain so to all other persons."[18] Deane in his correspondence with John Jay used the invisible ink supplied by James Jay. It was gallo-tannic acid and John Jay used the counterpart.[19] Deane was known to have used an invisible ink made from cobalt chloride, glycerin, and water for some of his intelligence reports back to America. It was made visible through the application of heat.

When the British occupied Trenton, New Jersey, in December 1776 an American officer was sent to the British under a flag of truce.

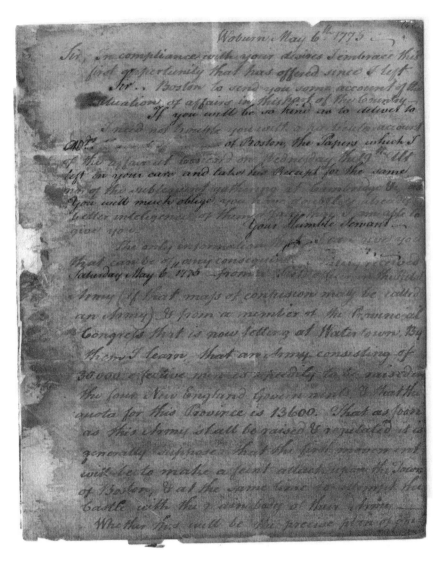

Invisible ink letter of British spy Benjamin Thompson at Woburn, Massachusetts, to an unknown person at Boston, May 6, 1775. It had been developed in the eighteenth century with a chemical reagent. What looks like a water stain is where the reagent was applied. Invisible ink letters become very brittle when developed and therefore were transcribed immediately. It is only the latter that typically survives, making this example of an actual invisible ink letter unusual and rare. (*William L. Clements Library*)

While there the officer was given an unsealed letter and asked to forward the letter to a gentleman in Philadelphia, Pennsylvania. When
he returned to Pennsylvania, the officer submitted the letter to
American army headquarters.[20]

George Washington asked Lieutenant Colonel Tench Tilghman,
military secretary, to inspect the letter. Tilghman thought he had seen
the handwriting before but the name was unknown to him. The letter
was mysterious and unintelligible. He apparently passed it around to
the headquarters staff. This most likely included Virginian Robert
Hanson Harrison, military secretary. Tilghman says most of the headquarters work at this time fell on the two of them. "This raised all our
suspicions and we were determined to unravel it." By chance the letter was held near the fire and "new characters began to appear and . .
. the whole sheet was fully written with some composition that
appeared when warmed." Tench Tilghman told James Tilghman, his
father, "it was from a gentleman nearly connected with our family and
gave an account to his friends of the intentions of the enemy. The
[Delaware] River was to be crossed upon the ice and the army
marched directly to Philadelphia. When every house, which the owners had left, was to be given up to be plundered, and the gentleman
pressed all his friends and acquaintance to remove in."[21]

Loyalist William Smith in New York City sent a letter "written with
lime juice on scraps of paper" to his brother, who lived north of the
city near the Hudson River. In the message, William Smith advised
his brother to "get away from navigable rivers in the spring and from
the inland frontier."[22] A secret correspondence in 1779 between
Bezaleel Kerr, who had been banished to New York, and his wife and
Aneas Urquhart, a merchant, in Philadelphia also used invisible ink.
The exact method used is unknown but Kerr instructed his wife "to
toast her letter well"; in other words, the heat of a fire would make the
invisible part visible.[23]

Invisible ink was made visible by the use of heat (fire) or a reagent.
The British army used a code system to identify letters containing
invisible writing and the process that was to be used to make it visible.
In some of the documents the letters are identified by the letters A, B,
C, and F. The letter "A" stands for acid, "B" for burn or heat, "C" for
code or cipher, and "F" for fire.[24] On one letter from British General

William Phillips to General Sir Henry Clinton, commander-in-chief of the British forces in North America, is marked with A, B, and C, indicating that three missives were sent and each one used a different method of transmission.[25]

In the secret negotiations between Benedict Arnold and Sir Henry Clinton, at least one letter was written in invisible ink. On May 21, 1779, Arnold sent a letter through Joseph Stansbury to Reverend Jonathan Odell in New York City. Odell and Stansbury were well acquainted and did the coding and decoding of the traitorous correspondence between Benedict Arnold and Major John André, aide to General Sir Henry Clinton. It seems that Murphy's Law was also true in the eighteenth century. Odell wrote a message to André about what happened to a letter written in invisible ink:

> I am mortified to death, having just received (what I had been so anxiously expecting) a letter from S—- [Joseph Stansbury], and, by a private mark agreed on between us, perceiving it contained an invisible page for you. I assayed it by the fire, when, to my inexpressible vexation, I found the paper, having by some accident got damp in the way, had spread the solution in such a manner as to make the writing all one indistinguishable blot, out of which not the half of any one line can be made legible. I shall use every diligence to forward a letter to him, and to instruct him to guard against the like accident in the future, and hope it will not be long before I shall receive a return.[26]

One of the problems with using heat to see the invisible writing is that the entire document becomes very fragile. Reverend Odell stated that "toasted paper becomes too brittle to bear folding,"[27] and he transcribed the letters for headquarters use. Because the invisible letters became so brittle and were routinely transcribed, most originals were not preserved.

The American spy networks also used disappearing inks. George Washington had supplied Major Benjamin Tallmadge with invisible ink and a reagent. Tallmadge was a case agent, operating one of several American spy networks in New York City. The invisible ink was for the use of his New York City spy Abraham Woodhull, code-named

Samuel Culper.[28] The reagent was for Tallmadge to read the invisible messages that he received. There is no record of the reagent having ever been given to spies. On April 30, 1779, Washington advised Tallmadge that he did not have any invisible ink but was going to try to obtain some.[29] In a June 13 follow-up on the invisible ink, Washington wrote to Tallmadge, "When I can procure more of the liquid C—r [Abraham Woodhull] writes for, it shall be sent, at present I cannot say when this may happen."[30]

However, just a few days after his initially telling Tallmadge that he had run out of ink, Washington advised Elias Boudinot at Basking Ridge, New Jersey, that he could get "a liquid which nothing but a counter liquor (rubbed over the paper afterward) can make legible. Fire which will bring lime juice, milk and other things of this kind to light has no effect on it. A letter upon trivial matters of business, written in common ink, may be fitted with important intelligence which cannot be discovered without the counter part, or liquid here mentioned."[31]

Major Tallmadge had to inform Washington that on July 2, Lieutenant Colonel Banastre Tarleton (accompanied by Lord Rawdon) led an expedition of British light horse and infantry to Bedford and Pound Ridge, Westchester County, New York. At Pound Ridge, they attacked Colonel Elisha Sheldon's 2nd Regiment of Continental Light Dragoons and New York militia accompanied by Tallmadge.[32] During the raid the British set fire to the meetinghouse, Major Lockwood's house, and, at Bedford, Mr. Hay's house.[33] The British won the skirmish and captured letters from General Washington along with Tallmadge's horse, most of his field baggage, and money that Washington had sent as payment for secret service work performed by Culper.[34]

On July 5, 1779, Washington responded, "I have just received your letter of the 3rd; the loss of your papers was certainly a most unlucky accident and shows how dangerous it is to keep papers of any consequence at an advanced post."[35] Washington's lost letter of June 27 mentioned George Higday, a low-level resident American spy who lived in New York City not far from the Bowery near the North (Hudson) River. Higday had provided some intelligence, and Washington wanted Tallmadge to find out if Higday could be trusted. Higday was arrested on July 13 by an order from General Sir Henry

Clinton and placed in the Provost and was still there on August 28, 1780, at which time he had spent 507 nights in jail.[36] Washington's letter of June 13 that mentioned the liquid was also captured, thereby alerting the British that the Americans were using invisible ink.

The supply of invisible ink continued to be a problem for Washington. On July 25, 1779, Washington sent Colonel Webb to Benjamin Tallmadge with all the white ink he had in a phial marked No. 1. There was very little prospect of getting any additional supply. In phial No. 2 was the reagent, which is applied to the dry paper with a fine brush. Tallmadge was instructed to send these to "C—r Junr" (Robert Townsend, alias Samuel Culper, Jr., a new member of the Culper spy ring). Tallmadge was also instructed that "no mention may ever be made of your having received such liquids from me or any one else. In all cases and at all times this prudence and circumspection is necessary but it is indispensably so now as I am informed that Governor Tryon has a preparation of the same kind, or something similar to it which may lead to a detection if it is ever known that a matter of this sort has passed from me." Washington also wrote that he wanted to know where the British and Hessian forces were located "in order to govern my own movements with more propriety."[37]

Benjamin Tallmadge of the 2nd Continental Light Dragoons painted by Ezra Ames circa 1800. In 1778, he became an American case agent who ran the Culper Spy Ring. His area of operations was in Connecticut and New York. (*William L. Clements Library*)

By September 24 Washington was giving instructions for Robert Townsend to write his information on the blank pages of a pamphlet; on the first and second pages of a common pocket book; on the blank leaves at the end of almanacs, or any new publication or book of small value. There was a problem with the ink; it was not easily legible unless it is written on paper of a good quality. Washington believed these books would pass the military checkpoints with less scrutiny than a letter. If Culper Jr. must send a letter, he was to "write a familiar letter, on domestic affairs, or on some little matters of business to his friend at Setauket or elsewhere, interlining with the stain, his secret intelligence or writing it on the opposite blank side of the letter." Washington suggested that if a letter contained invisible writing to send it without the date or the place but date it in the stain or by the manner in which the letter is folded, which he believed was the best methods for a letter. Washington believed that "the books, appears to me the one least liable to detection."[38]

George Washington at Morristown, New Jersey, on April 9, 1780, was again running out of his supply of invisible ink and its reagent. He wrote to James Jay that he found the liquid Jay had supplied to be very useful but he needed more. Washington instructed Jay that if the chemicals to produce the counterparts were available at a hospital that he was to procure them in Washington's name.[39] Jay on the 13th sent Washington a supply of "medicine" (invisible ink and reagent) in a little box. He apologized for the small quantity, but that was the last of what he had brought back from Europe. Jay reported:

> I have now the principal ingredients for the composition by me, and the rest may be procured: but the misfortune is, that I have no place where a little apparatus may be erected for preparing it. The composition requires some assistance from chemistry; an out house is so small, and so well inhabited, that there is not a corner left where a little brick furnace, which a mason could build in two hours time, can be placed. A log hut for the purpose might be soon run up, but it is also out of my power to effect this, neither bricks, boards nor lime are to be purchased here, nor a carpenter nor mason to be had without great difficulty, if at all. I beg you will not infer from hence that I would rather decline the undertaking. So far from that being the case, if you shall think it worth while, and will only direct [Lieutenant] Colonel [Udny] Hay to furnish the workman, and other requisites, I shall soon have the satisfaction of sending you such a supply that you may not only use it freely yourself, but even spare a little to a friend, if necessary, without the apprehension of future want.[40]

Jay on April 13 sent what "medicine" [invisible ink and reagent] that he had to Washington, who acknowledged that they arrived safely. Washington advised Jay that he had instructed Deputy Quartermaster General Lieutenant Colonel Udny Hay to assist James Jay in constructing a laboratory in a log building for making more invisible ink and its reagent.[41] Jay must have had his laboratory constructed because in a September 19 letter he apologizes to Washington for not getting the "medicine" to him sooner.[42]

Another occurrence of using invisible ink happened in Canada during the summer of 1780. American sympathizers in Montreal were headed by surgeon Boyer Pillon, who had a son in the American service. British Major Thomas Carleton was head of a counterespionage operation at Saint-Jean on the Richelieu River. He was the younger brother of General Guy Carleton.[43] Major Carleton had sent an agent from Chambly approximately

Portrait of John Jay published in London in 1783. Jay provided Washington with invisible ink and a reagent that had been obtained from his brother, Sir James Jay. In 1780, John Jay operated a laboratory to manufacture invisible ink for American spies. (*William L. Clements Library*)

eighteen miles into Montreal. During his clandestine activities, the agent discovered that Doctor Boyer Pillon of Montreal would shortly be sending a person with letters to the rebels.[44] The courier would be accompanied on the mission by three or four other comrades. On July 23, 1780, Major Carleton advised Swiss-born General Frederick Haldimand, who was 150 miles away at Quebec, that he wanted to surprise the party. However, Major Carleton after accomplishing the task needed to keep their capture a secret, or their plot and most likely his agent would become known.[45]

Haldimand quickly gave his approval of the plan to intercept Pillon's party. He cautioned Major Carleton to use enough men in his detachment to ensure that no one could escape. He expressed his hope that the failure of Pillon's party would discourage a "Mr.

Grenier," whom Carleton also suspected of being a spy, from making a similar attempt.[46]

Frederick Haldimand had served in the Prussian service before being appointed a lieutenant colonel of the 62nd (later 60th) Royal American Regiment of Foot with an effective date of January 4, 1756. He was sent to America and gained knowledge of Forts Edward, Oswego, and Ticonderoga from his service during the French and Indian War. After the war he had served in Pensacola, Florida. On June 27, 1778, he succeeded Sir Guy Carleton as governor of Canada.[47]

Haldimand sometimes micromanaged operations because of his experiences in the French and Indian Wars. On the 27th Haldimand decided to provide additional instructions. He recommended setting a trap in a deep part of the woods. Once Pillon's party had been captured they were to be tied up. During the night they were to be secured by both their hands and feet. In order to keep their captivity secret, provisions were to be sent to them by one or two of their guards. Haldimand instructed that the prisoners were to be separated until they are "minutely searched and examined which will require infinite cleverness and attention and as more is to be apprehended from the verbal messages these people may be charged with than the letters they bear, it will not be amiss after they are separated to threaten them with immediate execution for which the non-commissioned officers or persons you employ will have ropes prepared. They should likewise have pen, ink, and paper to prevent mistakes in names or circumstances related to them which might afterwards be denied."[48]

Pillon's plans in Montreal were on hold awaiting the return of Montreal merchant Pierre Du Calvet. Du Calvet, a French Protestant, had emigrated from France in 1758 and engaged in the fur and importing trade. He had been made a justice of the peace in June 1766 and continued in that capacity till the date for termination set by Parliament in the Quebec Act of 1774. Du Calvet thought of himself as being part of "the class of the leading citizens of Montreal."[49] He had traveled to Quebec to get a plan of the latest defenses of the city and to pick up letters. Major Carleton devised a plan where his spy would allow "himself to be seen as it were by accident by some royalists." Because of the discovery, Carleton believed Pillon would insist that the spy get out of Montreal quickly. This would provide the cover for the spy to bring him his intelligence report. True to the plan, the spy was suspected by royalists and Pillon did send him out of the city in a hurry. Before the spy left, Pillon quickly wrote a note in milk between the lines of a French song on September 7. When the milk dried the message became invisible. He provided the spy with the song sheet and told him that the application of heat would make the invisible message visible. The spy brought the song sheet to Carleton, who applied heat and made the secret message visible. Carleton then forwarded the song sheet to Haldimand on the 30th.[50]

British Lieutenant General Frederick Haldimand c. 1778 as painted by Sir Joshua Reynolds. (*National Portrait Gallery*)

Dr. Pillon's note was to General George Washington and the Marquis de Lafayette, telling them of him and his followers' readiness to support the cause of liberty. He related his plan to correspond by means of invisible writing on blank paper. The bearer would have the instructions on how to make the message visible. The letter was signed with just his first name, Boyer.[51]

Frederick Haldimand informed Lord George Germain that he "made it a rule to pretend ignorance" as often as he could, concerning people corresponding with the rebels. However, he took action when "their crimes [are] publicly known and I think it my duty to take notice of them, as a contrary course would betray weakness and would encourage others to follow their example, this was the case with Mr. Charles Hay of Quebec and Mr. Cazeau of Montreal." He gave the following observation, "The Province is surrounded by Enemies from without and as happens in all wars is infected with spies and secret enemies from within."[52]

Dr. Pillon and his group also concealed messages in a lead bullet which was to be thrown away in case of any danger."[53] This was not a situation Haldimand could overlook, and on September 28 he ordered Brigadier General Allan Maclean to arrest Dr. Pillon at daybreak in "as secret a manner as possible." All Dr. Pillon's papers were to be seized by the sheriff and an inventory made. Then the papers were to be sealed and shipped to Haldimand. Pillon was to be held in isolation in irons and brought to Quebec as quickly as possible by ship under the command of an officer who would be held responsible for his arrival. Dr. Pillon was to be held "in the hold or some part of the ship where no person can converse with him."[54]

Pierre Du Calvet was also arrested and held in confinement. General Haldimand had given instructions to Captain Le Maistre and Major Carleton to discover all of Du Calvet's activities.[55] In his search to discover the conspirators in Canada, Haldimand requested the assistance of now British General Benedict Arnold, who less than two months earlier had switched sides after a failed attempt to turn the American fortifications at West Point over to the British.[56]

When Dr. Pillon was confronted on October 20, 1780, with the letter to Lafayette and Washington, he admitted to being its author.[57] Pierre Du Calvet, being held on circumstantial evidence, would not see his freedom until May 2, 1783.[58] He instituted a lawsuit in London to recover damages against Governor Haldimand, but died at sea in 1786 before the case was resolved.

On July 16, 1782, Governor General Haldimand himself sent a letter that had a secret message written in milk between the lines and directly over several lines. It states in French that there are more than 5,900 regular soldiers "here," that Quebec is fortified, but that the people are so aroused that the 3,000 men at the French pavilion are worth 10,000. "One should distribute commissions to men at Chambly as well as in the lower gulf before (unreadable) to beat the royalists. Such wheat is scarce on the other side, (unreadable) to be found there, provided that its price is not raised by the subjects of the king. St. Jean cannot be guarded. It has no more than one cannon and a rather green voluntary force. On another opportunity, one of the writer's children will give some certain information if it is needed. People are aroused."[59]

Invisible inks were also part of the repertoire of British spies in Europe. Dr. Edward Bancroft was a British mole employed by Silas Deane, one of the American Commissioners in Paris, and was also a friend of Benjamin Franklin. Bancroft would write his reports in invisible ink for transmission to England. William Fraser, the Under Secretary at the Foreign Office, sent Lord Shelburne a letter written in what was described as white ink. The letter cannot be located so its source remains unknown. William Fraser was paid for secret service work out of the coffers of the Secretary of State's Office beginning at least from 1780.[60]

It is impossible to say which side used invisible ink more. Both sides had a good knowledge of its practice and the ability to use it.

Chapter 5

Ciphers and Codes

I t is true but hard to believe that at the start of the American Revolution, British Lieutenant General Thomas Gage, the fifty-six-year-old commander in chief of British forces in North America, had no code or cipher for confidential correspondence. He also did not have anybody at British military headquarters for North America in Boston with enough experience to devise one. No newcomer to the military, General Gage was in his thirty-fifth year in the military service, having worked his way up from a lieutenant to "captain general and governor in chief" of Massachusetts. He had distinguished himself in the French and Indian War. In March 1775, Gage had discussed with Governor General Guy Carleton at Quebec the need for them to communicate by a cipher. Gage was forced to admit that he did not have one and did not know anyone who did. He was forced to ask Carleton, his subordinate who was five years his junior, if he had a code that Gage could use.[1] There is no record that Carleton provided one. What General Gage wanted was either a code system—which is used for brevity or secrecy of communication, in which arbitrarily chosen words, letters, or symbols are assigned definite meanings—or a cipher—which is a secret method of writing, as by transposition or substitution of letters, specially formed symbols, or the like.

General Gage apparently advised the Earl of Dartmouth, the Secretary of State for the Colonies, of his predicament. On May 25, 1775, General Gage received from the Earl of Dartmouth at Whitehall in London two sets of a cipher and decipher which was known as "letter K." One copy of the cipher was to be sent "to the Major General who shall have a separate command at New York, it being His Majesty's intention that this cipher should be used, not only in your correspondence with me, but also with the officer having the separate command."[2]

Ciphers were not only for high-level communications, they could command a high cost paid to persons willing to use them. Several hundred new British guineas was the price the British paid for Dr. Benjamin Church Jr. to betray his fellow revolutionaries. Dr. Church was one of the political leaders of the revolutionary faction in Massachusetts.[3] In 1768 he built an expensive house in Raynham and was known to be short on cash. Just as King George had bought the loyalty of his opponents in Parliament, Thomas Hutchinson, the Royal Governor of Massachusetts, is believed to have bought Dr. Benjamin Church's services by 1772. Lord Dartmouth shortly after General Gage's arrival in Boston had encouraged Gage to set up an intelligence operation. "I take it for granted that you will have opportunity, upon the spot, of acquiring important intelligence," especially for indicting patriot leaders.[4] Dr. Church was a paid informant under Hutchinson's replacement, General Gage.

The plan had several stages. William Warden would leave the city of Boston by means of the customhouse boat and would travel north to Marblehead, where he would spend as long as six hours before making the return trip. While onshore, Warden received Dr. Church's intelligence reports in either Marblehead or nearby Salem.[5] Another courier used by Dr. Church was a woman by the name of Rachel, who may also have been his mistress.

Dr. Church reported to British headquarters on the activities of about thirty Whigs who formed themselves into a committee for the purpose of discovering the movements of British soldiers and procuring intelligence of the activities of the Tories.[6] Lieutenant General Thomas Gage submitted a March 4, 1775 report to Lord Dartmouth on intelligence titled "Machinations and Projects of these People," warning that the Massachusetts Provincial Congress was sending messengers to the other New England colonies to collect minutemen to oppose the King's troops.[7] The information mirrored what had been provided by Dr. Church. Gage also had intelligence from two other spies, Captain John Brown and Ensign Henry De Berniere of the 10th Regiment of Foot, whom he sent out in February on a fact-finding mission to Worcester. In mid-March he had sent them on another spying mission, but this time the objective was Concord. They had reported that Concord had the appearance of an armed camp and the northern road through Lexington was the best route for the British army to reach Concord.

With the failure of the British army's raid on Concord, Dr. Church was terrified that General Gage thought that he had led him into a trap and would cut off his remuneration. Just two days after the Battles of Concord and Lexington, during a Committee of Safety meeting at sunset at Jonathan Hastings's house in Cambridge, Dr. Church startled everyone when he announced his intention of going into Boston.[8] Now that an outbreak of hostilities had occurred and blood had been shed on both sides, going into British-held Boston was extremely perilous. Dr. Church's cover story was that he needed medicines for wounded American and British officers. The next morning, Saturday April 22, Church departed Cambridge by the overland route for Boston and returned on Sunday evening. Dr. Church went in a chaise to General Gage's residence at Providence House. He met privately with the general for about half an hour while all of the general's other business was put on hold. When the two exited their meeting they were seen talking like two old friends and not as an interrogator and his subject. Church was allowed free access to the city and General Gage even provided an officer by the name of Cane to assist him.[9]

Alice Fleming, Dr. Church's sister, sent a courier by the name of Timothy to her brother. Timothy acted like a mad man when he saw Dr. Church. Timothy feared he might be searched and restrained from returning to Boston because Dr. Church's visit to Boston had raised such a fuss. Dr. Church, fearing the attention that could be drawn to him as a result of Timothy's commotion, immediately destroyed his copy of the cipher he used to communicate with British headquarters. Dr. Church wrote to General Gage, "Caution on my part is doubly necessary as instant death would be my portion should a discovery be made, I perceive men of desperate fortunes. . . . Secrecy respecting me on the part of the General is indispensable to my rendering him any services and be the event what it may is necessary to the preservation of my life." He went on to say: "Send Rachel out soon with more practicable instructions, I can't see how 'tis possible to write again there is a close watch kept up, Contrivances shall not be wanting if necessary, send me the news." A letter written in Dr. Church's handwriting to General Gage stated, "The 25th of this month finishes a quarter," a reminder that his pay for services rendered was due on the 25th of the month.[10]

The Continental Congress appointed Dr. Church the director and chief physician of the first American army hospital at Cambridge, Massachusetts. He moved into the widow Penelope Vassall's house, which was also used as a hospital.[11] With John Adams, Samuel Adams, and John Hancock in Philadelphia and General Dr. Joseph Warren dead, Dr. Church, a British spy, was the most powerful politically connected person in Massachusetts.[12]

John Fleming, Dr. Church's brother-in-law and a loyalist printer in Boston, sent Church a letter in cipher requesting that Dr. Church move to Boston immediately because the British were determined to crush the rebellion.[13] Fleming told Church that "if you cannot pass the lines you may come in [by] Captain Wallace, via Rhode Island, and if you do not come immediately, write me in this character [cipher], and direct your letter to Major Cane, on his Majesty's service, and deliver it to Capt[ain] Wallace, and it will come safe."[14] A week later Dr. Church wrote in cipher to his brother-in-law via Major Edward Cane.[15]

Dr. Church sent his pregnant mistress, a prostitute, to Newport, Rhode Island, in late July to deliver the letter to Captain James Wallace of the HMS *Rose*, a British warship stationed at the Island of Rhode Island.[16] She carried Church's letter between her stocking and her leg to the Newport house of a former lover she had known in Boston, Godfrey Wenwood, a local baker who she thought was a Tory.[17] She had asked him to help her to contact Captain James Wallace, Mr. Charles Dudley (the Newport customs collector), or George Rome, who was a prominent loyalist merchant and ship owner.[18] Wenwood who was contemplating marriage to a local girl did not want the vestige of his wild nights in Boston coming to him. He told her how dangerous it was to see any of the men she mentioned. She gave Wenwood the letter addressed to Major Cane to make a secret delivery to one of the three Newport contacts.[19] Unsure of what to do, he contacted a friend by the name of Adam Maxwell, a school-teacher. Together they opened the letter but were unable to read it because of its unrecognizable characters. They decided that the safest course of action was not deliver a coded letter that they could not read.

Dr. Church, overwhelmed with fear that his letter to Major Cane had gone astray and fallen into the wrong hands, tried to resign from the Continental army on September 20. Claiming that his family needed him, he was able to procure a furlough to be away from camp. While he was at home Dr. Church most assuredly destroyed any evidence against him, just as he had done previously when the courier Timothy visited him. Four days later Washington sent information to Dr. Church that his request to resign was refused but he could extend his furlough and stay with his family for a few more days.[20]

Sometime in September Godfrey Wenwood in Newport received a very anxious letter from Dr. Church's paramour, who was in Little Cambridge.[21] Wenwood reasoned that someone had become aware that the ciphered letter he was holding had not made it to British Major Cane in Boston. Wenwood became apprehensive that the author of the letter had been and was still in contact with the British in Boston and this communication could be injurious to America. He and Maxwell took the coded letter to Henry Ward, secretary of the Whig government in Providence, Rhode Island. On September 26, 1775 Ward sent both of them with the ciphered letter to General Nathanael Greene, commander of the Rhode Island contingent of the Continental army surrounding Boston. Because Wenwood was known in Boston, Ward was afraid that the visitor's presence at Cambridge across the river from his paramour would tip off the spy, so he had him stop at Dedham. Wenwood was instructed to wait there in case he was needed. Maxwell continued the trip as instructed to General Greene, his former pupil, and delivered both Ward's and the ciphered letter to General Greene at Prospect Hill, Massachusetts.[22] Greene promptly passed the letters along to General Washington.

Realizing that the ciphered letter probably contained military intelligence and a spy was most assuredly in their midst, Washington "immediately secured the woman but for a long time she was proof against every threat and persuasion to discover the author. However, at length she was brought to a confession and named Dr. Church."[23] Washington ordered a special guard composed of a captain and forty men to place Dr. Church under house arrest at Mrs. Vassal's house.[24] General Greene had sent Mr. Gouch in search of Silas Downer, who had a reputation as an expert decipherer, and asked Ward to provide Downer with a horse and money and send him to the army headquarters as soon as possible.[25] He further instructed Ward not to tell anyone of Downer's undertaking except to Deputy Governor Cooke because the contents of the intercepted letter was unknown.[26]

Benjamin Thompson, later Count Rumford, engraved in 1797. He assisted British army deserters to return to Boston and wrote the first known invisible ink letter of the American Revolution. He may have assisted Dr. Benjamin Church Jr. to destroy his correspondence with the British. (*William L. Clements Library*)

When the news of Dr. Church's arrest reached the army, the rumor mill worked overtime and circulated a story that a deserter was picked up carrying Dr. Church's letter. In the letter Dr. Church supposedly wrote to British General Gage "not to be uneasy for he [Dr. Church] had killed more men in the hospital than the British had killed at Bunker Hill."[27]

Washington also ordered Dr. Church's papers seized. However it was generally believed that someone had gotten access to Church's papers at the widow Vassal's house prior to arrival of the guards. The visitor may have been another British spy, Benjamin Thompson, who on October 13 fled Woburn, Massachusetts, for the British warship *Scarborough* in Newport, Rhode Island.[28] Thompson and Dr. Church were acquainted.

There is another possibility as to what happened to Dr. Church's papers: Penelope Vassall's house contained a secret room. Dorothy Dudley in her diary wrote, "Major Appleton called my attention one day to a large panel in the wall near the fireplace opening which he stepped into the cavity and shut the door. I found it hard to believe my eyes as I saw him disappear in the wall, but afterwards made assurance doubly sure by peeping into the closet myself and discovered ample space for hiding treasures of any description, and for secreting a fugitive could he find air to keep him alive."[29] It is possible that no one had taken the documents but that they were concealed in the secret closet and destroyed by Dr. Church during his house arrest.

On Sunday morning October 1 Elbridge Gerry heard the news about the ciphered letter being intercepted.[30] He knew that Colonel Elisha Porter was an expert in deciphering and suggested to him that he tender his services to General Washington, who took him up on his offer. The ciphered letter was delivered on Monday evening to Colonel Porter. Unbeknownst to Washington, Porter asked Gerry's assistance in deciphering the letter.[31] At the same time a chaplain and former Harvard classmate of Dr. Church's, Reverend Samuel West, worked independently on the letter.[32] Both groups made identical translations of Dr. Church's ciphered letter that were delivered to General Washington on October 3, 1775.

Church had used a type of cipher known as monoalphabetic substitution. This cipher uses a different letter or character to represent each letter of the alphabet. Doctors James McHenry and Charles McKnight gave Church the bad news that his cipher was broken and his letter was translated.[33] The code that Dr. Church used was:[34]

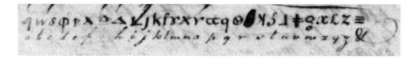

On October 3 a Council of War was begun consisting of Generals Washington, Greene, Heath, Lee, Putnam, Spencer, Sullivan, Thomas, and Ward. Washington informed the council of the discovery of Dr. Benjamin Church having a correspondence with the enemy in Boston by means of a ciphered letter that he said was decoded by Reverend West. He presented the council with the letter and the translation.[35] In the letter Dr. Church said that he has made three attempts to get this letter to the recipient. The last man was discovered, but his letter was hidden in the waistband of the man's breeches. The man was confined for a few days and some well-spent cash got him released. The ciphered letter stated that Dr. Church had gone to Salem to reconnoiter the situation and provided military information on troop strength and weapons. In his letter Church instructed that a response letter was to be sent to a confidential friend in Newport and addressed to fictitious Mr. Thomas Richards, merchant at Cambridge, but enclosed in a cover letter to Dr. Church. The cover letter was to say that Church, although a perfect stranger to the writer, had been recommended to him as a man of honor, and the writer took it upon himself to enclose the letter and entreating Church to deliver it.[36] The council decided there was sufficient evidence to continue and adjourned until the next day.

Church, knowing that he was in very grave trouble, wrote Washington that he knew his letter was deciphered and said it was written to his brother-in-law, John Fleming, who was a printer and an active loyalist. Church asserted that, when he was still in Boston, he obtained information from him on the British that he put to the American advantage. He said the story of the man being detained was to impress his brother-in-law and that he also lied about other things in the letter. Church asserted, "The end must apologize for the means." He said he concocted a scheme to have Fleming write to him under a feigned name and it was all part of his ploy to obtain intelligence from Fleming. Church says that he condemned "his heedless folly" and begged Washington "to shield him from undeserved infamy."[37]

The next day the war council called Dr. Church, who acknowledged that he was the author of the letter and the accuracy of the translation. He claimed that he was innocent as he was trying to impress the enemy with the size of the American army when it was in great need of ammunition in order to prevent an attack. The council unanimously found that Dr. Benjamin Church had carried on a "criminal correspondence" with the enemy. The council decided that because of the enormity of the crime and the extremely inadequate punishment available, that the selection of a punishment be deferred to the Continental Congress.[38]

The shock of Doctor Benjamin Church, one of the inner circle leaders of the rebellion and the highest-ranking politician still in Massachusetts, being found out as a British spy was inconceivable. His deed was overshadowed later only by Benedict Arnold's attempt to turn over West Point to the British. John Adams wrote from Philadelphia to his wife, Abigail, "The fall of Dr. Church, has given me many disagreeable reflections, as it places human nature itself in a point of bad light, but the virtue, the sincerity, the honor, of Boston and Massachusetts patriots in a worse.—What shall we say of a Country, which produces such characters as Hutchinson and Church?"[39]

The Continental Congress decided on November 7 that Dr. Church was to be held in close confinement without the use of pen, ink, and paper in some secure jail in the colony of Connecticut, and "that no person be allowed to converse with him except in the presence and hearing of a magistrate of the town or sheriff of the county where he shall be confined, and in the English language, until further orders from this or a future Congress."[40] Connecticut Governor Trumbull and his council ordered Dr. Church to be held at the Norwich jail.

Congress resolved that Dr. Benjamin Church be sent to the colony of Massachusetts where he was to post two bonds of not less than £1,000, "lawful money, for his appearance before such court as shall be erected for his trial, and at such time and place as such court shall direct, and to abide the judgment of the court."[41] Dr. Church on May 27, 1776, was removed from the Norwich, Connecticut jail and taken by Prosper Wetmore, Sheriff of New London County, to Boston and then to Watertown, Massachusetts.[42] Because he was unable to raise the money for the bonds, Dr. Church remained in jail in Massachusetts until the second half of 1777, at which time he was allowed to leave the United States. He set sail in a schooner under a Captain Smithwick to an island in the West Indies. He was never heard from again and was presumed lost at sea.[43] Dr. Church's wife went to England and filed pension requests in 1777 and 1782 and in support of her claim stated that her husband had provided certain services to the government. The British government gave Mrs. Church a pension of £150 per year for the services performed by her husband.[44]

General Sir Henry Clinton knew the importance of secure communications. He maintained a secret correspondence with Major

General William Phillips until Phillips's death on May 13, 1781. There are several extant letters of Sir Henry Clinton in which he discusses his personal ciphers.[45]

Not having a cipher could be a problem in communicating your instructions to your fellow officers and a major hindrance in conducting the war. General George Washington wanted to send a letter to Lieutenant General Luc Urbain de Bouëxic, Comte de Guichen, the French naval commander in the West Indies.[46] Since he had no cipher established with him, he had to get the Chevalier de la Luzerne to encipher his letter.[47] One might also need a cipher where one would not expect it. George Washington had such a problem and wrote from New Windsor on May 31, 1781, to Major General Marquis de Lafayette, "As you have no cypher by which I can write to you in safety, and my letters have been

Major General William Phillips was promoted through the ranks on his abilities. An expert in artillery, he was a confidant of General Sir Henry Clinton, and the two of them maintained a personal correspondence through masked letters. (*William L. Clements Library*)

frequently intercepted of late I restrain myself from mentioning many matters I wish to communicate to you."[48]

Spies stationed in the field sometimes think that the enemy may be closing in on them, and as they are easily disconcerted may want their codes or ciphers changed. Samuel Wallis was a British spy located in Muncy and Philadelphia, Pennsylvania. He wrote in a panicked letter on February 27, 1781, from Philadelphia that he wanted his controller to change his ciphers because of his fears.[49]

A basic cipher that was used was a simple substitution where one letter takes the place of another letter in the alphabet. The following design was an alphabetic transposition that was used during the American Revolution. Its basic format is to use n for a, m for b, etc.:[50]

a = n	h = i	o = y	v = w
b = m	i = e	p = v	w = s
c = l	j = d	q = x	x = z

d = k	k = c	r = t	y = o
e = i	l = b	s = u	z = y
f = h	m = a	t = r	
g = f	n = l	u = p	

Joseph Stansbury was a Philadelphia shopkeeper and poet who did the ciphering and deciphering for American General Benedict Arnold in his traitorous correspondence with British headquarters in New York City. When Stansbury sent the correspondence of June 7, 1780, from Benedict Arnold to George Beckwith, he used a simple transposition cipher of b = a, c = b, d = c, etc. (j and v were not always used in the eighteenth-century alphabet).[51] In the eighteenth century I and J were considered interchangeable. The following is their cipher:

Plain Text	A	B	C	D	E	F	G	H	I	K	L	M
Cipher Text	Z	A	B	C	D	E	F	G	H	I	K	L

Plain Text	N	O	P	Q	R	S	T	U	W	X	Y	Z
Cipher Text	M	N	O	P	Q	R	S	T	U	W	X	Y

Benedict Arnold also used a one-letter transposition cipher in his correspondence with his wife, Margaret "Peggy" Shippen Arnold. This cipher was a = b and b = c, and for proper names they used Brown and Entick's pocket *Dictionary* published in Philadelphia in 1777. An odd number denoted column one while an even number denoted column two.[52] It is the reverse of the preceding cipher.

Plain Text	A	B	C	D	E	F	G	H	I	K	L	M
Cipher Text	B	C	D	E	F	G	H	I	K	L	M	N

Plain Text	N	O	P	Q	R	S	T	U	W	X	Y	Z
Cipher Text	O	P	Q	R	S	T	U	W	X	Y	Z	A

The Reverend Jonathan Odell was Joseph Stansbury's counterpart in the ciphering and deciphering of the correspondence between Arnold and British headquarters. Odell wrote the instructions concerning a cipher used by Mr. L which stood for Mr. Lothario—none other than John André, who was the case agent running the Benedict Arnold correspondence at British headquarters. Mr. L's cipher was

"Reversing the alphabet, using the last as the first letter, in the first line, in the second line, using the last but one as the first, continuing to drop a letter each line in that manner to O inclusive, then beginning again as at first."[53]

The following would be John André's cipher chart if we assume he used the usual practice in the eighteenth century of I and J being the same letter as well as U and V. This system is a reversed eighteenth-century alphabet. The spy does not have to carry a chart as it is easy to remember and reconstruct as needed. As the spy writes his message he changes to the next line when he changes lines in the message. The spy would have to construct the table from scratch each time he wanted to cipher or decipher a letter. It would be too dangerous to keep a copy.[54]

A	B	C	D	E	F	G	H	I	K	L	M	N	O	P	Q	R	S	T	U	W	X	Y	Z
Z	Y	X	W	U	T	S	R	Q	P	O	N	M	L	K	I	H	G	F	E	D	C	B	A
Y	X	W	U	T	S	R	Q	P	O	N	M	L	K	I	H	G	F	E	D	C	B	A	Z
X	W	U	T	S	R	Q	P	O	N	M	L	K	I	H	G	F	E	D	C	B	A	Z	Y
W	U	T	S	R	Q	P	O	N	M	L	K	I	H	G	F	E	D	C	B	A	Z	Y	X
U	T	S	R	Q	P	O	N	M	L	K	I	H	G	F	E	D	C	B	A	Z	Y	X	W
T	S	R	Q	P	O	N	M	L	K	I	H	G	F	E	D	C	B	A	Z	Y	X	W	U
S	R	Q	P	O	N	M	L	K	I	H	G	F	E	D	C	B	A	Z	Y	X	W	U	T
R	Q	P	O	N	M	L	K	I	H	G	F	E	D	C	B	A	Z	Y	X	W	U	T	S

This chart is very similar to one that James Lovell had set up for use by American Major General Horatio Gates. Lovell's was a Vigenère cipher using the key word *James*. Any keyword can be used. A Vigenère cipher uses a table that lists the alphabet across the top and the side and each entry slips one letter (see next page).

The sender and the receiver agree on a keyword such as *George*. The keyword is written out and repeated as often as needed to complete the message. The message that is to be encoded, *James Long is a spy*, is placed below the keyword. Finding the point where the keyword letter and the message letter intersect in the Vigenère table yields the cipher letter. The cipher line is the message that is sent.

	a	b	c	d	e	f	g	h	i	k	l	m	n	o	p	q	r	s	t	u	w	x	y	z
a	A	B	C	D	E	F	G	H	I	K	L	M	N	O	P	Q	R	S	T	U	W	X	Y	Z
b	B	C	D	E	F	G	H	I	K	L	M	N	O	P	Q	R	S	T	U	W	X	Y	Z	A
c	C	D	E	F	G	H	I	K	L	M	N	O	P	Q	R	S	T	U	W	X	Y	Z	A	B
d	D	E	F	G	H	I	K	L	M	N	O	P	Q	R	S	T	U	W	X	Y	Z	A	B	C
e	E	F	G	H	I	K	L	M	N	O	P	Q	R	S	T	U	W	X	Y	Z	A	B	C	D
f	F	G	H	I	K	L	M	N	O	P	Q	R	S	T	U	W	X	Y	Z	A	B	C	D	E
g	G	H	I	K	L	M	N	O	P	Q	R	S	T	U	W	X	Y	Z	A	B	C	D	E	F
h	H	I	K	L	M	N	O	P	Q	R	S	T	U	W	X	Y	Z	A	B	C	D	E	F	G
i	I	K	L	M	N	O	P	Q	R	S	T	U	W	X	Y	Z	A	B	C	D	E	F	G	H
k	K	L	M	N	O	P	Q	R	S	T	U	W	X	Y	Z	A	B	C	D	E	F	G	H	I
l	L	M	N	O	P	Q	R	S	T	U	W	X	Y	Z	A	B	C	D	E	F	G	H	I	K
m	M	N	O	P	Q	R	S	T	U	W	X	Y	Z	A	B	C	D	E	F	G	H	I	K	L
n	N	O	P	Q	R	S	T	U	W	X	Y	Z	A	B	C	D	E	F	G	H	I	K	L	M
o	O	P	Q	R	S	T	U	W	X	Y	Z	A	B	C	D	E	F	G	H	I	K	L	M	N
p	P	Q	R	S	T	U	W	X	Y	Z	A	B	C	D	E	F	G	H	I	K	L	M	N	O
q	Q	R	S	T	U	W	X	Y	Z	A	B	C	D	E	F	G	H	I	K	L	M	N	O	P
r	R	S	T	U	W	X	Y	Z	A	B	C	D	E	F	G	H	I	K	L	M	N	O	P	Q
s	S	T	U	W	X	Y	Z	A	B	C	D	E	F	G	H	I	K	L	M	N	O	P	Q	R
t	T	U	W	X	Y	Z	A	B	C	D	E	F	G	H	I	K	L	M	N	O	P	Q	R	S
u	U	W	X	Y	Z	A	B	C	D	E	F	G	H	I	K	L	M	N	O	P	Q	R	S	T
w	W	X	Y	Z	A	B	C	D	E	F	G	H	I	K	L	M	N	O	P	Q	R	S	T	U
x	X	Y	Z	A	B	C	D	E	F	G	H	I	K	L	M	N	O	P	Q	R	S	T	U	W
y	Y	Z	A	B	C	D	E	F	G	H	I	K	L	M	N	O	P	Q	R	S	T	U	W	X
z	Z	A	B	C	D	E	F	G	H	I	K	L	M	N	O	P	Q	R	S	T	U	W	X	Y

An eighteenth-century Vigenère table would look like this if J and V are omitted.

Keyword	g	e	o	r	g	e	g	e	o	r	g	e	g	e	o
Message	J	A	M	E	S	L	O	N	G	I	S	A	S	P	Y
Cipher	P	E	A	W	Z	P	U	R	U	A	Z	E	Z	T	M

Since the intended receiver knows the keyword, the receiver can make up the three rows. The receiver writes down the cipher text on one line. Then the receiver writes the keyword and repeats it under each letter of cipher text. On a third line the receiver writes the letter where the two letters of the cipher and the keyword lines intersect in the table. When all the intersections are completed, the hidden message is revealed: *James Long is a spy.*

Cipher	P E A W Z P U R U A Z E Z T M
Keyword	*g e o r g e g e o r g e g e o*
Message	J A M E S L O N G I S A S P Y

Another type of cipher which was used by the Americans, British, French, and Hessians with slight variations in the American Revolution was called the pigpen cipher. It was later used by Napoleon's spies and was still in use during the American Civil War. Union soldiers who were being held in Confederate jails would use the pigpen cipher to communicate with those outside the jail. To construct a pigpen cipher, the alphabet was broken into a nine-square blocks that look like a tic-tac-toe game. The parties using the pigpen cipher had to agree on the placement of the letters in the pigpen. Any format could be used.

ABC	DEF	GHI
JKL	MNO	PQR
STU	VWX	YZ

Each letter of a message is indicated by drawing the position in the diagram where the letter is represented, and a dot to indicate which letter in that position. No dot would be the first letter, one dot would be the second letter, and two dots would be the third letter. It you wanted to send the word traitor, and then it would look like this:

TRAITOR

French Vice Admiral Jean Baptiste Charles Henri Hector, Comte d'Estaing, had a slightly different version of the pigpen cipher. His system employed the pigpen in an X arrangement. The first letter in the box gets a dot and is placed in the box, and no dot represents the second letter in the box. However a note on the back of the document indicates that U and V were the same symbol and there was no character for either J or Z (there was also no V).[55]

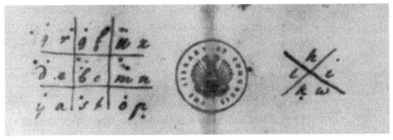

Lieutenant Johann Heinrich von Bardeleben of the von Donop Regiment used a pigpen cipher in his diary. In Bardeleben's system one dot would be the first letter, two dots would be the second letter, and three dots would be the third letter. The dots were placed below the horizontal line.[56]

ABC	DEF	GHIJ
KLM	NOP	QRS
TUV	WXY	Z

Prisoners of war during the American Revolution devised an unusual clandestine communication method. As the soldiers were naturally desirous of news of how the war was going and their prospects of getting released, they created means to communicate to each other. Captains Alexander Graydon and George Taylor of the 3rd Pennsylvania Battalion were captured with the surrender of Fort Washington on Harlem Heights on York Island (now Manhattan) on November 16, 1776.[57] Graydon was paroled on July 7, 1777. After paying for room and board he was taken from Long Island by a ship under a flag of truce to Elizabeth Town, New Jersey. Captain George Tudor 3rd Pennsylvania Battalion created a cipher for Graydon to use to send back what the soldiers desperately wanted to know. "The disguise was not in the character, but in the substitution of one piece of information for another,—for instance, a lady who was to be named, was to signify the army, and if that was strong and in a prosperous train, it was to be indicated by announcing the health and charming looks of the lady. There was a scale in the key, by which the intelligence might be graduated; and it was so contrived, as to admit of the transmission of pretty satisfactory information in a few important particulars." Alexander Graydon said that sending the letter was the first thing he did upon his getting home.[58]

One of the methods used by Sir Henry Clinton during the American Revolution was a numeric cipher where numbers equaled letters of the alphabet such as 62,53 used to represent H,C or Henry Clinton.[59] There is no explanation for the jump in numbers from 55 to 60 in this monoalphabetic substitution. One can only guess that it was to provide some additional security to the system.

Plain Text	A	B	C	D	E	F	G	H	I	K	L	M
Cipher Text	51	52	53	54	55	60	61	62	63	64	65	66
Plain Text	N	O	P	Q	R	S	T	U	W	X	Y	Z
Cipher Text	67	68	69	70	71	72	73	74	75	76	77	78

George Beckwith communicated with John André on July 13, 1780, by means of tiny strips of paper written in French. These strips of paper were one quarter-inch wide and could easily be sewn in the seam of a garment or placed between a book's binding and its cover, making detection nearly impossible. If the strips of paper were found, one had to be able to break the code and cipher in French and then translate the message from French to English.[60] This certainly complicated the job of anyone attempting to discover the message. The following is the system that was used:

French:	A	B	C	D	E	F	G	H	(I & J)	K	L	M	N	O	P	Q	R	S
Code:	G	X	N	Q	H	U	L	W	M	C	C	O	S	A	F	E	L	V

French:	T	U	V	W	X	Y	Z	(J'ai)	(et)	(Vous)	(le)(l'arme)
Code:	V	K	T	P	1	Z	4	9	5	3	\/

French:	(General)	(Magazine)
Code:	Q	T on top of a box

Lieutenant Colonel Nisbet Balfour of the 23rd Regiment of Foot on April 24, 1781, used the following cipher to instruct Captain Saunders to remain at Georgetown as American General Greene's army was before Camden and that Saunders was to join with Lord Cornwallis on his march if he could possibly get to him. If not then he was to wait at Georgetown for further orders.[61]

A=6	B=5	C=4	D=3	E=2	F=1
G=12	H=11	I,J=10	K=9	L=8	M=7
N=18	O=17	P=16	Q=15	R=14	S=13
T=24	U=23	V=22	W=21	X=20	Y=19

General Nathanael Greene and Colonel Henry "Light Horse Harry" Lee used a code to communicate in 1781 in the Carolinas. (See Appendix L for part of their code.)[62] In addition to ciphers there where also code charts where a number had a designated meaning or were words had an alternate meaning. All you needed to do was to find the word or number in a chart and the chart would give you the correct interpretation.[63] It is like today's postal zip code where the number replaces a town's name and state. Just like in the Johnny Rivers song *Secret Agent Man*, "they've given you a number and taken away your name."

American Major Benjamin Tallmadge of the 2nd Regiment of Continental Light Dragoons prepared a chart that did exactly as the song would say two hundred years later. In his chart 722 was Samuel Culper, 723 = Culper Jr., 724 = Austin Roe, 725 = C. Brewster, 726 = Rivington, 727 = New York, 728 = Long Island, 731 = Bergen, 732 = Staten Island, 735 = Connecticut, 736 = New Jersey, etc.[64] Tallmadge used John Entick's *New Spelling Dictionary* to develop a codebook for use in the Culper spy ring. Copies of the code were given to Culper Jr. and Sr. and General Washington.

The former colonial agent for New Hampshire, Paul Wentworth, worked as a British case agent running spies in France. His secret correspondence was accomplished in a mixture of both code and cipher. The agreed-upon method was written out by Lord Suffolk on December 5, 1776.[65]

Some of the systems used a cipher in addition to the basic alphabetic code representing words or phrases. Among the Clinton Papers is such a system that was used by two spies in 1781. Letters of the alphabet were represented by numbers. Single letters or lowercase letters stand for the names of persons or places. Double letters represent military units. Below are the substitutions of numbers for letters of the alphabet.[66]

A = 21   G = 31   M = 38   S = 64   Y = 41
B = 25   H = 35   N = 45   T = 62   Z = 49
C = 22   I = 28   O = 76   U = 80
D = 36   J = 34   P = 75   V = 73
E = 32   K = 23   Q = 78   W = 55
F = 27   L = 44   R = 72   X = 58

In addition to the alphabet, the spy code-named Squib also had the following representations available to him:

01 = then   3 = this   8 = for   93 = at   96 = them
2 = in   4 = under   9 = is   94 = from 97 = they
02 = where   7 = to   92 = you   95 = the   98 = will not

A numerical code containing 846 numbers was used by the Virginia delegates to the Continental Congress in 1782 in their official correspondence with the Governor of the Commonwealth.[67] A sample of the chart follows. A line over the number would make the word plural and a line under it doubles it.

1 bo   11 even
2 end   12 our
3 car   13 shall
4 part   14 F
5 has   15 be
6 the   16 France
7 his   17 rather
8 altho   18 give
9 may   19 effect
10 circumstance   20 execut

William Lee writing on June 17, 1779, was trying to set up an intelligence operation in England. He had extremely high hopes for his agent. He requested "to have immediate and accurate intelligence of every movement in the British Secret Cabinet, and of all secret intelligence that may be conveyed there from every quarter. In the prosecution of the plan, particular attention will be necessary to the Admiralty and Secretary of State's offices, tho' perhaps if a key could be found to the Secret Cabinet itself, it will be the shortest way of going to work, as well as the surest." He was going to pay his contact £200 sterling every quarter exclusive of expenses in sending the reports. He set up a response code that the person would write that would indicate they had taken the job. It was "I have received a letter of date —, the contents of which are agreeable and shall be complied with." The letter was to be directed Mr. Thomas Tomlin under a cover directed to "A Monsr. Richards, chez Mess. Frederic Miller et fils, Negociants, Frankfort sur Maine." It was to be franked in London and sent by the common post via Ostend.

William Lee also provided his hoped-for agent with a substitution alphabet for his reports.

Plain Text: A B C D E F G H I J K L M
Cipher Text: I J K L M N O P Q R S T U

Plain Text: N O P Q R S T U V W X Y Z
Cipher Text: V W X Y Z A B C D E F G H

William Lee wrote the following instructions, "In this alphabet use the letters (when writing) of the second line to mean the letters of the first line, and when reading, suppose the letters of the second line are always used for the letters directly above them in the first line. As for instance, King of France may be written thus sgvownnzivkm, and sometimes to render the deciphering almost impracticable & and ? may be occasionally be introduced between the letters in the same word, and are to have no meaning [nulls]."[68]

The British were also trying to set up a spy operation that involved the use of codes and ciphers. Lord George Germain in London had devised a plan to obtain intelligence from the French island of Martinique (which Germain called Martinico, its name at the time).

Because the Dutch were still neutrals at the time, vessels from St. Eustatius, a Dutch colony, were freely admitted to trade at Martinique.[69] The British undercover agent, a merchant at St. Eustatius, had to secure someone who would go to Martinique in a trading vessel to procure intelligence. If the agent knew when the trading vessel was returning from Martinique, he could have a vessel lying in wait for it between St. Lucia and Martinique. The captain of the trading vessel could be summoned to the British ship and provide his intelligence and then allowed to depart because he was a Dutch trader, that is, a neutral in the war, and maintain his cover. If they did not meet at sea then the intelligence from Martinique would be transmitted through St. Eustatius to a British agent on St. Kitts. Germain wrote that the person who collected the intelligence needed to keep a fast vessel operating between St. Eustatius and St. Kitts. A correspondent at St. Kitts should have a vessel at his disposal to get the information to the admirals. The document advised that these two people should establish certain phrases—a code—between them through which they might correspond without running the risk of being discovered.[70] It is unknown if this plan was carried out.

Ciphering and coding and the reversals were tiresome operations. Despite all the checking and rechecking, mistakes still got into the systems and frustrated those involved. British General Frederick Haldimand, who was in charge of the Northern Army at Quebec on November 23, 1778, proposed a cipher system that he and General Sir Henry Clinton could use for their documents.[71]

Haldimand did not get a response from Clinton so he tried again and sent a letter on May 26, 1779. He stated he was pretty certain about the safety of this letter and Mr. Gordon, the courier, was provided with the means to destroy the documents. Haldimand had another trick up his sleeve. He stated they would note the date on the intelligence letter. That number for the date would be used to count that number of lines from the top of the page. The resulting line would become the new line 1 and continue counting the lines down the page. He had proposed using a book that every British officer had, the British Army List. General Haldimand's system used the title page, which was the same in all editions except for the year of publication, which appears near the bottom of the page. Haldimand wrote, "I leave that out and I number the other lines of the page from 1 to 29 beginning at the top. I numbered in like manner every alphabetical letter in each line from left to right, but there being no Q in all the page, I represent that letter by one of the signs following ⊙ Ø which will signify alike the letter Q wherever they are found."

Haldimand also writes that he will not repeat a letter when it is doubled: "parallel," for example, will be coded as "paralel." He instructed, "Words are not separated because the letters once found out it will be easy with little attention and form the words. The writing is to be in column that is one figure under another from top to bottom. The first number of the column signifies the line of the book, The second denotes the letter in that line is meant. Here for cxample 4 2, the number 4 refers to the fourth line of the page used, and 2 signifies that the letter described is the second letter in that line."

[*By Permiſſion.*]

A

L   I   S   T

OF THE

General and Staff Officers

AND OF THE

OFFICERS in the ſeveral REGIMENTS
ſerving in NORTH-AMERICA,

Under the Command of His Excellency General
SIR WILLIAM HOWE, K. B.

With the DATES of their COMMISSIONS as they Rank
In each CORPS and in the ARMY.

NEW-YORK:
Printed by MACDONALD & CAMERON in Water-Street, between
the Coffee-Houſe and Old Slip-Bridge. 1777.

British Army List of the general and staff officers serving in North America with the dates of their commissions. It was a book that almost every officer had in order to know their seniority. Printed by Macdonald and Cameron, New York, 1777.

Haldimand provided a sample with a cipher. "I have certain intelligence of a detachment of Eight Thousand Rebels &c."[72]

Two years later General Haldimand wrote to General Sir Henry Clinton in New York "the cipher is a very tedious one but impossible to be discovered." In the same report he advises, "I wait for a vessel to send you a cipher less tedious and feel as safe."[73] He wanted to streamline the operation to the point quickly.

George Washington wanted all the collateral information he could gather. He had just received information from Jacob Bayley by way of James Lovell. Washington wrote Lovell, "I thank you for the trouble you have taken in forwarding the intelligence which was inclosed in your letter of the 11th of March. It is by comparing a variety of information, we are frequently enabled to investigate facts, which were so intricate or hidden, that no single clue could have led to the knowledge of them in this point of view, intelligence becomes interesting

4 – 2	– 14	– 3	9 – 5	– 1	20 – 4
11 – 1	– 25	9 – 5	13 – 7	11 – 2	6 – 5
– 8	7 – 11	– 6	– 25	– 20	– 4
22 – 6	– 12	9 – 1	– 26	4 – 4	13 – 1
– 3	– 13	– 2	– 27	5 – 4	– 16
20 – 16	– 14	3 – 1	– 28	– 1	– 21
– 7	4 – 1	11 – 6	11 – 2	25 – 3	– 23
– 15	– 2	– 5	– 17	– 7	27 – 9
– 1	6 – 1	– 20	6 – 2	– 1	– 10
– 5	– 2	– 8	– 12	– 11	

The cipher proposed by General Frederick Haldimand for use with the British Army List. The first number of each column signifies the line in the book and the second number identifies the letter in that line.

which but from its connection and collateral circumstances, would not be important."[74]

George Washington knew the importance of ciphers and codes in keeping his correspondence from prying eyes. He wanted to write to the Count de Guichen. As its contents needed to remain a secret from the enemy should the letter be intercepted and he did not have a system in place with the count, he wrote to Anne Césare, Chevalier de la Luzerne, asking his help to use his cipher. He also requested that the message be sent in triplicate as soon as possible.[75]

General George Washington had several alphabetic ciphers that he could use (illustration next page).[76]

William Heron (1742-1819) was a prominent citizen of Redding, Connecticut, and a double agent who played both sides to his advantage. In the winter of 1778–1779, American General Samuel Holden Parsons's headquarters were located in Esquire Betts's on Redding Ridge, Connecticut, diagonally across the wide main street from Heron's house. About 1780 he began his spying for the British as one of Oliver De Lancey's agents and at the same time was a trusted agent for Parsons.

British General and Royal Governor of New York James Robertson on September 21, 1780, wrote from New York to William Knox. In the letter he states, "I found means to have a conference with a man versant in the rebel councils. I give you what he related as I think it

General George Washington's four cipher alphabets. The fourth alphabet is French Admiral d'Estaing's pigpen cipher (see page 56). (*Library of Congress*) will explain the state of the country and convey you information, that might not be preserved in an abstract." The enclosure was a report from William Heron, who had come to New York City on September 4 under a flag of truce.[77]

Heron wrote in code and disguised handwriting to MΘ7911 3ΘLΘN213 (Oliver De Lancey) in care of Reverend John Sayre, New York, on October 1, 1780.[78] The document was deciphered by De Lancey and endorsed by Captain Beckwith.

Oliver De Lancey wrote to Heron on October 29, 1780, "I shall the next opportunity send the passport you require, or anything else you may desire. . . I shall be most obliged to you for a state of the army . . . to be sent in code."[79] When Herron did not venture to the city himself he used one Bulkly as a courier to De Lancey.[80]

Also available to the British during the American Revolution was a system which used a biblical theme. The following were some of the names:[81]

Augusta, Georgia	Simon
Bedford, Pennsylvania	Tyr
Congress	synagogue
Delaware River	Red Sea
Detroit	Alexandria
Fort Pitt [Pittsburgh]	Gomorrah
Susquehanna River	Jordan
Wallace's House in Muncy, Pennsylvania	Peter
George Washington	James
Wyoming, Pennsylvania	Sodom

The method of using musical notes or a harmonic alphabet to convey secret messages was published by Philip Thicknesse in 1772. Thicknesse claims it was created by Domingo Gonsales, a fictional astronaut from the book *The Man in the Moone* by Francis Godwin, published posthumously in 1638.[82] Gonsales was taken to the moon in a chariot towed by trained geese. The reader was told to send notes and no words in order to better hide the message. He clarified that any musician can convey notes by pitch class which express the first seven

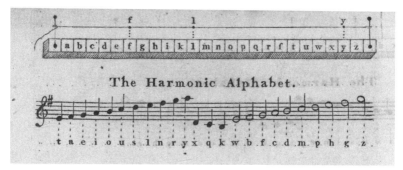

The Harmonic Alphabet was known at the time of the American Revolution, but ciphered music from the war has yet to be found. Sir Henry Clinton loved music and had a large collection of sheet music in New York. (*University of Pennsylvania, Rare Book and Manuscript Library of the Van Pelt-Dietrich Library*)

letters of the Latin alphabet: A, B, C, D, E, F, and G and know them by ear when the notes are toned. The correspondents need to fix the remaining part of the alphabet. He likened this to sign language. He suggested that the plain notes, the crotchets (quarter notes) and minums, alone make up the alphabet. He recommends ignoring the flats and sharps.

To provide the date of the message in this harmonic alphabet with no words, the first twelve lines represent the month. A dot placed in front of line four would indicate the month of April and a dash represent the day.[83]

Deciphering an encrypted letter is not an easy task. Intercepting a coded letter did not always result in successful deciphering. In one case the Americans had obtained a letter from Lord Cornwallis written in numeric code. They wanted to decipher it to find out the British military's plans. Despite their best efforts, Brigadier General Jethro Sumner had to inform Brigadier General William Davidson on October 11, 1780, "Several Gentleman have attempted but without success to decipher Cornwallis' figures."[84]

Also just because someone uses a cipher, it does not mean that they can decipher it. British General Sir Henry Clinton wrote to Lord

George Germain, British Secretary of State for America, on June 9, 1781, that they had intercepted some mail from Lieutenant General Jean-Baptiste Donatien de Vimeur, Comte de Rochambeau, commander of the French forces at Newport, Rhode Island, to the Chevalier de la Luzerne, French minister to the United States. The correspondence appeared to be very significant but they had not been able to discover the code key in order to decode the message.[85] A case of partial success was that of William Eden. In 1777 Anthony Todd, assistant director at the secret service office at the general post office in London, was sending Eden, Commissioner of the Board of Trade and Plantations, mail intercepts. As as result of the intercepted mail, Eden was trying to break Horace Walpole's cipher as well as another cipher.[86] (His progress in deciphering the letters is reprinted as an appendix.) Eden was successful with the alphabetic cipher, which is:

A B C D E F G H I K L M
N O P Q R S T U V W Y Z

N O P Q R S T U V W X Y Z
A B C D E F G H I K L X M

William Smith in a series of letters concerning deciphering in 1745 believed that the vowels a, i, and o had the highest frequency. He asserted that all the words of two letters were: *ah, ha, am, an, as, at, in, is, it, of, oh, ho, on, no, or, do, go, lo, so,* and *to.* He also observed that *to* is the only two-letter word that begins with "T" and the words *on* and *no* discover themselves by consisting of the same two letters, differently placed. He found that there are 373 three-letter words. Smith says that when he starts to decipher some text that he starts with "with, are, on, at, it, did, the, that, have, and, are, which, they, these, their, them, where, all, shall, with, those."[87]

In the English language today the most commonly used letters are ETAONRI and the least used letters are KXJQZ. The letters "I" and "J" were not considered separate letters at the time of the American Revolution and were used interchangeably. "V" was used in place of "U." July could have been written IVLY and be perfectly understood. Therefore, the most common letters at the time of the American Revolution would be ETAONRIJ and the least common would be

VKXQZ. There is also the pairing of letters such as TH, HE, AN, RE, ER, IN, and ON which repeat often. There is a high frequency of English words that begin with the letters A, O, S, T, or W and end in D, E, S, or T.[88]

Observing frequency and patterns are key tools in the task of deciphering messages but those who develop codes and ciphers always try to stay one step ahead.

Chapter 6

DICTIONARY CODES

B ecause of the need for greater security, codes became more involved than simple letter or number substitutions. Referencing specific words in a book known only to both writer and recipient created an additional level of security. These book codes typically used a dictionary, as they were readily available. These dictionary codes were used for private, diplomatic, and state military secrets. Dr. Wallis in 1737 stated "there is scarce a person of quality, but is more or less acquainted with it [writing in cipher and code], and doth, as there is occasion, make use of it."[1]

Mail in the eighteenth century was generally carried from one tavern to the next tavern by any person heading in the general direction of the recipient. This left the contents of any letter open to the perusal of prying eyes. Thomas Jefferson when he was only twenty years old wrote from Devilsburg, which was his playful name for Williamsburg, Virginia, to John Page on January 23, 1764, about the inability of writing a secret message.[2] His confidential correspondence was all about the attractive sixteen-year-old Miss Rebecca Burwell, whom he was courting.[3] In Jefferson's correspondence with John Page, a Virginia legislator and planter, he had disguised Rebecca's identity by referring to "Campana in die" (Bell in day), "R.B.," "Belinda," "Adnileb" (Belinda spelled backward), and "αδνιλεβ" which is Adnileb in Greek.[4] Because he feared that some of his mail had gone astray, he informed John Page that in their future correspondence he would use Thomas Shelton's *TachyGraphy, The Most Exact and Compendious Methode of Short and Swift Writing that Ever Beene Published by Any*. It had been first published in London in 1641 but had been reprint-

ed a number of times.[5] By March 20 Jefferson found out that his cause
was lost and Miss Burwell would shortly marry Jacquelin Ambler.[6]

Diplomatic matters were the more usual context for dictionary
codes. Silas Deane, Benjamin Franklin, and Arthur Lee were the trio
that Congress appointed in 1776 as its commissioners to the court of
France.[7] Arthur Lee in the summer of 1776 suggested a plan to the
Secret Committee of Congress for encoding dispatches between
Philadelphia and Paris. "This book is better than the last I sent you. It
is to decipher what I wrote you and for you to write by. This is done
by putting the page where the word is to be found and the letter of the
alphabet corresponding in order with the word. As there are more
words in a page than the letter of the alphabet the letter must be doubled or trebled to answer that. As thus, to express the troops: you write
359, kk 381, vv- ing, ed, s, & must be added when necessary, and distinguished by making no comma between them and the figures.
Thus, for betray'd put 33 ed x. The letters I use are abcde-
fghijklmnopqrstuvwxyz which are 26." Arthur Lee advised that he
would not use this procedure until he knew it had arrived safely. "You
can write to Mrs. Lee on Tower Hill in a woman's hand. If you have
both books say the children are well: if the first only, the eldest child
is well, if this, the youngest child is well. They will let this pass."[8]

John Jay, graduate of King's College and a delegate to both the
First and Second Continental Congresses, had an ardent sense of the
need for cryptology during the American Revolution.[9] While in
Philadelphia to gain expertise in military tactics, he purchased a copy
of Thomas Simes's *The Military Guide for Young Officers, Containing
a System of the Art of War* for £1.2.6 from Robert Bell's bookstore in
Third Street.[10] John Jay was elected President of Congress and served
from December 10, 1778, to September 28, 1779. Jay ended his term
as President of Congress because the day before he "was elected
Minister Plenipotentiary to negotiate a treaty of alliance and of amity
and commerce between the United States of America and his
Catholic Majesty [the King of Spain]."[11]

Realizing the need for secrecy, he wrote Robert Livingston on
February 19, 1780, and suggested they use Abel Boyer's *French
Dictionary*, thirteenth edition, which was printed in London in
1771.[12] They were going to use the second part, in which English
comes first. He also wanted Livingston to tell him if the letter was

inspected which would indicate that someone was in on their plan.[13] Jay told him, "It is not paged. You will therefore number the pages, marking the first page with number 1 and so on." The first column would be marked "c," the second "a," and the third "b." To arrive at the word, Livingston was to count from the top of the column to and including the word and then add "7" to the original number. Using Jay's plan, 279b23 would indicate the word at page 279, third column, and sixteenth word (23-7=16) down the column. Jay gave the following example, "the word abject is the third word in the third column of the second page, and is to be written in ciphers as follows 2b10."[14] It was a good plan, but Robert Livingston was unable to obtain a copy of the book.[15]

Entick's Spelling Dictionary was a very popular tool with both Americans and Britons for enciphering their correspondence. It listed all words but proper names and was readily available, being in its thirteenth edition during the Revolutionary War. With so many editions, it was absolutely necessary for both the sender and receiver to ensure they had the same edition.

John Jay used different additive words and formats with others. In his communications from the port city of Cadiz, Spain with Irish-born Charles Thomson, the Secretary of the Continental Congress, he instructed Thomson to add ten instead of seven to the word selected and add five to the page. Jay also instructed Thomson to count from the bottom up instead of from the top down. To identify the column they would use an underline under the first digit for the first column, the second digit would be the second column, and the third digit would indicate the third column. "The word abased is the sixth word from the bottom in the third column of the first page. And [it] is to be written as follows 16.6. The word abhorrent is the fifth word in the second column of the second page. Add ten to the place of the word [and] add five to the number of the page and put the _ [underline] under the second figure thus 15.7." He also supplied a list of words not used in the dictionary—the names of states, members of Congress, and a few others—that were expressed in Roman numerals. The extra words included:[16]

Connecticut	XX	North Carolina	XXXIV	Rhode Island	XVIII
Delaware	XXVIII	New Hampshire	XXIV	South Carolina	XXXVI
Georgia	XXXVIII	New Jersey	XXIV	Virginia	XXXII

Maryland	XXX	New York	XXII
Massachusetts	XVI	Pennsylvania	XXVI

Samuel Adams	XI
John Dickinson	VI
John Hancock	XXXIII
James Lovell	XXXIX
Roger Sherman	LVIII
George Washington	LXVIII
Rev. Jonathan Witherspoon	LXI

John Jay provided Robert Morris of Philadelphia with a cipher. He wrote, "Should the following cipher reach you safe we may afterwards write with less reserve. Entick's spelling dictionary printed in 1777 paged backwards — the last page in the Book is numbered 468, let this be page the 1st and mark the first page (which is the title page) 468 — Count the words from the top distinguishing the column, and a – over the first figure for the first column, and a - over the second figure for the second column — For Instance, the word absent is the fifth word in the first column of page 434, and is to be thus written 5.434. [Although the instructions said to put a – over the first figure for the first column this was not always done.] . . . Perhaps the dictionary may not contain all the words you may have occasion to use. The following alphabet will supply that defect":[17]

A = l   G = r   M = w   S = d   Y = j
B = m   H = s   N = y   T = e   Z = k
C = n   I = t   O = z   U = f
D = o   J = u   P = a   V = g
E = p   K = v   Q = b   W = h
F = q   L = x   R = c   X = i

John Jay made every system different. Jay also sent instructions on *Entick's Spelling Dictionary* to Philadelphia native William Bingham, one of the richest Pennsylvanians at the start of the American Revolution.[18] He instructed Bingham to add ten to the number of the word and twenty to the number of the page. Dots were used to indicate columns. They distinguished the first column by a dot over the first figure, and the second column by a dot over the second figure. For instance, the word duration is the first word in the first column of page 139, and must be thus written 159 11. Again, the word beauty is the tenth word in the second column of the 60th page, and must be written, 80 20. A substitution alphabet was provided for words not in the dictionary.[19]

William Lee was at Paris and had received his appointment as the Commissioner to the Courts of Berlin and Vienna when he realized he needed some cipher to use in his communications with Congress. He made that known to Charles Thomson, who used ciphers with John Jay, in his letter of November 24, 1777. Lee was not instructed to whom to send his reports for Congress and advised Thomson that they would be sent to him.[20]

The three brothers Arthur, Richard Henry, and William Lee were using Entick's *New Spelling Dictionary* with some codenames added to the book. Arthur Lee sent his brother Richard Henry Lee a copy of the book on November 25, 1777, under the care of Captain Wickes and told Richard Henry that this was the book "by which we may communicate our thoughts without danger from mischievous curiosity."[21] Their cipher used an Arabic number for the page, a letter for the column, and Roman numerals for the line. William Lee employed at least four different systems for encoding his correspondence. In addition to the dictionary code, he used two systems which were based on an alphabetic substitution and a cipher system of numbers used to identify persons, places, and certain transactions.[22]

In the secret negotiations between Benedict Arnold and Sir Henry Clinton, commander of the British forces in North America, some of the letters were in book or dictionary ciphers. Arnold and Joseph Stansbury, a merchant, used the first volume of Blackstone's *Commentaries on the Laws of England* of the fifth Oxford edition. Three number unit clusters were used to identify the words of the cipher. The first number is the page, the second is the line on the page identified by the first number, and the third number is the word in the line that is identified by the line. For example 45.9.8 would be page forty-five (45), line nine (9), and the eighth (8) word. To disclose the message, you would open the book, in this case Blackstone's *Commentaries*, to page 45, then go down to line 9, then counting from the left go to the 8th word. This is then the word identified for the message. They found the random order too time-consuming and then switched to Nathan Bailey's *Universal Etymological English Dictionary*, the twenty-first and twenty-fifth editions. Arnold also added seven to the line number for added security. However, he forgot to do this to his letter of July 13, 1780.[23]

Stansbury used similar ciphers with other correspondents. In Philadelphia on May 25, 1779, there were protests against the depreciation of Continental Currency and increasing prices. People could not afford the necessities of life and they were blaming the rich merchants such as Robert Morris, who had warehouses full of flour and was holding out for higher prices. Stansbury had fled Philadelphia, afraid that he would receive the wrath of the public. He had written to the Reverend Jonathan Odell on May 26, 1779, that "the confusion of a town meeting hath banished me to Moorestown for preservation." Moorestown, New Jersey, is about thirteen miles east of Philadelphia. In this letter Stansbury tells Odell that the cipher to his last two letters was based on Bailey's *Dictionary*, the twenty-fifth London edition. Odell in New York City in a response to the May 26 letter writes on June 9, 1779, telling Stansbury "to stick to your Oxford Interpreter," that is, his Blackstone's *Commentaries* that they had been using. Stansbury, still in Moorestown on June 9, 1779, wrote to Odell that there were problems with using Blackstone's and preferred Bailey's. With all the danger of conducting this clandestine exchange, Stansbury had the audacity to be temperamental.

On June 9, 1779, Stansbury at Moorestown wrote to Odell, "Mr. A. G. [General Benedict Arnold] is at present out of town on private business. I have some time since forwarded to Mr. Andrews [John André] a plan of trade which will, I hope, be to the satisfaction of the concerned." On the same day Odell in New York City had written to Stansbury that Lothario (John André) was impatient. Odell must have received Stansbury's letter of June 9 by June 13, because on June 13 Odell wrote to John André that the "plan of trade" was on its way. It would not be unusual for letters to pass each other moving on their secret way across New Jersey. When it did arrive, it was in cipher using Bailey's *Dictionary*, the twenty-first edition.[24]

Benedict Arnold used a one-letter transposition cipher in his correspondence with his wife, Margaret "Peggy" Shippen Arnold. This cipher was a = b and b = c etc. and for proper names they used Brown and Entick's pocket *Dictionary* published in Philadelphia in 1777. An odd number denoted column one while an even number denoted column two. The second number in the series appears to be a null.[25]

Patrick Ferguson wrote to Sir Henry Clinton from Savannah, Georgia, on February 19, 1780, and describes it, as a "Duty town," that is, there would be no liberty from work. This gives a clear picture of how the British perceived their latest conquest. He stated that "you will be much disappointed in the advantages expected from this expedition unless he who is to conduct it shall wave etiquette exert himself without regard to routine to procure every aid from every quarter, look more towards expedients than difficulties, lay himself out for extensive and frequent intelligence, avail himself as a man of real genius of the zeal experience and industry of the officers and loyalists who know the country."[26] On April 14, 1780, Sir Henry Clinton wrote to Colonel James Webster that "as Ferguson has a cipher, you may risque a letter to me by any opportunity."[27] On April 22, Ferguson did send a letter to General Clinton in cipher.[28] Clinton sent a response to Colonel James Webster, also in cipher.[29]

Another printed book that was used solely by the British during the American Revolution was the British War Office publication of the *List of the General and Field Officers as They Rank in the Army*. This system was very convenient as the book was readily accessible to British officers and the cipher used only the title page. A September 13, 1781, correspondence lists the first cluster as "22.6.7.8.39.5.9.17." The first number in this case 22 referred to the line down the page and the remaining numbers were the words in the line.

Although deciphering a dictionary or other book-based code could be more tedious than earlier simple codes and relied on the recipient's access to the same published edition, these systems offered a far more secure method of transmitting confidential information.

Chapter 7

DIPLOMATIC CIPHERS

O ne of America's first secret agents was fifty-four-year-old Charles Guillaume Frédéric Dumas. He was an acquaintance of Benjamin Franklin, who in 1775 requested that he report on the foreign ambassadors in his hometown of The Hague, the Dutch capital.[1] His task was to report on "the disposition of the several courts with respect to such assistance or alliance, if we should apply for the one, or propose the other." He was also to win Dutch support for American efforts in its War of Independence. He was cautioned to keep his activities "from the knowledge of the English ambassador, and prevent any public appearance, at present, of your being employed in any such business." The American commissioners at Paris paid Dumas £100 and later 200 louis d'or a year through the firm of Hornica, Fitzeau and Company in Amsterdam.[2]

Given the lack of privacy in the mail system and the British secret service office's practice of intercepting letters (see Chapter 3), Dumas was instructed to avoid the postal system. Sir Joseph Yorke, the British ambassador at The Hague, managed to intercept a letter in the summer of 1776 addressed to Dumas that revealed his status as a secret agent. With Dumas being located in neutral Holland, Yorke was unable to do anything. Dumas continued his correspondence for five more years with Benjamin Franklin, the Committee of Foreign Affairs, and John Paul Jones.[3]

Pierre Augustin Caron de Beaumarchais, the playwright known for *The Barber of Seville* and *The Marriage of Figaro*, prior to the American Revolution worked as a secret agent for Louis XV and XVI. While Arthur Lee was in London he was approached by Beaumarchais about a plan to ship goods from France to the United

States. Upon Beaumarchais' return to France, the French Foreign
Ministry employed him to run the operation. The company was funded by France, by Spain, and by Beaumarchais. Arthur Lee (using the
covert name of Mary Johnson) carried on a communication with
Beaumarchais partly in cipher.[4]

While Arthur Lee was in London, he was advised to get in touch
with Dumas in The Hague through a merchant in Rotterdam. Some
letters from Franklin to Dumas by way of Philadelphia or from France
were sent to the address of Mr. A. Stuckey, merchant in Rotterdam.[5]
Dumas was instructed that messages going to London were to be sent
by a trusted courier to Mr. Alderman Lee, merchant, on Tower Hill
and his correspondence to Benjamin Franklin in care of Messrs.
Robert and Cornelius Stevenson, merchants, at St. Eustatius, an island
in the Caribbean.[6] Some of Dumas and Benjamin Franklin's correspondence went through St. Eustatius. Franklin was to address these
Dumas letters "for Mr. Vryman; and on top an Envelope with the
address of Mr. Mr. Mr. Rey Libraire in Amsterdam."[7] The
Netherlands, which controlled St. Eustatius, was a neutral power in
the struggle between England and France. Smugglers and ships of all
nations were welcomed in its port. American and French ships could
enter the port and purchase or exchange goods and they were safe in
Dutch waters until the British declared war on the Dutch Republic in
1780.

Because of the need for secrecy in their communications, Dumas
provided Franklin with a cipher based upon a text of French prose.
The passage generated 682 letters and symbols and provided numbers
equal to the letters' frequency in French. It provided 128 different
numbers for the letter "e" and 44 for "o." It also did not use either "k"
or "w" in its transcription. To solve the problem of not having a "w,"
Dumas told Franklin to use two "u"s which he did. A later edition
added four numbers for "k."

Dumas' cipher would provide more security than an alphanumer-
ic substitution cipher, where every letter is replaced by one number
if used properly. However encipers including Dumas tended to use
the first listed number for a letter, defeating the purpose. Another
problem was that Dumas only enciphered the words he thought were
the most sensitive which allowed the decipherer to guess at what was
enciphered.

Dumas advised Franklin, "the words on which I composed it are in the book that I sent to you lately, of which I follow the editor, and ahead of I wrote on a white layer my idea on the government and the royalty, whose you mark me that it did not displease. I indicate it enough to you, I think. You will find these words in my Letter with Mr. *** who follows immediately the title page III, IV and V." Franklin needed to check the books that Dumas had sent him and look for a personal note on government and royalty written in the book after the editor's introduction. Dumas had sent the new Dutch published edition in French which he edited of Vattel's *Law of Nations* to Franklin on June 30, 1775.[8]

Charles Dumas prided himself to Franklin that this passage even had all the required punctuation marks such as ampersands, commas, hyphens, periods, and asterisks. To make the system easier for Franklin, Dumas made up sheets with 1,000 numbers. He told Franklin to "take one of these sheets, and to write along columns, since 1 up to 682, (which is a point) letters or characters of 13 lines indicated, each character beside its number." Dumas told Franklin to use C and K interchangeably and two V's for a W. Later the numbers 683, 692, 701, and 715 are used for the letter K. Because there were multiple numbers for letters, it provided a degree of security.

The first Dumas cipher text which came from Emer de Vattel's *Le droit des gens, ou Principes de la loi naturelle, appliqués à la conduite et aux affaires des nations et des* souverains (1775 Amsterdam edition) is as follows: "Voulez-vous sentir la différence? Jetez les yeux sur le continent septentrional de l'Amérique." These two sentences are translated into English as "Do you want to feel the difference? Glance at the continent of North America."

V	O	U	L	E	Z	-	V	O	U	S	S	E	N	T	I	R
1	2	3	4	5	6	7	8	9	10	11	12	13	14	15	16	17

L	A	D	I	F	F	E	R	E	N	C	E	?	J	E	T	T
18	19	20	21	22	23	24	35	26	27	28	29	30	31	32	33	34

E	Z	L	E	S	Y	E	U	X	S	U	R	L	E	C	O	N
35	36	37	38	39	40	41	42	43	44	45	46	47	48	49	50	51

T   I   N E N T S E P T E N T R I O N
52 53 54 55 56 57 58 59 60 61 62 63 64 65 66 67 68

A   L   D E L ! A M E R I Q U E . D A
69 70 71 72 73 74 75 76 77 78 79 80 81 82 83 84 85

Dumas also would use another cipher that contained 928 elements. It listed words that appeared in alphabetical order and values
for some of the most popular eighteenth-century English words. From
The Hague, Dumas practiced his new cipher with Franklin at Passy,
France, on February 8, 1780.[9] In order to hide identities he used the
following code names: For himself he used "Concordia"; the French
ambassador in The Hague was called "le grand facteur"; Vergennes,
the French foreign minister, was called the "le commis"; and Abbé
Desnoyer, a former Jesuit and the French chargé d'affaires at The
Hague, was a △ (triangle). Listing words in alphabetical order makes
the job of deciphering secret correspondence easier for the enemy.
Franklin was still using Dumas' cipher in August 1781 in their correspondence but was using primarily numbers in the first 100. It would
have been more secure if a great array of numbers had been used.[10]

Another European cipher came from Dr. Jacques Barbeu-
Dubourg, a contact for the American emissaries in Paris. He was a
close friend of Benjamin Franklin's from 1767 until Barbeu-
Dubourg's death in 1779. A committee of Dickenson, Franklin,
Harrison, and Morris instructed Silas Deane to search out the
English-speaking Dr. Barbeu-Dubourg and described him as faithful,
intelligent in affairs, prudent, secret, and capable of giving Deane
sage advice. Barbeu-Dubourg took an active part in arranging military
and financial aid from France.[11] He wrote to Franklin from Paris on
June 10, 1776, and provided him with a plan for routing their mail
and a cipher. He cited the probability that some of their mail would
be intercepted owing to the many English vessels at sea. His plan was
to send an original and two copies of the letter by different vessels.
This way he figured that at least one of the letters would get to
Franklin. He stated in his cipher, for

every letter there is represented by several different figures,
of which one will employ sometimes the one and some-

times the other to put the curious one in default. The
words will be distinguished by the interposition of a Greek
character [letter] without consequence; two of these characters will have the value of a comma, and three will be
worth a point [a period]. It will be necessary to obliterate all
these Greek characters to read the letter easily or confusion. Let us do in immediately the essay. 3,2,b, 19, 5, 23,
16, 12, g~, 44, 53, d, 10, 51, 4, 61, q, 36, 17, 6, 24, 71, 1, 1,
42, 28, 37, 33, m, 82, 54, 11, 9, 8, 47, 59, 88, 13, 69, here,
31, 92, w, 72, 34, 56, 73, s, 6, 94, 4, 20, f,, 100.

This is what Jacques Barbeu-Dubourg sent Benjamin Franklin in
French as a sample:[12]

3	2	b	19	5	23	16	12	g	44	53	d	10	51	4	61
m	a		f	e	m	m	e		e	t		d	e	u	x
q	36	17	6	24	71	1	1	42	28	37	33	m
f	I	L	L	E	S		V	O	U	S

"Ma femme et deux filles vous" translates to "My wife and two girls
you." The original copy of the cipher has become separated from the
original letter but the following is a partial reconstruction of the
cipher:[13]

1	2	3	4	5	6	10	12
S	A	M	U	E	L	D	E
16	17	19	23	24	28	33	36
M	I	F	M	L	O	S	F
37	42	44	51	53	61	71	
U	V	E	E	T	X	E	

James Lovell was an important figure in this type of American spycraft. Born on October 31, 1737 and educated at Harvard, James
Lovell was usher, or assistant teacher, at the South Latin School
under his father, master John Lovell, who sent his students home mid-
morning on April 19, the day of the Battles of Lexington and
Concord.[14]

Major Cane and Joshua Loring, Jr., sheriff, searched Lovell's papers and found he was involved in a prohibited correspondence. British General Gage had Lovell arrested on June 29, 1775, for being a rebel spy and placed him in a stone jail in Queen Street.[15] Also in the jail was John Leach, who "kept a navigation school in Boston previous to the revolution." It was said that he had thrice circumnavigated the globe. On July 17, 1775, General Gage ordered "a Garrison Court of Enquiry, at Concert Hall" and several individuals were brought before the court. James Lovell was accused of "being a spy, and giving intelligence to the rebels," and Leach of "being a spy, and suspected of taking plans." The accuser in this case, Captain Symmes, could not tell the schoolteachers apart.[16] Lovell would remain in jail and in December Captain Balfour, aide-de-camp to General Howe, advised Mrs. Lovell to inform her husband that to get his freedom he would have to be exchanged for Colonel Philip Skene and his son.[17] Lovell would be shipped to Halifax, Nova Scotia, and later exchanged. In February 1777 he was chosen a delegate to the Continental Congress. In May he was appointed to the Committee for Foreign Affairs where he deciphered Charles Guillaurme Frédéric Dumas' letters. Lovell remained on the Committee for Foreign Affairs until 1782 and at times was its only member.

Lovell deciphered intercepted British correspondence. He introduced to the American repertoire of secret writing a cipher system he developed that is based upon a key word. It uses a specified number of letters from the beginning of a key word and constructs an alphabet based upon those key letters. The alphabet continues in each column by starting after the key letter for that column. The individuals have to agree on the alphabet, that is, are I and J one or two letters and the use of ampersands and nulls. This type of cipher seems to have been created by Lovell. His ciphers were used primarily for diplomatic correspondence.

To encipher a document using Lovell's cipher start with the first column and find the letter of the alphabet needed and select the number along side of the first column that matches the letter chosen. This is the number for the first position. For the second letter go to the second column and find the letter needed and go across to the number. This will show the second position. For ciphers with more columns continue as before. For a third letter from a two column table, return to the first column for the third letter. Continue in this fashion. After an unciphered word or words, restart the cipher in the first column as done initially. Sometimes the numbers 28, 29, and 30 as well as any number(s) between 28 and 99 were used as nulls or blanks.[18] At the beginning of a passage when the number 28 was followed by 29, the normal order was used. However, 29 followed by 28 would signal that a message in reverse order would follow (line then column, but there were other reverse order variations). Users of Lovell's keyword system had to always keep in mind that when a ciphered passage is broken by unciphered or plain text, the next occurrence of ciphered text would return to the beginning of the first column; that is, you start all over as the first time in the letter.

Below are examples he used with Benjamin Franklin. Key letters are "COR" and with John Jay the key letters are "BY."[19]

Benjamin Franklin				John Jay		
1	c	o	r	1	b	y
2	d	p	s	2	c	z
3	e	q	t	3	d	&
4	f	r	u	4	e	a
5	g	s	v	5	f	b
6	h	t	w	6	g	c
7	i	u	x	7	h	d
8	j	v	y	8	i	e
9	k	w	z	9	j	f
10	l	x	&	10	k	g
11	m	y	a	11	l	h
12	n	z	b	12	m	i
13	o	&	c	13	n	j
14	p	a	d	14	o	k
15	q	b	e	15	p	l
16	r	c	f	16	q	m
17	s	d	g	17	r	n
18	t	e	h	18	s	o
19	u	f	i	19	t	p
20	v	g	j	20	u	q
21	w	h	k	21	v	r
22	x	i	l	22	w	s

23	y	j	m		23	x	t
24	z	k	n		24	y	u
25	&	l	o		25	z	v
26	a	m	p		26	&	w
27	b	n	q		27	a	x

After John Adams left to be one of the American representatives to French court, James Lovell wrote to Adams in November 1779 using a two-letter (key letters "CR") cipher key:

1	c	r
2	d	s
3	e	t
4	f	u
5	g	v
6	h	w
7	i	x
8	j	y
9	k	z
10	l	&
11	m	a
12	n	b
13	o	c
14	p	d
15	q	e
16	r	f
17	s	g
18	t	h
19	u	i
20	v	j
21	w	k
22	x	l
23	y	m
24	z	n
25	&	o
26	a	p
27	b	q

The message Lovell wrote to Adams was: "I can only say we are

27.	11.	12.	21.	16.	4.	14.	3.	21.	19.	18.	18.	26.
b	a	n	k	r	u	p	t	w	i	t	h	a

23.	19.	3.	7.	24.	13.	19.	2.	26.	1.	11.	8.
m	u	t	i	n	o	u	s	a	r	m	y

The latter owing very much to the

2.	15.	10.	11.	23.	25.	4.
d	e	l	a	y	o	f

13.	10.	25.	26.	3.	6.	19.	12.	17.
c	l	o	a	t	h	i	n	g"

The message was "I can only say we are bankrupt with a mutinous army. The latter [is] owing to the delay of cloathing." However, Lovell made an error in encoding the letter. Where the second "19" appears, Lovell used the wrong column. This certainly helped to confuse John Adams with the operation of the cipher.

Lovell in May 1780 instructed Adams that the cipher was based on a system of the alphabet square, with the key letters being the first two letters of the name of the family where he and John Adams had dinner the night before leaving for Baltimore. John Adams made a trip to Baltimore in January 1777, arriving there on the evening of February 1.[20] The family that he alluded to is the Cranches, close friends of the Adamses. John was a future brother-in-law of Richard Cranch. When Cranch was calling on Mary Smith, the daughter of Reverend William Smith of Weymouth, he brought John along and introduced him to Mary's younger sister— Abigail, his future wife.[21]

Lovell's system described a column of the alphabet of twenty-six letters beginning with the letter "a" and the ampersand. The second column begins with "b" and continues to the fourth letter "e." The third column begins with the letter "c" and continues again for four letters to "f." In a December 19, 1780, letter to Abigail Adams, Lovell explained the necessity for a cipher. He did not want any of his letters to John Adams thrown overboard, as was the practice when a ship was about to be captured by the enemy unless he so specified. "I am told letters from Holland have been thrown from vessels now arrived at Boston when only chased. Those losses at least might be avoided."[22]

In June 1780 Abigail Adams thanked Lovell for the alphabetical cipher that he had sent to her[23] but said she was not going to use it. She wrote, "I hate a cipher of any kind and have been so much more used to deal in realities with those I love that I should make a miserable proficiency in modes and figures." She told Lovell that "my friend [her husband John] is no adept in investigating ciphers and hates to be puzzled for a meaning."[24]

The ciphers that Lovell designed seemed to confuse the people to whom he wrote. In February 1782 John Adams was still having problems with Lovell's ciphers. Adams wrote to Robert Livingston that he did "know very well the name of the family where I spent the evening with my worthy Friend Mr. — — before we set off, and have made my alphabet accordingly; but I am on this occasion, as on all others hitherto, utterly unable to comprehend the sense of the passage in cipher. The cipher is certainly not taken regularly under the two first letters of that name. I have been able sometimes to decipher words enough to show that I have the letters right; but upon the whole, I can make nothing of it, which I regret very much upon this occasion, as I suppose the ciphers are a very material part of the letter."[25] Livingston responded by apologizing for the cipher and explained, "It was one found in the office and is very incomplete." He enclosed a new cipher and was hoping that he would find it easier to use. He also enclosed a set of blanks and asked Adams to complete them and provide it to former Continental Congressman Francis Dana, who was serving as secretary to Adams, thereby allowing all three of them to communicate in cipher. It was a great idea to use the same code, but Livingston forgot to send the code.[26] Adams noted, "The cypher was not put up in this duplicate, and I suppose the original is gone on to Mr. Dana in a letter I transmitted him from you some time ago, so that I should be obliged to you for another of the same part."[27] Dana wrote to John Adams on October 18, 1782, with the cipher. It used a key word "who" to operate the system.

	W	H	O
A	5	20	12
B	6	21	13
C	7	22	14
D	8	23	15

E	9	24	16
F	10	25	17
G	11	26	18
H	12	27	19
I	13	1	20
J	14	2	21
K	15	3	22
L	16	4	23
M	17	5	24
N	18	6	25
O	19	7	26
P	20	8	27
Q	21	9	1
R	22	10	2
S	23	11	3
T	24	12	4
U	25	13	5
V	26	14	6
W	27	15	7
X	1	16	8
Y	2	17	9
Z	3	18	10
&	4	19	11

It doing this cipher the key word "who" is written above the plain text, and taking the key word letter and the plain text letter and applying it to the chart results in a number. A very important rule was that when a number above 27 is used in the enciphering line then the key word starts over.

W	H	O	W		W	H	O	W	H
Y	O	U	R	Treaty	W	I	T	H	T
2	7	5	22	221	27	1	4	12	12

H	E		W	H	O	W	H	O
H	E	United	I	S	M	A	D	E
		Provinces						
19	9	225	13	11	24	5	23	16

The enciphered text is: 2.7.5.22.221.27.1.4.12.12.19.9.225.13.11. 24.5.23.16. The system also had words used in the columns in place of the letters and the numbers 221, 252, and 283 to stand for treaty. To decipher just reverse the process to fill in the blank boxes.

Abigail tried to help John.

> Mr. L—l [Lovell] not long since favored me with the sight of two Letters from you dated in February. With regard to the cipher of which you complain, I have always been fortunate enough to succeed with it. Take the two Letters for which the figure stands and place one under the other through the whole sentence, and then try the upper line with the under, or the under with the upper, always remembering, if one letter answers, that directly above or below must be omitted, and sometimes several must be skipped over. The contents of those Letters gave me a clearer idea of the difficulties you have had to encounter, than I before had conceived of.[28]

Despite the help, Lovell's cipher remained a mystery to Adams. He informed Francis Dana that "I have letters from the President and [James] Lovell, the last unintelligible in ciphers, but inexplicable by his own cipher; some dismal ditty about my letters of 26th July, I know not what."[29]

On February 24, 1780, James Lovell wrote from Philadelphia to Benjamin Franklin in France, "the Chevalier De la Luzerne [the French minister to the United States] expressed to me an anxiety because we do not correspond by Cipher. I early communicated to you from Baltimore a very good one, tho a little tedious like that of Mr. Dumas." Lovell even enclosed a sample of the cipher. He also annotated the letter that it was "to be sunk in case of danger" to ensure that the information did not fall into enemy hands.[30] The cipher to Franklin used the code key of "COR" (see page 82). The problems with Lovell's ciphers were caused by his attempt to force the ciphers on his recipients and his own mistakes in enciphering the letter.

Franklin wrote to Lovell that "the cipher you have communicated, either from some defect in your explanation or in my comprehension, is not yet of use to me; for I can not understand it by the little speci-

men you have wrote in it. If you have that of Mr. Dumas, which I left
with Mr. Morris, we may correspond by it when a few sentences only
are required to be writ in cipher, but it is too tedious for a whole
Letter."[31]

Benjamin Franklin had published in 1748 a book by George
Fisher called *The American Instructor*, which contained a section on
the uses of ciphers, codes, and secret writing.[32] Despite his background knowledge, Franklin was frustrated by both Lovell's system
and the enciphering errors. Franklin needed help and wrote to
Francis Dana on March 2, 1781, enclosing Lovell's cipher description
which Dana had wanted. Franklin wrote a copy of a paragraph of
Lovell's letter where Lovell had used the cipher. "If you can find the
key and decipher it, I shall be glad, having myself tried in vain."[33] On
March 6 Dana wrote to John Adams that he was going to try to decipher the passage. However, the day before he received Franklin's letter he received one from Lovell dated January 6, 1781, and was unable
to decipher it.[34] Lovell liked to give clues to the recipient that only the
two of them would know. The problem was Francis Dana could not
remember the key word.[35] Lovell wrote to Dana, "You begin your
alphabet by the three first letters of the name of that family in
Charlestown, whose nephew rode in company with you from this city
[Philadelphia] to Boston."[36] Dana wrote to Adams ten days later on
the 16th that he remembered the name.[37] The key word was "BRA."

Robert Morris writing from Philadelphia expressed his concerns
with the letters going to and from Benjamin Franklin. Because of the
quantity of letters being captured by the enemy, he wanted to use a
cipher for their correspondence. He said he would

> always be happy to hear from you but the mischief which
> arise from having letters intercepted are great and alarm-
> ing. I have therefore enclosed you a cipher and in the
> duplicate of my letters I shall enclose another, if both arrive
> you will use one and in case of your absence leave the other
> with such person as may supply your place, let me know
> however which cipher you use, whether it be No 3. or No
> 4. The bearer of this letter Major [David Solebury] Franks
> formerly an Aid de Camp to General [Benedict] Arnold
> and honorably acquitted of all improper connection with

him after a full & impartial enquiry will be able to give you our public news more particularly than I could relate them. He sails hence for Cadiz and on his arrival will proceed to Madrid where having delivered my letters to Mr. Jay he will take his orders for you. He will then wait your orders and I hope will soon after meet a safe opportunity of coming to America.[38]

Franks was scheduled to leave Philadelphia on July 13. Luckily his departure was delayed, so Robert Morris told Franklin: "If Major Franks had departed yesterday as was expected, he would have left the enclosed cipher behind, it was supposed to have been enclosed with the plans of the intended Bank, but was left out by accident."[39] After Franklin had received the ciphers and checked them out, he wrote to Robert Morris, "I imagine the old one preferable, which I left with you. At least it seems so to me, perhaps because I am used to it."[40]

Sample of a loyalist cipher alphabet from the Reverend Charles Inglis, rector of Trinity Church, New York City. (From Lossing, *The Pictorial Field-book of the American Revolution*, Vol. 1: 320)

In the eighteenth century, many people were afraid of reprisals should their correspondence be discovered. The Reverend Charles Inglis, rector of Trinity Church in New York City, wrote to Joseph Galloway, the former Pennsylvanian politician who was in London at the time, telling about the current conditions on the west side of the Atlantic Ocean. Inglis advised that loyalists had created their own cipher alphabets for communications among themselves and their friends abroad. He then provided a sample of one of the loyalist cipher alphabets and a sample message which are shown above and on the next page.[41]

An example of the loyalist cipher as transmitted. (*From Lossing, The Pictorial Field-book of the American Revolution, Vol. 1: 320*)

Benjamin Franklin had even received a cipher from John Paul Jones for their private correspondence in 1779. Jones had sent it from L'Orient, Brittany, as he was preparing to depart the port.[42] Although Franklin was not enthusiastic about learning new ciphers, he embraced the method all the same.

Chapter 8

DEAD DROPS

A procedure used by spies over the years to pass information to their contacts was through the use of a "dead drop." In the dead drop a spy places a message in a prearranged location—in a tree or under some rocks—and leaves it unattended. It remains there until an agent retrieves the correspondence from this agreed-on location and sends it to its final destination. The procedure can be reversed and the agent may leave instruction in a "dead drop" for the undercover spy to retrieve. "Dead drops" have never gone out of style and are still used today to pass information.

During the American Revolution, British General Sir Frederick Haldimand described the dead drop employed by his couriers carrying dispatches from Quebec, Canada, to General Sir Henry Clinton in New York City.[1] He states, "Meyers takes three men who with him will fix upon a certain tree, or spot wherein the letters are to be deposited in a small tin case to preserve them from the weather. One of these men will go on with him to [New] York [City], to carry and deposit your letters in the place fixed upon, who will at the same time take any that I may have sent for you by the other two men, whom I shall from time to time send with intelligence from hence, and to receive that you may intend for me."[2]

Haldimand feared that all his messages to Sir Henry Clinton using "dead drops" in the woods were not making their way to New York City. However, for unknown reasons, General Haldimand's messages of July 26 (concerning a diversion upon Lake Chaplain should the French attack), August 28, and September 8, 1780, did reach General Clinton in New York City.[3] On several occasions he sent additional copies of his secret correspondence with couriers who would travel overland from Quebec to Nova Scotia. From Nova Scotia they would travel by ship to New York City. As a backup to his backup plan Haldimand also sent copies of his dispatches directly by ship from Quebec to New York City. His letter of July 11, 1780, from Quebec to Hessian General Wilhelm von Knyphausen states, "I enclose you a duplicate of a letter in cipher with which I dispatched the runner who brought me yours of the 3rd of May, on the 6th." This duplicate was sent by the sloop *Delight* and received on October 4.[4] Haldimand's letter of November 15, 1780, to Sir Henry Clinton stated, "the inclosed are duplicates of notes I dispatched at different times thro the woods which perhaps may not have reached your Excellency." It was received by Ensign Prentice of the 84th Regiment of Foot, also known as the Royal Highland Emigrants, on August 19, 1781.[5] General Haldimand also wrote on the same day to General Sir Henry Clinton advising that Prentice is to winter in a warm climate and "he will have the honor to deliver to your Excellency duplicates of my letters conveyed by Ensign Drummond of the 44th Regiment [of Foot]." The letter is marked received by Ensign Prentice.[6] A message of Haldimand's for Sir Henry Clinton arrived in New York City being brought by two men from Albany who say they received it from a man who left Quebec on November 22, 1780, and apparently did not use the dead drop.[7]

Leaving messages in a dead drop in the New York wilderness continued to be a problem during the entire war. General Haldimand at Quebec wrote to Sir Henry Clinton in New York City on November 15, 1781, and advised "I have lately had the mortification to learn that the principal channels I have used to convey dispatches and procure intelligence are almost entirely broken up, owing to the imprudence of recruiting parties of the corps of loyalists and discoveries by emissaries and the desertions of rebel prisoners enlarged on parole. This will make our intercourse still less frequent than it is and I have to request your Excellency should you have any matters of importance to communicate to me that you will send duplicates by way of [Fort] Niagara or to strike upon [Fort Haldimand on] Carleton Island for though more tedious it is, at present, the most certain route."[8] This circuitous route would significantly delay communications between the two centers of British power in North America. In 1781 when

General Haldimand at Quebec had sent a letter to Sir Henry Clinton in New York City by way of Fort Detroit, it took fifty-two days to make the journey.[9]

On March 29, 1781, the British secret agent by the code name of Hudibras at Albany, New York, received a dispatch for General Sir Henry Clinton in New York City from General Frederick Haldimand at Quebec with a memorandum of instructions. Hudibras was Irish born Dr. George Smith. General Haldimand requested Hudibras to provide information on the general population as well as military defenses and supplies for Fort Stanwick and Albany and the status of the American and French armies. He wanted him to find out how information was getting out of Quebec and to whom it was going. He also wanted copies of newspapers when they could be sent. Hudibras was instructed to send his reports by the use of "some hollow tree or rock after the snow is gone, remote from the town, Should be fixed upon the messengers, where their intelligence would be mutually secreted and conveyed from and to this province and forwarded to New York if necessary. Provision should therefore be made by those who conduct the correspondence to convey dispatches and communicate intelligence between the two armies."[10] Dr. Smith was suspected and an order for his arrest was issued. He was trying to flee to Canada when he was seen at Bennington, Vermont. Smith then surrendered and on May 30, 1781 was being held at Bennington.[11] Smith believed one of General Sir Henry Clinton's domestics betrayed him to General George Washington.[12] Dr. Smith escaped from his confinement and made his way to New York City.[13]

Dead drops were used in Europe by both the Americans and the British. Lord Stormont, British ambassador to France from 1772 to 1778, reported from Paris and advised Lord Weymouth that Silas Deane, American commissioner to France, used a mail drop at the Germany, Girardot & Cie. trading firm. The firm of Germany, Girardot & Cie. was initially the banker to Deane and became Benjamin Franklin's banker upon his arrival in Paris.[14]

A dead drop was also used by a British double agent in France. Dr. Edward Bancroft had been a friend of Benjamin Franklin when they both were in London before the American Revolution. When Silas Deane arrived in France in June 1776, he wrote to Bancroft, his former teacher, under cover to Mr. Griffiths at Turnham Green near

London requesting that he come to Paris for a meeting. Bancroft made the journey to Paris where Silas Deane advised him of his mission on behalf of the United States.

Dr. Bancroft agreed to work for the American commissioners in carrying out their secret missions. In July 1776 Lords North and Suffolk offered Bancroft £500 and an additional £400 per year to work for the British government. Lord Suffolk also had promised Bancroft £200 a year for life if he would go to Paris and supply them with information on Deane's and Franklin's correspondence and the progress of any treaties.[15] His reports were to be sent through Paul Wentworth, an American who was a British case agent. Bancroft would now be collecting two salaries, one from American commissioners and one from the British government. He once threatened to discontinue his services to the American commissioners since he had not been paid. It was a bluff. If he did discontinue his job for the American commissioners as he threatened, he would also lose his British pay.

Dr. Bancroft started providing information to the British on August 14, 1776. He reported on a meeting that he attended on January 9, 1777 between the American commissioners and Charles Gravier, Count de Vergennes, French Minister of Foreign Affairs. Bancroft supplied Wentworth with a steady stream of reports. Dr. Bancroft lived with Benjamin Franklin for a year and all the while he was spying for the British. He was so thoroughly trusted by the American commissioners that he even had the keys to the secret documents.[16]

Bancroft used a dead drop in Paris to provide his information to the British ambassador David Murray, Lord Stormont. Bancroft wrote his reports in cipher and in invisible ink in the white spaces of letters written to a fictitious Mr. Richardson. His reports were deposited in a sealed bottle in a hole in a tree which was on the south terrace of the Tuileries along the Seine. The report was picked up at 9:30 p.m. every Tuesday by Thomas Jeans, who was Stormont's secretary. Jeans left Stormont's instructions for Bancroft in another bottle. All of Bancroft's reports from Paris went through Lord Stormont.[17] Should Dr. Bancroft be discovered and need to flee France, Lord Stormont kept a passport in the name of Stoughton for Dr. Bancroft's use.[18]

The Americans also used dead drops in their clandestine operations. A dead drop was used as part of the American Culper spy ring prior to the arrival of the French in Rhode Island in July 1780. Samuel Culper, Jr., who was actually Robert Townsend, would send messages from New York City, to Samuel Culper, Sr., who was Abraham Woodhull, in Setauket, Long Island, New York. At this point in time the messages were carried by Austin Roe, a local Setauket tavern owner.[19] Austin Roe upon returning to Setauket from New York City, a journey of over one hundred miles, would check on his cattle which were pastured in a field belonging to Abraham Woodhull. Roe would leave the documents that he brought from New York City in a box in this field. Abraham Woodhull passing through his own field would retrieve the documents. He would send them on their way across the Long Island Sound to Benjamin Tallmadge, who would forward the documents to General George Washington wherever he was at the time.[20]

Another use of a dead drop occurred during the time that Newport, Rhode Island was occupied by the British. Isaac Barker provided this service for fourteen months beginning in August 1778 until the British evacuation of Newport in October 1779. Barker pretended to be a Tory and observed British naval and troop movements. He also harvested information from a British cavalry colonel who was quartered in his house. Barker owned both his own farm and another which was named Paradise. The twenty-six-year-old Barker sent signals by means of the positioning of the barways at gaps in the stone walls running along Paradise Rocks located at Paradise farm. He was able to send approximately a dozen different messages which with a spyglass could be distinctly seen across the Sakonnet River at Little Compton.[21] One of the signals indicated that a messenger after dark could pass safely over the Sakonnet River. The first signal was leaving down a certain pair of bars. Afterward, for fear of exciting the suspicion of the enemy, the signal was changed, when an open window of Mr. Peleg Peckham's neighboring barn answered the same purpose. A small vault in the ground, near the shore, and at no great distance from Mr. Peckham's, covered with a flat stone and a "cleft [crack] in a rock," served as the dead drop. Letters and papers were regularly deposited and removed by the respective individuals engaged in the correspondence.

Lieutenant Seth Chapin of Shelburne's Additional Continental Regiment was stationed at Little Compton to observe the signals sent by Isaac Barker on his farm on the west side of the Sakonnet River and to service Barker's dead drop at North Point.[22] Chapin's whaleboat crew consisted of the pilot Hezekiah Barker and William Taggart of Middletown. The Taggart family prior to the British occupation had operated a ferry between Middletown and Little Compton and were very familiar with the river's hazards.[23] The intelligence received at Little Compton was given to William Wilkinson, secretary to General Ezekiel Cornell at Tiverton.[24]

General John Sullivan appointed William Taggart a major in charge of a flotilla of boats in May 1778. This naval activity of Taggart's ceased operation in the spring of 1779. For a time during the British occupation, a Hessian colonel and his retinue were quartered in the Judge William Taggart's farmhouse. They sometimes frequent-ed the Marquis of Granby Tavern in Newport, where other Hessian officers were quartered.[25] On other occasions, the (Hessian) colonel sent messages to his officers at the tavern by Taggart's black man, Cudjo. There Cudjo would talk with Gertrude Hegel, the German speaking servant, who repeated what she heard the Hessians say. It is unknown if Gertrude Hegel knew of her part in this spy operation. Cudjo relayed the information to his master, who forwarded it and intelligence gleaned from the colonel, to the American lines, proba-bly through his son William Taggart, Jr., and Lieutenant Chapin.[26]

The British knew there were spies in and around Newport but never suspected Barker. During the summer of 1779, the British attempted to stop this spying activity from the eastern shore of the Sakonnet River with a series of raids. On July 16, 1779, a loyalist raid was made at Little Compton, the base of operations for Chapin. The Americans lost one killed and four wounded. Five days later on July 21, some British soldiers landed at Sakonnet Point, and seized a guard squad of seventeen Americans including William Taggart Jr., another son of William Taggart's. Young Taggart was killed and the British burned Taggart's farm for his naval activities. On August 1, 1779, the British ambushed a militia patrol at Tiverton, Rhode Island, and killed one and wounded four Americans in an apparent attempt to strike at or capture General Ezekiel Cornell.[27] Despite the British efforts to stop the secret correspondence, Isaac Barker and Chapin continued to use their dead drop in passing the intelligence.

Dead drops figured in Philadelphia area activities as well. There is the story of Molly "Mom" Rinker, whose family had kept the Buck Tavern in Germantown. "Mom" bleached her flax atop a high rock in the Wissahickon Valley.[28] While performing this chore, she would sit and knit for hours on end, all the while observing British troop movements. She would put her information into the center of the skein of knitting yarn. She would allow the ball of yarn to fall over the edge of the rocks. She was being observed by the "Green Boys" who would retrieve the ball of yarn later from this dead drop and bring it to General Washington.[29]

Trees were also used as a dead drop on the western frontier. Simon Girty was a British agent who operated in the Ohio country. Nicknamed the "White Savage," he knew three Indian languages and was a renowned guide and woodsman.[30] Girty was given the rank of a Second Lieutenant in Captain John Stephenson's Company of Virginia Militia. George Morgan, Agent for the United Colonies, had appointed him as an interpreter to the Six Nations of Indians at Pittsburgh at the rate of 5/8 of a dollar per day on May 1, 1776. Part of his job was to provide intelligence and promote the public tranquility. By August 1, 1776, George Morgan had discharged Girty for bad behavior.[31] Girty was arrested for conspiracy to murder Whigs and accepting the British terms of reconciliation. He escaped from Pittsburgh on March 28, 1778, and eventually made his way to Fort Detroit. Girty became a courier carrying messages from a British spy at Pittsburgh and worked as an interpreter for the British to the Six Nations of Indians.[32]

Simon Girty had a major handicap in accomplishing his mission—it seems that he could neither read nor write. He could still carry messages. On February 7, 1779, he arrived at Fort Detroit bringing speeches from the Shawnee, Delaware, Wyandots, and the Six Nations just after a raid he led against Fort Laurens on the banks of the Tuscarawas River.[33] Secret messages from the loyalists in the area of Fort Pitt had been collected (possibly by his brother Thomas Girty) and placed in a hollow tree. On July 1, 1779, Colonel Daniel Brodhead, Commandant of the Western Department at Fort Pitt, wrote to Colonel Stephen Bayard, "Captain Brady and John Montour have gone with a party to capture Simon Girty, who is reported to be lurking with seven Mingo Indians near Holliday's Cove. [They went] express to Coshocton to seize Girty if he returns there."[34] However, they failed to capture Girty. The Reverend John Heckewelder, Moravian minister and an American spy, on July 8, 1779, wrote from Coshocton to Colonel Broadhead, "Girty had a packet of letters supposedly taken from a hollow tree. It is desirous that McCormick should read them for him."[35] Alexander McCormick had been a trader at Fort Pitt and in the Indian country from before the American Revolution. In 1777 he had a trading post at Half King's village (Wyandot Indians) near Upper Sandusky, Ohio.[36] McCormick agreed to assist Simon Girty in reading his secret mail. McCormick would then advise Colonel Brodhead with the information that he read to Girty thereby alerting him to what information was being supplied to the enemy. One of McCormick's reports was that "Simon Girty with eight Mingoes is gone to the inhabitants to fetch a packet of letters out of a hollow tree. I understand somewhere about Fort Pitt."[37] In these circumstances, a wise scout was as valuable an asset as an unbreakable cipher.

Chapter 9

HIDDEN COMPARTMENTS

S pies sometimes needed to transport written messages through enemy territory. A smugglers' tactic was sometimes used: hiding the contraband or message in a hidden compartment in an ordinary-looking object. The item had to be something that would normally be carried or worn so as not to draw attention to it. Some of the methods used involved placing the message in the waistband of a man's breeches, in false heels on shoes, in false handles on knives, and even in the hollow of a quill pen. John Wilkins in his book *Mercury, or the Secret and Swift Messenger* published in 1641 told of the early use of a hidden compartment. Harpagus the Mede, when he was trying to incite Cyrus into a conspiracy against his uncle the king, hid a message placed inside the belly of a rabbit. He provided a servant with the rabbit along with hunter nets. The servant was able to complete the journey inconspicuously despite all the guards on patrol in the countryside.[1] As mentioned earlier, the intercepted ciphered correspondence of Mary Queen of Scots in 1586 was hidden inside a beer barrel bung.

The use of hidden compartments was widespread during the American Revolution, and a careful examination of contemporary documents provides information on many of these occurrences. Dr. Benjamin Church was director general of the Continental army's medical department in 1775 as it was laying siege to the British in Boston. Dr. Church was also a spy for British General Thomas Gage in Boston. On at least one occasion Dr. Church's courier was carrying a letter to General Gage in the waistband of his breeches. He was suspected and stopped while still within the American lines but the hidden message he was carrying was not discovered.[2]

At the beginning of the American Revolution William Campbell was traveling on horseback and returning home with his wife and some gentlemen. When they were near his residence in western Virginia, he saw a shabbily dressed man walking with a small bundle tied to a stick which he carried over his shoulder. When they got within one hundred and fifty yards of the man, the stranger turned sharply and left the roadway trying to avoid them. Campbell and his fellow travelers took an angle that would allow their path to intercept that of the stranger. When the man realized that their paths were going to cross, he fled toward the river trying to escape. They chased after him and at the river they dismounted and continued after the stranger on foot until they caught him. They took their prisoner back to the main road on which they originally were traveling. When they reached the road they were joined by several of their companions. William Campbell questioned the stranger, who played the role of a fool. Campbell did not believe this ploy and had the man searched, including his bundle. He had the stranger change his clothes with those in the bundle. During the search of the clothes he was wearing, a pass and some other badly written papers were discovered. Campbell noticed that the prisoner was wearing a pair of very good shoes. The shoes looked too good and were examined. When the soles of the shoes were removed, a letter from the British commander in the area to the chief of the Cherokee Indians was found. A bladder had been used to keep the document from getting wet. The letter told the Indians to send their warriors to harass the Americans. The Indians if they did as requested were promised the return of their land. The letter said that the prisoner was honest and that the Indians should trust him. Campbell called a council and it was unanimously agreed that the spy was to be hanged. The spy was advised of the sentence and stated that the British commander had paid him a large sum of money to take the message to the Indians and to incite them to do mischief. The spy was hung till he died.[3]

Dr. John Connolly, Dr. John Smith, and Allan Cameron along with their unnamed servant were sent about November 13, 1775 by Lord Dunmore, the Royal Governor of Virginia, on a mission to raise an army at Fort Detroit and incite the Indians on the western frontier of Maryland, Pennsylvania, and Virginia against the Americans. They left Lord Dunmore at Norfolk on a flat-bottom schooner and landed south of Cedar Point near Dr. Smith's house.[4] They were to travel to Detroit on horseback and it is assumed they got the horses for their journey at Dr. John Smith's house. They were arrested at about 2 a.m. in a tavern about five miles west of Elizabethtown, Maryland, by the local minute men.[5] Since they were unable to provide a satisfactory explanation of their travels, they were taken to Frederick where they were stripped and searched. Even the soles of their shoes were opened looking for a document in a secret compartment. In Dr. Connolly's portmanteau a small fragment of a note on their mission was found. They were brought before the Committee of Observation on November 20, 1775. Dr. Connolly admitted their commissions from Lord Dunmore to avoid being lynched by a mob. Connolly's actions were determined to be of a traitorous nature. He was to be sent to the Council of Safety for trial. Additionally Cameron, Connolly, and Smith were to be sent to the Council of Safety for further interrogation. In the meantime Connelly's servant, who was not confined, had been able in the dead of night to destroy their commissions and the instructions that were hidden in the saddle's pillion sticks.[6]

Another case of false heels of shoes being used to hide letters happened in England. Israel Ralph Potter was born in Cranston, Rhode Island on August 1, 1744. He was a farmer, an assistant surveyor in New Hampshire, and had been on a sailing cruise all before he was thirty. He answered the call of the Boston alarm after the Battles of Lexington and Concord. He enlisted in the army and fought in the Battle of Bunker Hill, June 17, 1775, where he received several wounds. He was assigned to the crew of the Continental brig *Washington*, which was part of Washington's navy that was blockading the port of Boston. His ship was captured and he was taken prisoner to England. When the ship reached Spithead, he escaped.[7] He made his way toward London in the disguise of a beggar.

Israel Potter had met James Bridges and John Horne at the house of J. Woodcock, Esquire of Brintford, England at 8 p.m. and was sent to wait at White Waltham Town about thirty miles away until things were prepared.[8] When he returned on February 14, 1777, he was given a pair of boots with a false heel that held a letter for Benjamin Franklin. He then traveled to Charing Cross where he took a post coach to Dover. At Dover he took a packet to Calais and fifteen minutes after landing in France, he was on his way to Paris. He never knew the contents of the letter but believed that it contained the views of the British cabinet on American affairs. The letter or one of the letters carried was a letter of introduction to Benjamin Franklin.[9] Potter delivered the letter to Franklin and remained with him for an hour. Potter stayed in Paris for two days before being sent back to England by Franklin with a message concealed in the boot. Potter left Paris accompanied by Edward Griffis posing as his servant on their way to Nantes. Israel Potter made his way back to Woodcock's house and remained there in hiding. He made another round trip back to Franklin in Paris. On his third mission, he found out three hours before his arrival in Dover that war had begun with France. Because of the hostilities all communications with France were prohibited and he would be unable to cross.[10]

The lining of coats was also a useful place to hide things. Elkanah Watson was on a journey carrying $50,000, quilted in the lining of his coat, from John and Nicholas Brown of Providence to their mercantile agents in Charles Town, South Carolina, and Savannah, Georgia. At Morristown, New Jersey, he fell into company with two men going to Williamsburg, Virginia. On their approach of Philadelphia, they heard of the British capture of Philadelphia two hours earlier, so they crossed north of the city at Cowles' Ferry into Pennsylvania. Because of their inquiring of events, they were picked up as British spies but were released the next day and allowed to continue on their journey.[11]

In another example, when the British released Henry Williams from jail in July 1777 to act as their courier, a document was written on a small piece of silk paper and was sewed into a fold of his coat. As the British anticipated, Williams went to the first American officer with the hidden document, which contained misinformation.[12]

British General John Burgoyne, appointed to the command of the northern British army in Canada, arrived in Quebec in March 1777. His mission was to take control of Lake Champlain and the Hudson River area of New York and isolate the Massachusetts malcontents from the rest of the colonies. One of the main objectives was Fort Ticonderoga, strategically located overlooking the narrow passage between Lake Champlain and Lake George in northern New York. American Major General John Sullivan was believed to be in command at Fort Ticonderoga. If Sullivan could be turned to the British side then Fort Ticonderoga, the Gibraltar of the north, could be taken without resistance.

Peter Livius, chief justice of the province of Quebec and former chief justice of New Hampshire, sent a message to General Sullivan, a New Hampshire resident.[13] The message was hidden in the hollow space in a double bottom canteen. On June 2, 1777, he wrote to General Sullivan in an effort to convince him to come to the British side. Livius thought that Sullivan was a fairweather patriot. Livius based his assumption on Sullivan having been captured during the Battle of Long Island and his agreeing to be the bearer of Lord Howe's peace overtures to the Continental Congress in order to get himself exchanged.[14] In his letter Livius wrote that if Sullivan switched sides he would be pardoned, amply rewarded, and save his property from being confiscated.

Livius entrusted William Amsbury with the task of getting his letter to General Sullivan. Amsbury in the company of someone named Adams had left Montreal on June 4 with a British pass to go beyond their lines, letters to people in the United States, and a large amount of money.[15] He left Saint John, which is north of Lake Champlain on the Richelieu River, on the morning of June 5.[16] Amsbury took an old Indian trail from Canada. The Indians had used it to make their attacks on the frontier settlements on the Connecticut River which divides New Hampshire and Vermont. This route gave him the best chance of traveling undetected. Amsbury had made it as far as the Onion River in Vermont where an American scouting party captured him.[17]

On June 13, 1777, Amsbury was taken to Fort Ticonderoga and turned over to Major General Arthur St. Clair.[18] He had just taken command at Fort Ticonderoga the previous day. St. Clair wrote to General Philip J. Schuyler that he suspected that Amsbury was a spy. He based this assumption on the large amount of money including gold and silver that Amsbury had, his plan to search for a hidden map at Metcalf's, possession of a British pass made out for him, and his having been sent from Montreal. He also thought "there was no method more likely to procure them [Adams and Amsbury] an easy reception" than having them provide the intelligence to Sullivan of General Burgoyne's arrival. The Continental currency Amsbury was carrying was wrapped in a June 2 letter from Eph. Jones to his brother. Amsbury said that Michael Shannon wrote the letter. Shannon's name was found on a separate piece of paper that St. Clair says Amsbury was reluctant to surrender.[19] St. Clair sent Amsbury on June 15 by way of

Fort George, Lake George, New York, to Major General Philip Schuyler at Saratoga, New York.[20]

General Schuyler pointed out that the pass—written by M. Kirkman, Major of Brigade of the 2nd Brigade of British Infantry at Saint John's, to the commanding officer at the Isle aux Noix or any detached parts of the army—said "the bearer [Amsbury] and his companion [Adams] being employed on Secret Service" was enough to hang him as a spy and threatened to do so.[21] General Schuyler ordered Amsbury to be sent back to the guard, placed in irons, and taken to Albany. After the passage of some time, Amsbury pleaded for an audience with Schuyler which he granted. Schuyler cautioned him that if his information was frivolous that the execution would be accomplished. Amsbury's memory improved and he stated that British forces under the command of General Burgoyne were approaching St. John's. A detachment of British troops, Canadians, and Indians under the command of Sir John Johnson were to penetrate the country through the Mohawk Valley by Oswego. He also added that the Canadians were averse to taking up arms but were forced to do it and that no reinforcements had arrived from Europe.[22]

Also Schuyler's interrogation of Amsbury revealed that a "Mr. Levy, a Jew, had spoke to Amsbury to carry some things to Ticonderoga" which he agreed to do. On the 4th he met with Judge Peter Livius of Montreal who gave him a canteen with a false bottom concealing a letter for General Sullivan. While at Fort George, Amsbury had given the canteen to the servant of First Lieutenant and Adjutant Peter B. Tearse, of the 1st New York Regiment, to fill with water.[23] However the servant had not returned before he was taken away.

General Schuyler sent Second Lieutenant Bartholomew Jacob Van Valkenburgh of the 1st New York Regiment to get the canteen from the adjutant at Fort George.[24] He was instructed to bring the canteen under an armed guard to Fort Edward, New York, where they would meet the next morning.

At 10 a.m. on the 16th Lieutenant Van Valkenburgh delivered the canteen to General Schuyler. Schuyler opened the double bottom canteen in the presence of observers, who then signed the letter as witnesses. Later that day Schuyler sent the letter to General George Washington.[25] Schuyler devised a plan to send a reply back to Chief Justice Peter Livius as if it had come from General Sullivan.[26] On

June 17, 1777, Schuyler sent a letter from Albany to Congress advising them of his plan.

On Friday June 20 a response was ready. It claimed that Sullivan disapproved of the actions of Congress and was loyal to the king. It requested instructions from General Burgoyne and provided exaggerated troop strengths for the Continental Army in New Jersey and New York. Schuyler included some significant information received from spies from Montreal. This information could be verified by Peter Livius thereby giving credence to the rest of the information in the response. The letter indicated that correspondence should be directed to Major Henry Dearborn who was well known by Livius to the extent that Livius had twice made personal loans to Dearborn. Major Dearborn knew of the contents of the message as he was one of the officers who had verified its contents. A copy of the response was sent to Congress on June 25, 1777.[27] General Sullivan was at Rocky Hill, New Jersey, on the 21st when he received a letter written that day by George Washington informing him of the secret letter in the canteen. He immediately responded to Washington and referred to the letter from the "infamous Mr. Livius" and confirmed that it was in Peter Livius' handwriting.[28]

A soldier who was to have received physical punishment for attempting to desert to the enemy was duped into escaping and taking the letter with him. General William Howe sent a message on July 17, 1777, to General John Burgoyne which warned him that "there is a report of a messenger of yours to me having been taken, and the letter discovered in a double wooded canteen."[29] Howe's warning would explain why Dearborn received no response from Burgoyne. After the Battle of Bennington, Burgoyne wrote to Lord George Germain that two of his messengers to Sir William Howe had been hanged and that he did not know about the rest.[30] He was most likely writing about Adams and Amsbury.

General William Howe's message to General Burgoyne was made on two strips of paper that were rolled and hidden in the hollow shaft of a quill pen. Every educated person carried one much like people carry pens today. General William Howe's message was addressed to General Burgoyne who was descending from Canada with the goal of reaching Albany, New York. The message was dated at New York on July 17, 1777 and read:

Dear Sir, I have received yours of the 2nd ins{tant] and on the 15th, have since heard from the Rebel Army of your being in possession of Ticonderoga, *which is a great event carried without loss.* I have received your two letters viz. and from to Quebec your last of the 14th [of] May, and shall observe the contents. There is a report of a messenger of yours to me having been taken, and the letter discovered in a double wooded canteen, you will know if it was of any consequence; nothing of it has transpired to us. I will observe the [missing word possibly "secrecy"] in writing to you, as you propose in your letters to me. Washington is waiting our motions here, and has detached Sullivan with about 2500 men, as I learn, to Albany.- My intention is for Pennsylvania where I expect to meet Washington, but if he goes to the Northward contrary to my and you can keep him at bay, be assured I shall soon be after him to relieve you. After your arrival in Albany, the movements of the enemy will guide yours; but my wishes are that the Enemy be drove out of this province before any operation takes place in Connecticut. Sir Henry Clinton remains in the command here, and will act as occurrences may direct. Putnam is in the Highlands with about 4000 men. - Success be ever with you. Yours Etc. [Obedient Servant]. W[illiam] Howe[31]

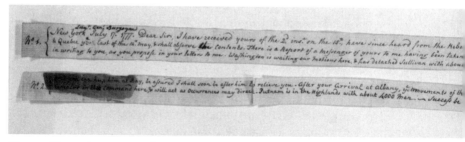

Two quill pen letters sent from General William Howe to General John Burgoyne, July 17, 1777. It told of Howe's plan to go to Pennsylvania. (*William L. Clements Library*)

Another popular method of secreting documents on the New York frontier was hiding a message inside a hollow bullet that was screwed together. On the frontier a man would not be conspicuous carrying a rifle, his powder horn, and a pouch of lead bullets. It was expected that a man would be out hunting for food for his family. The message-laden bullet would just be one among many in his pouch and would not draw attention. There are two documented cases of the British and one case of American collaborators employing bullets containing messages.

One cell of the rebel movement in Canada was being run by Dr. Boyer Pillon of Montreal. During the summer of 1780 British Major Thomas Carleton, younger brother of Guy Carleton, ran a counter espionage unit and sent an undercover agent into Montreal. During his clandestine activities, the agent discovered that Doctor Pillon would shortly be sending a person with letters to the rebels. Pillon, who had a son in the American service, was believed to be the chief orchestrator of the operation.[32] Pritchard, a person of whom we only know his last name, had somehow intercepted five letters being sent by those involved in the revolt against the crown and forwarded them to Carleton. Major Carleton after inspecting them advised that "there is a small slip cut of one of these letters, which you will perceive, is penned by Pillon and merchant Pierre Du Calvet that slip was to have been concealed in a lead bullet which was to be thrown away in case of any danger." A Captain Charlo was to be the courier of the message in the bullet.[33]

After British General Sir Henry Clinton had captured the American Forts, Clinton and Montgomery, on the Hudson River just

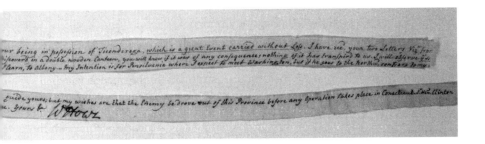

south of West Point, he dispatched couriers to General John Burgoyne who was heading south from Lake Champlain to Albany. On the morning after he sent Captain Alexander Campbell of the 62nd Regiment of Foot on a return trip to General Burgoyne.[34] During Campbell's journey south from General Burgoyne to Sir Henry Clinton, John Patterson had provided Campbell with horses and guides.[35] One of the guides was Abraham Volwyder, who successfully brought Captain Alexander Campbell in disguise into the city of Albany.[36] Captain Campbell made it safely back to General Burgoyne on the evening of October 16.[37]

Clinton was always one to send duplicate messages to ensure that one would get through. Captain Thomas Scott of the 53rd Regiment of Foot was one of the couriers between General Burgoyne at Freeman's Farm and General Sir Henry Clinton. Scott wrote in his journal of the difficulty he encountered in his travels. He had left General Burgoyne on September 27 and crossed to the east side of the Hudson River. He found that the Americans were guarding all the fords on the creeks to prevent loyalists from assisting Burgoyne. He got past the guards at night under the cover of a thick fog. Using guides and his compass, he finally located Sir Henry Clinton on October 9 at Fort Montgomery. Sir Henry Clinton sent him back to Burgoyne on the 10th. Captain Scott was frustrated in his efforts to get back to Burgoyne and spent his time hiding in the woods while trying to get a guide to help him locate Burgoyne. No guides were willing to take him the rest of the way as he was told Burgoyne was surrounded and had capitulated. On the 15th Captain Scott gave up trying to go north to get through to General Burgoyne and headed south. The next day he was picked up by a British vessel opposite Livingston Manor.[38]

Another courier was Lieutenant Daniel Taylor of Captain Stewart's Company in the 9th Regiment of Foot. He left from Fort Montgomery on the evening of October 8.[39] Taylor was wearing a blue camblet coat with white facings and silver epaulets. Because of the loss of the two forts to the British, the American troops were scattered throughout the countryside and attempting to meet and reform their ranks. With many American troops wandering about, Daniel Taylor was finding travel exceedingly difficult without being seen.

Phineas Shepard, a private in Colonel Samuel B. Webb's Additional Continental Regiment which was also known as the "Red

Coat Regiment", and some messmates were cooking breakfast in a field near the woods on October 9, 1777.[40] Due to a clothing shortage that existed amongst the American troops, Webb's regiment had been dressed in scarlet red British uniforms which had been captured in transport ships.[41] The captured British uniforms were made for use by the 9th, 20th, 29th, and 34th Regiments of Foot. The uniform was a scarlet red regimental coat faced with yellow trim and white waistcoat and breeches.[42]

General Sir Henry Clinton, Commander-in-Chief of the British army in North America from May 1778 to May 1782. (*William L. Clements Library*)

When Daniel Taylor and his traveling companion Isaac Van Vleek saw the men preparing breakfast wearing the scarlet red British army coats, they assumed Shepard and his mess mates were British soldiers.[43] Taylor and Van Vleek approached the men and asked to be guided to the general and "expressed great fears that the Yankees would catch them."[44] Shepard and his messmates assisted them but took them to the American camp near New Windsor. Taylor went up to the Lieutenant of the "Red Coat Regiment" and shook his hand saying that he was glad to see him. Lieutenant Howe held his hand firmly and informed Taylor that they were his prisoners.[45] Upon realizing his situation, Taylor immediately put something into his mouth and swallowed. Dr. Moses Higby was summoned and he gave Daniel Taylor a strong dose of tartar emetic (potassium antimony tartrate). The poisonous odorless compound had the desired effect as Taylor brought up the hidden item. It was a round silverish bullet,[46] and before anyone could stop him he swallowed it again. This time he refused to take the tartar emetic until American General George Clinton threatened to remove the object by surgery at the end of a bayonet. Taylor relented and the bullet was again brought forth. Upon inspection it was found to be in the shape and size of a one-ounce lead ball in two parts held together by a screw.[47] Inside the bullet was found a note which said,

Nous y Voici, and nothing now between us but Gates. I
sincerely hope this little success may facilitate your operation.
   In answer to your letter of the 28th of September by
C.C.[48], I shall only say, I can not presume to order, or even
advise, for reasons obvious. I heartily wish you success.
&:a H. C.[49]

   General Israel Putnam, nicknamed "Old Put," at an assembly of
the troops told them of the capture of a spy and the story of the
retrieval of the silver bullet. Putnam had the secret message read to
the troops. Upon completion of the reading, the army gave three huz-
zas, the eighteenth-century cheer. Six cannons were fired which were
answered by a discharge of seven cannons from the fort.[50]
   Colonel Lewis Dubois, commander of the 5th New York
Regiment, was the president of Daniel Taylor's court-martial, held at
the Heights of New Windsor on October 14, 1777. Most of Dubois'
5th New York Regiment had been captured at Fort Montgomery on
October 6 just a week earlier. When the charge of being a spy was
read to Taylor, he pled not guilty. He did admit to being an express
from General Sir Henry Clinton to General Burgoyne. He admitted
to carrying the news of the capture of Fort Montgomery and Dubois'
5th New York Regiment. The court-martial found Taylor guilty and
ordered him to be hanged.
   American Brigadier General George Clinton approved the death
sentence of the court-martial on October 16 and ordered the execution to be performed when the troops were paraded.[51] Daniel Woolsey
was Taylor's guard for several nights and at different times during the
day.[52] The paths of Phineas Shepard and Daniel Taylor crossed again.
Shepard, who was part of the group that captured Taylor, was given
the honor of being part of the guard detail that took Taylor to the gal-
lows.[53] Martiness Decker of the Orange County New York Militia was
the orderly sergeant for Taylor's execution.[54] In the meantime, the
troops had relocated to the vicinity of Kingston. Taylor was hanged
from an old apple tree near the old church at Kingston, New York, on
October 16, one day before General Burgoyne surrendered at
Saratoga.[55] Taylor stood on a hogshead barrel. The rope was affixed
around his neck, and when the rope was secured, the barrel was rolled

away. Taylor dangled from the apple tree until he died.[56]

Another method of using a hidden compartment was placing a note inside the cloth cover of a button. Covering wooden or base metal buttons with cloth that matched the coat was a fashionable practice of the time. Isaac Ogden's brother (believed to be Samuel who lived in Boonton, New Jersey) sent Christian Lownear with a message inside a button to Isaac in New York City. Lownear received two guineas for his mission.[57]

Hiding messages in buttons was also done by the Darraghs, a Quaker family, of Philadelphia. After the British took possession of Philadelphia on September 26, 1777, General Howe occupied the house of John Cadwalader opposite the two story wooden frame residence of William and Lydia Darragh at 177 Second Street.[58] The Darraghs attended the old

Genearl Sir William Howe, engraved for Murray's History of the American War in 1778. He was Commander-in-Chief of the British army in North America from April 1776 to May 1778. (*William L. Clements Library*)

Arch Street Meeting and then switched to the Free Quaker meeting.[59] William Darragh, a school teacher, wrote messages in shorthand on small pieces of paper which were then placed between the wooden button and its cloth cover. His Dublin-born wife, Lydia, would sew the messages in the coat buttons of John, their fourteen-year-old son. Being a child, John was permitted to pass and re-pass the sentries without being stopped. Once he reached American-held ground, he went to his older brother, Charles, to deliver the messages which were hidden in his cloth-covered buttons.

General Howe's staff used the back room of the Darragh residence as an adjunct meeting space to Howe's quarters across the street. On the evening of December 2, 1777 about 7 p.m. General Howe held a staff meeting at the Darragh's house. Lydia was told the meeting would run late and "they wished the family to retire early to bed; adding, that when they were going away, they would call her to let them out, and extinguish their fire and candles." Because of the unusual request her curiosity was piqued and she "put her ear to the key-hole of the conclave." Lydia overheard General Howe's staff meeting. During the meeting the forthcoming attack on the evening of the 4th on the American troops at White Marsh was discussed. When she overheard this, she went to her room as if she had been there all evening. When the officers knocked on her door she waited for the third knock, "having feigned to be asleep."

On December 3rd she obtained a pass from General Howe to travel out of the city to get flour which was in short supply in Philadelphia, as was firewood.[60] She was able to get through the lines, and may have made this journey a number of times because the Old Swedes Mill in Frankford was popularly known as Lydia Darragh's Mill.[61]

The American troops were ordered to stop farmers who were sneaking into the city to sell their goods for hard currency rather than accept the nearly worthless continental currency. The troops were to detain anyone leaving the city and to send them to headquarters. Most of the run-ins between the American and British patrols that were trying to slow the commuting to and from Philadelphia consisted of little more than firing some lead at each other with almost no damage.[62] Colonel John Jameson advised Washington that the mills at Pennypack and Frankford were furnishing great quantities of flour to the British that he was powerless to stop unless he was with the men on their side of the river day and night, "as they are a set of the greatest villains I ever heard of. Many of them have received bribes to let inhabitants pass, but no proof against any but one Hood and one Reade, both of whom deserted last week. . . . Captain Howard has took about 100 people going to market last week, mostly women."[63] With such a porous situation Lydia would not have had much difficulty getting to the Frankford Mill.

Adjutant General Major Baurmeister of the Hessian forces confirmed that on December 3, 1777, "the highways from Philadelphia to Germantown and Frankford, and the road to Trenton by way of Jenkintown, are open to anyone. Some Philadelphians have been appointed to give passes to loyalists, who are then permitted to pass the pickets. When returning, these people always bring foodstuffs with them. The rebel light dragoons frequently carry the women's packages on their horses as far as their vedettes.[64] From these people we receive most of the news about the rebels."[65]

Lydia left her bag at the mill and headed for the American lines to find her son. She encountered an American captain, Charles Craig of the light horse, who was on an intelligence gathering patrol and who knew her. He inquired where she was headed and she informed him that she was trying to find her son. She requested that he walk with her. He did and she informed him privately of what she heard about the forthcoming raid. The officer went to give the information to headquarters to warn General Washington.[66] Lydia went to the mill, picked up her flour, and returned to her home in British-occupied Philadelphia.[67]

Elias Boudinot was the Commissary General of Prisoners and he also managed some of the Continental army's intelligence mission. Boudinot stated he

> dined at a small post at the Rising Sun [Tavern] about three miles from the City [of Philadelphia]. After dinner a little poor looking insignificant old woman came in and solicited leave to go into the country to buy some flour. While we were asking some questions, she walked up to me and put into my hands a dirty old needlebook, with various small pockets in it. Surprised at this, I told her to return, she should have an answer. On opening the needlebook, I could not find any thing till I got to the last pocket, where I found a piece of paper rolled up into the form of a pipe shank [stem]. On unrolling it I found that General Howe was coming out the next morning with 5,000 men, 13 pieces of cannon, baggage wagons, and 11 boats on wagon wheels. On comparing this with other information I found it true, and immediately rode post to head quarters.[68]

Is Elias Boudinot's old woman Lydia Darragh, possibly because of exactness of the British forces and equipment? Could she have met both Boudinot and Craig? Yes, it is possible.

On December 5 when the British army arrived at White Marsh to attack, they found the Continental army well prepared. After a few skirmishes on the 6th and 7th, the British returned to Philadelphia. Although Darragh's information was not the only report of impending British attack, it did confirm other intelligence that Boudinot had received and helped Washington and the Continental army to fend off the British attack.[69] She was read out (disowned) of meeting in October 1782 for not attending meeting and for "joining with a number of persons, associated under a pretense of religious duty, so far as to attend their meeting."[70] Many histories claim it was for her spying ways, but it could not have had anything to do with her spying activities, which were not publicly known in 1782.

A hidden compartment played a key role for the British in New York. When word of the Pennsylvania Line Mutiny of January 1, 1781, reached British headquarters at 1 Broadway, General Sir Henry wanted to be sure that the mutineers were coming toward New York before he sent his troops into New Jersey in the winter and put them at risk. He never wanted to defeat the mutineers in a battle but wished to protect them with his troops if they were deserting in response to his proposals. Clinton needed answers and not just opinions, hearsay, and gossip. To get those answers he would send ambassadors to the mutineers. The response would help him determine the correct course of action. He had a number of options to send his ambassadors into New Jersey. They could be sent to Staten Island and cross over the short distance of the Arthur Kill to the swamps at Elizabeth Town or to any point of the almost unguarded coast southward to Perth Amboy. He could send them to the forts at Paulus Hook, De Lancey, and Sandy Hook in New Jersey. Another option was to have the navy put the spies ashore on the northern Monmouth County coast at Cheesequake or at South Amboy, Black Point, or Squan, where his secret service operations maintained contacts.[71]

It was a rainy January 4 evening at British headquarters where three copies of a proposal to the mutineers were being prepared by candlelight. His emissaries were given a message which was wrapped in a square sheet of lead of the kind used to preserve tea.[72] This method served the dual purpose of being weatherproof and would not draw undue attention, as a guard would assume it contained tea, which the Americans were boycotting. The proposals the envoys carried promised the mutineers everything but the throne of England if they would come to the British. General Clinton asked the mutineers to send a representative to Amboy, where a conference would be held. They also wanted the mutineers to move east of South River where they could easily be protected by the British army.[73]

As soon as the proposals were completed, Andrew Gautier, Jr., a British spy based in Elizabeth Town, New Jersey, was sent two copies to be forwarded to the mutineers. To ensure its arrival, one package containing the proposal was sent by way of Elizabeth Town and the other by way of Newark.[74] Uzal Woodruff of Elizabeth Town was most likely the other courier to Gautier. Woodruff was set ashore at Newark by a boat from the *Neptune*. The third proposal which was prepared on the 4th was given to John Mason, who was being released from a British jail after serving time for what he called "inadvertently plundering."

On Friday the 5th Oliver De Lancey sent an unidentified courier with a verbal message to the mutineers.[75] Since Henry Clinton was one to always cover his bases to excess, three more proposals to the mutineers were prepared as backups. De Lancey's job now was finding three more people willing to undertake this most perilous mission. He had John Stapleton, his assistant, try to send George Henry Playter, a four-year veteran of the espionage game who worked as a courier for Brigadier General Cortland Skinner. However, Playter complained to De Lancey that he had already been seen for two nights at a tavern, thus making him conspicuous, and he feared that his cover might have already been blown.[76]

From the second batch of proposals one was sent to the mutineers via Cornelius Hatfield, Jr., at Staten Island. Part of a large clan of Hatfields (also spelled Hetfield) from Elizabeth Town, New Jersey, Cornelius had worked as both a guide and a spy since 1776. Cavalier Jouet, who also was from Elizabeth Town, described him as being a very zealous loyalist, much employed at British headquarters, but a loose and drinking man not of the coolest sense.

Some time on January 5 two more proposals encased in tea lead were delivered to British couriers. One was given to Caleb Bruen, who was an American double agent.[77] Bruen was the go-anywhere do-anything individual for the British secret service. The British used him as a courier to Dr. John Halliburton, a British spy, in Newport, Rhode Island. By May 1780, Bruen was under the direction of Colonel Elias Dayton as part of his spy ring operating out of Elizabeth Town. Bruen's cover was that he was carrying on an illegal trade but was not believed to have much money. In November 1780 he was given a pass signed by thirty-six-year-old Lieutenant Colonel Tench

Tilghman, aide-de-camp and military secretary to General George
Washington, and allowed to pass to General Lafayette's quarters.
Many years after the war, Bruen would tell how he had volunteered
to carry the treacherous correspondence to the mutineers hoping to
find a way to serve the American cause. Bruen, upon his arrival in
New Jersey, went directly to Colonel Elias Dayton and told him everything.[78]

The other proposal to the mutineers that went out on January 6,
1781, was given to Thomas Ward who had deserted from the
American army on June 16, 1777. The British sent him on recruiting
and intelligence-gathering missions. Ward's cover was that he was selling cloth to the rebels.[79] His mission this day was to get a copy of the
proposal to Samuel McFarlan, who would take it the rest of the way.[80]
It would not be McFarlan's first spy mission, as he had been on an
undercover assignment to Albany in 1779. McFarlan was discovered,
incarcerated, and escaped.[81]

Another method of hiding a message was explained by Colonel
Daniel Brodhead in a letter dated March 27, 1781 at Fort Pitt to
General George Washington. "Since my last a small paper was
brought to me by some faithful Indians who found it neatly rolled up
in a powder horn which a disaffected person had lost near the waters
of Sandusky. I take the liberty to enclose a copy of it. I have discovered
the writer and put him in irons, but as too probably some of the garrison is concerned that he may escape before he meets the reward of his
demerit. Indeed this place is infested with such a set of disaffected
inhabitants."[82] The letter was dated January 21, 1781, from Pittsburgh
and is signed "Thomas Girty."[83] However it was actually sent by
Myndart Fisher, who confessed to having written it and sent it by a
Mr. Garrett Graverat (Graverod). Fisher was a civilian who was
employed as a guide. Thomas Girty, brother of Simon Girty, knew
nothing of the letter but was an easy target as he was an infamous fron-
tiersman and British agent. Fisher was sentenced to death but no
record of his execution has been found.[84]

Sometimes spies just hid the document on their person. John
Leach, who had kept a navigation school in Boston, was suspected by

the British of having communications with the rebels. British General Thomas Gage had him arrested and placed in the Boston jail. During his incarceration, his wife Sarah Coffin Leach was forbidden to carry letters to her husband. Sarah "sent . . . a note, in the foot of a stocking rolled up," telling him of a "Friend and relation, Mrs. B—" recovering from smallpox in the country.[85]

Even the best-hidden secrets could be vulnerable. John André, British Adjutant General, had left the safety of New York City to meet with American General Benedict Arnold to turn over the plan for the fortifications that comprise West Point to the British. André had come out on the Sloop *Vulture* with a pass and met Arnold on the shore on September 21, 1780.

Because the Americans were firing on the vessel, it had to move downstream and André was unable to reboard the ship. He changed his clothes within the American lines, and under a feigned name and in disguise, passed the American forts at Stoney Point and Verplanks Point. André proceeded on horseback with his pass and was taken at Tarry Town, out of uniform, on his way to New York City. Military intelligence was found hidden in his boot.[86] He was tried at a court-martial as a spy and found guilty. He was hung on October 2, 1780.

Also using this concealment methods were John Campbell and Robert Ross, British spies operating in the Spanish territory of New Orleans. Because they were under surveillance, they asked Alexander Graiden to carry a secret message to Colonel Hutchins, the British commander at Natchez.[87] Ross offered Graiden a good gratification for the trip but no specific fee was determined.[88] Graiden agreed and on May 11, 1778, requested a Spanish passport to travel to Punta Cortada. Bernardo de Gálvez, the governor of Louisiana, gave him the passport but ordered four men to meet him on the road and arrest him.[89] Graiden left New Orleans in the early afternoon of May 12th on Ross's horse carrying the letters of introduction. Graiden made it to William Dunbar's plantation about twenty leagues north of New Orleans. He was arrested on the night of the 13th.[90] At the time of his arrest, Graiden had the letter for Colonel Hutchins and others in his possession that Campbell and Ross had given to him. The arresting party took the letter addressed to Dunbar as well as the four letters left in the house of William Dunbar.[91]

Graiden was brought before Governor Gálvez early in the morning of the 14th and in the evening confessed that he was employed by Campbell and Ross to deliver a letter to Colonel Hutchins. On the night of the 15th, Pedro Olevaraz, Spanish aide-de-camp, arrested and confined Campbell and Ross to the public prison.[92] At the time of his arrest, Campbell discreetly took from his desk an anonymous letter that contained incriminating information on British intelligence operations and hid it in the waistband of his breeches.[93] When Campbell arrived at the prison, Sergeant Eugenio Alverez of the battalion stationed at the fort and Francisco Muños, jailer, wanted to search him. Campbell "raised many difficulties saying that he had no papers concealed about him." They discovered a folded letter in his breeches between his skin and his garter, which was delivered to Pedro Olevaraz.[94] Campbell would later claim "it was thro' inadvertency that he put the letter between his breeches and drawers and that he made no other opposition than what is natural to every one when a person puts his hand into his breeches that the suspicion of the letter having been sent with an intention to hurt him arose from circumstance of its not being signed."[95]

On June 2, 1778, the Spanish court ordered "Robert Ross, John Campbell, and Alexander Graiden to perpetual banishment from this Province and absolute prohibition to return to it." They were also required to pay 1,700 pounds sterling in fines and expenses by the Spanish.[96] John Campbell and Robert Ross were held in the prison till July 10, a total of fifty-five days.[97] Alexander Graiden was sent as a prisoner to Havana on the brig *Santa Theresa* commanded by Thomas de Herrera.[98]

Still, hiding messages in ordinary objects was unobtrusive and usually worked. Patrick Smyth lived on a fifty-acre farm at Fort Edward, Charlotte County, New York and owned a thirteen-acre piece of property at Kingsbury. Smyth had been the county clerk, assistant judge of common pleas, coroner, and deputy postmaster. As General John Burgoyne was making his decent from Canada in 1777, the rebels drove off all his livestock to keep them from falling into the hands of the British army and he was forcibly removed to Albany. After Burgoyne's surrender, his house was converted to a barracks and destroyed. He then became a courier between Generals Sir Henry

Clinton in New York and Frederick Haldimand in Quebec.[99] He was provided a pension and a house for himself and family in New York City.[100] He carried the dispatches in the handle of a large knife. When he submitted his memorial, he included his knife as evidence.[101]

Peter DuBois wrote a report on the character of Mr. Hector St. John. "In his small house he built upon his farm he had many private places artfully contrived (as he told his Carpenter) to secret his effects when he went abroad. In case at any time he might have dishonest Servants about him."[102] Hector St. John, better known by the name Crèvecoeur, was a Frenchman who arrived in New York City in 1759 and relocated in 1769 to Chester, Orange County, New York. He had been fined and imprisoned for loyalism. He was given approval to leave Chester on February 3, 1779 on the condition of his going to France. On going into New York City, he smuggled documents in secret compartments underneath various botanical plants. The plants were in boxes which had false bottoms in which he hid his papers. The papers were composed of twenty-four books of four sheets each that detailed petty tyrannies. "But upon taking them out on his arrival here [New York City], he found them very damp nearly wet from the moisture of the earth in the box above them which obliged him to take them out and dry them before a fire in his Lodgings."[103] He dined with William Smith on Feb 15th and William Smith summarized the information that St. John brought and sent it to General Robertson.[104] St. John was correctly suspected by the British of being an American spy and imprisoned in July 1779. Smith saw him looking out of the Provost on July 8, 1779. William Smith secured his release and in 1780, he sailed for France.[105]

In another case, a spy was unable to clear off where he hid his incriminating evidence. Jabes Sayers, an inhabitant of Newark, New Jersey, and a spy working for George Beckwith, came from Newark to New York City on the evening of March 21, 1781. He used the cover of smuggling provisions to the British to hide his espionage activities. If caught, a smuggler would be punished, but would not be put to death, as would a spy. Besides reporting on the American troop strength at Newark and Second River, Sayers told of "a man of the name of John Rogers, was taken a few nights ago, upon New Ark [Newark] Meadows; he is considered a spy, and Ensign Burnet who commands in New Ark; told the informant [Mr. Sayers] that Rogers had a pass from Sir Henry Clinton, some letters or papers, which he is thought to have carried out, were found concealed in a hay stack, near the place where he was taken."[106]

Patience Lowell Wright arguably had the most unusual hiding place. She was born in Bordentown, New Jersey, and ran away to Philadelphia when she was twenty. She returned to Bordentown after her marriage and stayed until her husband's death in 1768. She was a uniquely spirited independent woman. Before the American Revolution, she had set up studios in New York and Philadelphia sculpting portraits in wax. In 1772, she moved to London and opened a very popular studio. She was well known by powerful people and many sat for her. She was an eccentric who once called King George III "George," among other names, when he visited her studio. She claimed to have passed useful information to Benjamin Franklin and Congress by putting messages in wax heads that she periodically sent to her sister's shop in Philadelphia.[107] However, a comparison made of her letter dated September 3, 1774, and another one of the same date that probably arrived on the same ship indicated that her ability to gather accurate information needed much improvement. She reported that Sir Draper was coming to America, while the other letter indicates that he was only offered a position as a governor.[108] The British had found that she used Dr. Edward Bancroft's mistress to carry her letters to Benjamin Franklin in Paris. Some have speculated that she may have been used by the British to pass along misinformation.[109]

Chapter 10

Flags of Truce

Spies routinely used flags of truce to get themselves across into enemy territory, and once there would use any excuse to dawdle as long as they could and attempt to collect information from their local contacts. One of the known local contacts was Mrs. Jane Chandler of Elizabeth Town, New Jersey, the wife of Thomas Bradbury Chandler, a prominent Anglican clergyman and author.[1] He was a Loyalist and was attacked in 1775 by the Continental Congress in a pamphlet titled "What Think Ye of Congress Now?" He fled to England in 1775.[2] The Chandlers would most certainly have been well known to Cortland Skinner, the son of William Skinner, the Anglican clergyman at Perth Amboy, New Jersey.[3] It is suspected that Mrs. Jane Chandler was part of Loyalist Brigadier Cortland Skinner's New Jersey spy network.

British General Campbell who was in command of Staten Island would have refugee Tories bring over flags of truce on legitimate business to Elizabeth Town. Since they knew the area and the people, it was easy for them to accomplish their hidden agendas which included contacting their in place agents.[4] Prior to February 16, 1778, William Livingston had permitted Mrs. Jane Chandler to go into and return from New York because her son was reported to be at the point of death.[5] American General William Maxwell in a letter to Governor William Livingston on April 26, 1779, had the following to say about Mrs. Chandler: "In the way of giving intelligence to the enemy, I think her the first in the place. There is not a Tory that passes in or out of New York or any other way, that is of consequence but what waits on Mrs. Chandler, and mostly all the British officers going in and out

on parole, or exchange, waits on her-in short she governs the whole of
the Tories and many of the Whigs. I think she would be much better
in New York, and to take her Baggage with her that she might have
nothing to come back for."

People arriving with flags were always suspect. When American
General Richard Montgomery had surrounded the city of Quebec,
British General Guy Carleton refused to admit anyone into the city of
Quebec, even those carrying flags of truce. The city security net was
drawn so tight that it was said that not even a prostitute could get a
word into the city. The Americans were so desperate to contact their
friends in the city that they tied messages to arrows and shot them into
the city and hoped that they got to where they were intended.[6]

The outpost towns where flags of truce were accepted were also the
acknowledged locations for soldiers who had been exchanged to make
their return to their side of the line. British soldiers returning to New
York would wait in Elizabeth Town, New Jersey, for the next British
flag to come over from Staten Island, New York. While they waited in
Elizabeth Town, they would have contact with the citizens of the
town and pick up tidbits of information that they could bring back. If
a flag was not forthcoming and they tired of waiting, they would
arrange their own unauthorized transportation across the short
expanse of the Arthur Kill. The local military would be happy to see
them leave as they would be one less problem.

Soldiers on parole who were answering a call to return to their
units, or in their attempt to effectuate their exchange, crossed the lines
between the armies accompanied by flags of truce or in flag boats
established specifically to bring soldiers on parole across a body of
water. A parole was a promise given by a prisoner of war when he was
released that he would not bear arms or participate in the war until he
was exchanged.[7] There were soldiers like Captain Hankes, who had
traveled on his parole in February 1779 from Elizabeth Town to
Staten Island under a flag of truce and had picked up information in
New Jersey along the way. While he was on Staten Island James
Gambier took Hankes's deposition on what he had seen of the
American troops.[8] This was not an isolated occurrence, as Alexander
Phillips complained to Sir Henry Clinton on October 3, 1781, about
intelligence going out of the British lines that "others . . . sent from
here [New York] on parole make an excuse to return here to answer

their paroles and get what intelligence they can of your Excellency from us and then return to the rebels."⁹

Flags of truce were used on many occasions to distribute information. Richard Howe on the ship *Eagle* off Sandy Hook forwarded instructions to Sir Henry Clinton which had been sent as a circular from Lord George dated at Whitehall on February 19, 1778. The circular stated the King wanted General Clinton to print two legislative bills from the House of Commons and "to embrace every opportunity of circulating them by Flags of Truce or private persons among the rebel troops."¹⁰ Evidence that this was carried out comes from Colonel Tuffin Charles Armand who reported to General Scott that a Hessian captain came out with the flags almost every day "and never in right order." Either the Hessian captain or someone in the party that came with the flag of truce "put upon the door of one house in Taretown [Tarrytown, New York] one proclamation from G[ene]r[a]l Clinton."¹¹

In an effort to stop the flow of people and things across the lines, the commandant of New York City, Major General Robert Pigot, reissued a proclamation on February 17, 1777, previously issued by Major General James Robertson, which had the same hoped-for result. The proclamation required all people coming into New York City to immediately give their names. Anybody who came from an area controlled by the rebels and did not immediately report themselves to the general would be treated a spy as well as anybody harboring or concealing such an individual.¹²

Because of flags arriving on frivolous reasons from Connecticut, Major General Pigot issued an order on June 7, 1777, that "no flags of truce are permitted to land anybody, have any intercourse with the troops or inhabitants but be obliged to return from whence they came."¹³ The situation had gotten so out of control that both sides restricted the locations where they would accept flags of truce. The British would only accept flags at Staten Island, Paulus Hook, Kingsbridge, Morrisania, and those places on Long Island that were designated by Oliver De Lancey.¹⁴

On July 23, 1777, the new British commandant of New York, Major General Valentine Jones, restricted such travel to persons with suitable authorization, and completely prohibited it after sunset, on pain of military execution. He indicated that "many evil practices are carried on by persons passing and repassing to and from this city and the [New] Jersey shore in small craft."[15] Sir Henry Clinton issued a proclamation on February 13, 1778, concerning the movement of goods to Staten Island because "supplies of rum, salt, and other goods are frequently conveyed to the rebels, by the way of Staten Island." All vessels going to Staten Island were to land at Cole's Ferry and to report to Alexander Gardiner, wharf officer, before unloading their cargoes on Staten Island.[16]

American General William Maxwell in an April 26, 1779 letter to New Jersey Governor William Livingston stated that people who have been on the island came back "with the addition of seven devils more than they were possessed of before, by the connections they have formed on the other side, and no doubt but some of them is sent over to us by the enemy."[17]

General Alexander Leslie, British commander on Staten Island, advised General Sir Henry Clinton on August 3, 1779, that all people going to Elizabeth Town must come and go over at Decker's Ferry. After the lodging at Decker's Ferry quickly filled to capacity, the overflow was sent to a Mrs. Cuffey's, which was expensive as she did not keep a public house.[18] The local legislature would have set the price for accommodations at any inn, but since the accommodations were made at her residence, she could charge a rate as high as the traffic would bear.

William Lloyd of the 47th Regiment of Foot was the conductor of flags of truce between the British on Staten Island, New York, and the Americans at Elizabethtown Point, New Jersey. He held this position beginning on October 12, 1779 and continuing till at least June 30, 1780, when General Clinton noted that Lloyd was being overpaid. He had received ten shillings in New York currency per day.[19]

Major General James Pattison and Commandant of the City of New York issued a proclamation on July 12, 1779, that required all masters of ships and vessels arriving in New York to submit a report of all their passengers and letters to the police.[20] On January 10, 1781, Brigadier General Samuel Birch and Commandant of the City of New York issued another proclamation concerning the harboring in homes of people who had gone into the city and did not register. The proclamation indicated that General Pattison's proclamation of July 12, 1779, was being disregarded in some instances.[21]

It was not just the common soldier who would get tricked. American Brigadier General William Maxwell's assignment during the period of January to April 1777 was to oversee the area from Perth Amboy to Newark, New Jersey. He was instructed by General George Washington to be attentive to loyalists who now would swear allegiance to America but would be sending information to the British. He was also trying to collect enemy intelligence and kept a military detachment in Newark and Elizabeth Town for the sole purpose of obtaining information on the enemy's activities. Maxwell referred to people who passed between the lines as "licensed spies" and some were also double agents.[22] He sent a letter on April 10, 1777, from his headquarters in Westfield, New Jersey, to Major General Adam Stephen, which discussed their mutual problem of securing correct information. "I know how you must feel as I suffered just in something the same way my self by the scoundrel that remained in and about Newark. [It] is impossible for a man to divine these things in our degenerate days and he that will go blindfolded into such matters is worse than a fool. We have a very difficult card to play [and] we have often to act by the moon or twilight and leave the world to judge of it in clear sunshine." Apparently Generals Maxwell and Stephen both fell victim to a British deception and were duped into believing erroneous information. Maxwell had this same problem again in August 1778.[23]

General Samuel H. Parsons on December 13, 1779, was given the same job that General Maxwell had two years earlier of gathering intelligence and protecting the populous between Newark and Perth Amboy. Washington instructed him, "The detestable and pernicious traffic carried on with the enemy will demand your peculiar vigilance and attention. I entreat you to pursue the most decisive measures to put a stop to it. No flags are to be sent or persons suffered to go into the enemy without a permit from The Governor of the State or from Head Quarters."[24]

The problem of flags was not restricted to the area around New York City. John Page, lieutenant governor of Virginia, signed a report of the council meeting that they "are unanimously of opinion that a flag [of truce] ought not be permitted to carry any kind of merchandise not only as being contrary to the law of nations but as sending in our situation to establish a precedent which may be attended with mischievous consequences."[25] The problem with implementing that opinion is it would impact the practice of licensed smugglers, that is, spies who used smuggling to cover their true purpose.

The Americans did have some success in intercepting those individuals who were using the flags for cover for their smuggling or spying operations or both. A flag of truce came out from Boston on July 6, 1775, that was suspected of being a spy.[26] In 1780 John Adam, commissary of prisoners at Elizabeth Town, sent Brice, Davidser, Jones, Price, Ridge, and three others to Thomas Bradford, commissary of prisoners at Philadelphia. They had come from the British outpost at Sandy Hook in a flag boat to Shrewsbury, Monmouth County, New Jersey. There was no indication with the flag of truce what their business was. They had eight or ten pounds of tea and some sugar in their possession when they landed at Red Bank. They proceeded about five miles into the country before they were captured. Adam said that they were either spies or at least prisoners of war.[27] Abraham Skinner, commissary of prisoners at headquarters at Camp Tappan wrote on August 12, 1780, to Bradford that the prisoners sent to Bradford by Adam were to remain in confinement until he received orders from General Washington.[28]

Smuggling was practiced for the entire period of hostilities. On June 6, 1775, British sentries at the entrance to Boston stopped a team of horses pulling a wagon load of hay. When they checked under the hay, they found two calves, watches, a number of letters, some veal, several boxes of butter, two bushels of green peas, and some mutton.[29]

A report indicated that quantities of provisions found their way to the British from Shrewsbury and Middletown Point (Matawan) in Monmouth County, Perth Amboy in Middlesex County, and Elizabeth Town in Essex (now Union) County, New Jersey.[30] Most of the illegal trade known as the "London trade" from Perth Amboy and Middletown Point (Matawan) would have been smuggled in small boats out to the British armed provision ship, the 112 1/2 ton brig *Ranger* (Daniel Tinley, master) that was stationed off the southeast end of Staten Island.[31] *Ranger* was still at Princess Bay in 1781.[32] Governor Livingston wrote that there was an almost universal uproar over the flag boats that carried for the prisoners in New York. He stated that many times the complaints were not based on facts; however, these boats had been carrying private merchandise in addition to their official cargoes. The additional merchandise was used to trade with the enemy and bring back private goods. He suggested that Elias Boudinot should have an agent stationed at New Brunswick to certify the inventory the vessels are to carry to New York and what they are allowed to bring back. Livingston wanted the militia to intercept any smuggled items and the contraband would belong to the militia. He believed that the militia would diligently enforce the measure and would put an end to the smuggling.[33]

Flags were also being used as deceptive cover for covert operations in the Caribbean. Eliphalet Fitch, a Boston native and merchant at Kingston, Jamaica, imported provisions and timber from North America and cordage and clothes from England, and re-exported slaves to Cuba as the agent of the Spanish Royal Asiento Company. Prior to the American Revolution, Fitch smuggled British goods to the Spanish island of Cuba using the slave trade as his cover. During the early days of the American Revolution he also worked as a spy and supplied military intelligence to the American patriots. He contracted with Francisco Miranda, a Spanish official in Jamaica, to supply military stores to the Spanish using the cover of flags of truce for prisoner exchanges. The fact that Colonel John Darling, the governor of Jamaica, and Sir Peter Parker, a British admiral, were quarreling and not speaking to each other allowed Fitch to pretend that he had received permission for his flags of truce from one or the other.[34]

Sometimes a spy using the cover of a smuggler gets caught in the net put out to capture enemy spies. George Washington wrote to Joseph Reed and John Cox,

> I am informed, there is a certain Mr. Smith, who has been lately taken up by General Lincoln as a spy and sent to Philadelphia under that character; I believe, for several reasons that he is the man who was employed by you to act for us, in that capacity, and that the apprehending him is a mistake, which may be attended with ill consequences. Lest he should be precipitately tried and punished, I must beg you will interpose in the affair without delay, and if you find him to be the person I suspect he is, take measures to have

him released. I should be glad indeed, that some manage-
ment might be used in the matter, in order to turn the circumstance of his being apprehended to a good account. It
would be well to make him a handsome present in money
to secure his fidelity to us; and contrive his releasement, in
such a manner, as to give it the appearance of an accidental escape from confinement. After concerting a plan with
him, by which he will be enabled to be serviceable to us,
in communicating intelligence from time to time, let him
make the best of his way to the enemy, under the idea
above intimated, that is, as a fugitive from the persecution
and danger, he incurred among us, for his known friendship to the enemy. Great care must be taken, so to conduct
the scheme, as to make the escape appear natural and real;
there must be neither too much facility, nor too much
refinement, for doing too little, or over acting the part,
would, alike beget a suspicion of the true state of the case.[35]

Flags were also used to send people with counterfeit money to try
and wreck the value of the Continental dollar. During the American
Revolution it was a practice long tried by the British. The British forty-
four gun warship *Phoenix* stationed at New York Harbor had on board
a printing press on which counterfeits of the 1775 issue of
Continental currency were being produced. George and John Folliett
of Ridgefield, Connecticut, were charged in Superior Court,
Fairfield, Connecticut, with going on board the *Phoenix* and receiving counterfeit bills in January 1776.[36] The situation became so bla-
tant that the *New-York Gazette* of April 14, 1777 carried the following
advertisement:

> Persons, going into other colonies, may be supplied with
> any number of counterfeited Congress-notes, for the price
> of the paper per Ream. They are so neatly and exactly exe-
> cuted, that there is no risqué in getting them off. It being
> almost impossible to discover, that they are not genuine.
> This has been proved by bills to a very large amount, which
> have already been successfully circulated. Enquire for
> Q.E.D. [to see a sample] at the Coffee-House, from 11
> P.M. to 4 A.M. during the present month.[37]

David Farnsworth and John Blair were tried at a division court-martial convened by order of Major General Gates at Danbury, Connecticut, on October 8, 1778, with Brigadier General Patterson as president. They were found guilty for loitering about the army encampment as spies, and having a large sum of counterfeit money with them, which they had brought from New York.[38] The *Connecticut Current* of November 10, 1778, reports that they were held at the Hartford County Goal.[39] They were executed in Rocky Hill, Connecticut, during November 1778.[40]

Robert Townsend wrote a letter in invisible ink dated November 27, 1779, in which he reported that the British had obtained from Philadelphia "several reams of the paper made for the last emission (of paper Continental currency) struck by Congress."[41]

Stephen McPherson had been one of these agents who had come out of British-held Philadelphia under a flag of truce. Specifically he was a carpenter who had been sent to tend to the wagons. He had been arrested, charged, arraigned, tried, and acquitted of the charge of using counterfeit Pennsylvania currency. He was to have been sent back to Philadelphia when a flag was returning. However, the British army evacuated the city on June 18, 1778, and there would be no returning flag to Philadelphia, so he was held in jail. On July 3, 1778, McPherson wrote to Captain Thomas Bradford, commissary of British prisoners of war at Philadelphia, asking to be allowed to leave the Philadelphia jail and return to the British army.[42]

The practice continued when the British returned to New York City. A newspaper report of August 2, 1780, from Chatham, New Jersey, stated, "Within a few days past, upward of forty persons have been confined in Morris Town goal for being concerned in passing counterfeit money."[43] The British who hoped to undermine the American economy had sent them.[44] Richard Stevens, a counterfeiter, was arrested in 1780 and hanged in Morristown.[45]

In the summer of 1781 there was a great quantity of counterfeit money coming from New York City into New Jersey. Captain Asher FitzRandolph sent New Jersey Governor William Livingston six counterfeit bills of New Jersey money that came directly from New York. His information was that £4,000 of counterfeit New Jersey money was being passed. The person passing the money would get 2 1/2 percent from the Crown.[46]

Sometimes the people with the flags of truce had such obvious
ulterior motives that they were required to return immediately. One
case of the sort happened in Virginia. His Majesty's ship *Raisonable*
was stationed at Hampton Road, Virginia; because of her draft, she
could proceed no farther. The captain of the *Raisonable* sent a message to Sir George Collier, commodore and commander-in-chief of
the British fleet in America, that American Captain Peter Burnard
accompanied by two other men had arrived with a flag of truce and a
pass from Governor Patrick Henry dated May 13, 1779. Bernard was
to go to the ship and make application to the commodore of the
British squadron in Virginia to recover four runaway slaves of William
Armistead which were said to be on board some of the British ships.[47]
Commodore Collier notified Patrick Henry that the King's "ships in
Virginia was neither to entice Negro slaves on board, nor detain them
if they were found there; nevertheless, his Majesty's colors in all places
afforded an asylum to the distressed, and protection upon supplica-
tion. That be, however, could not seriously imagine three gentleman
would come upon so insignificant an errand as they pretend, but that
they were sent by Mr. Henry, as spies; notwithstanding which, as they
had approached under a flag of truce, it should not be violated, but
they, suffered to return; with an injunction, not to venture again to
gain intelligence through a channel which ought to be sacred, and
never prostituted to such purposes."[48]

General Lafayette while at Rawson's Ordinary on June 26, 1781,
complained, "Several people go into the enemy's lines, or upon flag
granted by county lieutenants. This practice is productive of many
evils, and I could wish to see it abolished by a proclamation or circular letter to the lieutenants of the counties."[49] On July 30, 1782,
George Kelly at Norfolk informed the governor that he had arrested
James Laughton and wanted to arrest John McLear, formerly of
Norfolk, who were put on shore from a ship and had gone into the
country without permission. Colonel John Newton also writing from
Norfolk on July 30, 1782, but to Colonel Davies stated that "Laughton
and McLear where British subjects, from Flags of Truce—Considers
the captain very culpable in permitting it—the persons 'so coming in'
should be regarded as spies."[50]

Virginia was not the only place that spy communications were
being accomplished using flags of truce. Washington in January 1782

wrote from Philadelphia to New Jersey Governor William Livingston that "a constant intercourse is carried on by water between the refugees and the inhabitants, but that, no force which I could spare would prevent, as they would, if kept out of one inlet make use of another for their purposes. It is in vain to expect the pernicious and growing traffic will ever be stopped, until the states pass laws agt. [against] it, making the penalty death. This I long ago foresaw and recommended. We are I believe the only nation who suffer their people to carry on a commerce with their enemy in time of war."[51]

Two weeks later George Washington wrote from Philadelphia to Brigadier General Elias Dayton on January 26, 1782, that "I am of opinion with you that the most flagrant abuses are committed under the cover of flags to and from New York[52] and am willing to adopt any measures to prevent a continuance of them. I have no papers with me but those of a late date, and therefore cannot refer to the instructions formerly given to you upon the subject. If I recollect them they were to put a stop to the practice of flags going and coming at stated times, and to suffer no persons to go on board or to land from the boats except those with proper passports. All letters to be delivered to the officer on guard at Elizabeth Town. If you think this mode or one similar to it will answer the purpose, you will carry it into execution and try the effect."[53] In May, Washington was complaining because of "an open intercourse between the City of New York and the County of Monmouth, by means of prostituted Flags of Truce."[54] In March 1783 Washington was complaining to Governor Jonathan Trumbull of Connecticut about "great quantities of provisions; meat and bread, in open day" that were being sent across the Long Island Sound to New York under the cover of flags of truce. Washington says this was happening "almost under the eye of your officers and troops stationed in that Quarter; in which Business, it is to be feared, your Commissioned Boats and Vessels, are not exempted from bearing a part."[55]

One of the accepted practices was that newspapers were routinely exchanged when flags of truce visited. Arranging to have proclamations and stories printed in the newspaper was one way of getting your message circulated in the enemy camp. A committee had prepared a proclamation of clemency for anyone who wished to return to the Royal Standard for General Sir Henry Clinton. James Rivington, the Royal printer in New York, published the proclamation in his *Royal*

Gazette on December 30, 1780. When the newspaper was exchanged at Elizabeth Town, the proclamation would also be distributed. Additionally spies would carry the handbills of proclamation to drop in the American camp. This proclamation was to even be translated into the German language for circulation to the Pennsylvania German-speaking population. William Smith, the Royal Chief Justice of New York, believed that 10 or 12,000 copies were going to be printed for a general distribution.[56] American Major General Israel Putnam, who had a sense of humor, once sent some newspapers with the following message, "Major General Putnam presents his compliments to Major General Robertson, and sends him some American newspapers for his perusal; when General Robertson shall have done with them, it is requested they be given to Rivington, in order that he may print some truth."[57]

Officers who were granted permission to try to effectuate their exchange would make the journey between the lines by accompanying the flags of truce since they were permitted to travel freely and openly. There was no need to use subterfuge. Captain William Bernard Gifford was in Colonel Elias Dayton's 3rd New Jersey Regiment. The British had captured him and Andrew McFarland at Elizabeth Town on January 25, 1780. During his captivity, Gifford married Nancy Voorhies at New Utrecht, Long Island, in 1780. On November 10, 1780 while at New Utrecht, Kings County, Long Island, New York, he told Oliver De Lancey, the adjutant general at British Headquarters, that he would go back into the American lines to settle his exchange and to provide military intelligence.[58] Gifford's plan was set in motion.

Gifford prepared a report dated November 28, 1780, and says "I have been at Trenton [New Jersey] dined and spent the evening with G. L. [Governor William Livingston] and several of the Council and assembly. . . . I shall set off for W. P. (West Point) to morrow."[59] Gifford looking to find a way to get his report into British headquarters in New York City found that British Lieutenant Thomas Hughes had just arrived in Elizabeth Town. Hughes had been exchanged and left Lancaster on November 22 to make his way back to New York City. Hughes and Lieutenant Brown were staying at a tavern in Elizabeth Town and awaiting transportation across the Arthur Kill to Staten Island. Hughes says that he met Gifford on November 30 and agreed to take his report to De Lancey in New York City. Hughes and Brown were taken across to Staten Island in a fisherman's canoe on December 2. Hughes finally reached New York City on December 4 and delivered Gifford's message to the adjutant general at British headquarters.[60]

The problem of people crossing the military lines never went away as De Lancey issued orders on March 27, 1783, that no person was to be allowed to come into the British lines unless they had a passport from the commandant of New York.[61]

Flags of truce and flag boats were a constant source of trouble for both sides because spies realized they provided a quick and safe method for them to get to the other side and return. Travel under flags of truce provided a channel for the distribution of counterfeit money for the British, and they provided a lucrative business for those on the lines willing to participate in the "London trade," as smuggling was called. Flags also served a much-needed purpose in the official movements of people and documents, both official military and personal correspondence, and the news of the day from the local or London newspapers between the two opposing sides.

Chapter 11

THE CULPER SPY RING

The Culper spy ring—primarily Abraham Woodhull and Robert Townsend writing as the fictitious father and son Samuel Culper Sr. and Jr.—would use Setauket, Long Island, as its fulcrum, working from New York City to Long Island and along the Connecticut coast.[1] Prior to the beginning of the ring, Judge Selah Strong of Setauket had been sending information to the American army in Connecticut. British Lieutenant Colonel Richard Hewlett wrote to Royal Governor William Tryon on September 3, 1777. that he had "authentic information lodged against a Justice Selah Strong by a gentleman from Connecticut." It was reported that the thirty-nine-year-old Strong had a correspondence with General Samuel H. Parsons. The report stated Strong had repeatedly sent intelligence to the rebels in Connecticut of the situation of the troops in this place by John and Cornelius Clark and Strong had "pretended to be our friend and several times given information of the last named persons being over but not until they were gone."[2] Selah Strong was arrested and sent to the infamous prison ship *Jersey*.

After the British adventure in Philadelphia was over and they evacuated the Quaker city and returned to New York City, General George Washington wanted to know more about what the British were planning. He already had intelligence reports coming to him from New York via Staten Island and Elizabeth Town but wanted more. He preferred to cross-check his information to be sure it was correct. He instructed Major Alexander Clough of the 3rd Continental Dragoons on August 25, 1778, to arrange "to obtain a true account of what was passing in New York."[3] Shortly thereafter

Clough was killed in action at Tappan, New York, on September 28, 1778.[4] Benjamin Tallmadge was then given Clough's assignment as a case agent overseeing spies. Tallmadge's sphere of operation was east of the Hudson River which included Westchester County, the Connecticut shore, and Long Island as a backdoor into New York City.[5]

Benjamin Tallmadge in his memoir wrote that the Culper ring started its operation in 1778 and continued its operation through to the summer of 1781.[6] Tallmadge said he kept one or more boats constantly employed in crossing Long Island Sound as part of this operation. Tallmadge while at Bedford, Westchester County, New York, wrote to General Charles Scott, "I have this moment received a letter from a gentlemen direct form Long Island, by the very gentlemen whom I made mention to you the other day to serve as a conveyance for Samuel Culper's letters. I doubt not it is authentic."[7] Tallmadge was addressed as John Bolton or "721" in the Culpers' correspondence.

George Washington wrote from Philadelphia on January 2, 1779, to Tallmadge on a change in procedures for handling the secret service letters. "There are regular expresses established between Danbury [Connecticut] and the head quarters of the army and you therefore need not in future send a special messenger the whole way. Send your letters to General [Israel] Putnam at or near Danbury, letting him know that they are to be forwarded with dispatch [and] I shall get them sooner than by a single express."[8]

There were times when the British army would disrupt communications. One incident was when British Lieutenant Colonel John Graves Simcoe of the Queen's Rangers was instructed on January 29, 1779, to go to Setauket where he was to visit the farms on the Drowned Meadow and the surrounding area. He was to determine how much good hay was being collected and the number of cattle that the farmers possessed. This agricultural census would provide the location of supplies should they be needed by the British military.[9] Having the British army scouring the countryside is not conducive to the execution of clandestine activities.

Sometimes one's own side can hinder an operation. Woodhull's letter of February 26, 1779, pleads for Colonel Benjamin Floyd's discharge and says that he be returned on his parole on February 16. "I

earnestly desire you would not forget. I am very likely to stand in need
of his services."[10] Woodhull tells in his letter of 427 eg (November 13),
1779, that "I have no love for Coll. Floyd nor for no Tory under heav-
en, but in my present situation am oblidge[d] to cultivate his friendship [to procure intelligence]."[11] Tallmadge had gone to Boston
where he had arrived by February 15, 1779, and was able to oversee
Woodhull's request.[12] Caleb Brewster, who after he arrived that day
(February 26, 1779) from Long Island, was at Fairfield, Connecticut,
when he wrote out an intelligence report and sent both letters forward
to headquarters.[13]

George Washington while at Middlebrook, New Jersey, wrote to
Benjamin Tallmadge on March 21, 1779, about the collection of
intelligence.[14] He advised that "as all great movements and the fountain of all intelligence must originate at, and proceed from the head
quarters of the enemy's army, C. [Samuel Culper, i.e., Abraham
Woodhull] had better reside at New York—mix with and put on the
airs of a Tory, to cover his real character and avoid suspicion." [15] The
British headquarters were at the Archibald Kennedy house at 1
Broadway in New York City.[16] Washington suggested that Woodhull
make an acquaintance "with a person in the naval Department, who
may either be engaged in the business of procuring transports for the
embarkation of the troops. or in victualling them."[17]

Culper's next letter dated April 10, 1779, from 10 (New York City)
gives some insight into his mind. He tells why he is working as a spy
and of his great fear of being found out. Woodhull writes, "I indevour
to collect and convey the most accurate and explicit intelligence that
I possibly can; and hope it may be of some service toward alleviating
the misery of our distressed Country, nothing but that could have
induced me to undertake it, for you must readily think it is a life of
anxiety to be within (on such business) the lines of a cruel and mis-
trustful enemy and that I most ardently wish and impatiently wait for
their departure." At the end of the letter he advises "No. 10 represents
N. York, 20 Setauket, 30 and 40 Post Riders."[18] This was the beginning
of the Culpers' writing in code.

Culper's next letter (April 12, 1779 at New York) acknowledges to
John Bolton (Benjamin Tallmadge) that he has received a vial of the
invisible stain.[19] This was the stain and reagent provided by James Jay,
brother of John Jay. The concept was not new but James Jay created

his own formula. Creating an invisible ink letter worked like this: The whitest paper was selected and the message was written in white ink; it then disappeared from view. The message could be written on a blank page of an almanac, in between the lines of some personal correspondence, or on the blank side of a letter. Culper was able to pass documents through the military checkpoints since the writing was not visible. When the document reached its destination, the counterpart (reagent) was applied with a fine brush to the paper over the invisible writing and the writing became visible. Culper was always asking for more of the invisible stain and Washington was having problems procuring more until 1780 when a laboratory was built for the purpose of manufacturing the agent and reagent.[20]

Travel to and from New York had its dangers. Tallmadge advised Washington that Culper (Woodhull) "was the other day robbed of all his money near Huntington, Long Island, and was glad to escape with his life."[21] George Washington in a letter dated June 13, 1779, to Tallmadge advised, "Should suspicions of him rise so high as to render it unsafe to continue in N[ew]— Y[ork]—. I would by all means wish him to employ some person of whose attachment and abilities he entertains the best opinion, to act in his place, with a request to be critical in his observations rather than a mere retailer of vulgar reports. To combine the best information he can get with attentive observation will prove the more likely means to obtain useful knowledge. A mode of conveying it quickly is of the utmost importance and claims much attention."[22] Washington's plea for more reliable intelligence was part of the same letter that was intercepted by the British that confirmed the Americans were using invisible ink. The British also intercepted a letter from Caleb Brewster to Benjamin Tallmadge of June 21, 1779, revealing that Anna "Nancy" Strong, wife of Justice Selah Strong, was part of the spy ring.[23]

Abraham Woodhull (aka Samuel Culper), in a letter from Setauket on June 5, 1779, advises that he is a suspected person and as such he can no longer go to the British army camp to gather intelligence. He advises that he is going to move from 10 (New York) to 20 (Setauket). "I shall endeavor to establish a confidential friend [Robert Townsend] to step into my place if agreeable direct in your next and forward the ink."[24]

Robert Townsend was an occasional roomer at Amos Underhill's. Amos on March 21, 1774, had married Mary Woodhull, the sister of Abraham Woodhull. Townsend also had business dealings with Benjamin Underhill, brother of Amos and husband to the daughter of Sylvanus Townsend. Townsend also boarded with Jacob Seaman, who was married to Margaret Birdsall, the daughter of Lieutenant Colonel Benjamin Birdsall. Lieutenant Colonel Birdsall was providing information to New York General Governor George Clinton.[25] This group of in-laws could be seen meeting and not draw suspicion to themselves. Later more relatives would be brought into the mix. Letters of December 31, 1779, and June 7, 1780, reached Culper through Joseph Lawrence of Bayside, Long Island. Joseph married Phebe Townsend in 1764 and their son Effingham Lawrence married Anne Townsend, daughter of Solomon Townsend, who was Robert Townsend's brother.[26]

Abraham Woodhull in his letter from 20 (Setauket) on June 20, 1779, advised that "I have communicated my business to an intimate friend and disclosed every secret and laid before him every instruction that hath been handed to me." He says that Townsend "is a person that hath the interest of our country at heart and of good reputation, character and family as any of my acquaintance. I am under the most solemn obligation never to disclose his name to any but the Post [courier] who unavoidably must know it. I have reason to think his advantages for serving you and abilities are far superior to mine."[27] Robert Townsend (who in joing the operation used the alias Samuel Culper, Jr. to distinguish himself from Woodhull, now known as Samuel Culper, Sr.) sent his first report from New York on June 29, 1779.[28]

A month later, Townsend's letter of July 29 states, "the times now are extremely difficult—guard boats are kept out every night in the North [Hudson] and East Rivers to prevent any boats from passing, and I am informed that some persons have been searched on Long Island; therefore whenever you think that my intelligence is of no service, beg you will notify me, 'till which time I will continue as usual." In this letter he acknowledges that he has received Tallmadge's dictionary [code chart]. Samuel Culper, Sr. was telling Samuel Culper, Jr., to give up his business in New York. He was in partnership with Henry Oakman in the firm of Oakman and Townsend which supplied ships and the public with dry goods and groceries.[29] In a letter of September 11, 1779, Townsend says it will be difficult to get out of the business because of his partner as he has no real reason to sell out. Therefore, he will stay in the business.

Abraham Woodhull's cipher letter (written as 722) of 29 (August) 15, 1779 from 729 (Setauket, Long Island) is a good example of the use of the cipher provided by Benjamin Tallmadge. It was one of the early letters to be written by the Culpers in cipher and they were also just getting used to using it. The letter reads:

> Sir, Dqpeu (Jonas) Beyocpu (Hawkins) agreeable to 28 (appointment) met 723 (Robert Townsend alias Samuel Culper, Jr.) not far from 727 (New York) & received a 356 (letter), but on his return was under the necessity to destroy the same, or be detected, but have the satisfaction to inform you that theres nothing of 317 (importance) to 15 (advise) you of. There been no augmentation by 592 (ships) of 680 (war) or 347 (land) forces, and everything very quit. Every 356 (letter) is opened at the entrance to 727 (New York) and every 371 (man) is searched, that for future every 356 (letter) must be 691 (written) with the 286 (ink) received. They have some 345 (knowledge) of the route our 356 (letter) takes. I judge it was mentioned in the 356 (letter) taken or they would not be so 660 (vigilant). I do not think it will continue long so. I intend to visit 727 (New York) before long and think by the assistance of a 355 (lady) of my acquaintance, shall be able to out wit them all. The next 28 (appointment) for 725 (Caleb Brewster) to be here is 1 of 616 (September) that it is so prolonged. It may be better times before then. I hope ther will be means found out for our deliverance. Nothing could induce me to behere but the ernest desire of 723 (Robert Townsend). Friends are all well, and am your Humble Servant, 722 (Abraham Woodhull alias Samuel Culper, Sr.).[30]

George Washington in a letter to Benjamin Tallmadge dated September 24, 1779 at West Point tells Townsend to stay in the business. "It is not my opinion that Culper junr. should be advised to give up his present employment. I would imagine that with a little industry he will be able to carry on his intelligence with greater security to himself and greater advantages to us, under cover of his usual business, than if he were able to dedicate himself wholly to the giving of information. It may afford him opportunities of collecting intelligence that he could not obtain so well in any other manner. It prevents also those suspicions which would become natural should he throw himself out of the line of his present employment."[31] Since he was supplying ships as part of his business, it was a good cover for his going down to the docks to try and drum up some business while checking out what was arriving and leaving the port. Washington also went on to explain how Townsend should send his information when using the liquid:

> He should occasionally write his information on the blank leaves of a pamphlet; on the first second &c pages of a common pocket book; on the leaves at such end registers almanacs or any new publication or book of small value. He should be determined in the choice of these books principally by the goodness of the blank paper, as the ink is not easily legible, unless it is on paper of good quality. . . . He may write a familiar letter, on domestic affairs, or on some little matters of business to his friend at Satuket or elsewhere, interlining with the stain, his secret intelligence or writing on the opposite blank side of the letter. But that his friend may know how to distinguish these from letters addressed solely to himself, he may always leave such as contain secret information without date or place; (dating it with the stain) or fold them up in a particular manner.[32]

Not all instructions were put in writing. Washington on October 9, 1779, called Tallmadge to headquarters and told him "These things are better settled personally than by letter."[33]

Townsend's letter of October 9, 1779, told that the British were much alarmed by a number of corroborating documents, and "they had great reason to expect [Count] D'Estaing [and the French fleet]. All the Men of War [warships] and a number of armed transports were ordered down to the Hook [Sandy Hook, New Jersey], with several old hulks to sink in the channel in case D'Estaing should appear. They had also two or three fire ships prepairing, and are building a very strong fort at the light house (at Sandy Hook, New Jersey)."[34] Townsend's update on October 21, 1779, advises that a number of vessels were being prepared to be sunk off of Sandy Hook, New Jersey. Four vessels had already been sent to the bottom of the sea.[35]

Abraham Woodhull wrote requesting more stain (invisible ink) and told about how he was captured and then released, but he also tells where he hid Culper Jr.'s letter. He wrote, "Soon after I left Hempstead Plains and got into the woods I was attacked by four armed men, one of them I had frequently seen in N[ew] York. They searched every pocket and lining of my clothes, shoes, and also my saddle, which the enclosed [Culper Jr.'s letter] was in, but thank Providence they did not find it. I had but one dollar in money about me. It was so little they did not take it, and so came off clear. Don't mention this for I keep it a secret for fear it should intimidate all concerned here."[36]

George Washington at Morristown, New Jersey, had Colonel Blaine take twenty guineas and two vials of stain and counterpart to Major Benjamin Tallmadge.[37] The stain and the money were for Culper Junior. Washington on February 5, 1780, requested, "It is my further most earnest wish, that you would press him to open, if possible, a communication with me by a more direct route than the present. His acc[oun]ts are intelligent, clear, and satisfactory, consequently would be valuable, but owing to the circuitous route thro' which they are transmitted I can derive no immediate or important advantage from them."[38] Washington again explained how he wanted the information to be sent. "He should avoid making use of the stain upon a blank sheet of paper (which is the usual way of its coming to me); this circumstance alone is sufficient to raise suspicion; a much better way is to write a letter a little in the Tory stile, with some mixture of family matters and between the lines and on the remaining part of the sheet communicate with the stain the intended intelligence, such a letter would pass through the hands of the enemy unsuspected."[39]

In response to Washington's request for a shorter route, Culper Jr. had selected his cousin James Townsend, who had gotten himself captured by the American army.[40] Culper Jr. did not hear back from his cousin and obviously realized the danger from exposure. Woodhull's (Samuel Culper Senior) letter of May 4, 1780, advised, "I have had an interview with C. Junr. [Culper, Jr.] and am sorry to find he declines serving any longer, as hinted in my last." He writes about replacements and states, "I have for some time suspected Daniel Diehel living with Hugh Wallace has been employed by 711 [George Washington]—If this be the case would wish to be informed of it."[41]

Washington wrote from headquarters at Morristown on May 19, 1780. concerning Townsend's wanting to quit this secret service:

> Dear Sir: Your favor of the 8th reached me a few days ago. As C_ junr, has totally declined and C_ Senr seems to wish to do it, I think the intercourse may be dropped, more especially as from our present position the intelligence is so long getting to hand that it is of no use by the time it reaches me. I would however have you take an opportunity of informing the (elder C_) that we may have occasion for his services again in the course of the Summer, and that I shall be glad to employ him if it should become necessary and he is willing.
>
> I am endeavoring to open a communication with New York across Staten Island, but who are the agents in the City, I do not know.[42]

Abraham Woodhull responded to Major Tallmadge on June 10, 1780. He indicated that he received George Washington's letter of May 19, 1780, the previous day (June 9). It gives some indication of the delay in mode of communications between Morristown, New Jersey, and Setauket, Long Island, about which Washington had been complaining. Woodhull is obviously upset at both the perceived value of the Culper spy work and Washington doubting his commitment. Woodhull states,

> I perceive that the former [the Culper Sr. and Jr. intelligence reports] he [George Washington] intimates hath been of little service. Sorry we have been at so much cost and trouble for little or no purpose. He also mentions my backwardness to serve. He certainly hath been misinformed. You are sensible I have been indefatigable, and have done it from principal of duty rather than from any mercenary end—and as hinted heretofore, if at any time

thers need you may rely on my faithful endeavours.

Samuel Culper [Sr.][43]

With the anticipated arrival of the French fleet, Washington want-ed to know of the disposition of the British troops on Long Island. On July 11, 1780, he sent a letter from headquarters now in Bergen County, New Jersey, to Major Tallmadge which instructed, "as we may every moment expect the arrival of the French Fleet a revival of the correspondence with the Culpers will be of very great importance. . . . You will transmit your letters to Gen[era]l Howe, who will forward them to me."[44] Tallmadge quickly writes back to Washington on July 14, 1780, from Cortlandt's Manor, that he would set out the next morning for Fairfield, Connecticut, where he would endeavor "to put matters on such a footing, as may answer your Excellency's expecta-tions."[45]

In response to Washington's request to restart the flow of intelli-gence, Tallmadge sent Caleb Brewster across Long Island Sound to find Samuel Culper, Sr. (Abraham Woodhull). However Woodhull was ill with a fever so Brewster contacted Austin Roe (code name 724), who was a local tavern owner. Roe set off for New York City to see Robert Townsend (Samuel Culper, Jr.). Because the British were also expecting the arrival of the French fleet, efforts were made to restrain anyone who might carry any information to the Americans. Townsend's plan to get both Roe and his intelligence information written in the invisible ink past the British guards was to send a letter addressed to a loyal British subject. He chose Colonel Benjamin Floyd at Setauket, Long Island, as the recipient. In the visible part of the letter, Townsend, as Samuel Culper, wrote that "the article you [Floyd] want cannot be procured as soon as they can will send them."[46] The messenger, Roe, would be returning empty-handed and would not stir any suspicion. Once Roe got to Setauket, he delivered the letter with the invisible part to Woodhull.

Normally Roe upon returning to Setauket from New York City would check on his cattle, which were kept pastured in a field belong-ing to Woodhull. Roe would leave his shipment in a box in the field. Woodhull passing through his own field would retrieve the docu-ments.[47] Both men had a legitimate reason to be in the field and would not draw attention to their activity.

The method used by Caleb Brewster to announce his arrival to Abraham Woodhull was the hanging of a black petticoat on a line across the creek on Strong's Neck. Woodhull would have Anna Smith Strong, wife of Judge Selah Strong, hang clothing out to dry on a specific clothesline. A black petticoat indicated that a message was ready to be picked up, and the number of handkerchiefs identified the cove on Long Island Sound where the messages could be found.[48]

Woodhull left Townsend's message and a letter he wrote to Tallmadge along with a letter to Brewster. Woodhull's message to Caleb Brewster was, "Sir, The enclosed requires your immediate departure this day by all means let not an hour pass: for this day must not be lost. You have news of the greatest consequence perhaps that ever happened to your country."[49] Woodhull advised that Admiral Graves had sailed for Rhode Island and would have nine warships along with one ship with fifty guns and two with forty guns. Also 8,000 troops were leaving for Rhode Island that day from Whitestone.[50]

The message reached Benjamin Tallmadge at 9 p.m. and he immediately got letters off to Generals Heath, Howe, and Washington with the information of the embarkation of the enemy troops and their expected destination.[51] The letter reached Alexander Hamilton, General Washington's aide-de-camp, at headquarters by 4 p.m. on July 21, 1780. Washington was away and not expected back till later that evening. Hamilton immediately sent a message of the British plans to Major General Marquis de Lafayette, who was on his way to Newport, Rhode Island, to meet Comte de Rochambeau, who was bring 6,000 troops.[52]

General Washington prepared a package that contained details of a plan of attack on New York City. Washington then arranged to have the package brought to a British outpost by someone the British trusted. The messenger claimed to have found the package along the road. The British reacted to the documents and expected an attack on New York and lighted their signal fires on Long Island.[53] The fleet upon seeing these beacons immediately changed course and set sail for New York City.[54] With the British and Hessians out of the way, the French army was able to safely land their men and artillery.

John Vanderhoven was one of Washington's spies in New York City. He operated through Staten Island and Elizabeth Town, New Jersey, and reported on a series of events from the July 21 to 25, 1780.

Using code name L.D., he relayed that the enemy was busy embarking the 22nd Regiment of Foot from Staten Island and they went up
the East River. He indicated that other troops embarked in the North
River and fell down and went up the East River. The entire fleet was
between the shipyards and Hell Gate. He told of the embarking of the
Hessians at East Chester on the Hutchinson River and that the ships
all passed through Hell Gate to Long Island Sound.[55] General
Clinton had not yet embarked but the engineers were loading thirty-
six 24- and 32-pound cannons and two mortars. It was said that the
French were at Rhode Island.[56] Vanderhoven's intelligence was correct but because of all the naval activity in New York Harbor going up
the East River, it appears that he was delayed getting back to Staten
Island and over to New Jersey.

    During the summer of 1780 a new member of the ring was added:
George Smith of Nissequogue, Long Island, who used the code name
"S.G." He worked both independently and at times as part of the
Culper spy ring.[57] He had served as a second lieutenant in Captain
Daniel Roe's Suffolk County company. In the summer of 1780 his
father died and he received permission to return from Stratford,
Connecticut, to Smithtown, Long Island.[58] He went to New York
where he was arrested, but acquitted in court.[59]

    With the French in Rhode Island and the need for fast communi-
cations, General Washington ordered Colonel Elisha Sheldon of the
2nd Regiment of Continental Light Dragoons to set up a chain of
express riders between New London, Connecticut, and headquarters.
Mr. Shaw of New London was to continue the chain by hired expresses from there to Tower Hill, Rhode Island.[60] Besides conveying messages from the French, it was to also bring the Culper correspondence. Sheldon advised that he had placed men at New London,
Lyme, Guilford, New Haven, Stratford, Green Farms, and Stamford,
or approximately every fifteen miles. Washington wanted to keep
Major General William Heath up to date on what was happening and
instructed Tallmadge to send messages to General Heath of anything
that seemed of interest to the French army and navy as well as sending the information to him.[61]

    Abraham Woodhull turned his attention to events happening in
the area of Setauket and Connecticut. In his letter of September 1,
1780, Samuel Culper advises that "Aiqlai Bqyim [George Howell] of

Southampton is now on your shore and positively a 23 [agent] for the 178 [enemy]."[62] He also stated that a boat loaded with provisions from New Haven met a number of refugees, one of the men's names being Trowbridge[63] who was intimately known to John Clark, and another person who left £20,000 of counterfeit money at Hartford and Middletown, Connecticut, but he did not know his name.[64] On September 18, 1780, he wrote, "I have made several discoveries of villany but have not time to write now. Forbid the boat man [Benajah Strong?] on with 725 [Caleb Brewster] to come any more, and desire Governor Trumbull immediately to grant him no favors, or else it will be too late."[65]

Woodhull's correspondence of October 14, 1780, continued the discussion of George Howell and he was happy that Howell, a close friend of Royal Governor Tryon, would be apprehended. Woodhull said Howell always got his requests for favors from the British. "You may rest assured that B. & J. Nwcluqp [H. & F. Muirson] are his bosom friends and know his heart. Not long since H[eathcote] Muirson told me he was very uneasy about him. Said he has been expected back for some time, asked me if I had not heard nothing about him and desired if possible to enquire after him. Said this was the second time he had been out in the service of the Government [as a spy] and was afraid he would be found out. He is largely in debt at 727 [New York City] and his departure appeared like one fleeing for refuge but it was all to cloak his villany."[66]

Benjamin Tallmadge in his letter of October 17, 1780, from Pine Bridge shed some more information on Aiqlai Bqyim [George Howell]. "I really believe he is a very dangerous man among us, and from the charges adduced aginst him by C. should suppose he ought to be apprehended. I am informed he has lately been to Rhode Island; his business may be guessed at. The person mentioned in C. Senior's letter as friends to Aiqlai Bqyim are the brothers of the person who had a permit from Genl. Parsons to cross with Lt. Brewster, but has since been prohibited agreeable to your Excellency's order through me. I am very confident Genl. Parsons was much deceived in the man."[67]

Woodhull would get very upset with Washington's not acting on his advice. Woodhull returned from New York on February 7, 1781, and the next day wrote, "It was not long ago that I declared to you a certain person being in your lines and in the Enemy's service, and but a few days ago he found his way into New York and waited on the Commander in Chief." He also went on about the fact that he has had only partial payment of his expenses and needs to be paid if they want someone placed in 727 (New York).[68]

The Culpers were always afraid of being discovered. The British were closing in on their operation. In addition to the previous information collected, more was coming to the light. Henry Vandycke, who was the keystone in a British spy ring that operated in Connecticut, reported on November 26, 1780 to Oliver De Lancey, who was the head of the British Secret Service operations, that "there is one [Caleb] Brewster who has the direction of three whale boats that constantly come over from Connecticut shore once a week for the purpose of obtaining intelligence. They land at Drawn Meadow bay."[69] More of the Culper ring was exposed when Nehemiah Marks sent in a report on December 21, 1780, from Flushing to Major De Lancey that the intelligence being brought back from Long Island by Lieutenant Caleb Brewster was coming from Austin Roe, Philip Roe at Round Meadow, and James Smith at Oldmans, who are the people involved with Brewster. Marks advised that he got this information from a commissioned officer in the rebel service who would do what ever he would to find out the particulars of the operation. Marks said he paid the officer for the information.[70] Marks advised on January 3, 1781, that he expected to hear from the rebel officer in about ten or twelve days. He said he wanted to get to the bottom of this affair.[71] Heron writing under the code name "Hiram" to Oliver De Lancey advised that "Private dispatches are frequently sent from your city to the chieftain here by some traitors, they come by way of Setalket where a certain Brewster receives them at or near a certain woman's."[72] British headquarters even had a detailed map of the area that was drawn in 1778.[73]

In April 1781 Abraham Woodhull had a visit from Robert Townsend, who no longer wanted to write the intelligence reports. Woodhull went to New York City in May 1781 to find someone to take Townsend's place but was unable to find anyone. Woodhull said he was thoroughly searched at the ferry to Brooklyn and told that some villain maintains a correspondence from New York. He was "greatly alarmed" and wanted out of his situation, deeming it too risky.[74]

Woodhull reports on May 27, 1781, that he had proposed the assignment to a person who had been mentioned in their last correspondence. That person could not take up residence in New York City but could only go there. Woodhull still could not get anyone to take Townsend's place. Austin Roe had just returned and provided the information in this correspondence.[75]

On June 4, 1781, Abraham Woodhull wrote as Samuel Culper from Setauket, Long Island, that, "We live in daily fear of death and destruction. . . . I dare not visit New York myself and those that have been employed will serve no longer, through fear." Woodhull would write one more letter and advised, "My circumstances would not admit me to undertake to visit the several quarters of the Enemy."[76] This was the cessation of operations for the Culper ring.

Benjamin Tallmadge during the summer of 1783 went into New York City under the cover of a flag of truce "to take some steps to insure the safety of several persons within the enemy's lines, who had served us faithfully and with intelligence during the war." While there he even dined with General Carleton, the British commander-in-chief. He also visited with Abraham Woodhull.[77] He also requested the outstanding bill from Woodhull, who responded on July 5, 1783.[78] Tallmadge advised Washington of the debt owed for secret service work.[79] Washington agreed that he believed that Culper spent the money and therefore should be paid; "but the services which were rendered by him (however well meant) were by no means adequate to these expenditures. My Complaints on this head, before I knew the amount of his charges, you may remember were frequent; and but for the request of Count de Rochambeau, who told me that he had put money into your hands, and would continue to furnish you with more for the purpose of obtaining intelligence through this channel, I should have discontinued the services of S. C [Samuel Culper, i.e., Abraham Woodhull] long before a cessation of hostilities took place, because his communications were never frequent, and always tedious in getting to hand."[80] Tallmadge did receive the money, totaling £201, 5 shillings, 9 pence, on December 4, 1783 to pay off his spies.[81] It was part of the cost of doing business during a war.

Chapter 12

"Traitor of the Blackest

Dye"

B enedict Arnold's attempt to turn West Point over to the British during the American Revolution is the story told to every elementary school child. General Nathanael Greene says Arnold "was a traitor of the blackest dye."[1] However as part of his negotiations for a better deal in turning over the great stronghold, Arnold first became a British spy providing military intelligence to the British. The story of the negotiations involving over sixty letters used several of the technologies available to spies. It also demonstrates the difficulty of trying to maintain a correspondence and secrecy at a distance. Over time, as more people handle the correspondence during the course of its delivery, the possibility of detection is increased.

Benedict Arnold was an exceptional officer who had led his troops on an unbelievable journey through the Maine wilderness to Quebec and performed heroically against Lieutenant General John Burgoyne's troops in northern New York. If the war had ended with General Burgoyne's surrender at Saratoga on October 17, 1777, Arnold would have been a great American hero. At the time he was being blocked out of a promotion by politics. Congress had decided to limit each state to a maximum of two major generals. Since Connecticut already had their two, Benedict Arnold could not be promoted no matter what he did. Arnold was forced to watch people with lesser ability and weaker credentials being promoted ahead of him. Congress on February 19, 1777, promoted five majors general; Benjamin Lincoln, Thomas Mifflin, Arthur St. Clair, Adam Stephen, and Lord Stirling while passing over General Benedict Arnold.[2] General Washington informed Arnold of the promotions and said he was "at a loss whether you have had a preceding appointment, as the news papers announce, or whether you have been omitted through some mistake."[3] Washington was apparently informed verbally by General Nathanael Greene of the events that led to Congress' actions. He then informed Arnold, "General Greene, who has lately been at Philadelphia, took occasion to inquire upon what principle the Congress proceeded in their late promotion of general officers. He was informed, that the members from each state seemed to insist upon having a proportion of general officers, adequate to the number of men which they furnish, and that as Connecticut had already two major generals, it was their full share. I confess this is a strange mode of reasoning, but it may serve to show you, that the promotion which was due to your seniority was not overlooked for want of merit in you."[4] Arnold's feelings of betrayal by the politicians are understandable.

Congress was also accusing him of mishandling the accounting of $66,671 advanced to him for his 1775 expedition to Canada of which more than $55,000 was not properly documented. Arnold claimed to have given the money, called into question by Congress, to officers and other people for public use. Arnold did not have large holdings of fixed assets (real estate) to support him while Congress dawdled with his reimbursements. He watched as the money Congresses owed him dwindle to 10 percent of its face value because of the depreciation of the Continental dollar.

Arnold, who had suffered debilitating injuries at the Battle of Saratoga, was unable to take a field command. On May 28, 1778, Washington had assigned Arnold to the command of Philadelphia as soon as the British left the city.[5] This was no small responsibility. Philadelphia was the largest city in North America and second only to London in population in the British Empire. Philadelphia was the capital of the new United States and therefore its seat of power. The military commander of Philadelphia would need the wisdom of Solomon to appease all the interested parties in Philadelphia: Congress, the State of Pennsylvania, the city's business merchants, and the general public all had their own interests which were in conflict. They probably would have driven Solomon mad.

On June 19, 1778, Washington had instructed Arnold, "You will take every prudent step in your power to preserve tranquility and order in the city and give security to individuals of every class and description; restraining, as far as possible, till the restoration of civil government, every species of persecution, insult, or abuse, either from the soldiery to the inhabitants or among each other." Arnold was to adopt measures he considered "most effectual, and at the same time least offensive, for answering the views of Congress."[6]

Congress had asked General George Washington to prevent looting or the "removal, transfer, or sale of any goods, wares, or merchandise in possession of the inhabitants" until Congress and the State of Pennsylvania could "determine whether any or what part thereof may belong to the King of Great Britain or to any of his subjects."[7] All military goods and supplies left by the British would be confiscated. Arnold as the military governor complied with Congress' request and ordered the city's shops closed until further notice to prevent the removal, transfer, or sale of items that were needed by the quartermaster and commissary for the army. The shops remained closed for a week. This naturally angered the citizens of Philadelphia since they could not buy the merchandise in the shops and the merchants could not sell their wares. Arnold was quickly making many enemies. Congress did not vote Arnold a budget for the administration of the city until October 28, 1778.[8]

On June 23, 1778, four days after his arrival and before the shops could reopen, Arnold had entered into a secret written agreement with James Mease, clothier general, and his deputy clothier general William West. It stated, "by purchasing goods and necessaries for the use of the public, sundry articles not wanted for that purpose may be obtained, it is agreed by the subscribers that all such goods and merchandise which are or maybe bought by the clothier general, or persons appointed by him, shall be sold for the joint equal benefit of the subscribers and be purchased at their risk." This was to be a very lucrative arrangement for the trio. Mease and West could buy very large quantities of merchandise for the army using the government's money, then sell anything not needed by the army for whatever price they could get. Since goods and supplies were scarce and the retail price was higher than the wholesale price the clothier general was paying, there was a significant profit to be made. Mease and West had to pay the government only the original purchase price. This secret agreement allowed the trio (Arnold, Mease, and West) to keep all the profit for themselves. It also allowed them to purchase items the army did not even want but that they could sell.

The deal came to light and the Pennsylvania Council prepared a list of charges against Arnold. On February 9, 1779, the Pennsylvania Council sent copies of their resolves to Congress and had them published. The situation was getting nasty and public. The Pennsylvania legislature wanted to take back the control of the state. Arnold and the council were accusing each other of improper conduct. Arnold was accusing the council of purposely waiting until he had left Pennsylvania on his way to Poughkeepsie and then made their charges. The council claimed that Arnold had left so that they could not deliver the charges until he had taken flight. Arnold in the latter part of February met with General George Washington at Middlebrook, New Jersey. Washington had recommended that Arnold demand a court-martial.

Congress "resolved, therefore that the Commander in Chief be directed to cause the said Major General Arnold to be tried by a Court Martial for the several misdemeanors with which he so stands charged, in order that he may be brought to punishment if guilty; or if innocent, may have an opportunity of vindicating his honor.[9]

Congress voted on February 16, 1779, to postpone Pennsylvania's motion to suspend Arnold from command as the military governor. Congress' committee did not report till March 17, 1779, because Pennsylvania was slow in producing the evidence. The report indicated that only the first, second, third, and fifth charges were eligible for a court-martial.[10] Arnold demanded that a court martial be speedily convened and he wanted an immediate decision. On March 17 Arnold resigned his position as military governor of Philadelphia. His letter stated that for the recovery of his health and wounds, and for the settlement of his public as well as private affairs he had, with the permission of General Washington, resigned his command in the city of Philadelphia to Brigadier General James Hogan of North Carolina.[11]

On April 20, 1779, Washington set the starting date for the court-martial for May 1.[12] There were delays and cross charges between Benedict Arnold and Joseph Reed, President of the Pennsylvania

Council, as to the cause for the delays. On April 27, Washington had to again postpone the event until either June or July.

On May 5, 1779 Benedict Arnold wrote a crazed hysterical letter to George Washington. It is the keystone to the puzzle to understand Arnold's state of mind as a disabled war hero. In the letter Arnold mentions the ungrateful countrymen and the ingratitude of Congress. These certainly are the inner feelings of a man who feels betrayed. He says he has nowhere to turn. He feels that the cause for which he has fought, for which he "having made every sacrifice of fortune and blood, and become a cripple in the service of my country," has turned against him. Why would he (or you) be loyal to someone or something that has stabbed you in the back? Would you not want to distance yourself from that ungrateful people who injured you? Would you not want to cut the ties that bind you and that ungrateful person together? Would you care what happens to the party that hurt you? Certainly you do not mind if they got the same treatment they gave to you. Would not REVENGE be considered? Would not revenge taste good?

Arnold's letter makes his perspective clear:

> If your Excellency thinks me criminal, for heaven's sake let me be immediately tried and, if found guilty, executed. I want no favor; I ask only Justice. If this is denied me by your Excellency, I have nowhere to seek it but from the candid public, before whom I shall be under the necessity of laying the whole matter. Let me beg of you, Sir, to consider that a set of artful, unprincipled men in office may misrepresent the most innocent actions and, by raising the public clamor against your Excellency, place you in the same situation I am in. Having made every sacrifice of fortune and blood, and become a cripple in the service of my country, I little expected to meet the ungrateful returns I have received from my countrymen; but as Congress have stamped ingratitude as a current coin, I must take it. I wish your Excellency, for your long and eminent services, may not be paid with the same coin. I have nothing left but the little reputation I have gained in the army. Delay in the present case is worse than death.[13]

Arnold's letter reveals his feelings of betrayal, ingratitude, and help-lessness. He certainly is not going to be loyal to a cause and Congress which in his mind has betrayed him.

Congress had not reimbursed Arnold for his money that was spent in the attack on Quebec. His prospects of ever seeing his money were growing dim and if he ever received it then devaluation would have made it worthless. During his negotiations with Sir Henry Clinton, he kept upping the ante as his financial situation worsened. Carl Van Doren, author of *The Secret History of the American Revolution* which first published the correspondence between Arnold and Clinton, gave his opinion in a personal letter to Howard Peckham, Director of the William L. Clements Library at the University of Michigan, of Arnold's motives. Van Doren stated, "I have given up all belief that he [Arnold] changed out of principle. At least in my handling Arnold is more like Shakespeare's Iago than any other well known figure of fic-tion or history."[14]

Clinton wrote a memorandum after the war about Arnold and says that "G[eneral] Arnold supported the Rebellion as long as he thought the Americans right; but when he thought them wrong particularly by connecting themselves with France he told them so, opened a corre-spondence with me offering his services in a manner I would accept them. He gave me most important information . . . his conduct does not seem to have been influenced by any interested motives."[15] Clinton wrote that "Arnold offered either to join or give information or be otherwise serviceable in any way we wished."[16] Clinton in writ-ing on October 4, 1780, to his sisters states that Arnold made the first move and offered his services "without any overtures from me."[17]

Joseph Stansbury after the war stated that Benedict Arnold had sent for him about the month of June 1779. This would have been a year after the British evacuation of Philadelphia on June 18. Arnold was aware of those individuals who had been appointed to positions of importance when the British army had occupied the city. Stansbury had been appointed to oversee the city watch (patrolling guards) and one of the managers of a lottery—both positions of trust. Stansbury had sold Arnold expensive dining room furniture when he had moved into the Penn family home at 6th and Market Streets in Philadelphia. The British army trusted Stansbury and he was shrewd enough to operate successfully after the Continental army took control of

Philadelphia. Stansbury advised that Arnold told him of his wishes to open a line of communications to the commander-in-chief of the British forces. Stansbury further said that he secretly went to New York City with Arnold's offer of his services to British General Henry Clinton.[18]

Stansbury, with the probable assistance of his fellow author the Reverend Jonathan Odell, had a meeting with John André on May 10, 1779, a mere five days after Arnold's hysterical letter to General George Washington. It would have taken a couple of days for Stansbury to make the trip from Philadelphia across New Jersey to New York City.

Benedict Arnold's message that Stansbury carried to André was totally unexpected. André in a letter written to British General Henry Clinton stated that it was "such sudden proposals." Later that day André provided a written response to Stansbury that said,

> On our part we met Monk's[19] [Benedict Arnold] over-
> tures with full reliance on his honorable intentions and dis-
> close to him, with the strongest assurance of our sincerity,
> that no thought is entertained of abandoning the point we
> have in view. That on the contrary, powerful means are
> expected for accomplishing our end. We likewise assure
> him that in the very first instance of receiving the tidings or
> good offices we expect from him, our liberality will be
> evinced; that in case any partial but important blow should
> be struck or aimed, upon the strength of just and pointed
> information and co-operation, rewards equal at least to
> what such service can be estimated at will be given. But
> should the abilities and zeal of that able and enterprising
> gentleman amount to the seizing an obnoxious band of
> men, to the delivery into our power or enabling us to attack
> to advantage and by judicious assistance completely to
> defeat a numerous body, then would the generosity of the
> nation exceed even his most sanguine hopes; and in the
> expectation of this he may rely on that honor he now trusts
> in his present advances. Should his manifest efforts be
> foiled and after every zealous attempt flight be at length
> necessary, the cause for which he suffers will hold itself

bound to indemnify him for his losses and receive him with the honors his conduct deserves.[20]

André in his response seems to have promised Arnold that he would indeed be handsomely rewarded if he was able to accomplish a major coup. Arnold would also be compensated according to his efforts if he made a good faith effort but failed in his attempts.

The method first used to carry on communications between the conspiring parties was to be a cipher, using a volume of Blackstone's *Commentaries*. Three numbers identify the words of the cipher; the first number is the page, the second is the line on the page, and the third number is the word in the line. For example 45.9.8 would be interpreted as page forty-five (45), line nine (9), and the eighth (8) word. The coded cipher would appear as clusters of three number units on the page and use as many clusters as was needed to encode and decode the message.

Van Doren tells us that André planned to bury messages in letters written to Peggy (Shippen) Arnold and her friends. There is a draft letter from John André to Margaret Chew believed to be dated in May 1779 and marked with the letter "A." If the letter was sent, it would indicate that it contained a hidden part that needed acid or a reagent to make it visible.[21]

Next was a letter written before May 23, 1779, from Benedict Arnold that was sent under Stansbury's name to John André. Arnold used Bailey's *Dictionary*, twenty-first edition. Stansbury says he paged the dictionary for Arnold beginning with "A" and paged each side, resulting in 927 pages. One is added to each page, line, word. "Zoroaster will be 928.2.2 and not 927.1.1. Tide is 838.3.2 and not 837.2.1." Arnold the following week was off to camp and from there he was to send his correspondence directly "to Col[onel] Edward Antill to your care. He was going to use the signature AG or a name beginning with A."[22] This way André would intercept the letter to American Colonel Edward Antill of the 2nd Canadian Regiment, which was also known as Hazen's Regiment. Antill was taken prisoner at Staten Island on August 22, 1777.[23]

The ploy worked, as Benedict Arnold's letter of May 23, 1779, to John André made it safely to him. It did use Bailey's *Dictionary*, twenty-first edition, and was successfully decoded. Arnold acknowledges that Stansbury's proposal did come from him and that his proposals were agreeable to Sir Henry Clinton. Arnold reported that Congress could only raise 3,000 to 4,000 militia to defend Charles Town during an attack.[24]

The next letter, dated May 26, 1779, was from Stansbury writing under the name of Paliwoledash from Moorestown, New Jersey, because he had been banished from Philadelphia. The first paragraph tells the decoder (Reverend Jonathan Odell) to use page 46 of the fifth Oxford edition of his copy of the first volume of Blackstone's *Commentaries* to solve the second paragraph, which is in code. The second paragraph tells Odell to use Bailey's Dictionary, twenty-fifth edition, to solve two other letters that Stansbury sent. Bailey's Dictionary was paged to the right beginning with "A," and "An Integer is added to the paging column and line, and that is the word." Odell left a notation and signed it "Yoric."[25] The postscript is "Integer, I presume, means only a single figure as in no case can there be requisite a number larger than 9 to denote the word in a line of a Dictionary Column."[26]

Sending messages over long distances usually resulted in some technical difficulties. On May 31, 1779, Reverend Jonathan Odell had to advise John André that a letter written on May 21, 1779, in invisible ink had gone terribly wrong. Using a "private mark agreed between" himself and Joseph Stansbury on the letter to indicate that "it contained an invisible page," the message would require heat to make it visible. When Odell held it near the fire he "found that the paper, having by some accident got damp on the way, had spread the solution in such a manner as to make the writing all one indistinguishable blot, out of which not the half of any one line can be made legible."[27]

Odell wrote to Stansbury and put the letter in the form of a business deal to hide the true intent, stating, "our little matters of trade and commerce; for thus our correspondence, though secret, will be harmless, and we shall no cause to repent our choices." He also told him to "stick to your Oxford Interpreter" (that is, his Blackstone's *Commentaries*). Odell wanted Stansbury to stop using invisible ink.[28]

Odell pointed out that the correspondence was passing en route between himself and Joseph Stansbury, a situation that could cause confusion. He wanted a quicker way of getting through the bureaucracy to get his translation to André. He tried to get the cooperation of Captain John Smith, General Clinton's secretary, but got nowhere. He then had to tell André that he had apparently given André's personal cipher to Stansbury to use.[29] John André's personal cipher was "Reversing the alphabet, using the last as the first letter, in the first line, in the second line, using the last but one as the first, continuing to drop a letter each line in that manner to O inclusive, then beginning again as at first."[30]

John Rattoon, a South Amboy tavern owner and a British mole who used the code name of Mercury, was the answer to Odell's problem.[31] Rattoon provided intelligence, secreted messages across the lines, and arranged for guides to take spies to their destination. Captain George Beckwith tells about the handling of communications with a certain party (Rattoon) in the Raritan Bay area of New Jersey when he was handling the intelligence operation in New York. The messages had come through "the armed vessel stationed off the Raritan [River]." This would be the British ship at Princess Bay, Staten Island.[32] Beckwith wrote that the commander of the vessel had been instructed "to forward all letters, without exception, which he may receive through this channel to Richmond Redoubts . . . and from thence such letters are to be sent immediately to New York." The commander was instructed to use his seamen instead of the troops when they had to land on the Jersey shore. The messages were to be given to someone in whom he had the highest trust. Messages received were to be placed in a second cover and marked to the care of Captain George Beckwith.[33] This degree of safety was to protect the identity of an extremely reliable and valuable agent.

Rattoon brought the next letter dated June 9, 1779, to the Reverend Jonathan Odell in New York City.[34] It was in code using Blackstone's *Commentaries*. Stansbury said that he lost his copy of Bailey's *Dictionary* when he had to move and wanted another copy.[35] Odell informed John André of what he was doing. He sent a response back to Stansbury by way of South Amboy, New Jersey, where the contact was John Rattoon. A duplicate copy was given to Mrs. Gordon, who was accompanying Mrs. Chamier to Philadelphia.[36]

The next letter that used a cipher was John André's offer to Benedict Arnold of a reward of twice as many guineas should Arnold bring over a corps of 5,000 or 6,000 men. He also related that General

Clinton was looking for intelligence that would produce such a stroke.[37] Arnold sent a letter dated June 18 in code keyed to Blackstone's *Commentaries*, fifth Oxford edition, volume I. He was sending intelligence that General Sullivan with 5,000 men was going to western New York to destroy the Indian settlements. He also advised that Washington had 5,000 men in New Jersey and another 3,000 to 4,000 up the North or Hudson River.[38]

The next piece of correspondence came from Joseph Stansbury, who signed the letter as Jonathan Stevens. It was dated July 11, 1779, and was in code keyed to Bailey's *Dictionary*, twenty-third edition, 1773. Odell must have complied with his June 9 request for a copy. However Stansbury says that he is doing it "sans integer."[39] Odell later clarifies that "sans integer is that he does not make the addition of a unit to his numbers as his partner had done."[40] So now Arnold is encoding his letters with an additional number to the location of the word and Stansbury is not.

Stansbury advised that he gave André's letter of mid-June offering money to Arnold, who was being called Gustavus. However, the offer was not good enough. Arnold wanted guarantees for his effort even if they did not result in positive success for the British. Stansbury says he received a list of questions from Mr. Cox, who is believed to be Daniel Coxe. Daniel Coxe was in contact with Samuel Wallis, a British spy in Pennsylvania, and gave Wallis the first money for Arnold. Arnold reported that General Sullivan had taken 5,000 men with him and they were about sixty miles from Wyoming, and that it was believed that Detroit was the destination.[41] General Benjamin Lincoln had 3,000 regulars and 500 militia and was "not likely to collect an army of consequence."[42]

The next letter brought by Mercury (John Rattoon) was keyed to Bailey's *Dictionary*, twenty-third edition, and was transcribed. One of the problems with so much correspondence is that Rattoon believed that he was now under suspicion, having crossed the lines into New York so frequently. Benedict Arnold even found time to send in a shopping list of items for his wife, Peggy, whom he called Mrs. Moore. Odell advised John André that Arnold and Stansbury were using Bailey's *Dictionary*, twenty-third edition, which is a different edition from the copy that Odell originally sent to André. Odell believed that André originally had a twenty-third edition and told him to use it.[43]

Built around 1765, Mount Pleasant in Philadelphia's Fairmount Park was owned by Benedict Arnold while he was military governor of Pennsylvania and conducting traitorous correspondence with the British. John Adams called it the "most elegant seat in Pennsylvania." (*Lisa Nagy*)

For whatever reason, another copy of the twenty-third edition could not be found in New York. Stansbury sent a copy by way of John Rattoon to Odell with a bill for $60 for the book. Odell cautioned André to use the edition that André took with him after visiting with Odell.[44] The shipment for Peggy Arnold was sent and a second parcel was prepared and ready to be sent on December 24, 1779.[45]

John André wrote two letters at the end of July which he sent to Odell for enciphering. The first letter concerned the efforts of Samuel Wallis, but he was too far away for them to respond. The other letter went to Benedict Arnold concerning the negotiation of terms for Arnold's efforts. Stansbury's response was keyed to Bailey's *Dictionary*, twenty-third edition. Other letters transpired but only drafts and transcribed copies are extant and give no clue as to how they were sent.

Stansbury wrote a letter believed to be sent on December 3, 1779, that was a mixture of plain text, code, cipher, English, and French. He reported the army was going into winter quarters but only had four days' supply of flour. "Fhp [Philadelphia] has not enough flour to subsist her inhabitants." There was a militia call for 2,500 men to turn out in North Carolina but no more than 1,000 were expected to answer the summons. He also warned them that "some insect of your place hath written the President of Congress that the October packet was arrived, the contents not transpired, but that your officers looked very blue."[46]

The correspondence stopped as the armies went into winter quarters and very little aggressive action would occur. No one wanted to fight a sustained campaign during winter, when armies healed and prepared for the spring campaign to begin. The American army, camped at Morristown, would suffer through the lack of food and proper clothing. Private Joseph Plumb Martin described winter encampment as "the time again between grass and hay, that is, the winter campaign of starving."[47] Starvation would be their hut mate for the next several months. This winter would be called the "hard winter" as it was the coldest in the eighteenth century.

The British army officers, in contrast, prepared for the winter season of balls and plays in New York City. Everyone in the city complained of fuel shortages, that is, firewood to keep them warm through the long cold winter months, and of price gouging by the woodcutters.

Come spring, activity in camp escalated. It was time to get ready to reengage the enemy. Everything had to be prepared to be able to move on short notice. Joseph Stansbury was sent to New York to reestablish the chain of correspondence. When he arrived in New York, he found that General Sir Henry Clinton was at Charles Town and Hessian General Wilhelm von Knyphausen was in charge of the British forces in and around New York. Before leaving for South Carolina, General Clinton had left instructions with Jonathan Odell that all letters that he received from Mr. Moore (Benedict Arnold), when deciphered, were to be sent to Captain George Beckwith at Morris House.[48] Stansbury appears to have met with Beckwith, an aide to General Knyphausen. General Knyphausen's response to Mr. Moore was that he did not believe that he could speak on such an important matter for General Clinton but would cultivate their communication. He procured two identical rings and two pocket dictionaries and gave a ring to Stansbury to give to Arnold. It is unknown which pocket dictionary was provided. The dictionary was for Stansbury to use for his correspondence by cipher. Among the British headquarters' documents is a memo that summarizes the previous year's correspondence. There was to be an indemnification for Arnold and family for "the loss of his private fortune for £5,000 sterling, ye

A letter dated July 15, 1780 from Benedict Arnold to John André in code and John Odell's decoded transcription. (*William L. Clements Library*)

debt due him by the community (Congress) for "£5,000 sterling to be made good or whatever part is lost, and to have a New York-raised battalion here upon the common footing."[49]

The next letter, dated June 7, 1780 was from Arnold to Captain Beckwith and was keyed to the small pocket dictionary. It was actually addressed "G. B. Ring executor to the late John Anderson [John André], Esquire to the care of James Osborn [Jonathan Odell]." What a profound statement it would be in just a few months. Arnold writes, "If I meet a person in my mensuration who has the token agreed upon, you may expect every intelligence in my power which will probably be of consequence." He was asking for a meeting with someone who had the other identical ring and also directly asked for a meeting with an officer.[50] Accompanying Arnold's letter was one from Joseph Stansbury, which was also keyed to the small dictionary. It contained a copy in cipher of a proclamation to the Canadians.[51] The document used both a small dictionary and a cipher which was a = b, b = c, c = d, d = e, etc. The original proclamation had been prepared by General Marquis de Lafayette and sent by Washington, who was at Morristown, to Benedict Arnold in Philadelphia on June 4. With it were instructions to get a printer to make a proof copy with a possible final run of five hundred copies.[52]

The correspondence continued with only extracts of the letters available. In one of the extracts Arnold indicated that he was to have command of West Point and that there were only 1,500 soldiers there. However, American General Clinton was bringing 1,200 more soldiers from Albany. Arnold also provided a description of the state of the defenses. In a letter to Stansbury dated July 7, 1780, he asked for a direct answer to his request for an interview with Major General William Phillips. It was keyed to the small pocket dictionary and decoded by Jonathan Odell.[53]

John André was the adjutant-general of the British army in America when he conducted the correspondence with Arnold. He was executed as a British spy. (*William L. Clements Library*)

Another method used for secret correspondence by spies and in this case General Benedict Arnold was to write in a disguised handwriting. His letter of July 11, 1780 was accomplished in this fashion. It was signed as "J. Moore to John Anderson [John André] merchant to the care of James Osborn [Jonathan Odell] and to be left at Mr. [Jonathan] Odell's," thereby trying to make it harder to unscramble should it be intercepted.[54] Arnold's letter of August 30, 1780 from Gustavus to "John Anderson [John André] merchant to the care of James Osborn [Jonathan Odell] and to be left at Reverend Mr. [Jonathan] Odell's" was also accomplished in a disguised handwriting.[55]

Another letter in code was sent by Arnold the next day which was keyed to the small pocket dictionary. It too was decoded by Jonathan Odell. Both of these letters were brought by Samuel Wallis.[56] Arnold mentioned his spy reports providing intelligence and that he would soon be in command of West Point. He reported that Washington with the arrival of the French troops planned to attack New York "as the first object." He reiterated his "wish [for] an interview with some intelligent officer in whom mutual confidence can be placed."[57]

On July 15, 1780 Benedict Arnold responded to an undated letter from John André, keying his letter to the small pocket dictionary, but did not add seven to the line number used in his letter. Arnold was now upping the ante. He now wanted £10,000 sterling in case of loss and £100 per year for life. He also wanted an additional £20,000 sterling if he could turn over West Point and its garrison to Sir Henry Clinton. He said, "I think will be a cheap purchase for an object of such importance. At the same time I request a thousand pounds to be paid my agent—I expect a full and explicit answer."[58] The old problem of letters passing each other as they made their way across New Jersey was happening again. Responses were actually several letters behind. James Osborne {Reverend Jonathan Odell} wrote to Mr. Stevens {Joseph Stansbury}[59] to be relayed to Mr. Moore (Arnold) that Sir Henry Clinton shall reward him for his efforts "but indemnification (as a preliminary) is what Sir H[enry]: thinks highly unreasonable." Clinton was willing to pay Arnold for his action but was not going to guarantee him a large endowment before he exerted any effort on behalf of the cause. Clinton was also agreeing to a meeting at West Point by a flag of truce. "Mr. Anderson [John André] is willing himself to effect the meeting either in the way proposed or in whatever manner may at the time appear most eligible."[60]

A sick Captain George Beckwith had traveled from the Morris House to New York City to meet with Samuel Wallis who was anxious to return. Beckwith gave Wallis the 200 guineas that Mr. Moore (Arnold) requested be paid to his agent. He told André that he hoped to get reimbursed for the expense.[61] Odell advised André that he believed that Samuel Wallis was sent by Mr. Moore "chiefly with a view of ascertaining whether Mr. Stevens [Stansbury] or your humble servant [himself] had faithfully conducted the correspondence."[62]

General Benedict Arnold sent two letters (July 30 and August 5, 1780) addressed to Margaret Arnold but written with the intention of them going to his contacts in New York City. Should his correspondence to his wife be discovered, he would be accused of being careless in divulging to her the plan to attack New York, Washington's movements, supply problems. At this point he would not be thought of as a British spy.

Finding dependable couriers could be challenging. A letter in Jonathan Odell's handwriting of an August 14, 1780, from Stansbury to Odell was encoded and transcribed but no information exists as to what was used. The letter states that "Mr. Moore [Arnold] commands at West Point, but things are so poorly arranged that your last important dispatches are yet in her hands, no unquestionable carrier being yet to be met with." The August 14 letter took nine days to clandestinely travel from Philadelphia to New York City with it being delivered by John Rattoon, the South Amboy tavern owner.[63] The communication problem was that Arnold was at West Point, New York, and his letters were sent to Philadelphia and then across New Jersey to New York City, and the reverse for letters from New York to him. On August 27 George Beckwith advised John André that he believed that Benedict Arnold had taken over command of West Point.[64]

Arnold wrote a letter which Stansbury, using the name of Thomas Charlton, encoded and sent on August 25. It reached Odell on September 3. It told

An image of Benedict Arnold published by Thomas Hart, London, in 1776. He was both a hero and traitor during the American Revolution. (*William L. Clements Library*)

that Washington was planning to attack New York. However there was a problem. For the last three days there was no meat for his men because the commissaries were selling the meat to the French, who paid more.[65]

The only letter remaining with encoded letters was one sent by Benedict Arnold to British headquarters—a short code note that was keyed to a small dictionary. It provided the British with enough information to potentially ambush Washington and capture him. The translation was done by the Reverend Jonathan Odell and provided his date of September 15, 1780. The note told of Washington's travel via "King's Ferry on Sunday evening next on his way to Hartford, where he is to meet the French Admiral and General. And will lodge at Peak's Kill [Peekskill, New York]." It is unknown if the British had tried to ambush Washington. If they did they were waiting in vain, as Washington did not follow his publicized agenda.[66]

On September 20, 1780, Major John André boarded the *Vulture*, a British sloop of war in the Hudson off Teller's Point. He was to wait for an American ship to pick him up and take him to Colonel Elisha Sheldon's headquarters of the 2nd Regiment of Continental Light Dragoons. It was not until the night of the 21st that Major André was picked up by Joshua Smith and taken to meet with General Benedict Arnold. Major André wore his uniform as instructed by General Clinton in order that he would not be taken for a spy.

André and Arnold met on the shore near Haverstraw, New York. They proceeded to Joshua Smith's house behind American lines. Arnold gave André the plans of West Point containing the placement of troops and other military intelligence. Their conference was completed in the morning. However, the *Vulture* was fired upon by the Americans and forced to move, thereby stranding Major André behind American lines. Arnold wrote a pass in the name of John Anderson for André to use to get back to New York by a land route.

André decided it was best to change out of his uniform and travel in disguise. On September 23, Joshua Smith left André's side near Pine's bridge, over the Croton River. They thought that André had "clear sailing" to the British lines. Around 9 a.m. he was stopped near Tarrytown in neutral territory by some militia men. André said, "I was taken by three volunteers who, not satisfied with my pass, rifled me and, finding papers, made me a prisoner."[67] When news of Major André's capture reached Benedict Arnold, he fled to the protection of the British.

A board of inquiry was held with Major General Nathanael Greene as president. The board determined that André changed clothes within the American lines and "under a feigned name and disguised habit passed our works at Stoney and Verplank's Point the evening of the twenty second of September instant and was taken the morning of the twenty third of September instant at Tarry Town in a disguised habit being then on his way to New York and when taken he had in his possession several papers which contained intelligence for the enemy." They also determined that "Major André Adjutant General of the British Army ought to be considered as a spy, from the enemy, and that agreeable to the law and usage of nations, it is their opinion he ought to suffer death."[68]

An attempt was made to trade Major John André for Benedict Arnold. A letter done in a disguised handwriting dated September 30,

1780, believed to be from Alexander Hamilton to General Sir Henry Clinton, offered this exchange. It is endorsed by General Sir Henry Clinton that it came from "Hamilton, W[ashington's] aid de camp, received after A[ndre's] death."[69]

Washington approved the sentence of the board of inquiry and "directs the execution of the . . . sentence in the usual way this afternoon at five o'clock precisely."[70] Major John André had requested to be shot but was refused. If he were permitted to be shot then he would be considered a gentleman, and no gentleman could be a spy. As a spy he was only entitled to be hung, and so he was.

Chapter 13

DECEPTIONS AND SMUGGLERS

L andon Carter, a Virginia planter, cautioned a twenty-three-year-old George Washington in 1755 never "trust too far to the information of those who may be benefited by deception."[1] It may have been the best piece of advice Washington ever received. It served him well both in his business dealings and during the Revolutionary War. When Captain Thomas Hanson Marshall offered his land for sale, Washington believed that Marshall "will practice every deception in his power to work me (or you [Lund Washington] in my behalf) up to his price, or he will not sell. This should be well looked into and guarded against."[2] During the Continental army's retreat across New Jersey in 1776, Washington was convinced, "I do not doubt but that they [the British army] are well informed of everything we do."[3] He instructed John Cadwalader to "keep a good look out for Spies, endeavor to magnify your numbers as much as possible" so that his army would appear stronger than they were.[4]

Washington was always mindful that the British army had more money and was able to put more spies and double agents in the field than he could. He constantly confirmed one spy's report with information collected from other sources such as deserters or other spies. Although Washington hated deception, even where the imagination only is concerned, he used deception during the American Revolution to his advantage whenever he could.[5]

At Boston, just weeks after George Washington took command of the Continental army, it was discovered the American supplies of gunpowder were in disastrously short supply. To prevent British spies from discovering this shortage, gunpowder casks weighing a ton and a half supposedly shipped by John Brown of Providence, Rhode Island, were filled with sand and brought to the American supply depots at Cambridge, Massachusetts, and Mystic, Connecticut.[6] This was an effort to convince the British spies that the American army had a sufficient supply of gunpowder and had the ability to prosecute the rebellion.

Another bit of deception at Boston was conducted by Goodwin and Enock Hopkins, ferryman.[7] The loyalists were saying they are

> as bad rebels as any. . . . I have seen them bring men over in disguise and they are up in town every opportunity they have gathering what intelligence they can and when they return communicate it to the rebels the other side, and they again to the Rebel Officers. And the men that go in the fishing boats are equally as bad, for they will get a pass from the admiral for a boat and perhaps four men, they will take three fishermen and one rebel, and as soon as they get below they will land the rebel and take another on board, so he comes up in the stead of him that they carried down, and sees and hears what he can, and then returns the same way that he came.[8]

William Stoddard in Boston on June 15, 1775, provided instructions on how to smuggle people and supplies through Boston's defenses using the ferrymen. He advised Captain James Littlefield of Watertown, Massachusetts, that he received a fishing pass from the admiral "for your boat and three men, to come in and out of this harbor [Boston], which I now send you. You will carefully observe the pass; you must observe to go a fishing from Salem, before you come up here [to Boston], and then you may come in and go out. I hope you will not meet with any obstruction at Salem." He reminded him "to bring up veal, green peas, fresh butter, asparagus, and fresh salmon. Mr. Miles went away yesterday in the afternoon, by water, in order to come to you, and we suppose he is with you before this. I hope you have received a cloak, with a bag of brown sugar, I sent over yesterday by Mr. Hopkins's son." He continued his request for items to be smuggled into Boston. "I shall be much obliged to you, if you can, before you go for Salem, send me some fresh butter, and half a bushel of green peas. I now send you two dollars in this letter, and an osnaburgh bag, by Mr. Hopkins's son, to put the peas in."[9]

Many New Englanders had received their training in smuggling by avoiding paying sugar duties. They had imported molasses from which they made rum primarily from the French Caribbean islands. When England imposed the Sugar Act and its high duty on all imported sugar, molasses, and rum, the New England shippers, with the aid of the local customs officials who profited from the contrivance, were able to smuggle most of the molasses without paying the tax.[10] It was alleged that in one year the custom collectors accepted £17,000 in bribes.[11] Governor William Franklin of the colony of New Jersey advised the Board of Trade in London on the subject of the Sugar Act that "the Custom House Officers (upon finding that the North American Colonies could not do without that Trade, as our own West India Islands did not afford a sufficient supply) entered, as I am told into a composition with the merchants, and took a dollar a hogshead, or some such matter in lieu of the duties imposed by Act of Parliament."[12]

The Americans at Boston had small pieces of paper printed which compared conditions in the American camp at Prospect Hill with the British position at Bunker Hill.[13] The papers were wrapped around a musket ball in order that they would "fly well." On August 24 Lieutenant Scott and two others went near to the British sentries and threw the papers among them.[14] The intent of this operation was to entice the British solders to come over to the American side.

Prospect Hill	Bunker's Hill
I. Seven Dollars a Month	I. Three pence a day
II. Fresh provisions and in plenty	II. Rotten salt pork
III. Health	III. The Scurvy
IV. Freedom, ease, affluence and a good farm.	IV. Slavery, beggary and want

George Washington's victories at Trenton and Princeton had electrified the morale not only of his men but the average citizen and deflated those of his enemies. Public opinion had gone from the certainty of doom and disaster to jubilation and hope. Washington stated his original plan after these victories "was to have pushed on to [New]

Brunswick, but the harassed state of our own troops (many of them having had no rest for two nights and a day) and the danger of loosing the advantage we had gained by aiming at too much, induced me, by the advice of my officers, to relinquish the attempt but in my judgment six or eight hundred fresh troops upon a forced march would have destroyed all their stores, and magazines; taken (as we have since learnt) their military chest containing £70,000 and put an end to the war. The enemy from the best intelligence I have been able to get, were so much alarmed at the apprehension of this that they marched immediately to [New] Brunswick without halting."[15]

Washington two days later reported to Congress that "the severity of the season has made our troops, especially the militia, extremely impatient, and has reduced the number very considerably. Every day more or less leave us. Their complaints and the great fatigues they have undergone, induced me to come to this place [Morristown], as the best calculated of any in this quarter, to accommodate and refresh them."[16] Washington described the British as being "in great consternation, and as the panic affords us a favorable opportunity to drive them out of the Jerseys."[17] He instructed Major General William Heath at Peekskill: "you should move down towards New York with a considerable force, as if you had a design upon the city [New York City]. That being an object of great importance, the enemy will be reduced to the necessity of withdrawing a considerable part of their force from the Jerseys, if not the whole, to secure the city."[18]

The British held positions a few miles away from Morristown with encampments at New Brunswick, Perth Amboy, and the land between. The British also held the strongholds of New York and Staten Island. In order to keep the British army at bay, Washington also had to use deception. He needed to create a phantom army to convince British General Howe that his five incomplete regiments were twice their number and more.

Colonel Elias Boudinot, a lawyer and resident of Elizabeth Town, New Jersey, who worked with Washington on intelligence and deception, left a journal that reveals how diligently and ingeniously Washington labored to impress on General Howe an exaggerated estimate of his strength. Boudinot says that one of the tricks was "Washington distributed them [his soldiers] by 2 and 3 in a House, all along the main roads round Morris Town for miles, so that the general expectation among the country people was, that we were 4000 strong."[19]

Howe wanted to know the strength of the American forces at Morristown and sent a New York merchant of some character as a spy into the American camp. The merchant told sad tales of the treatment he had received from the British and therefore deserted from them. Based upon several circumstances, the adjutant general believed that the merchant was really a spy and applied to General Washington for an order to confine him. Washington checked into the circumstances and found the suspicions well supported. He ordered the adjutant general to go home and immediately draw up returns from every brigadier general in the army of the number of their brigade, making the army to consist of about 12,000 effective men. The reports were placed in the paper holes on his desk.

The adjutant general was instructed to get introduced to the spy and invite him to lodge with him. He was to get the New York merchant to have supper with him alone and told him "about 9 o'clock in the evening to have an orderly servant to call on him with positive orders that the adjutant should attend the general in haste that then he should make an excuse to the gentn [gentleman] suspected as a spy and leave him alone about half an hour. This was done and in the interval as was suspected the spy, took a copy of the returns, and the next morning went with them to New York."[20] This game of deception made British General Howe believe that he would face much stiffer resistance then would occur if he chose to attack the American army at Morristown. The ploy worked and bought the American army time to heal its wounds, recruit more soldiers, and prepare for the next season of campaigning.

A British Colonel Luce had been captured at Elizabeth Town. He was moved to and confined on parole in a house in Morristown. Luce was able to obtain accurate information of the American army's situation at Morristown. He then broke his parole and returned to New York City. He advised General Howe of the real strength of the American army. Howe refused to believe him and showed him the copies taken by the spy from the adjutant general's desk. Howe accused Luce of having gone over to the rebels and was going to have him hanged. Luce made his escape. He was "mortified and chagrined with having broken his parole and at the last disappointed and treated with contempt and great severity, he took to drink and killed himself by it in the end."[21]

Alexander Hamilton described the situation at Morristown as an "extraordinary spectacle of a powerful army straitened within narrow limits by the phantom of a military force and never permitted to transgress these limits with impunity."[22]

Washington was not the only American general playing the deception game. After the battle of Princeton, Captain McPherson of the 17th Regiment of Foot was found on the battlefield wounded in the lungs and left for dead. While his recovery was still in doubt, he requested that a friend be allowed to come from British-held New Brunswick to American-held Princeton to help him make out a will. General Israel Putnam agreed.

A flag of truce was sent to New Brunswick with instructions that the return visit was not to take place until after dark. In order to prevent the arriving British officer from spying on his post and finding out that he had but fifty men under his command, Putnam had candles placed in all the rooms of Nassau Hall (the College of New Jersey, now Princeton University) and in every vacant house in the town.[23] While the visitor was with Captain McPherson, the fifty soldiers spent the evening being marched from different quarters past the house where McPherson stayed sometimes altogether and at other times in smaller groups. The visitor on his return to New Brunswick reported that General Putnam had between 4,000 to 5,000 men under his command at Princeton.[24]

Governor Thomas Johnson, Jr., of Maryland had heard that the British were trying to recruit "pilots to assist in bringing the [British] fleet round from New York to Delaware." On April 1, 1777, he proposed the idea of giving the British the impression that Congress was attempting to engage the pilots familiar with New York and they were going "to be put on board a French fleet which was daily expected to arrive off Delaware." He believed leaking this information would slow the attack by the British on Philadelphia.[25]

Washington was mindful that the British could also play the deception game. In May 1778 when it was believed that the British army would end its occupation of Philadelphia, Washington instructed General Marquis de Lafayette to be ready to pounce on the rear of the British army as they departed the city. However, he cautioned him against being deceived by the British for it would "be attended with the most disastrous consequences."[26]

The British did try to trick him. British General Sir Henry Clinton even misled his own generals as to his actual plans. He wrote in an undated letter (believed to have been written in 1779) to Campbell, "as it is intended to make an attempt upon the Province of S[outh] Carolina with a considerable corps early in October and as the whole are to assemble for that purpose in Port Royal . . . you will obtain all the information you can from G[eneral] Prevost respecting his [plan] of operation against C.T. [Charles Town]. . . . I wish him to suppose we are going to the W.I. [West Indies]."[27]

The British navy also practiced a bit of deception when it was to their advantage. American Captain John Burnell, commander of an American armed sloop *Montgomery*, took refuge in the port of Cherbourg, France, with his ship and one of his prizes, thereby putting himself under the protection of the King of France. An armed vessel belonging to the King of England had cruised some days in front of the entrance to the Port. They did so in disguise and anchored near the French fort. They pretended to be a smuggler chased by a British cutter.

Captain Burnell, thinking he was safe in view of the French fort, went on board the pretended smuggler with a Mr. Morris, one of the ship's officers, at about 4 p.m. on June 15, 1777.[28] When the Baltimore resident stepped on board, "immediately the deck was filled with armed men before concealed, many of them with the officers in the uniform of the British marine who attempted to seize him". He broke loose and dove into the water and tried to swim to the French pilot boat that brought him. "The English Captain ordered his men to point their guns into the said pilot boat, and threatened a full discharge upon the said boat, if they offered to assist or take in the said Burnell, which obliged them to desist, while the English retaking him, got him again on board, put him immediately in irons in the hold." They quickly set sail and departed with Burnell and Morris.[29] Burnell was taken to Mill Prison. Benjamin Franklin quickly was applying to the French ministers to reclaim Burnell as being under the protection of a French fort, because France was not at war at this time.[30]

Later that year Henry Laurens, President of Congress, advised Washington of intelligence brought to him by Richard Beresford of South Carolina. Beresford brought information he received before he left New York City from Robert Williams, an attorney from South Carolina, who was interested in his own concerns and those of the crown. Williams claimed to have received the intelligence during a conversation at New York with British peace commissioner and former Royal Governor George Johnstone of the colony of West Florida.[31] The British after the end of the hurricane season were going to send a part of their naval squadron with 10,000 men to attack South Carolina. They were to land at Beaufort, Charles Town, or Port Royal. Washington believed that the information was a deception, but prudence called for them to guard against it.[32]

Washington, in setting up a spy operation in March 1779, cautioned Major Benjamin Tallmadge, the case agent, that "S-C-r" [Samuel Culper. alias of Abraham Woodhull] should be leery of deceptions by the British.[33] Washington cautioned Congress that information they were receiving concerning departing British ships from New York City could not be trusted. He believed that the British might leak false information, which they did in an attempt to deceive the American spies.

Washington again used inflated numbers in August 1779 to deceive the British. He arranged for American General Robert Howe to have Howe's spy, who was playing the role of a double agent, deliver to the British approximately the same inflated numbers that Washington had earlier fed to the British. Washington did not fully trust Howe's man, Elijah Hunter. Washington told Howe,

> but still there are some little appearances about him that give me distrust, and as the enemy have it more in their power to reward certain services than we have in the way which is most tempting, I always think it necessary to be very guarded with those who are professedly acting as double characters. This has hitherto prevented my doing any thing for the man in question in the way of office, least it might really put it in his power to do us mischief; but as the pretext upon which he applies is plausible and may be honest, I shall endeavor to find some place which will answer

the purpose and by keeping him mostly remote from the army, leave it the less in his power to turn it to our injury. We must endeavor to make it his interest to be faithful, for as it is apparent he means to get something by the business, and will even receive double wages, we must take care if possible not to let motives of interest on the other side bear down his integrity and inclination to serve us. Few men have virtue to withstand the highest bidder.[34]

Elijah Hunter was given the job of forage master for the Continental army. He operated on the east side of the Hudson River, usually at Bedford and Verplank's Point. Just as Washington said, Elijah Hunter was kept out of the main American encampment thereby limiting the damage he could do if he leaned more on the British side of the question. His American case agent was Colonel Elisha Sheldon of the 2nd Regiment of Continental Light Dragoons. His British case agent was Royal Governor William Tryon.[35] In writing to the British Hunter sometimes used the code name of "Joshua." Royal Governor Tryon would send Hunter's letters through William Smith to General Sir Henry Clinton.[36] William Smith was appointed the chief justice of the Province of New York Supreme Court in 1763. From the time William Smith came into New York City in August 1778, he was a case agent handling British spies for British headquarters. He at times prepared drafts of proclamations and reviewed intelligence and reported directly to General Sir Henry Clinton, commander-in-chief of British forces in North America.

On August 8, 1779, Elijah Hunter turned over a letter from Colonel Banastre Tarleton of the British partisan corps to George Washington for his inspection. It was sent back on the 12th along with an American troop return which Washington personally prepared for Hunter with inflated numbers. Washington advised Hunter,

for the reasons I mentioned to you the other day I have not the least objection to our real strength being known, and it will be well for you to inform that you came by the knowledge of it from inquiry and your own observations of the troops when under arms upon which you formed an average estimate of the force of each regiment in the different

Fake status return of the American army prepared by George Washington for Elijah Hunter, a double agent, to take to the British. (*Library of Congress*)

Brigades; to give your account, the greater air of probability you may observe that the Officers are very incautious in speaking of the strength of their regiments. As the amount of the inclosed return exceeds that which I showed you when here, you may be at a loss how to account for it. In that was included only such troops as are on this spot; to the present one is added those under the command of Lord Stirling Gen[era]l Howe and the Light Infantry. There are about 3000 Levies coming on from Massachusetts and Connecticut, 500 of which are already arrived.

The report indicates that the total strength of the Continental army as 17,010, present and fit for duty, exclusive of the detachment on Sullivan's expedition.

Washington tells Hunter that "boats sufficient to transport at least 5000 at a turn are now lying at the fort [West Point], New Windsor and Fishkill Landing and can be assembled in two hours at any time." The weekly return of the Continental army, for August 14, 1779, shows a total of rank and file and noncommissioned officers of 16,316; but when the absent sick and those on command were subtracted from the rank and file fit for duty, the total shrinks to 9,532.[37]

Elijah Hunter sent a letter at Verplank's Point dated June 6, 1779, to General Clinton stating that he received a message containing his orders. In response he says that he went to Fishkill the previous morning and went to see American Governor Clinton of New York and found him at "Mr. Naigts" in the Highlands.[38] In an August 21, 1779, letter dated at Bedford, New York, from Elijah Hunter to Governor Tryon, he stated that he had not lost his allegiance to the crown. Also on August 21 Elijah Hunter wrote to John André. The purpose of the letter was to extract money from the British and information that he could peddle to the Americans. General Alexander McDougall paid Hunter for his American secret services.[39] At times Hunter used the services of Mary Campbell as his courier. Over time George Washington changed his opinion of Elijah Hunter. Washington said the recommendations given in Hunter's favor by John Jay (then President of Congress) and Major General McDougall were such as induced him to repose great confidence in Hunter. George Washington in 1783 wrote a letter of recommendation of Hunter's spy activities.[40]

In September 1779 Washington was having a difficult time determining if the British were running another deception through his spies. He wrote to General Benjamin Lincoln in South Carolina,

> The enclosed extracts contain substantially the most authentic intelligence I have received of the enemy's motions and designs. You will perceive they are making large detachments and that the Southern states are spoken of as a principal object. The particular corps too which are mentioned point that way: They would not separate their grenadiers and light infantry but for some important *coup de main*; and this I imagine is the manner in which they would proceed against Charlestown: Nor do I see where except with you they can intend to employ their cavalry. But there may be a mistake in this part of the intelligence, from the difficulty of ascertaining corps with precision, and some movements among those which are specified may have occasioned a deception.[41]

Another effort involved deceiving the Canadians into believing that a combined American and French army was going to invade Canada. Washington wrote to General Lafayette,

> We talked of a Proclamation to the Canadians. If it is not already done, I think it ought not to be delayed. It should be in your own name, and have as much as possible an air of probability. Perhaps it will be more plausible to have two different kinds struck; one intimating to them that the arrival of a French fleet and army in the River St Lawrence, to cooperate with these states is to be expected by the way of Rhode Island where they are to touch for to answer. Some important purposes, and dwelling on the happy opportunity it will afford them to renew their ancient friendships with France, by joining the allied arms and assisting to make Canada a part of the American confederation with all the privileges and advantages enjoyed by the other members; cautioning them by no means to aid the enemy in their preparations for defending the Province. The other proclamation should be drawn on the supposition of the fleet and army being already arrived, and should contain an animating invitation to arrange themselves under the allied banners. In both proclamations you should hold yourself up as a French and American officer charged both by the King of France and by Congress with a commission to address them upon the occasion. It may indeed be well to throw out an Idea that you are to command the corps of American troops destined to cooperate with the French armament. The more mystery [there is] in this business the better. It will get out and it ought to seem to be against our intention.[42]

George Washington instructed Benedict Arnold to draft "a proclamation addressed to the inhabitants of Canada. You will be pleased to put this into the hands of a printer whose secrecy and discretion may be depended on and desire him to strike off a proof sheet with the utmost dispatch, which you will sent to me for correction." Washington was going to order 500 copies once a final version was ready. He stressed to Arnold: "The importance of this business will sufficiently impress you with the necessity of transacting it with every possible degree of caution. The printer is to be particularly charged not on any account to reserve a copy himself or suffer one to get abroad." Washington had planned that the Chevalier de la Luzerne would provide a number of letterheads "with the Arms of the King of France, on which it is proposed to print the proclamation if the paper will admit."[43]

American General Benedict Arnold, calling himself Mr. Moore, at Philadelphia wrote to British Captain George Beckwith in New York City in cipher. The ciphered letter was keyed to a small dictionary which probably came the previous month from General Wilhelm von Knyphausen by way of Captain George Beckwith. Arnold sent with his letter a copy of the secret proclamation to the residents of Canada.[44] Sir Henry Clinton forwarded the translation of the proclamation to Lord George Germain in England in his dispatch of August 31, 1780.[45] Meanwhile Arnold had told Washington, "I have therefore sealed up the original draught, [of the proclamation] with a proof sheet similar to the one enclosed, which I have left with Mrs. Arnold, to be delivered to your Excellency's Order."[46]

British headquarters considered sending Baron Nicholas Dietrich de Ottendorf into New Jersey during the Pennsylvania Line Mutiny in January 1781.[47] He was from Lusayia, Saxony, and was a professional German soldier. He had been a lieutenant under Frederick the Great in the Seven Years War (known as the French and Indian War in North America). He had been commissioned as a major by Congress on December 5, 1776, to raise an independent corps in the Continental army. General Arthur St. Clair did not think that Ottendorf had any chance of raising a corps as Ottendorf neither spoke English nor had the financial resources needed to accomplish the task.[48] Ottendorf did have difficulty completing the corps as predicted and General Washington had Ottendorf replaced by Lieutenant Colonel Charles Armand Tuffin, Marquis de la Rouerie, on June 11, 1777. Ottendorf decided to try his luck with the enemy and had gone over to the British by April 5, 1780.[49] While in New York he had overextended his credit and was arrested for his debts.

Joshua Loring, commissary general for prisoners on January 14, 1781, proposed sending Ottendorf out to the Pennsylvania mutineers.

Loring wanted to use deception to send a spy to New Jersey. Loring supplied Ottendorf with a parole and a letter to American Major Adams, who was the commissary of prisoners at Elizabeth Town, New Jersey. Loring had also arranged for Sergeant Lloyd using either a boat from the ship *Neptune* or a sloop that was available to escort Ottendorf to Elizabeth Town. Loring in the letter reminded De Lancey that Ottendorf "having been detained here on account of his debts, will be good cloak, and I do not see any cause there will be for suspicion, unless it happens from his own imprudence, I think him rather a weak man for any capital undertaking, and therefore your caution to him may not be unnecessary. If you do not approve of the within method suppose he should be landed at Bergen Point [Fort De Lancey] and pretend that he had made his escape in some of the market boats from this city, he would easily find his way to Eliza[beth] Town."[50] However the unfolding events of the Pennsylvania Line Mutiny appear to have precluded his mission as no documentation of it could be found.

Elizabeth Town was also a good place to have returning British soldiers smuggle documents across the lines. Individuals had managed to smuggle letters cross the lines. A letter to Mrs. Kempe (possibly Grace Coxe Kempe) dated October 2, 1778, was written on a piece of paper one inch by 14 1/2 inches and folded into eight panels each approximately 1 3/4 inches long.[51] Grace Galloway while in American-held Philadelphia kept up a secret correspondence with her husband in British-held New York City.[52] Joseph Galloway was in the Pennsylvania assembly (1757–1775 except for 1764) and was also its speaker (1766–1774). He was the second most powerful politician in Pennsylvania behind Ben Franklin. In 1774 he was a delegate to the First Continental Congress and became a volunteer secret agent for the Crown. A letter dated Nov. 27, 1778, was sent to New York City through a Mrs. Potts.[53] One letter from him has been preserved and was written on a piece of tissue paper the size of a postage stamp.

As part of the propaganda war New York Royal Governor General William Tryon had proclamations made to entice American soldiers to desert. When John Cunningham "was last a[t] Morris T[own] he saw many of General Tryon's late Proclamations offering pardons to deserters. Some Women carried them out they cannot fail being publicly known. Tho' he saw none in the hands of the soldiers."[54] Women spies were not considered as dangerous as male spies. Aaron Burr wrote that "there are a number of women here of bad character, who are continually running to New York and back again. If they were men, I would flog them without mercy."[55]

Sex was a tool used by some female spies to accomplish their mission. Ann Crocheron of Staten Island is one of those women who used her beauty and brains to her advantage. She was able for a long time to gain entrance anywhere without suspicion using her assets. She provided information usually late at night to both Generals Sir William Howe and Sir Henry Clinton. She was able to enter British headquarters at 1 Broadway without being questioned by the guard on duty which would indicate that she was a frequent visitor. Her activities as a British agent led to the capture of a number of Continental soldiers whom she enticed to her home. She pretended to be frightened and heartbroken when they were arrested and taken into custody.[56]

Miss Jenny was a French seamstress who spied for the British on the French forces on the east side of the Hudson River north of New York. In August 1781 she reported having received some of her intelligence from the mistress of General Rochambeau's son.[57] Women and children were used as spies throughout the war. General Charles Lee stated, "Women and children had learnt the art and practiced with address the office of spies."[58]

Deception was also part of the repertoire used by the Spanish. Bernardo de Gálvez, Spanish Governor of Louisiana since 1777, had intercepted some letters in 1778. They led him to believe that the British had plans to attack New Orleans.[59] In one of the letters John Stephenson had written to an Irish friend in New Orleans warning the English there to leave Louisiana as soon as possible, "because a black cloud is forming above it, which will soon discharge its burden."[60] Also Alexander Ross expressed his sorrow that William Dunbar had purchased a plantation in Louisiana, "I would not have given a rial for it, or anything in Spanish territory. Sell it at once, for I expect to see a different set-up on the Mississippi [River] soon."[61]

Louisiana Governor Gálvez decided to plan a deception strategy which would provide the British in the colony of West Florida with something about which to worry. He wrote a circular letter to all his commandants stating that there was an advance unit of 2,000 soldiers who were preparing to descend on the British settlements along the

Mississippi River. He hoped that British spies would discover the circular and spread the word. The ploy worked just as Gálvez planned. Gálvez observed after the circulars were distributed "those who formerly menaced us are [now] looking for our friendship today."[62]

Nonetheless, the waterways remained a vulnerability. Washington wrote from Philadelphia to New Jersey Governor William Livingston that "a constant intercourse is carried on by water between the refugees and the inhabitants, but that, no force which I could spare would prevent, as they would, if kept out of one inlet make use of another for their purposes. It is in vain to expect the pernicious and growing traffic will ever be stopped, until the states pass laws agt. [against] it, making the penalty death. This I long ago foresaw and recommended. We are I believe the only nation who suffer their people to carry on a commerce with their enemy in time of war."[63]

It wasn't only the Americans that were having problems. The British commandant of New York, Major General Valentine Jones, on July 23, 1777, restricted such travel to persons with suitable authorization, and completely prohibited it after sunset, on pain of military execution. He indicated that "many evil practices are carried on by persons passing and repassing to and from this city and the [New] Jersey shore in small craft."[64] Sir Henry Clinton issued a proclamation on February 13, 1778 concerning the movement of goods to Staten Island because "supplies of rum, salt, and other goods are frequently conveyed to the rebels, by the way of Staten Island." All vessels going to Staten Island were to land at Cole's Ferry and to report to Alexander Gardiner, wharf officer, before unloading their cargoes on Staten Island.[65]

John Page, Lieutenant Governor of Virginia signed a report of the council meeting record of March 4, 1780 that they "are unanimously of opinion that a flag ought not be permitted to carry any kind of merchandise not only as being contrary to the law of nations but as sending in our situation to establish a precedent which may be attended with mischievous consequences."[66] Colonel John Newton also writing from Norfolk, Virginia on July 30, 1782 but to Colonel Davies stated that "Laughton and Mc Lear where British subjects, from flags of truice—Considers the Captain very culpable in permitting it—the persons 'so coming in' should be regarded as spies."[67]

As part of the British plan to divide the colonies, General John Burgoyne was to take the Northern British Army on an expedition from Canada south through Lake Champlain and Lake George to the Hudson River and Albany, New York. The British army in New York City was to proceed north up the Hudson River. Lieutenant Colonel Barry St. Leger was to come from the west down the Mohawk Valley and the three forces would meet at Albany. The forty-year-old Irishman, St. Leger was a seasoned soldier having spent half his life in the service. He had fought in the French and Indian War at Louisburg and Quebec. St. Leger was very fond of liquid refreshment of the alcoholic kind. He had the soul of a gambler and was always ready to place a wager or two. St. Leger started out from Montreal on June 23, 1777, and by July 25 his army of 1,800 souls, of which 1,000 were Indians, was at Oswego, New York, on Lake Ontario and ready to begin his descent. They would travel overland to Fort Stanwix at present day Rome, New York. Fort Stanwix was a leftover relic from the French and Indian War and was reported to be in a ruinous condition. St. Leger was expecting to make short work of the fort and make his push quickly to Albany. General Philip Schuyler, the great administrator, had foreseen the need to repair the fort and protect the western flank. He had somehow managed to find the means to upgrade the fort. Colonel Peter Gansevoort of Albany took over command of the fort and pressed the garrison to restore the fort. In the short time available they worked wonders in bringing the fort back into condition. The fort was now ready for battle and was renamed Fort Schuyler in honor of General Philip Schuyler.

St. Leger's forces emerged from the woods before Fort Stanwix on August 3, 1777, and proceeded to surround the fort. St. Leger realized that the condition of the fort had changed and he was not going to take the fort without his artillery. St. Leger then sent crews to cut a six-teen-mile-long road to get his artillery to the fort. A relief militia column under native New Yorker Brigadier General Nicholas Herkimer had formed at Fort Dayton, which was about thirty miles east of Fort Stanwix.[68] On August 4, they pushed on toward Fort Stanwix but St. Leger had 400 Indians and some loyalists prepare a trap. St. Leger's forces lay in waiting at a ravine near Oriskany Creek. A battle ensued but at the apex a sudden downpour occurred and produced a lull in the battle of an hour. During this lull General Herkimer, wounded in the leg, reorganized the militia. He stationed the men behind trees. The Indians and loyalists broke off their attack after six hours. Herkimer's band survived but they were unable to relieve the fort. General Herkimer's leg had to be amputated and as the result of a poor operation, he died on August 16.

Generals Benedict Arnold and Philip Schuyler were determined to save the fort. Arnold set off with about 950 men and was outnumbered by St. Leger's forces by almost two to one. Arnold decided to use a hoax. He was aware that the Indians held mentally deranged people in high esteem. The Indians believed they could foretell prophecy. The Americans had arrested a half-demented Tory by the name of Hon Yost Schuyler, a distant relative of General Schuyler. Hon Yost Schuyler had been charged as a British spy, tried, and sentenced to die. He was offered a stay of his execution if he agreed to participate in General Arnold's plan to convince the Indians that he was coming with 3,000 soldiers. To insure Hon Yost Schuyler's performance, his brother Nicholas was held as security.[69] Hon Yost Schuyler's coat was shot full of bullet holes to add to his mystique. He was sent out with a friendly Oneida Indian who was in on the plot. He arrived at St. Leger's camp, terrified and babbling that he had just barely escaped from an overwhelming American army and they were coming to Fort Stanwix. The Indians could see his bullet-riddled coat. When the Indians asked Hon Yost Schuyler how many men were coming, he babbled, shook his head and pointed to the leaves on the trees. The Indians believed his ranting. They panicked and fled despite St. Leger's attempts to get them to stay. Without his Indians St. Leger could not maintain the siege as the panic spread to his own troops and the army fled toward Oswego and their boats on Lake Ontario.[70]

Another person acting deranged was Nancy Hart, who lived in the back country in a log cabin on Wahatchee Creek in what is now Elbert County, Georgia. One of the stories about her says that in January 1778, she reconnoitered the British garrison at Augusta, Georgia, by pretending to be a mad or crazy woman.[71] She has been described as being six feet tall, ugly, vulgar, illiterate, strong, and cross-eyed. Her attributes did not hurt her disguise as soldiers probably kept their distance.[72]

Sometimes people can deceive themselves into thinking a real document is a fake. During the British army's advance on

Philadelphia from the Chesapeake, they won a decisive battle at Brandywine on September 11, 1777. A troop return of the strength of the Continental army dated September 10, 1777 was captured by the British. It listed that General George Washington had 12,900 men plus militia and two regiments of light horse fit and ready for battle. British Captain John Montresor wrote in his journal some of their staff believed the reports were false and were prepared for the deception.[73]

Washington did feed false troop returns to the British whenever he saw an opportunity. Washington wrote at 10 a.m. on November 4, 1777, and advised that he had received Major John Clark's letter of 8 p.m. the previous evening and "think you have fallen upon an exceeding good method of gaining intelligence and that too much secrecy cannot be used, both on account of the safety of your friend and the execution and continuance of your design, which may be of service to us." Washington made up a false return of the strength of the Continental Army, with a brief memorandum of his intended movements, and Clark's spy carried it in to Sir William Howe on his next trip.[74] Clark responded at 6 p.m. that he just received Washington's letter from the morning and stated that he would comply. He reported that he had personally gone below Marcus Hook and Chester to view the British ships and that he had friends observing their activities with good glasses.[75]

During the celebration of the French alliance at Valley Forge, a loyalist spy was discovered. A member of Washington's staff decided it would be more beneficial to take no action against the spy but to allow the spy to return to Philadelphia and report on the excellent drilling by and the condition of the American army.[76]

Lieutenant General John Burgoyne wrote from Quebec on May 14, 1777 to General Sir William Howe that he would write letters to him that he intended to fall into American hands in a game of deception. Such letters will be "dated at the bottom and two strokes after the name of the place."[77] General Howe decided to participate in this strategy to also deceive Washington of his movements by means of a false letter. Howe had Colonel William Sheriff approach Henry Williams in the *Provost* to be a courier to General John Burgoyne in Canada with the promise that Williams would get a great reward.[78] Howe and Sheriff knew Williams would take the letter directly to the

Americans. Even if he did not, no harm would be done. At first Williams declined but eventually decided to accept the mission with the intent to deliver the document to the first American officer he could find. Henry Williams was given six half Joes (Portuguese coins) prior to his departure.[79] The document dated July 20, 1777, was written on a small piece of silk paper and was sewed into a fold of his coat. At the bottom of the letter was the sign: "*New York July 20th.*"

Major General John Burgoyne who surrendered at Saratoga. (*William L. Clements Library*)

In this fake letter General William Howe tells Burgoyne: "To General [John] Burgoyne. Our destination is changed. Instead of going to S.D., we shall in three days sail for B.N. Regulate your conduct accordingly. [General William] Howe."

In the real letter Howe writes, "I am now making demonstrations to the southward, which will I think have the full effect in carrying our plan in[to] execution."[80] Howe hoped that Washington would think that his move toward Philadelphia was a deception and he would have little opposition to capture the American capital. Philadelphia was his objective in 1776 but he was unable to accomplish it. With Washington's victories at Princeton and Trenton, he was disgraced and was forced to draw his army back to New Brunswick and Perth Amboy.

Henry Williams left New York City on July 22 and brought Howe's letter to General Philip Van Cortlandt in East Chester, New York. Van Cortlandt sent him on to General Israel Putnam at Peekskill. Williams caught up with Putnam on the 24th and advised him that he thought the letter was a hoax and it was intended to fall into their hands. Putnam immediately sent Williams's deposition and the note to General George Washington at the Clove on the west side of the Hudson River near Nyack. On the 25th Washington writing from Ramapo, New Jersey, stated, "A stronger proof could not be given that the former [Howe] is not going to the Eastward, than this letter adduces. It was evidently intended to fall into our hands, the complexion of it, the circumstances attending it etc., evinces this beyond a doubt in my mind. I therefore desire that no time be lost in sending Generals Sullivan and Lord Stirling with their divisions" to Philadelphia.[81] Howe's plan to hoodwink Washington failed.

George Washington had plans for another deception to solve a problem situation after the war. While in retirement at his home at Mount Vernon in 1785, Washington had a subscription to the Philadelphia newspaper. However, the paper did not always reach its destination at Mount Vernon. Lafayette informed George Washington that Mathew Carey, late printer of the *Volunteer Journal* in Ireland, was going to become the publisher of a Philadelphia newspaper. Washington contacted Carey and "requested that your weekly production might be sent to me." He also informed him of his delivery problem and the deception that was needed to resolve it. Washington said "It has so happened that my gazettes from Philadelphia, whether from inattention at the printing or post offices, or other causes, come very irregularly to my hands; I pray you therefore to fold it like, and give it the appearance of a letter, the usual covering of your newspapers will do. I have sometimes suspected that there are persons who having stronger desires to read newspapers than to pay for them, borrow with a pretty heavy hand: this may be avoided by deception, and I know of no other way."[82]

Chapter 14

Going Incognito

O ne type of deception that was used by spies was going incogni-
to. This could be something as simple as Nathan Hale changing from his military uniform to that of a Dutch schoolmaster. Spies
who were recruited out of the military obviously had to get out of their
uniforms, if they had one, to accomplish their mission. Many more
cases of this type of action exist then are represented here. Some male
spies chose to wear women's clothes, enemy uniforms, or in one
unusual case his own uniform in order to deceive and become invisible to the enemy.

Before the Battles of Concord and Lexington, British General
Thomas Gage had sent Captain David Brown, Ensign John De
Berniere, and John (Howe?) on an intelligence-gathering mission
through the counties of Suffolk and Worcester, Massachusetts, specifically to check out Concord. They set out from Boston on the ferry to
Charlestown disguised like countrymen in brown clothes with reddish
handkerchiefs around their necks. They stopped at Brewer's Tavern
just past Watertown. Their disguise did not help them as a black
woman working in the tavern saw their map and recognized Captain
Brown.[1] About the same time the British in Montreal had sent two
regular lieutenants in disguise to Boston to find out what was happening.[2] Later that summer Lieutenant Colonel Allen McClean, who
was on half pay from the British military, came to New York City
under pretense of taking possession of some land north of the city. He
went to Boston on the real estate matters and returned to New York.
He then went in disguise though the country to Oswego. There "he
boasted of his exploit, put on a red coat, seemed to take upon him
some command, and went to Canada with Colonel Guy Johnson."[3]

When the American army invaded Canada and were attacking Montreal, British General Guy Carleton hid on board a vessel fleeing the city. He went dressed like the six Canadians who were in the boat with him. He was successful and made it to Quebec.[4]

Captains Noah Phelps and Ezra Hicock went into Fort Ticonderoga in disguise on May 9, 1775.[5] . Phelps pretended to be a countryman who wanted a shave from the British fort's barber. While there they scouted out the fortifications and the laxity of the sentinels and the poor condition of the fort and then reported the information to Ethan Allen.[6] Benedict Arnold and Ethan Allen then led the raid that captured Fort Ticonderoga and its cache of cannons. The cannons were brought by General Henry Knox to Boston and placed on Dorchester Heights, forcing the British to evacuate the city of Boston for Halifax, Nova Scotia.

At Halifax the British planned to take New York City and the North also known as the Hudson River and divide the colonies. The British army and navy had arrived off of Sandy Hook, New Jersey, in July 1776 and then began landing troops unopposed on Staten Island, New York. The Continental Congress on August 14, 1776, heard a report from a committee appointed to devise a plan for encouraging the Hessian mercenaries and other foreigners to quit the British army. Benjamin Franklin on August 28, 1776, wrote to General Gates that "the Congress being advised that there was a probability that the Hessians might be induced to quit the British service by offers of land, came to two resolves for this purpose, which, being translated into German and printed, are sent to Staten-Island, to be distributed, if practicable, among those people."[7] The resolves that were passed stated "that these states will receive all such foreigners who shall leave the armies of his Britannic majesty in America, and shall chuse to become members of any of these states; that they shall be protected in the free exercise of their respective religions, and be invested with the rights, privelleges and immunities of natives, as established by the laws of these states; and, moreover, that this Congress will provide, for every such person, 50 Acres of unappropriated lands in some of these states, to be held by them and his heirs in absolute property." Furthermore they resolved that the committee "be directed to have it translated into German, and to take proper measures to have it communicated to the foreign troops. In the meanwhile, that this be kept secret."[8]

Swiss-born Protestant Herman Zedwitz was an unscrupulous individual.[9] Before the Revolutionary War, Zedwitz while in London had
promised to sell cut diamonds in a setting for Rudolphe Ernest
Hartmann, a German businessman who was a stranger to the city.
Zedwitz took possession of the diamonds and absconded with the fortune. Hartmann initially tried to get James Le Ray, a New York City
merchant, to recover his money but without any success.[10] Hartmann
then tried to get Benjamin Franklin to intercede on his behalf in
recovering his money. Franklin sent Hartmann's requests to America
but did not know if the requests had been received.[11]

Herman Zedwitz was commissioned a major in the 1st New York
Regiment on July 15, 1775. On September 4, 1775, Zedwitz co-led
two battalions of New York soldiers up to Fort Ticonderoga at Lake
Champlain.[12] They then continued on to Canada. During the attack
on Quebec he had been wounded falling from the city walls. In
March 1776 Zedwitz was elected lieutenant colonel of the 1st
Battalion of the New York Regiment by the Continental Congress.[13]
When Zedwitz returned to New York, he brought prisoners back from
Canada.[14] Because he was fluent in German, Lieutenant Colonel
Zedwitz had been given the job of translating the aforementioned
August 14 resolves of the Continental Congress into German for the
intended clandestine distribution to the Hessians on Staten Island.[15]

In New York City on August 21, 1776, Zedwitz paid a visit to
Captain Bowman. While there he conversed with Augustus Stein and
inquired if he was in the military, and Stein informed him that he was
not. Zedwitz commented that Stein could then go wherever he
pleased and said that he needed to talk to him. With Stein's ability to
travel, Zedwitz wanted to use him as a courier to New York Royal
Governor William Tryon. The next day Zedwitz returned and talked
to Stein about accumulating money and travel. Stein told Zedwitz
that he was "poor but had always found a good living in the country."
The conversation was cut short when Captain Bowman returned.
Stein offered to meet Zedwitz later at Zedwitz's house but was told
"that would not do," and they parted. On August 23 Zedwitz sent a
man to collect Stein and bring him to camp. After Stein entered his
tent, Zedwitz told him that "he believed we were all lost." Stein
assured him that he was of the same opinion. Stein said during the
Zedwitz's later court-martial that Zedwitz wanted him "to go to Long

Island with a letter to Governor [William] Tryon that he [Zedwitz] had intelligence from him by the means of a woman and he would strongly recommend me [Stein] to the Governor." Stein agreed to the task.

On the 24th, Zedwitz called on Stein but Captain Bowman was around and so the letter could not be passed. Zedwitz looked at Stein, who gave him a wink that he would meet him later in camp. Stein got to camp about 1 p.m. when Zedwitz turned over his letter for Governor Tryon. Upon completion of the exchange, Stein left camp and went immediately to Captain Bowman's house and broke open the letter and read it. When Captain Bowman arrived, Stein told him that he had something that needed to be communicated to the general. They went and saw Captain Hamilton, who delivered the letter to Washington.[16] The letter to Royal Governor Tryon of New York informed him of the Continental Congress' resolves and their planned distribution to the Hessians. Zedwitz also told of seeing four villains at General Washington's house. They had fourteen bottles of a mixture "as black as ink" and they were going to poison the watering place on Staten Island. They were to receive from General Washington £1,000 if they accomplished this mission. Zedwitz also offered to serve as a British spy and used this story to make himself appear more valuable to Governor Tryon.[17]

Peter Kinnan was in Colonel Ephraim Martin's Regiment in General Heard's Brigade and was the keeper of an order book.[18] His job was to attend daily at headquarters and to transcribe the orders so that they could be given to the individual regiments. Peter Kinnan wrote on August 25, 1776, that a special court-martial was going to start that day at noon, at Mrs. Montagnies's, for the trial of Lieutenant Colonel Zedwitz, charged with "carrying on a treasonable correspondence with the enemy." The court was to be composed of a Brigadier General and twelve field officers; General Wadsworth was to be president of the court.[19] As part of his defense Zedwitz provided a statement of his military service.[20] Augustus Stein's deposition on August 25, 1776, was taken and he confirmed the events and the copy of Zedwitz's letter to Governor Tryon.[21] Zedwitz was found guilty of attempting to give information to the enemy and was sentenced to jail for the duration of the war.

The Continental Congress on November 22, 1776, ordered Herman Zedwitz relocated to the new jail at Sixth and Walnut Streets in Philadelphia.[22] New Jersey Governor William Livingston, unaware of Congress' resolution, wrote on November 30 to David Rittenhouse requesting to send Zedwitz from the Burlington, New Jersey, jail where he was being held to the new jail in Philadelphia.[23] Mrs. Juliana Zedwitz had filed a claim for the salary that was due her husband prior to his conviction and Congress approved the disbursement of two months' pay for Zedwitz's prior service.[24] At some point Zedwitz was taken from the Philadelphia jail and relocated to the jail at Reading, Pennsylvania. He escaped from Reading and was making his way to the British in New York City and freedom when he was captured in May 1779 dressed in women's clothes near Morristown, New Jersey.[25] Zedwitz submitted petitions that were referred to the Board of War. He requested and "was released on parole because of health and sundry reasons. He was eventually deported."[26]

The papers containing the Continental Congress' resolves were printed with "tobacco marks on the back, that so tobacco being put up in them in small quantities, as the tobacconists use, and suffered to fall into the hands of these people [Hessians], they might divide the papers as plunder, before their officers could come to the knowledge of the contents, and prevent their being read by the men."[27]

George Washington believed that the documents "would produce salutary effects. If it can be properly circulated among them; I fear it will be a matter of difficulty."[28] Christopher Ludwick, a German-born Philadelphia baker, was given the mission to infiltrate the Hessian camp on Staten Island disguised as a deserter and distribute the tobacco handbills prepared by the Continental Congress, which were aimed at encouraging desertion.[29] He made it safely to Staten Island on August 22, 1776, with the assistance of Joshua Mercereau.[30] The Mercereau family was already operating a spy ring on Staten Island.[31] However Ludwick returned the next day disappointed with the results.[32] George Washington advised Congress, "The papers designed for the foreign troops, have been put into several channels, in order that they might be conveyed to them, and from the information I had yesterday, I have reason to believe many have fallen into their hands."[33] Lawrence Mascoll was paid on August 23, 1776, for going into the enemy's line on Staten Island to obtain information and may have been the other channel Washington referred to who conveyed the papers to the Hessians.[34]

Washington informed John Hancock, president of the Continental Congress, on August 29 about Ludwick's lack of success. "As to the encouragement to the Hessian officers, I wish it may have the desired effect, perhaps it might have been better, had the offer been sooner made."[35] Some of the leaflets, which were dated August 14, did reach their objective. Some of the special papers were received by members of Colonel Friedrich Wilhelm and Freiherr von Lossberg's brigades on Staten Island.[36]

Another attempt was made in upstate New York to entice the Hessians to switch sides, or so said Jacob van Alstyne, who was at the capture of British General John Burgoyne and his army. Van Alstyne was an adjutant and quartermaster of a regiment of Rensselaer County militia, under Colonel Stephen J. Schuyler and Lieutenant Colonel Henry K. van Rensselaer.[37]

General Gates employed John Tillman as a German interpreter. "Tillman was a generously proportioned German who resided at Albany, New York, after the war. Tillman was asked to select an appropriate individual to 'go into the British camp as a spy…to circulate letters among the Hessian soldiers, to induce them to desert and to bring on an engagement in such a manner as Gates desired. Tillman selected Christopher Fisher, a native-born private' of German descent in Colonel Schuyler's New York Militia Regiment who was reported to be a shrewd fellow. After being informed of the risks and consequences, 'Well,' said Fisher, 'if you will not advise me how to proceed, then I must act on my own judgment.'"[38]

After the battle on October 7, 1777, Christopher Fisher entered Jacob van Alstyne's tent and showed him "a purse of gold and his discharge from the service." Van Alstyne wanted to know what happened. Fisher told him "he approached the enemy's picket with a sheep upon his back, which had been killed for the occasion." The guard wanted to know where he was from and why he was visiting the camp. Fisher told him that he lived a few miles away—and "that the d—d Yankees had destroyed all his property but one sheep, which he had killed, and was then taking [the sheep] to his friends." The guard permitted him to enter the camp. In the British camp, he was again questioned about his visit by an officer. In order to gain his confidence Fisher said, "the rebels are preparing to give you battle, and if you will go with me, I will convince you of its truth." Off they went to a prearranged location where a body of Morgan's rifle corps were putting on a show upon the orders of General Gates. Fisher pointed out the moving frocks of Morgan's men in the woods. He was then accepted as a loyalist and allowed to move about the British camp where he spent several hours with the soldiers who spoke German. When encouraged to enlist, he claimed to be a pacifist and was needed at home to protect his family against the rebels. During a battle, he made his escape.[39]

Stephen Edwards used the same ploy of using women's clothes as Herman Zedwitz. Edwards lived in Shrewsbury Township, Monmouth County, New Jersey. In September 1778, he joined the Associated Loyalists in New York. Colonel George Taylor sent him back home. His return was noted and he was suspected. Captain Jonathan Forman of the light horse was sent to arrest him. On Saturday night Captain Forman went to Edwards's father's house near Eatontown, New Jersey. Edwards was found in bed with his wife while he wore a woman's nightcap. Under the bed were Edwards's clothes that had his written instructions from Colonel George Taylor. Edwards denied that he was a spy. He was arrested and taken to Monmouth Court House (now Freehold), New Jersey. On Sunday he was tried and convicted as a spy. Then on the following day, Monday, at 10 a.m. he was hung until dead. His parents arrived in Monmouth Court House a few moments after he died and took his body back.[40] The Pennsylvania Evening Post reported on his execution and stated that Edwards had requested to say goodbye to his wife, children, and his two aged parents who were at Monmouth Court House. The newspaper stated that this request was "inhumanly denied him."[41]

Another incident of changing one's appearance to pass through hostile territory occurred while the Northern army of the Continental army was in Canada. Aaron Burr, a Newark, New Jersey, native and lawyer, passed though the colony of Quebec late in 1775 dressed as a priest in order to get to Major General Richard Montgomery.[42]

There is also the story of Joseph Badger's exploits at the north end of Lake Champlain. During July and August 1776 a New Hampshire militia regiment was raised to assist the ongoing war effort in Canada and the unit was placed under the command of Colonel Joshua Wingate. The New Hampshire militia regiment joined the Northern

Army in upstate New York sometime after General John Sullivan had made his successful retreat from Canada back to northern New York with the remnant of General Richard Montgomery's Army.[43] The British had called off the campaign because of the oncoming winter season and had taken a position at St. John's, Canada. Lieutenant Badger and three rangers who had been in the French and Indian War were sent on a scouting mission to determine the British army's intentions. They embarked in a boat and landed near St. John's under the cover of darkness. The scouting party captured a Canadian who informed them that the British were having a ball that evening. Two men stayed at the boat with their prisoner while Badger and a ranger went to the fort and captured a young British officer who had just come out of a house they were observing. They drew their pistols, sprang upon him, and took him as their prisoner to the boat.

When Lieutenant Badger realized that he and the young officer were the same size, he had the prisoner strip. Badger then got dressed in the British officer's uniform and went to the ball. Badger then collected military information during his conversations from others attending the ball. Lieutenant Badger brought back the news that Sir Guy Carlton was discontinuing his advance and going into winter quarters.[44]

George Washington instructed Colonel Daniel Morgan of the 11th Virginia Regiment on June 13, 1777, to take post at Van Veghten Bridge. It crossed the Raritan River between present-day Bound Brook and Manville, New Jersey. Washington wanted Morgan to attack any movement by the enemy. He had an idea to confuse the enemy by using some of the newly formed Corps of Rangers that were placed under Morgan's command. He told Morgan, "It occurs to me that if you were to dress a company or two of true woods men in the right Indian style and let them make the attack accompanied with screaming and yelling as the Indians do, it would have very good consequences especially if as little as possible was said, or known of the matter beforehand."[45]

Colonel William Patterson of the Lancaster County Pennsylvania Militia employed Gershom Hicks, a married man with two children, to go undercover in the disguise of an Indian. Patterson had Hicks supplied with a suit of Indian clothes. George Washington sent instructions to Colonel Zebulon Butler of the 2nd Connecticut

Regiment who was at Wyoming, Pennsylvania, Major Barnet Eichelberger, of the Pennsylvania militia, who was at Sunbury, Pennsylvania, and to the commanding officer at Fort Willis. They are to allow the bearer of Patterson's pass to "pass and repass [the lines] without interruption, and without search of their Canoes or baggage; they are farther to be supplied with five days provision on their applying for it; and you will afford them any other assistance their circumstances may require." Patterson's pass said:

> This will serve as passport for Gershom Hicks who may appear in Indian Dress, and the officer commanding will receive him.
>
> W[illiam] Patterson.
>
> 25th March, 1779.[46]

Gershom Hicks went up to Shamong where he met with a group of twenty-five whites under the command of a Sergeant and about thirty Indians.[47]

The British also sent soldiers in disguise. British Colonel John Simcoe led a raid from Staten Island to destroy Washington's boats that were being built at Van Veghten's Bridge and on Somerset Court House, New Jersey. Before reaching Somerset Court House and setting fire to the boats on October 28, 1779, Colonel Simcoe's corps was dressed to look like American Lieutenant Colonel George Baylor's Dragoons. They played the role so well they even drew rations and forage at an American army post.[48]

There were rumors that Russian soldiers had debarked on Staten Island.[49] Even General Charles Lee thought that Russians were going to be involved.[50] The British had been trying to obtain Russian mercenaries for some time; however, General Sir William Howe stated he heard that the deal was not accomplished due to the interference of the French.[51] Zechariah Hawkins,[52] innkeeper at Derby, is believed to have been the organizer of local raids on American stores at Derby and New Haven, Connecticut. Notably, the raiders were to wear green uniforms and be identified as Russians.[53]

In Europe, the French spy Beaumarchais went from France to England undercover using the name of Dr. Duval while wearing common clothes and a great wig as his disguise. Although not a change of clothes but a clothing deception of sorts was the four-month extended stay of Lewis J. Costigan in British-held New York City. Lieutenant Costigan of the 1st New Jersey Regiment was captured in January 1777.[54] He was placed on parole in New York City which allowed him to walk around the city in his Continental army uniform. He was exchanged on September 17, 1778, and no longer bound by his parole. At the request of Major General Lord Sterling and Colonel Matthias Ogden, Costigan did not leave New York City immediately as he should have. He continued his usual travels around New York City in plain sight in his American military uniform, collecting information and sending his correspondence through Colonel Ogden and Lord Sterling to George Washington using the code name of "Z."[55] If his espionage activities were to be discovered, he could not be treated as a spy since he was in uniform. He would have been a prisoner of war. He remained in New York City for four months until January 17, 1779. Costigan also went secretly back into New York City in April 1779 for three days and nights to collect intelligence.[56]

James Alexander used a disguise to aid in his act of revenge. Alexander had been a prisoner of loyalist Colonel James Grierson, who mistreated him. During the siege of Augusta, Georgia, Alexander decided to get his revenge. Alexander changed into a disguise and went into British-held Augusta. When Colonel Grierson had stepped out on to a balcony on a log house, James Alexander shot him to death.[57]

Cases of soldiers traveling in disguise were not unusual, although the nature of the disguise was often not described, but can be assumed to be some kind of civilian clothing. British Captain Alexander Campbell of the 62nd Regiment of Foot, a courier between Burgoyne and Sir William Howe and Sir Henry Clinton, is said to have been brought in disguise by a guide, Abraham Volwyder, to Albany.[58] Lieutenant William Clark in the 3rd New Jersey Volunteers moved in and out of the American lines in disguise for over five years until he was shot near Woodbridge, New Jersey, in 1782.[59]

Chapter 15

EUROPEAN SUBTERFUGE

D eception was an old game played in Europe. Finding the truth sometimes was like watching a game of three-card monte where the dealer or barker shows a card and then the victim or mark has to find the designated card. Behind what card is the truth? King George III and Prime Minister Lord North were able to silence their detractors by buying them off. The propaganda war in London was won at the cost of £200 a year. Henry Bate, the editor of *The Morning Post* newspaper, stopped being a critic of Prime Minister Lord North in exchange for some cash.[1] Bate was released from jail for libeling the King and received annual payments of £200 from the King's secret service fund.[2] King George wrote comments on closing out Lord North's secret services accounts that the worthless Mr. Bate had received £3,938.8.11.[3] When Alexander Wedderburn had made too vociferous an attack on the administration in favor of John Wilkes and liberty, he was offered the job of solicitor general in 1771 to quell his attacks. Wedderburn went from an opponent to one of the King's strongest supporters. It got him a promotion on June 11, 1778 to attorney general of England, a position he held until July 21, 1780. The month before in June 1780 he was made chief justice of the Court of Common Pleas with the title of Baron Loughborough. Lord North stated that Alexander Wedderburn had "the gift of accommodating conscience."[4] Junius wrote of him, "As for Mr [Alexander] Wedderburn, there is something about him which even treachery cannot trust."[5]

   John Bew, a bookseller, printer, publisher, and stationer at Paternoster Row, London, in 1777 published *Letters from General*

Washington, to several of his friends in the year 1776. In which are set forth a fairer and fuller view of American politics, than ever yet transpired, or the public could be made acquainted with through any other channel. It claimed to a collection of letters that purported to be from George Washington to friends and family in Virginia written in 1776. The fictitious letters attempted to lead the reader to believe that Washington had no confidence in the cause of American Independence and was discouraged. There was no way the English public could verify any of the statements in the letters. The rumor mills in England were always telling that Washington had been captured or killed and that the members of Congress were in disagreement over the war. The letters gave credence to the gossip of the day.

The purpose of the pamphlet was to assist the ministry by making the general public and Parliament believe that it would be an easy and quick war, thereby making it palatable to the English people. To help add credibility to the documents, Bew claimed to have received them from a friend serving with Brigadier General Oliver De Lancey Senior. This friend claims to have obtained the letters after the capture of Fort Lee, New Jersey, formerly known as Fort Constitution, on November 20, 1776.[6] The friend recognized an acquaintance among the prisoners; it was William Lee, George Washington's mulatto servant. The story says that William Lee had been left at Fort Lee because of his indisposition, which prevented him traveling with his master. The story says William Lee (also known as Billy Lee) had been entrusted with a small portmanteau that belonged to George Washington. Upon inspection it was found to contain some stockings, shirts, an almanac used as a journal from Washington's arrival in New York City, and some letters, which were the ones Bew published. It was reported that there was two letters from Martha Washington, one from Mr. Custis, some long ones from Mr. Lund Washington, who was George's cousin and lived at Mount Vernon, and drafts of responses to them.

The letters were clever forgeries written by someone who knew Washington's life in Virginia in detail. Washington did have a slave by the name of William Lee who was a boy purchased for £61.15 in 1768. William "Billy" Lee was Washington's constant companion during the war. Historian Worthington Chauncey Ford stated that

Washington had sent all his papers to Philadelphia in August 1776 to prevent them from falling into British hands. The public papers were not returned to him until after December 1776 thereby making it highly unlikely that any of his letters would have been available to fall into British hands at Fort Lee in New Jersey.[7]

John Bew's publication was reprinted by James Rivington, the royal printer in New York City. An ad appeared in the *Royal Gazette* of March 14, 1778, and lists a pamphlet of these letters and to which was added the letter of Reverend Jacob Duché, rector of Philadelphia's Christ Church, to George Washington which was delivered by Mrs. Ferguson.[8]

Tench Tilghman writing to his father told him, "the letters published under General Washington's signature are not genuine."[9] George Washington wrote to his boyhood friend Bryan Fairfax, son of William Fairfax, that the British "are practicing such low and dirty tricks, that men of sentiment and honor must blush at their villainy, among other maneuvers, in this way they are counterfeiting letters, and publishing them, as intercepted ones of mine to prove that I am an enemy to the present measures, and have been led into them step by step still hoping that Congress would recede from their present claims."[10]

Richard Henry Lee sent a copy of the pamphlet of forged letters to Washington on May 6, 1778. Lee states, "'Tis among the pitiful arts of our enemies to endeavor at sowing dissention among the friends of liberty and their country, with me, such tricks will never prevail."[11] Historian Worthington Chauncey Ford also quotes a letter Washington wrote to Richard Henry Lee on February 15, 1778, "I have seen a letter published in a handbill at New York, and extracts from it republished in a Philadelphia paper, said to be from me to Mrs. Washington, not one word of which did I ever write."[12]

Mathew Carey was the publisher of the *American Museum* and was going to publish a letter supposedly written by George Washington. Prior to publication in 1788, he contacted Washington to check the authenticity of the letter. Washington responded,

> Sir: In reply to yours of the 20th of this month, I have to observe, that the fragment of the letter in question, supposed to be written by me, is spurious, and that there was a

pamphlet containing a great many letters of the same
description, published in New York at the same time. It
should farther be observed, that this publication was made
soon after several of my letters were really intercepted with
the mail and that the pretended copies of them not only
blended many truths with many falsehoods, but were evidently written by some person exceedingly well acquainted
with my domestic and general concerns. Advantage was
adroitly taken of this knowledge to give the greater appearance of probability to the fiction. From these circumstances you will perceive, Sir, how prudently you have
acted in making an application to me previous to your
meditated republication. Otherwise I might have found
myself under the necessity of denying that they were genuine; from any apprehension, that, being thus preserved in
a manner under my eye and with my acquiescence, they
must have assumed the seal of veracity in the estimation of
posterity. For whatever credit some of those letters might be
thought to have done to my literary or political talents, I
certainly cannot choose to avail myself of the imposition.[13]

George Washington again had to address the issue of the spurious
letters. Once more he stated the letters were forgeries

with a view to attach principles to me which every action of
my life have given the lie to. . . . I never wrote, or ever saw
one of these letters until they issued from New York, in
print; yet the author of them must have been tolerably well
acquainted in, or with some person of my family, to have
given the names, and some circumstances which are
grouped in the mass, of erroneous details. But of all the
mistakes which have been committed in this business,
none is more palpable or susceptible of detection than the
manner in which it is said they were obtained, by the capture of my mulatto Billy, with a portmanteau. All the army,
under my immediate command, could contradict this; and
I believe most of them know, that no attendant of mine, or
a particle of my baggage ever fell into the hands of the
enemy during the whole course of the war.

Washington asked Benjamin Walker to contact James Rivington and find out who were the authors of the letters.[14]

The *Monthly Review or Literary Journal* of 1777 believed that the letters were faked.[15] The article states that the author was "a Mr. V___, then a young Episcopal clergyman, who came from New York, in order to make his fortune here, in the character of a loyalist." The person referred to was the Reverend John Vardill, who may have contributed to the penning of the letters but did not have the detailed information on Washington's life to be the sole source of the letters. Also the journal does not provide any source for the conclusion.[16]

William Carmichael was an assistant to Arthur Lee, one of the American commissioners. Carmichael was of Scottish ancestry and born at "Round Top" near Chestertown in Queen Anne's County, Maryland. He became an assistant to Arthur Lee when the war broke out. Lee had sent him to America by way of France and he had taken ill in Paris and remained there. He lived with Silas Deane and worked as his confidential secretary. Carmichael was not one to keep secrets or choose his friends wisely. Jacobus Van Zandt, a New Yorker and a British spy, was able to get information from Carmichael after plying him with alcohol "which sets him chatting like a madman and completely off his guard."[17] Carmichael and Joseph Hynson, a fellow Marylander who would become a British spy, had a very close friendship. Their mistresses even lived in the same building in London.[18] Lieutenant Colonel Edward Smith, a British spy, was told that Carmichael promised to "tell any little thing that you may wish to know" and he therefore made overtures to Carmichael.[19] Arthur Lee suspected Carmichael of being a British spy but he thought every one else was a British agent, including Dennis Deberdt, James Jay, John Langdon (a New Hampshire politician), William Molleson (a Maryland merchant), and Paul Wentworth. Arthur Lee was correct about Carmichael and Paul Wentworth. Charles Gravier, Count de Vergennes, the French Minister for Foreign Affairs, suggested that Carmichael was the source of information that had been leaked to the British, which led to his return to the United States in May 1778.

Carmichael gives us the insight as to the origination of the forged letters. He wrote to Charles W. F. Dumas, an American spy in Amsterdam, that "A junto of refugees from various parts of the [North American] continent, who meet daily in Pall Mall, London, to do this dirty work of government to earn the pittance but scantily afforded to each of them. At the head of this junto were [Thomas] Hutchinson, [Dr. Myles] Cooper, [Reverend Thomas Bradbury] Chandler, [John] Vassel, and others who would not be named but for their infamy. They have forged letters lately under the name of General [George] Washington, which the good, silly souls of Europe will swallow as genuine, unless contradicted in different gazettes."[20] Thomas Hutchinson was a former Royal Governor of Massachusetts from 1771 to 1774. Reverend Dr. Myles Cooper was an Anglican priest and President of King's College from 1763 to 1775. Reverend Dr. Thomas Bradbury Chandler, an Anglican priest, had been the rector at St. John's Church in Elizabeth Town, New Jersey. On May 10, 1775, he had taken refuge on the British warship *Kingfisher* (Captain James Montague) that was in New York harbor. On the 24th he left on the *Exeter* for Bristol, England, with Dr. Myles Cooper and Rev. Samuel Cook. John Vassal was a member of the Council for Massachusetts with residences in Boston and Cambridge, Massachusetts. None of the members of the junto identified was from Virginia and would not have known the very personal information included in the letters.

Other sources also indicated that the authors of the letters were believed to be John Randolph and Reverend John Vardill.[21] John Vardill was born in New York City in 1749 and graduated from King's College (now Columbia University) in New York City in 1766. He had been the assistant minister at Trinity Church in New York City and professor of Natural Law at King's College. He went to Oxford and received a master's degree in 1774. He wrote several loyalist pamphlets in New York using the pseudonym of "Poplicola" and in England "Coriolanus."[22] He became a spy for the British when he was promised a salary and a position as the King's professor of Theology when the rebellion ended. He was given an office at 17 Downing Street near the Prime Minister. He recruited and was the control agent for several spies. The British government rewarded him for his spy work with a £200 annual pension.[23] Vardill did not know Washington's personal background, however.

John Randolph of Williamsburg, Virginia graduated from the College of William and Mary, went to London in 1745 to study law at the Middle Temple in London, and returned to Williamsburg to practice law in 1749. He became the King's Attorney General in 1766

when he was just thirty-nine years old. A man of excellent literary culture and fashion, he had been a close friend of Virginia Governors
Francis Fauquier and Lord Botetourt. He left Virginia for England in
late 1775. His son Edmund stayed in Virginia, joined the American
army, and served as an aide-de-camp to General George Washington
from August 1775 to March 25, 1776.[24] John Randolph knew
Washington and his circle of friends extremely well. John "Jack"
Randolph knew Washington's personal information in more detail
than the other suggested authors and most likely was heavily involved
with the creation of the letters. Worthington Chauncey Ford says that
he observed a note on a New York copy of the letters in the handwriting of Pierre Eugène Du Simitière, a famous portrait painter at the
time of the American Revolution, that said, "Spurious: wrote in
London by Mr. Randolph of Virginia." However he does not tell us
where he saw this notation.[25]

George Washington never did find out for certain who created the
forged letters. However, he did have an opinion as to their author and
I believe he was correct. Tench Tilghman, secretary and aide to
Washington says that Washington "suspects Jack [John] Randolph for
the author, as the letters contain knowledge of his family affairs that
none but a Virginian could be acquainted with."[26]

The Americans also created fake letters. Some officer in the
American army who was up along the North (Hudson) River in a *jeu
d'esprit*, a lark, penned a factitious letter attributed to British General
Sir Henry Clinton. It was printed as a copy of an intercepted letter of
Sir Henry's. The fake letter gained credence and was believed to be
true for a period of time. John Adams says the letter first arrived in
Europe accompanying a letter of John Jay in a Philadelphia newspaper at L'Orient, France. Samuel Wharton sent a copy of the letter to
Benjamin Franklin who sent it on to Charles Dumas and to
England.[27] Dumas had arranged to have British General Clinton's letter printed. Dumas' friend John Luzac published the *Gazette de
Leyde* at Leiden United Provinces (Netherlands). Benjamin Franklin
was suspicious of the letter as "whether some parts of it were really
written by him [Clinton], yet I have no doubt of the facts stated, and
think the piece valuable as giving a true account of the State of British
and American affairs in that quarter. On the whole it has the appearance of a letter written by a general who did not approve of the expe-

dition he was sent upon who had no opinion of the judgment of those who drew up his instructions." The author of the letter never heard Franklin's opinion of his handiwork: "if not genuine it is ingeniously written."[28]

John Adams had sent a copy by Mr. Jennings to William Lee in Brussels. Lee adds to the story about copies that appeared in Dutch newspapers. A contradiction of its authenticity appeared in the *Gazette de Haye* which implied that the contradiction came from Sir Joseph Yorke, the British ambassador to the Netherlands.[29] The *Gazette de Leyde* agreed to a degree as to the letter being spurious.[30] This was followed by the *Courier du Bas-Rhin* published at Cleves, Wesel (Prussia), which originally assured its readers of it being authentic, was now back-pedaling as to its veracity. William Lee says the *Courier du Bas-Rhin* was considered one of two house organs of the Prussian government.[31] After the surrender of Charles Town, South Carolina, the *Courier du Bas-Rhin* published on June 24, 1780, that the letter of General Sir Henry Clinton was a fake. It said, "donc il vaut mieux se bien défendre et se bien battre, que de supposer des letters, qui ne peuvent abuser le public qu'un moment." (thus it is better to be well defended and to fight well, to suppose letters, which can deceive the public only one moment).[32]

Benjamin Franklin manipulated spies by planting misinformation which he knew could sway public opinion or meet his own purposes. One such instance occurred when he sent a report about a Hessian mutiny from Paris on May 1, 1777, to John Winthrop of Boston. Franklin stated,

> The conduct of those princes of Germany who have sold the blood of their people, has subjected them to the contempt and odium of all Europe. The Prince of Anspach [Christian Friedich Karl Alexander, Margrave of Brandenburg], whose recruits mutinied and refused to march, was obliged to disarm and fetter them and drive them to the sea side by the help of his guards; himself attending in person. In his return he was publicly hooted by mobs thro' every town he passed in Holland, with all sorts of reproachful epithets. The King of Prussia's humor of obliging those princes to pay him the same toll per head

for the men they drive thro' his dominions, as used to be paid him for their cattle, because they were sold as such, is generally spoken of with approbation; as containing a just reproof of those tyrants.[33]

John Thornton was secretary to Arthur Lee, American commissioner to France along with Benjamin Franklin at Paris. Thornton has also been a British spy since February 1777 reporting on naval matters, finances, and correspondence between France and Spain. He was paid by Thomas Lord Sydney at the rate of £100 per year which was raised to £200 for his British secret service activities. Thornton was able to deceive Arthur Lee with false military information while claiming to spy on the British.[34]

British General John Burgoyne had surrendered his army at Saratoga on October 17, 1777, and the prospects for a quick end to the war had evaporated. Lord North sent Paul Wentworth, who spoke perfect French, on a mission to Paris to direct the spy operations on site and to try to see if the American commissioners would accept a peace short of Independence. Wentworth had been recruited by William Eden, Under Secretary of State, as a secret agent in 1772. He sent his reports to Lord Eden and used numbers for people. Franklin was called "72." At the outbreak of the American Revolutionary War, Wentworth was given a salary of £500 per year and an expense account to provide information and recruit other Americans as secret agents.

Paul Wentworth's secret correspondence was accomplished in a mixture of both code and cipher. The agreed upon method was written out by Lord Suffolk on December 5, 1776.[35] His transposition cipher was:

a = o	g = u	n = b	t = h
b = p	h = v	o = c	u = i
c = q	i = w	p = d	w = k
d = r	k = y	q = e	x = l
e = s	l = z	r = f	y = m
f = t	m = a	s = g	z = n

Wentworth also had a codebook of which the following is a sample:

Alliance	1
Admiral	2
Ambassador	3
Amboy	4
Albany	5
America	7
Army	8

Wentworth also gave the tense of the words that he used. A horizontal line through a number such as ~~837~~ would indicate a future tense, a perpendicular line would indicate a past or past perfect tense, and no line would indicate the present tense. He also had eleven symbols at his disposal:

+ = and	= from	≈ = our	= = the, he
~ = to	ϴ = not	⁻⁻o = we	D = them
- = of	= I	o⁻⁻ = with	

Beaumarchais, whom the French Foreign Ministry employed to handle covert shipments to America, reported the arrival of Paul Wentworth. Charles Gravier, Count de Vergennes, the French Foreign Minister, had been trying to complete the negotiations with the American ambassadors and now a new player entered the contest. The French ministry suspected Wentworth of being a British spy and had his own servants spying on him.[36] Benjamin Franklin had refused to meet directly with Wentworth because it would cast doubts of his creditability with Vergennes. He had Silas Deane met with Wentworth instead. Franklin knew this information would cause Vergennes to pressure Louis XVI to make a deal with the Americans before they could come to terms with the British. Franklin knew that France did not want to see England and the Americas reunited. Deane rebuffed Wentworth's inquiry as to whether the Americans would agree to a peace without independence. Lord Stormont, British ambassador to France, had Wentworth accompany him to Versailles and presented him to Louis XVI under the cover of a wealthy businessman, which he was. Vergennes was unsure of what Wentworth's motives were. Wentworth was invited to dinner by Vergennes in order to check him out. Wentworth's elusiveness made Vergennes very uneasy. Franklin's ploy had worked. Wentworth tried again to see Franklin and again was put off.

Word from Spain was received on December 31, 1777, that Spain would not join France in a war with England. Franklin in order to turn up the heat on France agreed to a meeting with Wentworth on January 6, 1778. Paul Wentworth asked the same question of Franklin as he had asked Deane. Franklin's reply was that after the British had burnt towns and mistreated prisoners, the only condition for peace was independence. On January 7 Franklin was advised that the King's Council had met and voted to recommend to Louis XVI to accept both an alliance and a treaty of commerce with the new American states.

After Paul Wentworth's face-to-face negotiations with Benjamin Franklin, the French police shadowed him at the opera and other public places. Wentworth had a minder wherever he went and his friends shunned him because of all the attention he was attracting.[37] Vergennes had recently paid off the 40,000 livres debt of Jean Louis Favier and then convinced him to spy on Wentworth, his old friend. They had known each other from when Wentworth was an agent for the colony of New Hampshire in 1773 and 1774. Favier had passed Lord Stormont on the stairs to Wentworth's lodgings. Wentworth confirmed Lord Stormont's visit and that Wentworth had negotiations with Franklin. Favier passed the information on to Vergennes. Wentworth claimed that he had withdrawn from the negotiations because of the excessive American demands. Wentworth had offered to be a partner in Favier's financial speculations and invited him to dinner at his mistress' house in rue Traversière along with other ladies and gentlemen.[38]

On January 8, 1778, Conrad Alexandre Gérard, a secretary of the Count de Vergennes, personally visited the American commissioners and inquired what would it take for them to not listen to any more overtures from England. The commissioners had previously proposed to France a treaty of friendship and commerce. Gérard left the room to allow the commissioners to compose a response. Benjamin Franklin started to write out a reply. The commissioners were reading it when an impatient Gérard entered, was handed Franklin's answer, and agreed to the treaty. He advised them that the other questions could wait. Gérard then shook Franklin's hand and told him, "I am at liberty to tell you the treaty will be concluded." Paul Wentworth returned to London without the answer he had been sent to obtain. He had lost in this game of Spy vs. Spy.

Chapter 16

DECEPTIVE BATTLE PLANS

Deception in battle plans during the American Revolution carried the highest stakes—success if it worked and the greatest dangers if the strategy failed.

The United States and France signed a Treaty of Amity and Commerce on February 6, 1778. However, the expected French troops would not arrive in North America for two more years. Charles Louis d'Arsac, Chevalier de Ternay led a fleet of forty-four sail and 6,000 troops that left from Brest, France. On July 10, 1780, they arrived at Narragansett Bay, Newport, Rhode Island. The inhabitants were so overjoyed with their arrival they illuminated the town in celebration.[1] However it would be another year before the Comte de Rochambeau and the French army commenced offensive military operations.

After the Franco-American treaty, the British had switched to a southern strategy for the war. The British at the time held East Florida, which was a constant threat to Georgia and South Carolina. In March 1778 a British expedition under the command of British Lieutenant Archibald Campbell of the 71st Regiment of Foot (also known as Fraser's Highlanders) captured Savannah on December 29, 1778. In the fall of 1779 General Sir Henry Clinton, British commander in chief in North America, sailed from New York with an army of some 8,000 men. After a classic European siege the British captured Charles Town, South Carolina, the fourth largest city in the United States, on May 12, 1780. General Clinton received word of a possible combined American and French attack on New York City. Clinton left Charles Town and took 4,000 soldiers with him. General Lord Charles Cornwallis was left to command the British forces in the south.

Congress appointed Major General Horatio Gates as commander of the southern army. Congress was hoping for another Saratoga where General Gates had defeated British General John Burgoyne in the fall of 1777. When Gates joined his troops on July 25, 1780, the southern army consisted of 3,050 men of whom approximately half were regulars and the other half were militia from North Carolina and Virginia. General Cornwallis' decisive victory at the Battle of Camden, South Carolina, on August 16, 1780, resulted in an estimated 250 soldiers killed and 800 wounded, most of whom were captured. Alsatian-born Continental Major General Johann DeKalb who first came to America as a spy for France was mortally wounded and died on the 19th. Only about 700 men of the American southern army reached North Carolina in flight.[2]

Following the defeat, the command of the southern army was turned over to General Nathanael Greene. After taking command he orchestrated a masterful retreat before British General Lord Cornwallis' army. The retreat and the Battle of Guilford Courthouse on March 15, 1781, severely weakened the southern British army.

General Lord Cornwallis in a partially ciphered letter of May 5, 1781, to Lieutenant Colonel Banastre Tarleton tells that all his letters to General William Phillips were in the new cipher since he didn't have the old one.[3] That Cornwallis was having trouble getting intelligence information is clearly stated in his ciphered letter of May 8, 1781, from Crowell's plantation near the Tarr River, to Lieutenant Colonel Tarleton. Cornwallis instructs Tarleton to be "fixing every possible channel of intelligence at any price." Cornwallis' intelligence network was so deficient that he was unable to determine the location of British Major General William Phillips and his troops. In a ciphered letter of May 8, 1781, to Phillips, Cornwallis wrote, "I can learn no satisfactory accounts of you. . . . I wish to join you. . . . Let me hear from you at every possible opportunity."[4]

With a weakened army and tired of chasing American General Greene around the Carolinas, Lord Cornwallis decided to open a new phase of the war. He took his troops to Virginia. After attacking several American positions around Richmond and Petersburg, he eventually took a defensive position at Yorktown, Virginia.

Washington, who was at New Windsor, New York, on April 22, 1781, wanted to keep General Lafayette, who was in Virginia, informed of events, but "the accidents to which letters are liable, forbid me, unless I could write to you in cipher." Washington wanted to bring him up to date, "but I dare not attempt it in a common letter."[5] A month later Lafayette still did not have a cipher by which Washington could write to him "in safety, and [because] my letters have been frequently intercepted of late I restrain myself from mentioning many matters I wish to communicate to you."[6] Obviously this was not the way to be running an army at war.

General Lord Charles Cornwallis, a print made after a portrait by John Smart in 1786. (*William L. Clements Library*)

James Moody, a British spy who had been a resident of Sussex County, New Jersey, knew the routes through the mountains across northern New Jersey that the American express riders had to use to get General Washington's mail to the Continental Congress in Philadelphia and beyond. Moody was a man of patience who would hide out in the woods for days until the express riders arrived and then relieve them of their mail pouches.

On April 9, 1781, Washington's analysis of the army's situation was that "we are at the end of our tether, and that now or never our deliverance must come."[7] The army had experienced the reduction of 2,467 men because of the Pennsylvania Line mutiny.[8] There had been threats from the Massachusetts sergeants of a mutiny on January 17.[9] It was followed by the New Jersey Line mutiny, which had to be put down by force.[10] It was at this time that General George Washington and Lieutenant General Rochambeau learned that Admiral François Joseph Paul de Grasse was bringing a French fleet to the Caribbean.

Rochambeau and Washington agreed to a strategy meeting to be held on May 21 in Wethersfield, Connecticut.[11] Generals Du Portail, Knox, and Washington established their headquarters at the Joseph Webb House. The Comte de Rochambeau and his officers stayed at Stillman's Tavern. The two delegations met at the Webb House the next day. Washington wrote in his diary "fixed with Count Rochambeau the plan of campaign," which was a joint assault on New York.[12]

Washington wrote to John Sullivan on May 29, 1781, informing him that he had a meeting with Rochambeau at Wethersfield. Washington said he saw advantages to Sullivan's plan, which was an expedition against Canada. However he cites the lack of supplies as well as the "languid efforts of the states to procure men, and the insuperable difficulties in the way of transportation, would I apprehend, have rendered the scheme (however devoutly to be wished and desired) abortive in the first instance." Washington cites another reason "which makes the attempt you have suggested, *absolutely impracticable* with the means you propose, but which I dare not commit to paper, for fear of the same misfortune which has already happened to some of my letters."[13]

On May 31, 1781, George Washington wrote to the Marquis de Lafayette in Virginia: "Upon a full consideration of our affairs in every point of view, an attempt upon New York with its present garrison . . . was deemed preferable to a Southern operation as we had not the command of the water." The British with a superior naval force in the Chesapeake could force their way to General Cornwallis and extract his army from Virginia. The letter contained considerable detail on the proposed campaign, including the vital information that "above all, it was thought that we had a tolerable prospect of expelling the enemy or obliging them to withdraw part of their force from the Southward, which last would give the most effectual relief to those States."[14]

The letters to Colonel Elias Dayton at Chatham, New Jersey, May 28, to Sullivan on the 29th, and to Lafayette on the 31st were among thirteen letters, including some of George Washington's dispatches to Congress and correspondence of the French command, which were captured in Sussex County, New Jersey, by the British on 3 June.[15] British spy Moody arrived at Clinton's headquarters in New York City on the 4th with the captured mail and was rewarded by the elated Clinton with 200 guineas.[16] Frederick Mackenzie wrote in his diary, "The capture of this mail is extremely consequential, and gives the Commander in Chief the most perfect knowledge of the designs of the enemy."[17] Clinton was "elated" when he informed William Smith on the 6th of the capture.[18] General Sir Henry Clinton said this mail led him to adopt a "policy of avoiding all risks as much as possible, because it was now manifest that, if we could only persevere in escaping affront, time alone would soon bring about every success we could wish."[19] The reason the documents which identified an attack on New York were believed was because of the intercepted letter of May 29, 1781, from General Washington to Dr. John Baker his dentist. It requested "a pair of pincers to fasten the wire of my teeth." Washington also requested "scrapers as my teeth stand in need of a cleaning and I have little prospect of being in Philadelphia soon."[20]

Based upon the intercepted mail Sir Henry Clinton wrote to Lord George Germain on June 9, 1781, shortly after coming into possession of the above Washington letter: "I shall act offensively or defensively, as circumstances may make necessary. But by some lately intercepted dispatches . . . your Lordship will perceive that it is not likely the choice will be left to me for some months to come." Clinton estimated Washington's combined force as 20,000 men fit for duty and was convinced that his forces were very inadequate. "My present Force is 9997 rank and file fit for duty." However, he was "under no apprehensions, while our fleet is superior to that of the enemy and I can draw reinforcement from Chesapeake. For should it be otherwise, and the enemy command Long Island Sound, such force might be passed over into that Island, as might make our situation here more critical."[21] Clinton feared an attack on New York City from Long Island just as the British did in 1776. Should that be the case with an American and French combined fleet in command of the water around York (now Manhattan) Island and possession of Long Island and the Bronx, his army could be starved into submission.

Admiral de Grasse sailed on March 22 from Brest for the West Indies on the *Ville de Paris*. On June 8 Rochambeau learned of Admiral de Grasse's arrival in the Caribbean with his fleet of warships. It was agreed that de Barras would keep his small French fleet at Newport, Rhode Island and be ready to deploy. On June 13, Washington reminded Rochambeau, "Your Excellency will be pleased to recollect that New York was looked upon by us as the only practicable object under present circumstances; but should we be able to secure a naval superiority, we may perhaps find others more practicable and equally advisable."[22] Admiral de Grasse's message to

Rochambeau arrived on June 15 that he would be bringing the main French fleet to American waters as early as July 15. The focus of the military campaign was still to attack New York.

On June 18, the Bourbonnais regiment dressed in their uniform, which was white with black facings, departed Providence Rhode Island under the command of Marquis de Laval de Montmorency for their new encampment near the North River. They were followed by the Royal Deux Ponts on the 19th, the Soissonnois on the 20th, and the Saintonge on the 21st. Ezra Birch raised a company of teams to move the French army baggage and stores from New Town, Connecticut, to White Plains, New York.[23] When the French army detachments reached the Continental army at White Plains, the destitute appearance of the Continentals and the large number of blacks shocked the French. Upon arrival Rochambeau changed his opinion and believed that they would not be successful in their attempt to take New York. The problem facing the combined Continental and French armies was that the British had command of the seas. New York was an island and any French naval attempt to cross the bar off Sandy Hook would leave their ships open to fire from both the British ships positioned in Raritan Bay and a British battery on Sandy Hook. If the combined armies went south, General Cornwallis could escape to the sea. Neither of their options was going to work.

Sir Henry Clinton believed that the French navy was going to connect with its troops already on land. He had advised Sir George Brydges Rodney on June 28, 1781, that "De Grasse [has] intention of coming here during hurricane months, and that this post [New York City] will be his first object."[24]

George Washington at Dobbs Ferry on July 21, 1781, wrote to Jean-Louis Aragon de Sibille and thanked him for translating his letter to Lieutenant General D'armée Navale du Roi Comte de Grasse and ciphering parts of it. De Sibille was the secretary and interpreter to the Comte de Rochambeau. Washington stressed that it was important to keep its contents a secret.[25] Washington's letter to de Grasse gave information on the junction of the American and French armies and their strength as well as that of the British. It also told what the plan of operations would be.[26] The enciphered letter was sent to Brigadier General David Forman of the New Jersey militia. Forman was instructed to have lookouts at the heights of the Navesink in

Monmouth County near Sandy Hook. Forman was to deliver the enciphered letter upon the arrival of the French fleet and to establish a chain of expresses for quick communications from the Monmouth coast to George Washington at Dobbs Ferry, New York.[27]

While Washington was contacting De Grasse, Oliver De Lancey ordered Lieutenant Colonel Edmund Eyre on July 29, 1781, to send people from his post to gather intelligence. He wanted them to go toward Sneden's Ferry and find out if any troops had crossed the Hudson River.[28] Eyre immediately gave the assignment to Thomas Ward, who that day left for Bergen County and sent two men toward Kings Ferry.[29] He took a command of 150 men with some of them on horseback and a brass cannon and followed behind them as far as Liberty Pole. He reported that he sent for a very intelligent person whom he had understood to be at Kings Ferry on the 28th. This person advised him that there were no troops at King's Ferry nor had there been for some time. He had seen heavy cannons and mortars on the move from West Point toward White Plains. This person further advised that he was not allowed to cross at Dobbs Ferry but made to cross at Kings Ferry, and that there were rumors of a siege of New York and an attack on Fort Lee, New Jersey He also stated that George Washington reconnoitered Fort Lee in disguise. Ward said that intelligence from another informant, who says he got his information from Colonel Dayton, reported that an attack was planned on Fort Lee.[30]

Washington sent Connecticut native Sergeant Daniel Bissell of the 2nd Connecticut Regiment into New York posing as a deserter to gather intelligence on August 14, 1781. While in New York Bissell became ill. The only way he could get medical attention was to enlist in the British army. It was months before he could get out of a British hospital. He found himself a supply sergeant and was not able to make his escape to safety in Newark, New Jersey until 1782.[31]

De Grasse and his fleet of ships of the line departed Cape François on August 5.[32] De Grasse decided he was going to the Chesapeake Bay and would stay in the local waters no later than October 15 due to the hurricane season. August 14 was a day of cool temperature but filled with hot news. A vessel that had come into New York City during the night from the Chesapeake in fifty hours reported that Lord Cornwallis had taken post at Yorktown, Virginia. It was on this day that Rochambeau and Washington learned of de Grasse's new plan of going to the Chesapeake with all his ships and troops.[33] De Grasse had changed the game . The plan of an assault on New York could not be executed without the French fleet, and they were not coming to New York. The new campaign would be to take the combined American and French armies to Virginia and lay siege to Cornwallis' army. The combined French fleets of de Grasse and de Barras, who would sail from Newport to the Chesapeake, would be used to close the avenue of escape by the sea for General Cornwallis. Washington sent a dispatch to General Lafayette and set the orders for expedited communications with the south. He told Samuel Miles,

> If there is a chain of expresses established, that the con-
> veyance may be depended upon in the shortest conceivable
> time, you will have them instantly forwarded by that mode.
> If there is no such establishment, I must request you will
> forward the letter immediately by a trusty, active express,
> with orders to ride night and day and to call on the magis-
> trates, or military officers for horses and assistance, and to
> deliver the letter to the Marquis at the earliest possible peri-
> od. You will be pleased to acknowledge the receipt of this,
> noting the moment when it comes to hand, and informing
> me of the mode of conveyance by which you have expedit-
> ed the dispatches for the Marquis [de Lafayette].[34]

Because of the change in targets, General Washington decided to use what in modern times would be called the "deception battle plan." The approach has five elements: (1) clear objective, (2) known enemy assumptions, (3) method selection (operational options), (4) execution, and (5) exploitation.

The first step in running a successful deception battle plan is to have a clear objective of what you are going to do and what you want the enemy to do. During World War II, British Lieutenant General Frederick E. Morgan in the spring of 1943 became chief of staff to the Supreme Allied Commander and responsible for planning the invasion of northwestern Europe. The objective was to make a land-ing in France and establish a beachhead. There were only two acceptable beaches that were within range of Allied air cover and close to England. They were the Pas de Calais and Normandy.

Morgan wanted the Germans to concentrate their efforts at the wrong beach, the Pas de Calais. They also wanted the Germans to hold their Panzer tanks in reserve in the rear waiting for the attack at the Pas de Calais. The misleading approach gave the Allies the advantage. During the Operation Desert Storm, General H. Norman Schwarzkopf Jr. used the deception battle plan in liberating Kuwait from Iraq. The objective was to move Iraq's best-trained troops, the Republican Guard, so that Schwarzkopf would turn their flank and attack across the desert. Schwarzkopf wanted them to be defending the two obvious choices of approach: the Shatt al Arab waterway (Arvand River) and the route north from Saudi Arabia into Kuwait.

General George Washington's objective was to quickly take the combined American and French armies across New Jersey by stealth in order to avoid being attacked by the British during their march. If he could get his forces to Pennsylvania, they would be too far ahead for the British forces in New York to prevent them from going to Virginia. Once in Virginia they would combine with Lafayette's troops and soldiers from the French fleet for an attack on General Cornwallis. The second part of his objective was that he needed a specific plan for British General Sir Henry Clinton. He knew exactly what he wanted Clinton to do: keep the crown forces in New York and out of New Jersey. Washington's objective met the first element of the deception battle plan.

The second part of the deception battle plan is to know the enemy's assumptions. In World War II, the Germans knew there was going to be a landing at either the Pas de Calais or Normandy. They believed that it would be at the Pas de Calais. It would have been their choice as it was a shorter route between England and France and the men would be exposed to enemy attack on the English Channel for a shorter period of time. The German military operations up to this point in the war had been quick moving strokes and the Pas de Calais would fit that modus operandi. The Allies needed to help convince the Germans that their assumption was correct. In Desert Storm, the Iraqis had recently completed a war with Iran over the crucial Shatt al Arab waterway. They thought this was the key target. It was an important channel for oil exports of both Iran and Iraq. To them an attack across the desert in the west was the least likely plan. This repositioning of the Republican Guard allowed General Schwarzkopf to run what he called his "Hail Mary," a reference to a long distance throw in American football. General Schwarzkopf wanted to attack across the desert and assault the Republican Guard from their rear.[35]

In the American Revolution British General Clinton was already predisposed to think that the combined American and French troops were going to attack New York. British General Frederick Haldimand at Quebec had earlier that year been reporting that the American campaign plan for 1781 was to attack either Canada or New York City. Haldimand, using intelligence he received, informed Clinton that there was not going to be an attack on Canada that year but New York was the objective. Clinton also had the American mail that was intercepted in early June that confirmed that the objective was a combined American and French attack on New York. His spies were telling him the same story, that New York City was the campaign objective for the combined American and French armies. About a month earlier the British were able to intercept a report from Stewart, rebel commissary which stated that he gave out 8,000 rations. This led Clinton to believe that Washington had at least 5,000 men with him. Clinton stated that the ministers in England were always ready to believe the lowest estimates of Washington's forces.[36] Washington's plan was to let Clinton continue to believe what he already held to be true: that New York was where the attack would occur. He had to make the deception fit Clinton's assumptions.

If Clinton held the belief that New York would be attacked then he would not venture his forces into New Jersey to fight the combined American and French forces. Clinton was busy preparing to defend New York, waiting for an attack that would never come. He had the Hessian Grenadiers busy fixing "the fort at Hell Gate for the defense of that passage from the [Long Island] Sound."[37] Sir Henry Clinton stated that "had they [the combined American and French forces] intended New York an attempt upon Staten Island was probable and if it succeeded we should have been in a scrape."[38] A person by the name of Hamilton who came into New York City from the Clove (also known as the Ramapo Pass) on Tuesday August 28 told of seeing both Rochambeau and Washington with their armies at Paramus on Saturday. He said the men talked of an attack on Staten Island but he believed they were going southward.[39] Another report came in on Friday night that American and French armies were in motion.

Captain George Beckwith in New York reported the information from an unidentified person from Hackensack who was the previous day (August 20, 1781) in the company of American Major John Mauritius Goetschius of the Bergen County New Jersey Militia that the American troops were on their way to Baltimore, Maryland.[40] Beckwith later on the 21st reported that the informant is a near relative of "Captain Sobriscoes" (Zabriskie?) and was reliable. Captain Beckwith advised that if they were going to Delaware, they would go by way of the Newark Mountains and if their goal was Staten Island then they will go to Elizabeth Town and "Gen[era]l [Cortland] Skinner will of course have it in his power to clear up this matter this night."[41] The talk among the Hessians was that the combined American and French forces "have gone for Rhode Island [and] others think they are both crossed the North River."[42] If they had gone to Rhode Island, they could be preparing to attack eastern Long Island.

On August 18 the 54th Regiment of Foot was brought from Paulus Hook back to New York City and camped with the 38th Regiment of Foot. On the 19th the British were moving more units into consolidated positions. Dresden-born John Charles Philip von Krafft said that "all these changes led us to anticipate, a few days hence, some as yet unknown expedition" by General Clinton. On the 23rd the Hessian troops knew that the American and French armies were somewhere in New Jersey. On Saturday night of August 25, the 57th Regiment of Foot marched from Laurel Hill and was sent to Staten Island.[43] On the 26th, the 42nd Regiment of Foot (the Black Watch) was sent to Bedford and the Hessian Grenadiers were sent to Denyce's Ferry at the Narrows where they could quickly be sent to Staten Island.[44] On the 29th, the Hessian Grenadiers, 37th, 42nd, and 54th Regiments of Foot were all placed on orders to be ready to move.[45] On September 4 orders were sent to the 17th, 37th, 42nd, and 43rd Regiments of Foot and the English Light Infantry, Grenadiers, Hessian Grenadiers, Yagers, the Body regiment, Prinz Carl, and the Garrison regiment of Bienau to be ready to embark.[46]

The British were always sending out spies to try and determine Washington's next step. The British had a heightened interest in the activities of the American and French armies to determine when the attack would occur. They needed to know if the attack would come at King's Bridge at the north end of York Island. Would the assault on

New York come from Long Island or Staten Island? The answers that the spies would bring back would determine the course of action for the British defense. On Saturday evening August 18, William Sproule and Jacob Browers proceeded three miles above Paramus and discovered that the French were on the march to Philadelphia and were currently between the Clove and Paramus.[47] Ezekiel Yeomans, who had been a resident of Kakiat in Orange now Rockland County, New York, returned to the British lines late on the night of August 23 and filed his report on the 24th that the greatest part of Washington's army had passed to the west side of the Hudson River and that the rumor was that they were going to Philadelphia.[48] However these reports only partially met the preconceived ideas at British headquarters. It was believed that if Staten Island was the target, the American and French armies would move south as if headed to Philadelphia, and then turn or come back to make the assault. Both sides had crossed the Arthur Kill which separates New Jersey and Staten Island to accomplish their military objective in the past. The British had made numerous raids from Staten Island into New Jersey in which they attacked Elizabeth Town and Newark. They also crossed prior to the Battle of Springfield. Lieutenant Colonel John Simcoe in 1779 crossed to Perth Amboy before making his raid at Somerset Court House. The Americans had attacked Staten Island before. General Nathanael Greene led 600 men on a raid on Staten Island. General John Sullivan staged a raid on Staten Island on August 22, 1777. The most recent was a raid the previous winter.[49] Naturally the locals in New York City were worried about an attack from the combined American and French forces. The scuttlebutt was that General Clinton was unprepared should there be an attack on New York City in force.[50]

The third part of a deception battle plan is the method selection. In other words, what options are available and what will be used. In World War II there was "FUSAG," a totally fictional First United States Army Group that was located in England poised for a landing at the Pas de Calais. The army was equipped with fake rubber balloon tanks, a small detachment of real soldiers, constant radio traffic, and inflatable landing craft. German prisoners of war who were being released through the Swedish Red Cross were "accidentally" (on purpose) allowed to see some of the staged activities of FUSAG which they then reported back to German command. The clincher was assigning American General George S. Patton to command FUSAG. The Germans believed that Patton was the most aggressive of the Allied generals and he would have been their choice to lead the landing. In Scotland another army was practicing for winter mountain warfare. It indicated a possible assault across the North Sea to German-occupied Norway. Because of the threat to Norway, possible German reinforcement for France had to stay and defend Norway. In the Mediterranean there was the threat of an Allied attack on the Balkans. It kept more possible reinforcements away from the scene of the action. The Allies were able to convert a group of German spies into double agents. The double agents in England sent back to Germany information about the plans for a landing at Pas de Calais, which is what the Germans wanted to hear.

During Desert Storm, Marines were practicing amphibious landings while American naval vessels searched the water for mines in preparation for a landing. As in World War II, false and high volume radio traffic was used to reinforce the Iraqi military's preconceived ideas of where the Allied forces were and what they were planning. During Desert Storm, a new possibility was available. General Schwarzkopf manipulated the information that was provided to the television news reporters. These reports were used to further convince the Iraqis that their assumption of the Allied plan was correct.

During the American Revolution the operation was on a smaller scale but Washington did have options available to him in running his deception. Washington writing after the war says, "much trouble was taken and finesse used to misguide and bewilder Sir Henry Clinton in regard to the real object, by fictitious communications [letters], as well as by making a deceptive provision of ovens, forage and boats in his neighborhood, is certain." Washington intentionally deceived his own men as to what was the objective. "Nor were less pains taken to deceive our own army; for I had always conceived, when the imposition did not completely take place at home, it could never sufficiently succeed abroad."[51] Dr. James Thacher wrote in his journal that "Our destination has been for some time matter of perplexing doubt and uncertainty; bets have run high on one side, that we were to occupy the ground marked out on the Jersey shore, to aid in the siege of New York, and on the other, that we are stealing a march on the enemy, and are actually destined to Virginia, in pursuit of the army under Lord Cornwallis."[52] Washington had previously made marches under the cover of darkness to make an escape. After the Battle of Long Island, he moved the army across the East River at night in August 1776 to escape annihilation by General Howe. On January 2, 1777, he escaped from Trenton and General Cornwallis and proceeded to engage the enemy at Princeton the next day.

Washington had to make things for Clinton to see to feed his opponent's assumptions; but they could not be obvious or Clinton would realize it was a deception. He could then run a counter-deception and set a trap for Washington. General Clinton could also re-float the pontoon bridge. The British army had used the pontoon bridge across the Schuylkill River on December 10, 1777, to span a distance of 434 feet. It was also used at Spuyten Duyvil Creek (also known as Spiking Devil and Spijt den Duyvil) across a span of 160 feet.[53] It was used a third time in June 1780 to bring British soldiers quickly across from Staten Island to make a push on the American stronghold at Morristown. It resulted in the Battle of Springfield on June 23, 1780. Washington did not want to fight a battle in New Jersey as he wanted to get the troops to Virginia as fast he could. Washington had very little time to implement his plan. He had to move the army to the south as fast as he could to ensnare Cornwallis at Yorktown, Virginia, before the French fleet departed.

Washington said he used fictitious communications during this deception. A story of false mail during this time period concerned a young Baptist clergyman by the name of Montagnie. Washington had instructed him to carry the mail by crossing over at Kings Ferry and then go by way of Haverstraw and the Ramapo Pass (also known as the Clove) to Morristown. The Ramapo Pass was an area with a high probability of his being intercepted by a loyalist. As Montagnie feared, he was caught and relieved of the mail he carried that indicated a plan of attack on New York City. He was taken to New York and confined in a sugar house.[54] Washington in furthering his plan of deception sent detachments to repair the road toward King's Bridge and the northern end of York Island as if preparing to attack that post.[55]

In order to ensure secrecy Washington decided to have Brigadier General Chevalier Louis Le Bègue de Presle du Portail sent to General Lafayette in Virginia to personally inform Lafayette of the army coming to Virginia to engage British General Cornwallis.[56] This way there would be no chance of a letter being intercepted by the British or the leakage of information through gossip in camp which would be picked up by British spies.

One of the extremely important methods available to Washington was to feed misinformation to spies. Misinformation could stop your enemy from attacking by making your army appear larger than it was, as Washington did at Morristown in 1777. Misinformation could keep your enemy from leaving its fortifications because of a fear of being attacked by a phantom army. Washington wanted British General Sir Henry Clinton to fear an attack by the combined American and French armies and the soon-to-arrive French fleet.

Washington noted in his diary On August 19, "French bakery to veil our real movements and create apprehensions for Staten Island."[57] In the French army, bread was a significant part of their diet. Building bake ovens for the French army indicated that the French planned to be in the area for an extended period of time as if they were expecting to conduct a siege. George Washington on August 19 gave orders to Colonel Elias Dayton to take the New Jersey Continental Line and Moses Hazen's 2nd Canadian Regiment to march and take post on the heights between Chatham and Springfield for the purpose of covering the French bakery at Chatham, New Jersey. Dayton was to supply this small guard for the bakery to veil Washington's real intention and create British trepidation for Staten Island.[58] The French bakery was built on the Passaic River at Chatham. Rochambeau wrote that the ovens were to supply the French army on the march.[59] As part of the deception strategy preparations for ovens were also to be made for the army near Sandy Hook.[60]

Jonathan Trumbull, Jr., one of George Washington's aides-de-camp, noted in his journal on August 21, "French ovens are building at Chatham in [New] Jersey. Others [ovens] were ordered to be prepared at a place near the Hook [Sandy Hook, New Jersey]. Contracts are made for forage to be delivered immediately to the army on their arrival at the last mentioned place. Here it is supposed that batteries are to be erected for the security and aid of the fleet, which is hourly expected. By these maneuvers and the corresponding march of the troops, our own army no less than the enemy are completely deceived."[61]

As early as August 15 it was planned for a detachment to go to Perth Amboy to collect the bricks for the ovens for Chatham.[62] There was an artillery post at the Billopp's House on Staten Island opposite Perth Amboy that observed the activities in the city. Collecting the bricks at Perth Amboy would insure that the task would be seen by the artillerists at the Billopp House on Staten Island who would send the information to British Headquarters. British General Sir Henry Clinton believed that the enemy forces taking position at Chatham were a threat to Staten Island.[63]

As part of his deception strategy George Washington had thirty boats built in the North (Hudson) River. The boats were mounted on carriages and taken in the line of march. The British army had two armed boats patrolling the North River.[64] If a British spy saw the boats on the carriages on the march on the west side of the North River, the spy would report back to British headquarters that some amphibious operation was involved. This would feed Clinton's idea of a water assault on either York or Staten Islands. In June intelligence had been received in New York City that carriages were being built on the Hudson River north of New York.

The fourth element, execution, is actually carrying out the deception. During World War II, planes dropped chaff which simulated on radar a large fleet of ships approaching the Pas de Calais. The planes dropped both real and dummy parachutists, which resulted in the German army spending their time trying to track down real and fake soldiers. The Allied army landed at Normandy and was able to establish a beachhead and move inland before the Germans realized there was no landing at the Pas de Calais. The deception plan worked as it kept the Germans holding their forces in reserve waiting for an attack at the Pas de Calais that never happened. In Operation Desert Storm the Iraqis were waiting for a northern strike from the east that never took place. General Schwarzkopf was able to execute his "Hail Mary" play so successfully that the army advanced 100 miles in 100 hours and liberated Kuwait City.

During the American Revolution the Americans on August 19 began their march to the south from the camp at Phillipsburg, New York.[65] The lack of horses and bad condition of the horses in the French army was part of the reason for delaying the departure until the 19th.[66] Intelligence of the French army's movements reached the

British in New York City on the 20th.[67] On the same day the troops arrived at Kings Ferry and crossed the Hudson River. Washington crossed in the evening after supper and lodged at the White House. While there Washington wrote several letters to the states but did not send them. He wanted to keep the real operation he was running a secret as long as possible. If he sent the letters, they might be intercepted, or upon delivery the information might make its way to a British spy and be forwarded to British headquarters in New York City. One of the letters was to Governor William Livingston of New Jersey requesting that the state raise 500 militiamen.[68] Washington while at Philadelphia on September 3 would write to the governors of Delaware, Maryland, and New Jersey advising them of the movement of the armies going to Virginia and asking if he could rely on them for supplies for the armies moving south.[69]

Because of the deception, all of Washington's discussions about where they were going were focused on Staten Island and Sandy Hook. By keeping the deception a secret even from most of the officers and all of the enlisted men, Washington reduced the chance of an accidental leak of the deception and the real plan to British spies, who were always about.

On August 21 Washington instructed Colonel Sylvanus Seely, Morris County New Jersey Militia, that he was to follow the directions of General Benjamin Lincoln. Seely was to proceed to Connecticut Farms when Lincoln's troops marched for Springfield. Seely was to remain there and keep constant patrols on the Arthur Kill "as far as [Perth] Amboy till the French Army has passed Princeton and then act under the orders he may receive from Governor [William] Livingston."[70] Seely is to keep a vigilant lookout both by land and water toward York Island. He is to forward to Washington anything he sees or any intelligence from there that is important to send to him by express.[71] Washington wanted to be certain that British General Sir Henry Clinton was not running his own deception battle plan and letting Washington walk into a trap.

On August 24, Washington began calling out troops in Delaware and Pennsylvania to be ready to march; he also instructed Brigadier General David Forman of the Monmouth County militia to continue to observe the British fleet at Sandy Hook.[72] Washington needed to know the moment they left the Hook to head to Virginia to extract Lord Cornwallis and his army.[73]

To find out if his deception was working, Washington wrote to Elias Dayton on August 24 and instructed him "to use your best endeavors to obtain intelligence from York and Staten Island, that we may know what effect our late movements have produced; ascertain the strength of the enemy on Staten Island; and whether any troops have arrived from Virginia. What boats could, on an emergency, be procured between New Ark [Newark] and [Perth] Amboy for transporting troops if they should be required." He even directed that he wanted any expresses that Dayton would send to "come from Chatham by the two bridges at the fork, to Pompton and thence along the common road to this place [Kings Ferry]."[74]

On the 27th Colonel Sylvanus Seely of the New Jersey militia received the orders to begin his march from Dobbs Ferry. He was to go by way of New Bridge through Acquacknack to Springfield.[75] Once at Springfield he was to take orders from Major General Benjamin Lincoln.[76] Colonel John Lamb with his 2nd Continental Artillery Regiment and the Rhode Island regiment were to go to Chatham by way of Pompton.[77] The design of the combined American and French armies' movements started to circulate among some of the French officers on the 27th.[78]

Philip van Cortlandt was instructed to take boats to Springfield and report to General Benjamin Lincoln.[79] In all, thirty boats were mounted on carriages and transport to enhance the deception strategy as a preparation for the attack on Staten Island. On August 28 Washington informed van Cortlandt, "As the army will march tomorrow morning before you probably have arrived, you will be pleased when you reach Colonel Cook's to make yourself acquainted with the best road leading above the [Watchung] mountains towards Trenton, this you will pursue at least to Bound Brook, and from thence will continue the most direct route to Trenton, with your regiment and all the stores and other articles which have been committed to your charge. You will keep your destination a perfect secret for one or two days at least."[80] Washington was not going to allow the march of the army to Virginia to be slowed. He detested the practice of impressing supplies from the public as it created disgruntled individuals if not enemies. He instructed Colonel Timothy Pickering, quartermaster general, "In all cases on the present march, where the draught horses or cattle of the army shall fail, or where an additional number shall be

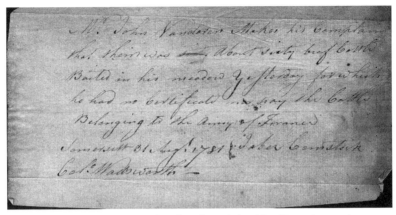

The French army grazed 60 beef cattle in John Van Doren's meadow near Somerset, New Jersey, while on the march to Yorktown in August 1781. This letter states that Van Doren complained on August 31, that he neither received a certificate nor pay for his loss. (*Private Collection*)

absolutely necessary, and cannot be procured by hire, or in any other way, except by military force; you are hereby authorized and directed to impress such numbers of horses or oxen as shall be required to perform the public service, taking care to have it done in such a manner, as to secure the property of the owners as well, and with as little damage and inconveniency as the circumstances will admit."[81]

On August 27, Washington advised Colonel Samuel Miles, deputy quartermaster general who was at Philadelphia, to get watercraft together at Trenton "in consequence of a total alteration in our plans, and the movement of a large body of troops to the southward." These vessels were for taking the troops to Christiana, which is now known as Wilmington, Delaware. "I have delayed having these preparations made until this moment, because I wished to deceive the enemy with regard to our real object as long as possible, our movements have been calculated for that purpose and I am still anxious the deception should be kept up a few days longer, until our intentions are announced by the army's filing off towards the Delaware."[82]

Also on the 27th Washington wrote from Chatham to Congress that he would be in Philadelphia in a few days with a "very considerable detachment of the American army and the whole of the French troops for Virginia."[83]

In New York the men of the Hesse-Cassel Jaeger Corps believed "Washington plans to attack New York" except Colonel von Wurmb. The colonel had been given the authority to employ spies. His spies reported that "the commissary had ordered forage and bread as far as Trenton and along the Delaware River; an American woman, mistress of a distinguished French officer, was sent to Trenton, where she is to await the arrival of the army."[84] It is believed this woman was the mistress of Donatien Marie Joseph de Vimeur, Vicomte de Rochambeau, who was the son of Jean-Baptiste Donatien de Vimeur, Comte de Rochambeau. She had followed the French troops to New York from Rhode Island.

When a deception strategy is used, there is always the possibility of a counter-deception. Washington's intelligence was that the British "have been throwing Troops upon Staten Island."[85] He had to wonder if the British had discovered his deception and were preparing to attack his troops while on the march; on the other hand, perhaps they had bought his deception strategy and were preparing to defend Staten Island. Only time would tell. British General Sir Henry Clinton was running a minor deception of his own at the time. He had arranged for a sham deserter to deliver to Rochambeau a letter from Chatelleux which cast uncertainty on Rochambeau. The sham deserter went as a friend to Rochambeau. Clinton was hoping to upset the French chain of command. Clinton noted that the sham deserter was sent back to obtain more information.[86]

When Washington knew he was taking the bulk of the army south to Virginia, he had prepared letters to the governors informing them of the repositioning of the army in Virginia but delayed sending the letters until the last possible moment. Now that he had arrived at Trenton and could no longer keep his intentions hidden, he sent the letters on August 29 to General Heath to be distributed.[87]

When the French troops reached Pompton on the 26th, Rochambeau sent Jacques Pierre Orillard de Villemanzy, the French commissary of war orders, to work on establishing the bakers' ovens and to bring up supplies for the ovens.[88] "He was let into the secret and told that it was our intention to nourish the army from that bakery in its march to Philadelphia." Villemanzy was instructed that they needed to convince the enemy that the design was for an attack on Staten Island. "He did so well with this that he caused himself to be fired upon by the English batteries [on Staten Island, New York] in trying to collect the bricks which were at the mouth of the Raritan [Perth Amboy, New Jersey]."[89] On the 29th, Washington assured Antoine Charles du Houx, Baron de Viomenil, that a subaltern and twenty-five militia men had been ordered to protect the bakery and four hundred men would be nearby.[90] Washington had issued instructions ten days earlier to Colonel Elias Dayton to accomplish this task.[91]

Comte de Rochambeau painted from life in 1787 by John Trumbull. (*William L. Clements Library*)

Oliver De Lancey had heard that a body of troops were moving to Newark and ordered Major Thomas Ward, commanding the Loyal Refugee Volunteers at Bergen Neck, New Jersey, to send out as many people as he could to find out what was happening.[92] Ward sent two men (David Demaree and Green) to Smith's Clove in what is now Rockland County and two other men to Newark. Ward advised that the men had difficulty getting to Newark and were due back shortly. Because of the delay in getting the men over, he also sent out John Moore the previous night, the 23rd, into New Jersey. Ward stated that Moore was able to pass among the rebel troops without being detected, which would lead us to believe that he had done this type of espionage work before.[93]

Washington wrote in his diary for August 29, 1781: "The whole [army] halted as well for the purpose of bringing up our rear as because we had heard not of the arrival of Count de Grasse and was unwilling to disclose our real object to the enemy." He wrote on the "30th as our intentions could be concealed one march more. Idea of marching to Sandy Hock to facilitate the entrance of the French fleet within the bay."[94] Washington allowed this rumor to circulate that they were going to help the French fleet get over the bar. He had already put out the rumor of building batteries for that purpose.[95] It was one lie verifying another lie. Washington was using all his operational options.

Colonel Sylvanus Seely, commander of the three-month militia, had received private information from New York by a spy that told of Admiral Graves departing New York from Long Island where he took on board Grenadiers. Writing from Connecticut Farms, New Jersey he advised that he asked his person to try and get the names of the ships that sailed and what regiments they carried.[96] Colonel Sylvanus Seely was sent on patrol to Perth Amboy to observe the British and reported no major activity on September 10. Seely, the farmer, innkeeper, and storekeeper, noted in his diary the sailing of a British fleet on September 18.[97] It was the return of the British fleet under Admiral Thomas Graves from the Battle of the Virginia Capes. Seely reported to General Washington on October 14 the British fleet were making the greatest preparation to sail. The fleet had assembled at the watering place off of northeastern Staten Island. From his spy he reported: "the British officers say that they mean to lay the French onboard and by their being so well manned they expect to over power them."[98] Seely was still on post at Connecticut Farms when he reported the British fleet of twenty-four ships with two to three thousand troops finally sailed from Sandy Hook about 10 a.m. on October 17.[99]

George Knox, a former brevetted captain in the 9th Pennsylvania Regiment, resigned his commission on April 20, 1780, and took up residence at Newark, New Jersey.[100] Lieutenant Knox was brevetted a captain by Congress on July 26, 1779 for his heroism that he displayed in leading the forlorn hope at Stony Point "braving danger and death".[101] The forlorn hope were the first soldiers to attack a fortified position with a very high mortality rate and very few survivors.

Knox entered the refugee post at Bergen Neck on September 4th "to offer his services to government in the military line." Knox on September 5, 1781 told the story that Washington was below Philadelphia, which the British knew to be true, and took only 600 to 900 men with him, which the British knew to be false, and that the New England troops were about the Highlands under General Heath. Knox was suspected of being an American spy and was taken prisoner. He was delivered to Joshua Loring, British commissary of prisoners. Knox then wanted to be placed on parole in order to arrange an exchange, and if he could not then he claimed he would sell his estate and come to New York with his family.[102]

British headquarters were concerned with what Washington was doing. Where they still going to attack New York? The bake ovens were at Chatham indicating a prolonged assault on New York. Was Washington's trip southward a diversion? Was he going to double back? They began to send some of their spies in the field to gather the intelligence to determine what was the real plan. Nehemiah Marks was requested to intercept the dragoon that carried the American dispatches. He advised Oliver De Lancey on September 4, 1781, that he needed three men to man his boat if he was to send two volunteers, John Marks Smith and Lockwood, to hide out in the Connecticut countryside in order to intercept the dispatches.[103] Marks writing to De Lancey from Fort Franklin at Lloyd's Neck, Long Island, told about his trip to Connecticut and that he only saw a black slave. The slave reported that 1,000 foot soldiers and some light horse would come near to King's Bridge. The slave's master "bid him tell me that meant to stop our troops going to the southard by their pretending to attack up at King['s] Bridge."[104]

Isaac Ogden, a refugee from Newark who had worked in Brigadier Cortland Skinner's spy network, received an intelligence report from New Jersey. The spy reported on a conversation with Bill Livingston, the son of New Jersey Governor William Livingston. Also mentioned in this report are two other reports which have not been located, dated Saturday (September 8, 1781) and Tuesday (September 11), which is evidence that the unnamed spy was routinely sending in reports.[105] Joseph Gould had sent in a note on the American line of battle, that was endorsed as coming from Gould and was received on September 16, 1781.[106] Gould, probably the author of the aforementioned reports, was described by John André as "my old friend" and that he could be depended upon.[107] Gould was working for the Americans by May 1, 1780, thus dealing with both sides.[108] Brigadier General Cortland Skinner reported on March 15, 1781, that he was unable to hear anything about Gould and that they had probably seen the last of him.[109] Gould must have explained his absence and regained the trust of the British. He may have been sent by Colonel Elias Dayton of the 2nd New Jersey Regiment, his American controller, to deliver "black intelligence," that, is false or misleading information.

The British were trying to set up another mail interception. Major Thomas Millidge of the 1st Battalion of the New Jersey Volunteers advised Major Oliver De Lancey on September 16, 1781, of a plot to seize the American mail. Isaac Sweasy and Nathan Horton were to meet with Constant Cooper, who was being exchanged. Cooper was to try to get to carry the mail and then allow Nathan Horton or Isaac Sweasy to steal the mail. If Cooper could not get the assignment of taking the mail then he was "to procure the best intelligence which he is to deliver to Sweasy and Horton who are very capable to perform the business." Cooper believed that if he were exchanged with two people from Newark with whom he was acquainted, he could use them to write to their friends. The friends in turn would write to the rebel commissary, Major Abraham Skinner, trying to get them exchanged.[110]

Washington had traveled all the way to Chester, Pennsylvania, when he finally received word of the safe arrival of de Grasse and his fleet in the Chesapeake Bay.[111] At this point Washington knew his successful deception strategy had given them the chance to capture Cornwallis and his army in Yorktown.

The French minister Luzerne reviewed the French troops in Philadelphia on September 6. Afterward Luzerne invited the dignitaries and officers present to dine with him. Among the dignitaries were the President of Congress Thomas McKean and Charles Thomson, Secretary of Congress. When they were seated at the table an express arrived with the information of de Grasse's arrival in the Chesapeake and that de Grasse had opened communications with General Lafayette. The news brought everyone in Philadelphia great joy.[112]

The fifth element of the deception battle plan is exploitation of your plan. During World War II, the Allies had so convinced the Germans that the landing at Normandy was a deception that they were still waiting for the landing at the Pas de Calais. The Panzer tank corps was being held in reserve as the Allies started moving out from the beachhead. In Desert Storm the Coalition forces were able to continue the destruction of the Iraqi army after the liberation of Kuwait.

In the American Revolution, British General Sir Henry Clinton had advised Cornwallis on August 27, 1781, that Washington's movement might be to take a defensive position at Morristown "from whence he may detach to the southward."[113] Clinton still believed that the bulk of the American and French troops were going to take up position in New Jersey and some troops would go to Virginia but certainly not the bulk of them. As long as de Grasse's destination was uncertain, Clinton believed that the allies would probably not move their entire force to the south. It was not until September 6, when Clinton received Cornwallis's letter of September 4 and Sir Edmund Affleck's letter of September 5 announcing de Grasse's arrival off the Capes, that "Mr. Washington's design in marching to the Southward remained no longer an object of doubt."[114]

Washington's deception was run so effectively that the British were trying to sort out who was still in the area. They did have some help from the Philadelphia newspapers of September 5, which reported that Washington's troops passed Philadelphia on the 3rd and the French troops on the 4th and 5th. The regiment of Soisonnois was to be reviewed in Philadelphia on the 5th. The Philadelphia papers were circulating in New York City on the 14th.[115]

Captain Ludwig August Marquard, aide-de-camp to Lieutenant General Wilhelm von Knyphausen, had been running an intelligence gathering operation out of Morris House since February 1781.[116] On September 22, 1781, he advised Major Oliver De Lancey that reports of Sheldon's Dragoons having crossed the Hudson River were not true. His information told him that 1,000 continentals and militia were at North Castle, New York, and were coming south to attack the refugees.[117] Marquard's intelligence on the 2nd Regiment of Continental Light Dragoons, also known as Sheldon's Dragoons and Sheldon's Horse, was basically correct. The bulk of the Dragoons did stay in Westchester County; however, twenty of the men did accompany Washington to Yorktown. Marquard followed this up with an intelligence report on the 24th on the situation on the east side of the Hudson.[118]

General Sir Henry Clinton noted the tardiness of the British navy in repairing their ships to take his army to Virginia to remove General Cornwallis and his army.[119] British headquarters was busy trying to keep track of American and French troop movements. An intelligence report on the movements of Major General William Heath came from South Amboy on September 24, 1781, to Sir George Beckwith. The spy, Rattoon, advised, "your friend Sol Harper is where he wrote you last. If an army of yours would come into the Country it would alter the face of things."[120] Rattoon gave information that he obtained from a gentleman in Jersey, which had been written by Major Dayton to his friends.[121] Captain George Beckwith reported that two spies, sent out to Maryland and Pennsylvania on September 10 to obtain intelligence, had returned on September 27. They advised that the French and New York troops had marched by land to Baltimore, Maryland. What they heard was that they were going to proceed to Annapolis and then join up with the American army in Virginia.[122]

Before Washington had left the Hudson Highlands, he sent instruction to General William Heath that he was to take command of the troops being left behind. "The Security of West Point and the posts in the Highlands is to be considered as the first object of your attention. . . . Altho your general rule of conduct will be to act on the defensive only, yet it is not meant to prohibit you from striking a blow at the enemy's posts or detachments, should a fair opportunity present itself. . . . The uncertainty which the present movement of the army will probably occasion with the enemy, ought to be increased by every means in your power, and the deception kept up as long as possible."[123]

Jacob Van Wagoner had gone to Fort De Lancey at Bergen Point where he was trying to find out the military strength of the post. He questioned the men who were cutting wood as to the amount of ammunition and guns at the fort and if they were kept in working order. He then dawdled about the post till sundown. When he left he had talked a recent deserter from the rebels, Andrew May, into going with him to his house. May thought that Van Wagoner's activities were strange and returned to the loyalist refugees and inquired about Van Wagoner. Captain Ward had that night sent Captain Charles Homfray to Bergen with a parole. It was there that Homfray saw Van Wagoner coming through Bergen on his way home. Homfray called to Van Wagoner but he would not acknowledge it. Homfray was shortly after taken prisoner. A report of the incident was completed on October 6, 1781, outlining the accusations against Jacob Van Wagoner.

At dawn on the September 7 Fort De Lancey was attacked. The Americans were repulsed and they were followed during their retreat along the bay road. At about two in the afternoon, Captain Ward saw two men in a canoe crossing the bay. He then hid until the boat landed and Mr. Van Wagoner and Garret Frealin had disembarked. During questioning they claimed to have seen no one and to have only gone as far as the ferry house. Captain Ward later received reliable information that they had been in Newark and had met with rebel officers. Van Wagoner was apprehended by Captain Ward then ordered on October 8 to be confined on board the *Clinton* galley. Van Wagoner remained there until David Mathews, Mayor of New York, became security for his release. Ward's report stated that Garret Frealin had escorted a deserter from New York to Bergen where he tried to get a resident to take the deserter to Newark for sixteen dollars. When the resident refused, Frealin took the deserter himself.[124]

General Sir Henry Clinton had managed to keep in contact with General Lord Cornwallis by means of ciphered letters sent with messengers who made the trip from New York to Yorktown in small boats. Based on his correspondence with Cornwallis, Clinton on September 26, 1781, told Lord George Germain he thought that Cornwallis had sufficient supplies and would be able to hold out until the end of October.[125] Clinton was sending duplicative messages in case some did not get through. However the messages he sent to Cornwallis on September 26 and October 3 were intercepted. One of the couriers was driven ashore near Little Egg Harbor, New Jersey.[126] The courier had managed to hide his document under a rock before he was captured and taken to Philadelphia. After being interrogated and given a promise of a pardon, he agreed to turn over the document he was transporting. After much stalling by the courier, the document was brought to Philadelphia on October 14, 1781. James Lovell was a member of the Congressional Committee of Secret Correspondence who developed a number of codes and ciphers. Lovell, an experienced cryptologist, quickly decoded the document. Because Clinton and Cornwallis were still using the same cipher known to Lovell from previously intercepted letters, it was an easy task.[127] The message stated that Clinton hoped to cross the bar at the entrance to lower New York harbor on October 12 but that this plan was subject to change, and if Cornwallis advised him, they would continue in their attempt to reach him even to the middle of November.[128]

Prior to Lord Cornwallis's arrival at Yorktown, Virginia, the Americans had intercepted some of his ciphered messages that he used to communicate with the officers under his command. General

Nathanael Greene sent the intercepted documents to Congress because no one at his headquarters could decipher them. Because of Lovell's experience with codes and ciphers, the documents were given to him to solve. He broke the cipher but the documents were too old to be of any help. He did send the cipher solution to General George Washington at Yorktown through General Greene in case the same cipher was being used between Cornwallis and Clinton.

During the siege of Yorktown the Americans had intercepted a letter from General Cornwallis to General Clinton. Washington wrote to Lovell advising that the British cipher that Lovell had sent him on September 21, 1781 worked. Washington wrote on October 6, "[my] secretary has taken a copy of the ciphers, and by help of one of the alphabets has been able to decipher one paragraph of a letter lately intercepted going from L[or]d Cornwallis to Sir H[enr]y Clinton."[129] The September 8 letter from Lord Cornwallis was captured by the brig *Sea Nymph* of Philadelphia from a dispatch boat off of Cape Charles, Virginia, on September 10. The letter was brought to General Mordecai Gist at Baltimore on September 23 and he sent it the next day to Washington.[130] The deciphered letter provided Washington with the conditions inside the British fortifications at Yorktown.

The following is the cipher between British Generals Sir Henry Clinton in New York City and Lord Cornwallis in the south.[131]

line	a	b	c	d	e	f	g	h	i	k	l	m
1	19	9	17	13	16	7	12	8	14	15	26	4
10	23	22	6	19	9	17	13	16	7	12	8	14
14	5	24	29	1	25	23	22	6	19	9	17	13

line	n	o	p	q	r	s	t	u	v	w	x	y	z
1	18	21	3	2	11	5	24	29	1	25	23	22	6
10	15	26	4	18	21	3	2	11	5	24	29	1	25
14	16	7	12	8	14	15	26	4	18	21	3	2	11

The aforementioned cipher was good for the first page of the document. Any number above 30 was a null, that is, it had no value. The change in the numbers occurred after a series of four to seven nulls appeared in the document.[132] Lovell also reported that the British were using Entick's *Dictionary* of 1777 printed in London by Charles

Dilley marking the page, column, and word as 115.1.4. which would be page 115, first column, fourth word.[133]

Additional operational assistance came from James Rivington, the noted publisher of the semi-weekly *Royal Gazette* in New York City. Rivington provided the signals of the British navy in 1781 to American Major Allen McLane who brought them to Washington.[134] The signals would have provided the French navy with a quicker read on the planned movements of the British navy during the Battle of the Capes on September 5, 1781. Knowing what the signals meant, the French could respond as soon as they were given by the British navy and prepare their defense and offense accordingly.

It was not the first time that the Americans had acquired the British naval signal codes. In October 1775 William Foster, master of the ship *Jenny* of 325 tons with a cargo of coal, 100 butts of porter, and 40 live hogs sailed from London bound for Boston.[135] As it approached Boston in early December it was intercepted by Captain John Manley of Washington's schooner *Lee* of 74 tons.[136] Captain William Foster, realizing he was going to be taken, threw overboard some arms along with his most important papers, which were retrieved before they sank. Among the papers were the private British naval signals. Captain Manley brought the ship and the documents into Beverly, Massachusetts. Captain William Bartlett in the port sent Stephen Cabot to notify Washington of the capture on December 9, 1775.[137] The papers had not arrived on the 11th when Washington in turn told John Hancock of the papers being retrieved.[138]

Captain John Manley went back out to sea, but now on the schooner *Hancock*.[139] While in Nantasket Road he captured two transports from Whitehaven, England: the *Happy Return* of 130 tons with James Hall, commander, and the *Norfolk* of 120 tons with Jonathan Grendal, master, bringing coal, potatoes, and pork to Boston on January 26, 1776.[140] After he brought them into Plymouth, a packet of intercepted letters from the transports as well as the private signals of the men of war and transports were sent to Congress under Captain John Manley's name. When Congress received them on February 9, 1776, it had copies made and sent them to Admiral Esek Hopkins and to the delegates of each colony.[141]

Naval signals used the position of pennants and lanthorns (lanterns) and the firing of guns to transmit instructions from one ship to another ship. For example on the American expedition to Quebec in 1775, the following naval signals were used:

> For speaking with the whole fleet—Ensign at main topmast head
>
> For chasing a sail—Ensign at fore topmast head
>
> For heaving to—Lanthorn at mast head and two guns if head on shore and three guns if head off shore
>
> For making sail in the night—Lanthorn at mast head and 4 guns
>
> In the day for making sail, jack at foretopmast head. For dispersing and every vessel making the nearest harbor— Ensign at main peak
>
> For boarding any vessel – Jack at main topmast head and the whole fleet to draw up in line as near as possible.[142]

Admiral Richard Howe in the *Eagle* off of Chester sent a letter on December 13, 1777, to Captain Pownell of the *Apollo* informing him of the sequence in which their naval signals would change.[143] Howe's letter provided the following sequence of rotation:

Mar.	April	May	June	Jan.	Feb.
Sept.	Oct.	Nov.	Dec.	July	Aug.

The British also used signals at Staten Island to advise of approaching vessels. At the western flagstaff, they would display a blue square flag at half staff for a returning British fleet of warships while an enemy fleet would be a red square flag over a blue square flag.[144]

British Major Charles Cochrane requested to be in the first vessel that attempted to reach Lord Cornwallis at Yorktown, Virginia. He also offered to bring back Cornwallis' response. In his request to Clinton, Cochrane stated it was of much importance to him to get there.[145] The smoke and sound signal that Major Cochrane was to use if General Cornwallis was still at Yorktown was "One great smoke and one gun at one minute intervals."[146] Major Cochrane arrived at Hog Island east of the Virginia's Northern Cape on the evening of October 8.[147] He had been delayed by blowing weather when he was at the Delaware Bay. On Tuesday morning he sent in a report and advised that he had spoken to a messenger who had left Yorktown the previous Tuesday.[148] Cochrane left Hog Island at 10 a.m. on October 9.[149] Many ships traveling into the Chesapeake Bay would stop at Smith Island off the southeast tip of Virginia's eastern peninsula to pick up pilots to navigate the waters. John Dennis on Smith Island was Cochrane's contact.[150] Cochrane said that any person who they might pickup from Cape Charles or Cape Henry would have a token if they were to be trusted.[151] It will be "a Halfpenny with a strong mark upon it and either of the four letters A, B, C, [or] D wrote upon it."[152]

Major Cochrane, who had only arrived at Yorktown on October 10, carried a message by whaleboat from Yorktown dated October 11, 1781, at noon from Cornwallis to Clinton and reached Clinton on the morning of the 16th. Mr. Carey was also sent out from Yorktown and had a duplicate of the October 11 message.[153] Carey was instructed to go to Smith's Island and wait for the fleet. He was picked up in a small whaleboat and arrived on the 28th.[154] The message stated, "I have only to repeat what I said in my letter of the 3rd, that nothing but a direct move to York River, which includes a successful naval action can save me."[155]

Cornwallis did surrender to the combined American and French forces on October 19, 1781. The British fleet under the command of Rear Admiral Graves did not leave Sandy Hook, New Jersey, until October 19 and arrived off of Cape Charles on the 24th.[156] General Clinton immediately on arrival sent Lieutenant Blanchard instructions to take a whaleboat to contact John Dennis at Smith's Island and collect his information on position and strength of the French fleet and see if any information had arrived from Lord Cornwallis. He was to find out "if any of the boats from New York or the York River are there" and, if so, "to order them to us."[157] He was told "You must return as soon as possible."[158]

Blanchard brought back John Mehollom, an inhabitant of Machapungo, who stated he had heard that Cornwallis had surrendered.[159] James Rider, an African American, left Yorktown on the 18th in a four-oared boat in company with a Captain McDaniel and his crew of the sloop *Tarleton*.[160] James Robinson, an African American who was the pilot to the *Charon* man-of-war, left Yorktown with Rider when he heard of a treaty to surrender Yorktown. Robert Morsse left Yorktown with Rider and Robinson. Morsse, Rider, and Robinson were picked up by the British fleet on the 24th and told of the surrender of Cornwallis.[161] The frigate *Nymph* out of New York brought a letter from Cornwallis dated the 15th that convinced Clinton that what he was being told was the truth.[162]

After the fall of the left redoubt, Mr. Caldwell left Yorktown on the 15th in a small vessel and was instructed to stay at Smith's Island until the arrival of the fleet. After the firing had ceased, he sent a person to go near Yorktown and the person brought back the information of the surrender.[163]

Sir Henry Clinton sent a report to Lord George Germain from the ship *London* off the Chesapeake Bay on October 29, 1781, the day the fleet went back to New York. Clinton says that he received the information that Cornwallis had proposed terms of capitulation on the 17th from the pilot of the *Charon* and from some people they had picked up off the shore.

After Cornwallis' surrender Clinton clearly placed the blame on the British navy. In his report he stated the surrender could "have possibly been prevented could the fleet have been able to sail at or within a few days of the time we first expected. At least I am persuaded we should have saved to His Majesty's Service great part of that gallant army together with its respectable chief whose loss it will be now impossible I fear to repair."[164] Obviously he was not going to mention how Washington tricked him into staying in New York while the combined American and French armies marched across New Jersey. Washington's objective was a quick and unmolested march from New York through New Jersey to Virginia. Washington, Frederick Morgan and H. Norman Schwarzkopf Jr., used the deception battle plan to achieve their military objectives.

CONCLUSION

Codes and ciphers have never gone out of fashion. The pigpen cipher was used during the American Civil War. The breaking of the German Enigma machine and the Japanese purple cipher machine's ciphers during World War II have become famous. The deception battle plan was used during both World War II and Operation Desert Storm with success.

Even Hollywood got into using an alphabetic transposition in the movie *2001, A Space Odyssey*. The computer's name was HAL; when a simple alphabetic transposition is made, the secret name of IBM for the computer is revealed.

In the 1950s, hollowed-out coins were used in New York City by Rudolph Ivanovich Abel, a Russian spy, to hide messages.[1] Robert Philip Hanssen, an FBI agent who was spying for the Russians, was caught on February 18, 2001, after he had left material at a dead drop under a wooden bridge near his home. The FBI asserted that Hanssen had used the dead drop at least twenty times.[2]

British spies in Moscow were alleged to have used a fake rock containing a transmitter which received and sent intelligence as the agents passed the rock.[3] It was revealed in 2009 that al-Qaeda used e-mail accounts to pass information and a "10-code" to pass telephone numbers. In the "10-code" system the actual telephone number is subtracted from 10 and the resulting new numbers are sent. The process is reversed to obtain the real number.[4]

10-code	10	10	10	10	10	10	10	10	10	10
real telephone number	5	5	5	1	2	3	4	5	6	7
new telephone number	5	5	5	9	8	7	6	5	4	3

Modern adaptations of the technology used during the American Revolution are being used in today's world. To find them, one needs only to pay attention to the news.

APPENDIX A

McLane–Rivington Communications

The events leading to the 1781 meeting of James Rivington and Major Allen McLane on Long Island.

During 1781 James Rivington, the noted publisher of the semi-weekly *Royal Gazette* in New York City provided the signals of the British navy to American Major Allen McLane. Major McLane traveled from Shrewsbury, New Jersey, to Long Island to pick up the codes and then took them to General Washington.[1] No method has been put forth as how the two made initial contact to set up this exchange. Here is a possibility. The following are advertisements that appeared in the *Royal Gazette*. They might be the key to how contact was made.

Beginning on July 11, 1781 on page three column three was the following ad:

> The person to whom Mr. Lemuel Nelme wrote a letter dated Fish-Kill, April 27 (which did not come to his hand till yesterday the 10th of July 1781) takes this earliest opportunity to desire he will immediately obtain permission to come to New York, where he will receive intelligence of matters momentous and interesting to himself, and be enabled directly to return to his native country, and enjoy the happiness of meeting his parents, proper information; and directions are left with the printer, to whom Mr. Nelme will be pleased to repair as soon as he shall have met with this advertisement.[2]

The ad appeared in Rivington's newspaper through August 4.[3]

It is an interesting ad to be sent from British-controlled New York to someone in the American-controlled area along the Hudson River north of New York. It requests that the person come to New York to receive

1 Crary, *"The Tory and the Spy:* The Double Life of James Rivington", *William and Mary Quarterly*, volume 16, number 1, January 1959: 68.

2 *Royal Gazette*, July 11, 1781 (#499) p3c3.

3 *Royal Gazette*, July 14, 1781 (#500) p1c1; July 18, 1781 (#501) p1c1; July 21, 1781 (#502) p1c1; August 1, 1781 (#505) p4c3; and August 4, 1781 (#506).

important "intelligence." It also indicates that the person would be able to return quickly to his "native country" or state. People at the time thought of themselves first as New Yorkers or Pennsylvanians and not Americans. It also identified the printer (Rivington) as the contact. Another tidbit is the choice of the name Mr. Lemuel Nelme. A Mr. Lemuel Dole Nelme had written a book in 1772 called *An Essay Towards an Investigation of the Origin and Elements of Language.* It was a speculative book on the origin of languages and alphabet symbolism—that is, ciphers—which is the language of spies.

Two ads which appeared in the September 29 newspaper draw attention. On page two, column three, one reads, "The person to whom Nimrod wrote the two letters, begs leave to inform him that he received them this morning, and acknowledges himself much obliged to him, but earnestly wishes to have an immediate interview at any place Nimrod may by letter appoint. Nimrod may depend upon the honor of the author of this advertisement, in every respect." The ad is actually dated September 25 in print. The ad indicates that two letters were received on September 25 and requests for an immediate meeting at a place to be pointed out. Nimrod is depicted in the Bible as a nation-builder, among other attributes.

In the same newspaper on the next page, page three, column three, is a notice but it has a finger printed in the margin pointing to it. It says: "The printer feels much concern at being obliged to make use of paper on which this gazette is printed, its quality so very mean and disgraceful, is entirely owing to a want of supply from the mill on Long Island, which he hopes will be early enough for the next publication."[4] Rivington, using the cover of an apology, appears to be identifying his paper mill on Long Island as a place for a meeting that he identified on the previous page. He also indicates that he would be there only until the next publishing date. It is known that American Major Allen McLane did meet Rivington on Long Island, where Rivington turned over the British naval codes. Neither McLane nor Rivington left any written letters or journal evidence as to what series of events led to their meeting on Long Island. Rivington may have left this trail of events in his *Royal Gazette* newspaper. Although there is no certainty as to how contact for the meeting happened, this series of events is plausible.

4 *Royal Gazette*, September 29, 1781 (#522) p2c3 and p3c3.

APPENDIX B

CULPER SPY RING CODE

1	a	35	assume	69	business
2	an	36	attempt	70	battery
3	all	37	attone	71	battalion
4	at	38	attack	72	british
5	and	39	alarm	73	camp
6	art	40	action	74	came
7	arms	41	accomplish	75	cost
8	about	42	apprehend	76	corps
9	above	43	abatis	77	change
10	absent	44	accommodate	78	carry
11	absurd	45	alternative	79	clergy
12	adorn	46	artillery	80	common
13	adopt	47	ammunition	81	consult
14	adore	48	be	82	contest
15	advise	49	bay	83	contract
16	adjust	50	by	84	content
17	adjourn	51	best	85	Congress
18	afford	52	but	86	captain
19	affrent	53	buy	87	careful
20	affair	54	bring	88	city
21	again	55	boat	89	clamour
22	april	56	barn	90	column
23	agent	57	banish	136	detain
24	alter	58	baker	137	divert
25	ally	59	battle	138	discourse
26	any	60	better	139	disband
27	appear	61	beacon	140	dismount
28	appoint	62	behalf	141	disarm
29	august	63	bitter	142	detect
30	approve	64	bottom	143	defense
31	arrest	65	bounty	144	deceive
32	arraign	66	bondage	145	delay
33	amuse	67	barron	146	difficult
34	assign	68	brigade	147	disapprove

148 disregard
149 disappoint
150 disagree
151 disorder
152 dishonest
153 discover
154 december
155 demolish
156 deliver
157 desolate
158 during
159 ear
160 eye
161 end
162 enquire
163 effect
164 endure
165 enforce
166 engage
167 enclose
168 equip
169 excuse
170 exert
171 expend
172 expose
173 extort
174 express
175 embark
176 employ
177 explore
178 enemy
179 example
180 embassador
91 copy
92 cover
93 county
94 courage
95 credit
96 custom

97 compute
98 conduct
99 comply
100 confine
101 caution
102 conquer
103 coward
104 confess
105 convict
106 cannon
107 character
108 circumstance
109 clothier
110 company
111 confident
112 committee
113 continue
114 contradict
115 correspond
116 controversy
117 commission
118 commissioner
119 constitution
120 date
121 day
122 dead
123 do
124 die
125 damage
126 doctor
127 duty
128 drummer
129 daily
130 dispatch
131 distant
132 danger
133 dislodge
134 dismiss
135 dragoons

136 detain
137 divert
138 discourse
139 disband
140 dismount
141 disarm
142 detect
143 defense
144 deceive
145 delay
146 difficult
147 disapprove
148 disregard
149 disappoint
150 disagree
151 disorder
152 dishonest
153 discover
154 december
155 demolish
156 deliver
157 desolate
158 during
159 ear
160 eye
161 end
162 enquire
163 effect
164 endure
165 enforce
166 engage
167 enclose
168 equip
169 excuse
170 exert
171 expend
172 expose
173 extort
174 express

175 embark
176 employ
177 explore
178 enemy
179 example
180 embassador
181 engagement
182 experience
183 evacuate
184 Farm
185 face
186 fate
187 false
188 friend
189 fin
190 find
191 form
192 fort
193 fleet
194 famine
195 father
196 foggy
197 folly
198 frugal
199 faithful
200 favour
201 faulty
202 foreign
203 forget
204 fulfil [sic]
205 factor
206 favorite
207 fortune
208 fortune
209 forget
210 foreigner
211 fortitude
212 fortify
213 formiable

214 foundation
215 february
216 get
217 great
218 good
219 gun
220 go
221 gain
222 guide
223 gold
224 glory
225 gunner
226 gloomy
227 govern
228 grandieure
229 guilty
230 guinea
231 gallant
232 gazette
233 grateful
234 glacis
235 general
236 garrison
237 gentlemen
238 glorious
239 gradual
240 grenadier
241 hay
242 he
243 his
244 him
245 haste
246 hand
247 hang
248 has
249 have
250 head
251 high
252 hill

253 hope
254 hut
255 horse
256 house
257 happy
258 hardy
259 harvest
260 horrid
261 horseman
262 human
263 havock
264 healthy
265 heavy
266 honest
267 hunger
268 honor
269 harmony
270 hazardous
271 hesitate
272 history
273 horrible
274 hospital
275 hurrican [sic]
276 hypocrite
277 [document damage]
278 [document damage]
279 [document damage]
280 I
281 if
282 in
283 is
284 it
285 ice
286 ink
287 into
288 instance
289 island

290 impress
291 improve
292 incamp
293 incur
294 infest
295 inforce
296 instance
297 insnare
298 instruct
299 intrigue
300 intrust
301 instant
302 invest
303 invite
304 ignorant
305 impudent
306 industry
307 infamous
308 influence
309 infantry
310 infantry
311 injury
312 innocent
313 instrument
314 intimate
315 illegal
316 imagin
317 important
318 imprison
319 improper
320 incumber
321 inhuman
322 inquiry
323 interview
324 incorrect
325 interceed
326 interfere
327 intermix
328 introduce

329 immediate
330 impatient
331 incouragemt
332 infection
333 irregular
334 invalid
335 indians
336 june
337 july
338 jury
339 jealous
340 justify
341 january
342 key
343 king
344 kill
345 know
346 law
347 land
348 love
349 low
350 lot
351 lord
352 light
353 lart
354 learn
355 lady
356 letter
357 levy
358 levies-new
359 liar
360 lucky
361 language
362 limit
363 liquid
364 longitude
365 latitude
366 laudable
367 legible

368 liberty
369 lottery
370 literature
371 man
372 map
373 may
374 march
375 mast
376 make
377 met
378 me
379 my
380 much
381 move
382 mort
383 mine
384 many
385 mercy
386 moment
387 murder
388 measure
389 method
390 mischief
391 mistake
392 molest
393 majesty
394 meditate
395 memory
396 messenger
397 misery
398 moveable
399 multitude
400 miscarry
401 misfortune
402 miserable
403 mercenary
404 majority
405 minority
406 memorial

407 missterious [sic]
408 manufacture
409 moderator
410 minsterial
411 name
412 new
413 no
414 not
415 night
416 never
417 needful
418 number
419 neither
420 nothing
421 neglect
422 nation
423 navy
424 natural
425 negative
426 negligence
427 november
428 necessary
429 nobility
430 oath
431 of
432 off
433 on
434 or
435 out
436 offer
437 office
438 onset
439 order
440 over
441 obstruct
442 obtain
443 observe
444 occur
445 offense

446 omit
447 oppose
448 obligate
449 obstinate
450 obviate
451 occupy
452 operate
453 origin
454 ornament
455 overcome
456 overlook
457 overtake
458 overrun
459 overthrow
460 obedience
461 objection
462 october
463 obscure
464 occasion
465 opinion
466 oppression
467 opportunity
468 obligation
469 pay
470 peace
471 plan
472 put
473 port
474 proof
475 please
476 part
477 paper
478 pardon
479 party
480 perfect
481 pilot
482 prudent
483 publish
484 purchase

485 purpose
486 people
487 pleasure
488 produce
489 prison
490 progress
491 promise
492 proper
493 prosper
494 prospect
495 punish
496 pertake
497 perform
498 permit
499 pervert
500 prepare
501 prevail
502 preserve
503 pretend
504 promote
505 propose
506 protect
507 provost
508 pursue
509 passenger
510 passion
511 pension
512 period
513 persecute
514 poverty
515 power or powerful
516 prosperous
517 punishment
518 preferment
519 production
520 pursuant
521 pensioner
522 Parliament
523 persecution

524 practicable
525 profitable
526 particular
527 petition
528 profession
529 proclaim
530 provision
531 protection
532 quick
533 question
534 quantity
535 quallity [sic]
536 rash
537 rain
538 run
539 rule
540 read
541 rise
542 random
543 ransom
544 rather
545 real
546 riot
547 robber
548 ready
549 ruin
550 ruler
551 rapid
552 reader
553 rebel
554 rigor
555 river
556 receit
557 refit
558 regain
559 rejoice
560 relate
561 request
562 relax

563 redoubt
564 rely
565 remit
566 reprieve
567 repulse
568 reward
569 retract
570 resign
571 ratify
572 recompence
573 regular
574 regulate
575 rigorous
576 recital
577 recover
578 remember
579 remittance
580 represent
581 rebellion
582 reduction
583 remarkable
584 reinforcemt
585 refugee
586 sail
587 see
588 sea
589 scheme
590 set
591 send
592 ship
593 safe
594 same
595 sky
596 secret
597 seldom
598 sentence
599 servant
600 signal
601 silent

602 suffer
603 sudden
604 surprise
605 summer
606 speaker
607 steady
608 submit
609 surpass
610 sanction
611 sensible
612 singular
613 soldier
614 sovereign
615 security
616 seventy
617 August
618 september
619 surrender
620 serviceable
621 security
622 severity
623 society
624 superior
625 the
626 that
627 this
628 these
629 they
630 there
631 thing
632 though
633 time
634 to
635 troops
636 thankfull [sic]
637 therefore
638 timber
639 tory
640 transport

641 trail
642 traitor
643 transgress
644 translate
645 terrible
646 tyranny
647 vain
648 vaunt
649 vouch
650 vacant
651 vary
652 venture
653 vital
654 vulgar
655 value
656 virtue
657 visit
658 valiant
659 victory
660 vigilant
661 vigorous
662 violent
663 volenteer [sic]
664 valuable
665 voluntary
666 up
667 upper
668 upon
669 unto
670 unarm
671 unfit
672 unheard
673 unsafe
674 uniform
675 uncertain
676 uncommon
677 unfriendly
678 unfortunate
679 wind

680 war
681 was
682 we
683 will
684 with
685 when
686 wharf
687 wound
688 wood
689 want
690 wait
691 write
692 who
693 wish
694 whose
695 wages
696 warlike
697 welfare
698 willing
699 winter
700 water
701 woman
702 writer
703 waggon [sic]
704 weary
705 warrant
706 yet
707 you
708 your
709 yesterday
710 zel
711 Genl Washington
712 Genl Clinton
713 Tryon
714 Erskine
715 Vaughan
716 Robinson
717 Brown
718 Genl Garth

719 North, Lord
720 German, Lord
721 Bolton John
722 Culper Saml
723 Culper Junr.
724 Austin Roe
725 C. Brewster
726 Rivington
727 New York
728 Long Island
729 Setauket
730 Kingsbridge
731 Bergen
732 Staten Island
733 Boston
734 Rhode Island
735 Connecticut
736 New Jersey
737 Pensylvania [sic]
738 Maryland
739 Virginia
740 North Carolina
741 South Carolina
742 Georgia
743 Quebeck
744 Hallifax
745 England
746 London
747 Portsmouth
748 Plymouth
749 Ireland
750 Corke
751 Scotland
752 West Indies
753 East Indies
754 Gibralter
755 Fance
756 Spain
757 Scotland

758 Portugal

759 Denmark

760 Russia

761 Germany

762 Hanover

763 Head Quaters

Alphabet		Numbers	
a	e	1	e
b	f	2	f
c	g	3	g
d	h	4	i
e	i	5	k
f	j	6	m
g	a	7	n
h	b	8	o
i	c	9	q
j	d	0	u
k	o		
l	m		
m	n		
n	p		
o	q		
p	r		
q	k		
r	l		
s	u		
t	v		
u	w		
v	x		
w	y		
x	z		
y	s		
z	t		

DIRECTIONS FOR THE ALPHABET

N.B. The use of this Alphabet is when you wish to express some words not mentioned in the numerical Dictionary. For instance the word heart, would be expressed thus *bielv*. look the [sic] letters of the real word in theirs column of the alphabet and then opposite to them, let those letters in the second column represent them; in this case always observe to draw a line under the word, as *fwv* stands for but. Numbers are represented by their opposite letters which must have a double line under them as *fikm* is 2456. & *nqu* is 790. . . .

Direction for the numerical Dictionary. In the numerical Dictionary it is sufficient to express a part of a sentence only in figures, to make the rest perfectly unintelligible, as all words meaning must be sought for. & if not to be found, & the word not proper to be wrote, then the alphabet must be used-When numbers are used always observe to put a period after the number thus 284. stands for it & 295. inforce. It will often happen that the same word may need to be changed thro the different moods, tenses, numbers. Thus if you would express the word Introduce the number would be 328. if you would express the word in introduced make a small flourish over the same 328. Horse is repres. by 255. Horses 255. kill by 344. killed by 344. impress by 290. impressed by 290, in such cases the fore going & subsequent parts must determine the word.

APPENDIX C

MARQUIS DE LAFAYETTE'S NUMERICAL CODE*

*GWP, General Correspondence, Marie Joseph Paul Yves Roche Gilbert du Motier, Marquis de Lafayette, 1779-80, Numerical Code.

1. Halifax
2. New Found Land
3. Penobscot
4. Savannah
5. New York Island
6. Long Island
7. Georgia
8. Carolina
9. New York Harbor
10. Spanish Ships
11. Dutch Ships
12. French Money
13. Spanish Money
14. Dutch Money
18. French Troops in the West
   Indies
19. America
20. Southern States
21. France
22. Spain
23. Holland
25. Jamaica
26. West Indies
28. French Ships
40. Peace
42. Negotiations
44 - May
45. June
46. New York
47. Charles Town
49. July
50. August
51. September
54. October
60. King of France
62. French Ministers
63. British Fleet

64. British Ships
65. Great Britain
66. Congress
71. Maritime Superiority
72. Continental Troops
80. Chevalier de la Luzerne
81. Count de Rochambeau
82. Count de Grasse
84. French Troops in the North
115. Russia

Appendix D

British Headquarters Code Book (Undated)[*]

A

a=1

and=2

above=3

about=4

abscond=5

abundance=6

acceed=7

abroad=8

accept=9

amount=10

acknowledge=11

acquaint=12

act=13

admit=14

admiral=15

adapt=16

advance=17

advantage=18

advise=19

against=20

aid=21

alarm=22

all=23

alliance=24

ambassador=25

America=26

Amsterdam=27

ammunition=28

angry=29

amuse=30]

Antigua=31

answer=32

approve=33

April=34

arms=35

army=36

appoint=37

arise=38

artillery=39

articles=40

assent=41

assure=42

at=43

attack=44

Augustine=45

avoid=46

authentic=47

away=48

also=49

axe=50

B

backward=51

bad=52

base=53

battalion=54

battle=55

Barbados=56

boat=57

Bermuda=58

be=59

begin=50

belong=61

betray=62

believe=63

bind=64

better=65

Boston=66

blame=67

Bordeaux=68

brass=69

Brest=70

bribe=71

bring=72

British=73

beef=74

by=75

business=76

broadcloth=77

bandanas=78

before=79

brother=80

broke=81

bright=82

Broom Sr.=83

Broom Jr.=84

bays(cloth)=85

blankets=86

C

camp=87

capitulate=88

Canada=89

cargo=90

[*]CP 234:8 British headquarters code book. Spelling is as the original. M. is used for Mr.

Carolina N.=91
do S.=92*
captain=93
carry=94
cast=95
certain=96
change=97
Change Bills of=98
cheap=99
cheat=100
choose=101
cloathing=102
coast=103
collect=104
colonies=105
come=106
commerce=107
commission=108
communicate=109
complain=110
comply=111
conclude=112
condition=113
confess=114
confide=115
confirm=116
congress=117
consent=118
consult=119
contain=120
content=121
contradict=122
convenient=123
converse=124
convey=125
convoy=126

copy=127
correct=128
correspond=129
council=130
court=131
crown=132
credit=133
cruise=134
Connecticut=135
camblets=136†
calamine=137
calico=138
chintz=139
can=140
came=141

D

day=142 dead=143
Deane B=144
["]Simon=145
Duer Col.=146
decide=147
declare=148
defeat=149
defend=150
defense=151
Delaware=152
delay=153
deliver=154
demand=155
depart=156
desire=157
destroy=158
detach=159
determine=160
discourage=161
dispatches=162

distress=163
divide=164
Domingo St.=165
doubt=166
Dutch=167
do=168
done=169
doing=170

E

each=171
East=172
effort=173
embargo=174
embark=175
engage=176
employ=177
enough=178
end=179
England=180
English=181
equal=182
escape=183
establish=184
enterprise=185
evade=186
every=187
event=188
excuse=189
expert=190
expedition=191
express=192
express–193
engagement=194
Europe=195

F

fail=197

*"Do" stands for ditto or the same as stated above.
†Camblets is a variant spelling of camlet which is a plush fabric.

faithful=198
false=199
fall=200
far=201
fear=202
few=203
fight=204
finances=205
find=206
first=207
fishermen=208
flag=209
fleet=210
flight=211
Florida=212
fellow=213
for=214
forbid=215
forces=216
foreign=217
form=218
fort=219
fortify=220
fortnight=221
France=222
Franklin Dr.=223
French=224
friend=225
frigate=226
from=227
fulfill=228
fund=229
furnish=230
fringe cloth=231

G

gain=233
Gates Gen.=234
gazette=235
Georgia=236

general=237
give=238
go=239
good=240
government=241
grant=242
great=243
Granada Isl.=244
guard=245
Guadeloupe=246
guilty=247

H

Halifax=248
Hamburgh=249
Hampshire New=250
harbor=251
Havannah=252
he=253
high=254
his=255
hinder=256
Holland=257
hope=258
hostilities=259
House of
Commons=260
House of Lords=261
hurry=262
Hudson River=263

I or J

Jamaica=264
jealous=265
Jersey New=266
ill=268
immediate=269
immense=270
impatient=271
import=272
important=273

impossible=274
improbable=275
in=276
into=277
incline=278
image=279
increase=280
independence=281
Indies East=282
Indies West=283
indigo=284
infantry=285
inform=286
inhabit=287
injure=288
insist=289
insult=290
insure=291
inland=292
interest=293
intercept=294
interpose=295
interview=296
invade=297
Ireland=298
Irish=299
iron=300
island=301
it=302
June=303
July 304
January=305
just=306
join=307
invade=308

K

keep=309
Kepple Adl.=310
king=311

know=312
knowledge=313
Kersey=314*
L
land=315
language=316
last=317
Lee Henry=318
Lee Arthur=317
Lee William=320
less=321
letter=322
levy=323
least=324
limit=325
Lisbon=326
little=327
loan=328
Long Island=329
ditto Sound=330
loose=331
low=332
let=333
leather=334
lead=335
M
mail=336
maintain=337
make=338
made=339
many=340
March=341
may=342
most=343
more=344
Martinico=345
marine=346

Maryland=347
Massachusetts=348
met=349
meet=350
memorial=351
militia=352
minister=353
ministry=354
money=355
mouth=356
more=357
mortars=358
move=359
much=360
miracle=361
my=362
me=363
mine=364
N
name=365
Nantes=366
nation=367
navy=368
near=369
never=370
necessary=371
negotiate=372
Nantes=373
new=374
news=375
New York=376
next=377
night=378
north=379
North Lord=380
November=381
not=382

nothing=383
now=384
never=385
no=386
none=287
New London=388
O
obey=389
oblige=390
obtain=391
occasion=392
of=393
off=394
offensive=395
offer=396
officers=397
old=398
omit=399
open=400
oppose=401
order=402
our=403
out=404
over=405
P
packet= 406
Paris=407
Parliament=408
particulars=409
partner=410
party=411
pass–412
passage=413
pay=414
peace=415
Pennsylvania=416
people=417

*Kersey is a woolen fabric used for coats. It is also a ribbed fabric used for hose and trousers.

permit=418
policy=419
possession=420
position=421
post=422
post office=433
Portsmouth=434
do New Eng=435
preliminary=436
prepare=437
prevent=438
private=439
privateer=440
prison=441
procure=442
profit=443
promise=444
procure=445
prove=446
propose=447
protect=448
provide=449
purchase=450
pursue=451
push=452
Putnam Gen.=453
privilege=454
Q
quantity=455
Quebec=456
queen=457
question=458
quick=459
quiet=460
R
raise=461
receive=462
reconcile=463
recover=464

remit=465
reduce=466
refit=467
refuse=468
regiment=469
reject=470
remain=471
remit=472
remove=473
renounce=474
report=475
resign=476
resolve=477
restore=478
result=479
return=479
retire=480
retreat=481
return=482
rice=483
rise=484
ribbons=485
red=486
river=487
Rhode Island=488
ruin=489
Russia=490
run=491
rum=492
ratify=493
right=494
read=495
S
safe=496
sale=497
save=498
say=499
sea=500
see=501

seen=502
seal=503
seamen=504
scarlet=505
secret=506
secretary=507
secure=508
seize=509
sell=510
send=511
settle=512
ship (Merch)=513
Ship (War)=514
sign=515
sink=516
sloop=517
schooner=518
silk=519
slow=520
small=521
soldiers=522
soon=523
south=524
Spain=525
speak=526
speech=527
speed=528
spy=529
stand=530
stay=531
still=532
stop=533
strong=534
stack=535
submit=536
subsidy=537
succeed=538
sudden=539
suffer=540

sufficient=541
sum=542
supply=543
sure=544
surrender=545
suspect=546
suspense=547
suspend=548
system=549
sound=550

T
Take=551
tax=552
tardy=553
tell=554
term=555
tent=556
thanks=557
the=558
their=559
they=560
those=561
think=562
thousand=563
theatre=564
timid=565
to=566
tobacco=567
town=568
transcribe=569
translate=570
transport=571
treat=572
treatment=573
treaty=574
troops=575
trust=576
try=577
turn=578

tea=579

V
vessel=580
violate=581
violence=582
Virginia=583
visit=584

U
undertake=585
understand=586
unlucky=587
upon=588
urge=589
us=590
use=591
utmost=592

W
wait=593
want=594
war=595
Washington Gen=596
Washington Col=597
watch=598
we=599
weak=600
week=601
well=602
west=603
when=604
where=605
will=606
with=607
write=608
worse=609

Y
yesterday=610
you=611
Yours=612
young=613

There are no entries for
the letter "Z".

ADDITIONS
Continental
Currency=614
committee=615
gold=616
Guinea=617
state=618
silk=619
time=620
taffeta=621
silver=622
dollars=623
pounds=624
Webb Jos. M.=625
Webb Saml. Col=626
Webb Jno Capt=627
if=628
but=629
Philadelphia=630
bill=631
invoice=632
retain=633

APPENDIX E

BRITISH HEADQUARTERS CODE BOOK, 1779*

A
above=50
about=51
abroad=53
abscond=54
absent=55
abundance=56
accede=57
accept=58
amount=59
acknowledge=60
acquaint=61
act=62
admit=63
admiral=64
adapt=65
advance=66
advantage=67
advise=68
asent=69
aid=70
alarm=71
all=72
alliance=73
ambassador=74
America=75
ammunition=76
Amsterdam=77
amuse=78
Annapolis=79
angry=80
answer=81

Antigua=82
appoint=83
approve=84
April=85
Aranda Ct=86
arms=87
army=88
arrive=89
artillery=90
articles=91
assent=92
assure=93
at=95
attack=96
Augustine=97
avoid=98
authentick=99
away=100
B
backward=101
bad=102
Baltimore=103
base=104
battalion=105
battle=106
Barbados=107
boat=108
begin=109
belong=110
Berlin=111
Bermuda=112
believe=113

betray=114
better=115
bind=116
blame=117
bombard=118
Boston=119
Bordeaux=120
Brest=121
bribe=122
bring=123
British=124
Burgoyne=125
buy=126
by=127
business=128
C
cabinet+129
Calais=130
Camden Ld=131
camp=132
capitulate=133
Canada=134
cargo=135
Carolina=136
cannon=137
captain=138
carry=139
cast=140
certain=141
change=142
cheap=143
cheat=144

*CP 49:15, British headquarters code book. Spelling is as the original. M. is used for Mr.

Chesapeake Bay=145
choose=146
clothing=147
coast=148
collect=149
colonies=150
come=151
commerce=152
commission=153
communicate=154
complain=155
comply=156
conclude=157
condition=158
confess=159
confide=160
confirm=161
congress=162
consent=163
consult=164
contain=165
content=166
contradict=167
convenient=168
converse=169
convey=170
convoy=171
copy=173
correct=174
correspond=175
council=176
court=177
credit=178
crown=179
cruise=180

D
date=182
day=183
dead=184
Deane Silas=185

Deane
Simon=186
decide=187
defend=190
declare=188
defeat=189
defense=191
Delaware=192
delay=194
deliver=195
demand=196
depart=197
desire=198
destroy=199
detach=200
determine=1
discourage=2
dispatches=3
distress=4
divide=5
Domingo St.=6
doubt=7
Dover=8
Dublin=9
Dunkirk=10
Dutch=11

E
each=13
East=14
easy=15
ebb=16
=17
effect=18
elect=19
embargo=20
embark=21
engage=22
emperor=23
employ=24
enough=25

end=26
England=27
English=28
equal=29
escape=30
establish=31
enterprise=33
evade=34
every=35
event=36
excuse=37
expert=38
express=39

F
fail=201
faithful=202
false=203
fall=204
far=205
fear=206
few=207
fight=208
finances=209
find=210
first=212
fish=213
flag=214
fleet=215
flight=216
Florida=217
fellow=218
for=219
forbid=220
force=221
foreign=222
form=223
fort=224
fortify=225
fortnight=226
France=227

Franklin Dr.=228
French=229
friend=230
frigate=232
from=233
fulfill=234
fund=235
furnish=236
fringe=237

G

gain=238
Gates Gen.=240
gazette=241
general=242
Georgia=243
Germain L G=244
Germany=245
give=246
go=247
good=248
government=249
grant=250
great=251
Granada Isl.=252
guard=253
Guadeloupe=254
guilty=255
gunpowder=256

H

Halifax=257
Hamburg=258
Hanover=259
harbor=260
Havannah=261
Harve de Grace=262
he=263
Hesse=264
high=265
hinder=266
Holland=267

hope=268
hostilities=269
House of
Commons=270
House of Lords=271
Howe Gen.=272
Howe Ld=273
hurry=274

I or J

Jamaica=275
jealous=276
Jersey New=277
ignorant=278
ill=279
immediate=280
immense=281
impatient=282
import=283
important=284
impossible=285
improbable=286
in=287
incline=288
image=279
increase=290
independence=291
Indies=292
indigo=293
infantry=294
inform=295
inhabit=296
injure=297
insist=298
insult=299
insure=300
intend=301
interest=302
intercept=303
interpose=304
invade=305

Ireland=307
iron=308
island=309
it=310
June=311
July 312

K

keep=313
Kepple Adl.=314
king=315
know=316

L

land=317
language=318
last=319
Lee Arthur=320
Lee R. Henry=321
Lee William=322
Lee Gen.=323
less=324
letter=325
levy=326
limit=327
Lisbon=328
little=329
loan=330
London=331
Long Island=332
loose=333
L'Orient Port 334
low=335
lonesome=336
Lord=337
loss=338

M

Madrid=339
mail=340
maintain=341
make=342
many=343

March=344

marine=345

Martinico=346

Marseilles=347

Maryland=348

Massachusetts=349

may=350

meet=351

memorial=352

militia=353

minister=354

money=355

mouth=356

more=357

mortars=358

most=359

move=360

much=361

must=362

N

name=363

Nantes=364

nation=365

navy=366

Nukar M=368

necessary=369

negotiate=370

neuter=371

new=372

news=373

New York=374

next=375

night=376

North Lord=377

nothing=378

now=379

number=380

O

obey=381

oblige=382

obtain=383

occasion=384

of=385

off=386

offensive=387

offer=388

officer=389

old=390

omit=391

open=392

oppose=393

order=394

our=395

P

packet= 396

Paris=397

Parliament=398

particular=399

partner=400

party=401

pass=402

passage=403

pay=404

peace=405

Pennsylvania=406

people=407

permit=408

policy=409

position=410

possession=411

Poland=412

post=413

post office=414

Portsmouth=415

Portugal=416

preliminary=417

prepare=418

prevent=419

private=420

privateer=421

prison=422

procure=423

profit=424

promise=425

prove=426

propose=427

protect=428

provide=429

Prussia=430

purchase=431

pursue=432

push=433

Put=434

Q

quantity=435

quality=436

Quebec=437

queen=438

question=439

quick=440

quiet=441

quit=442

R

raise=443

receive=444

reconcile=445

recover=446

remit=447

reduce=448

refit=449

refuse=450

regiment=451

reject=452

remain=453

remove=454

report=455

resign=456

resolve=457

restore=458

result=459

retain=460

retire=461

retreat=462

return=463

rice=464

rise=465

river=466

Rhode Island=467

ruin=468

Russia=469

S

safe=470

sail=471

sale=472

Sandwich Ld=473

Sartain M.=474

save=475

say=476

sea=477

seal=478

seamen=479

secret=480

secretary=481

secure=482

seize=483

sell=484

send=485

settle=486

ship Merch=487

Ship of War=488

sign=489

sink=490

sloop=491

slow=492

small=493

soldiers=494

soon=495

south=496

Spain=497

speak=498

speech=499

speed=500

spy=501

stand=502

still=504

stop=505

Stormont Ld=506

strong=507

stocks=508

submit=509

subsidy=510

succeed=511

sudden=512

suffer=513

sufficient=514

sum=515

supply=516

sure=517

surrender=518

suspect=519

suspense=520

suspend=521   T

Take=522 tardy=523

tax=524

tell=525

terms=526

tent=527

thanks=528

the=529

their=530

they=531

think=532

thousand=533

theatre=534

timid=535

to=536

tobacco=537

Toulon=538

town=540

transcribe=541

translate=542

transport=543

treat=544

treatment=545

treaty=546

troops=547

trust=548

try=549

turn=550

Turks=551

V

Vergennes Ct=532

Versailles=553

vessel=554

Vienna=555

violate=556

violence=557

Virginia=558

visit=559

U

undertake=560

understand=561

unlucky=562

unto=563

upon=564

urge=566

utmost=567

W

wait=569

want=570

war=571

Washington Gen=572

watch=573

we=574

weak=575

week=576

will=577

west=578

when=579

where=580

who=581
will=582
with=583
write=584
Y
yesterday=585
you=586
Yours=587
young=588
year=589
yield=590
Postscript
Adams Jn=591
— —Sam=592
— —Thos=593
Africa=594
Asia=595
and=596
Arnold Gen.=597
but=598
Banister [Tarleton]
Col.=599
before=600
brother=601
Carmichael Wm=602
Chaumont M.=603
Carrol[l] M.=604
continent=605
continue=606
Duer Col. [W}=607
Europe=608
exclusive=609
freight=610
Gerard M.=611
Harvie Col.
[John]=612
Henry Gov.=613
if=614
minute=615
Newfoundland=616

Nova Scotia=617
Payne Thos.=618
Philada [Philadel-
phia]=619
ratify=620
right=621
state=622
turkey=623
time=624
Willson M. 625
Also
Holker M.=626
Miralles D. Juan=627
Smith Wm.=628
Jay M.=629
Morris M. Rob.=630
do Govern
[Gouverneur]=631
Also
brandy French=632
do apple=633
do peach=634
coffee=635
corn=636
molasses=637
gallon=638
rum=639
sugar=640
salt=641
wheat=642
bushel=643

There are no entries for
the letter "Z".

APPENDIX F

PAUL WENTWORTH'S CODE BOOK*

A

Alliance-1

Admiral-2

Ambassador-3

[Perth] Amboy-4

Albany-5

America-7

Army-8

Artillery-9

Arms-10

Ammunition-11

Answer-12

Arnold Gen.-13

Aranda Ct-14

Amsterdam-15

Assembly-16

Antigua-18

B

Baltimore-19

Battalion-20

Bay of Delaware-21

Bay of Chesapeake-22

Barbadoes-23

Berlin-24

Bermuda-25

Beaumarchais-26

British-27

Boston-28

Brest-29

Burgoyne Gen.-30

Bordeaux-31

Brass-32

C

Cargo-33

Canada-34

Carmichael-35

Carolina South-36

Carolina North-37

Camden Ld.-38

Chatham Ld.-39

Chaumont-40

Clinton Gen.-41

Charlestown S. Car-42

Choiseul-43

Colours-44

Congress-45

Commerce-46

Cloathing-47

Court-48

Connecticut-49

Calais-50

D

Deane-51

Delawar County-52

Dieppe-53

De Coudray-55

Du Chaffaulh-56

Dublin-57

Dover-58

Domingo St.-59

Dunkirk-60

E

Embargo-61

Emperor-62

Empress-63

England-64

Enterprize-65

Expedition-66

Earl-67

F

Fishermen-68

Fleet-69

Fort-70

France-71

Franklin Dr.-72

Florida W.-73

Frigates-74

G

Garnier-75

Gates Gen.-76

Georgia-77

Germain Ld.-78

Germany-79

Glasgow-80

Grand Sr. Geo.-81

Grand M.-82

Grantham Ld.-83

Grenades-84

Guadeloupe-85

Gunpowder-86

H

Hampshire-87

Halifax-88

Hamburgh-89

Hanover-90

Hancock-91

*Stevens, Facsimiles, Volume 1, # 1, December 5, 1776

Hesse Capel-92
Howe Ld.-93
Howe Sir Wm.-94
House of Lords-95
   of Commons-96
Havanna-97
Holland-98
Hudson's River-99
He-100

I

Jersey New-101
Jersey Isl.-102
Jamaica-103
India East-104
India West-105
James River-106
Independency-107
Indigo-108
Ireland-109
Iron-110
Izard-111

K

King-112
Kingsbridge-113

L

Lake-114
Lee Gen.-115
Lee Arthur-116
Lee Alderman-117
London-118
Long Island-119
Liverpool-120
Lord-121

M

Massachusetts-122
Maryland-123
Manufacturers-124

Marsailles-125
Martinque-126
Maurepas-127
Mansfield Ld.-128
Memorial-129
Ministry-130
Money-131
Mouth-132
Mortars-133

N

Nantes-134
New Orleans-135
New York-136
Nova Scotia-137
North Ld.-138
North or Northern-139
Neuter-140

O

Officers-141
Ohio-142
Oswego-143

P

Paris-144
Peace-145
Pennsylvania-146
Philadelphia-147
Pistols-148
Porthsmouth-149
Portugal-150
Packet Boat-151
Pensacola-152
Potowmack River-153
Petersburg-154
Privateer-156
Prisoners-156
Poland-157
Propositions-158

Projects-159
Prussia-160
Putnam-161

Q

Quaker-162
Quebec-163
Queen-164
Quilts-165
Quarrel-166
Quantity-167

R

Regiment-168
Rice-169
River-170
Rescounter-171
Rhode Island=172
Rochfort-173
Russia-174

S

Sandwich Ld.-175
Seamen-176
Ships of Line-177
   Sartine M.-178
Soldiers-179
Shelburne Ld.-180
Spain-181
Suffolk Ld.-182
Stormont Ld.-183
Subsidy-184
Staten Isl.-185
Sterling Ld-186
Sullivan Gen.-187
Six Nations-188
Stanwix-189
Stocks-190
Bank Stock-191
India Do-192[*]

[*]"Do" stands for ditto or the same as stated above.

Appendix G

Baron von Steuben Cipher*

A=2124, 5168	2165=ab	2789=1
B=2125, 5169	2167=ac	2792=2
C=2126, 5171	2168=ad	2793=3
D=2131, 5191	2169=ae	2796=4
E=2129, 5179	2175=af	2798=5
F=2132, 5192	2176=ag	2814=6
G=2133, 5193	2178=ah	2815=7
H=2134, 5194	2179=ai	2817=8
I=2135, 5195	2184=al	2819=9
J=2136, 5231	2185=am	2831=10
L=2137, 5232	2186=an	2851=50
M=2138, 5234	2187=ap	2859=100
N=2139, 5235	2188=ar	2862=1,000
O=2141, 5241	2189=aq	2863=10,000
P=2143, 5252	2312=as	2864=100,000
Q=2145, 5253	2313=at	3237-accepts
R=2146, 5254	2314=au	4574=Franklin
S=2147, 5256	2315=ax	4576=Washington
T=2153, 5263	2317=ax	5414=America
U=2154, 5264	2318=ay	5432=Quebec
V=2156, 5265	2319=az	5446=France
X=2158, 5268	2321=ba	5447=England
Y=2159, 5269	2341=be	5453=Miralez
Z=2161, 5271	2342=bi	6491=Jy

*The cipher was originally in French and does not use the letters k or w except in borrowed words. This is a partial transcription. The "Baron von Steuben Cypher" is in the Morristown National Historical Park Collection. A complete transcription is in Weber, *United States Diplomatic Codes and Ciphers*: 278-281 as WE002.

Appendix H

Comte de Rochambeau's Cipher*

A	615	1	sive
B	422	13	si
C	140	19	war
D	581	20	teen
E	283	21	pro
F	539	22	for
G	44	24	an
H	64	26	it
I	263	28	gr
J	263	33	these
K	542	34	or
L	290	36	tion
M	605	38	must
N	118	50	per
O	6 ?	52	land
P	511	54	either
Q	?	66	op
R	53	69	les
S	233	71	to
T	225	73	se
U	570	80	ea
V	570	83	those
W	300	86	pu
X	?	92	take
Y	484		
Z	294		

Nathanael Greene Papers 57:25, Comte de Rochambeau to Nathanael Greene, April 6, 1782. This cipher/code was also used with Robert Morris and George Washington.

APPENDIX I

KEY OF WALPOLE CYPHER IN THE HAND OF WILLIAM EDEN, 1777[*]
(This was an attempt by Eden to break [Horace] Walpole's "cipher.")

4=arrive
5=acknowledge
9=America
army
artillery
ammunition
13=answer
24=bank
41=Burgoyne
53=colonies
54=congress
58=court
60=Mr. Deane
70=dispatches
72=Dover
76=last
81=engagement
84=England
88=express
89=fall
94=express
96=France
/promise
97=Franklin
operations
99=frigate

107=here
119 House of Lords
120 House of Commons
124 Jamaica
128=independency
138=list
143=letters
144=little
158=Maurepas
161=ministers
162=money
163=north
165=Nantes
167=New York
168=now
170=next
172=Lord North
178=neglect
180=parts
181=pay
182=peace
192 prisoners
273=week
94=negotiations/
274=west
202=quickly

203=quiet
204=quarrel
205=quantity
209=retreat
210=return
211=report
213=rise
215=rescouster
223=sell
224=sailed
228=Lord Shelburne
233=soon
234=Spain
238=stock
240=some kind of stock
241= some kind of stock
242=Lord Stormont
244=stopt
246=stand
268=vessels
272=war

[*]Stevens Facsimiles, 139, Auckland Manuscripts, Key of Walpole Cypher in the hand of William Eden, 1777 Walpole's is actually a code, not a cipher.

Appendix J

An Attempt to Decipher a Code of Unknown Origin by William Eden, 1777[*]

9=advise
10=acknowledge
27=all
30=ambassador
32=America
33=Lord Amherst
37=angry
38=answer
50=at
52=any
55=absolute
61=burn
71=begin
75=believe
87=Brest
93=be
95=Burgoyne
99=by
100=business
117=certain
139=commerce
140=consequence
151=conditions
156=Charles Town [S.C.]
159=communications
163=contents
175=deal

185=drew
188=Mr. Deane
201=delivery
205=conjecture
208=continue
213=dispatches
216=do
219=doubt
230=effect
236=embark
239=employ
240=determine
248=discovery
256=express
264=fluctuations-fell
270=few
274=first
281=follow
282=from
289=final
303=frigate
304=from
309=French
311=Garnier
316=Ld George Germain
318=~~get~~
319=give

320=go
321=good
324=government
327=Mr. Grard
329=great
338=had
346=have
348=he
353=his
358=Howe
359=House of Lords
360=House of Commons
361=hurry
364=desist
374=immediately
381=instant/important
392=in
395=incog-concealed
400=informed
415=insurance
430=kept/keep
442=know
443=live
448=letter
451=returned
453=L
458=letter

*This is William Eden's guess as to what each number means. Number 188 was originally Carmichael but changed to Deane. Stevens Facsimiles, 237, Auckland Manuscripts, Cipher with Key in the hand of William Eden, 1777.

459=The King

470=London

472=lose

473=L'Orient

476=memorial

477=maintain

480=make

482=Ld. Maurepas

504=ministers

508=money

509=month

510=money/move

516=our

523=near

530=news

536=morning

540=Ld North

542=not

544=money-business

545=now

549=oblige

566=opened

568=oppose

570=orders

575=out

577=packet

582=Paris

597=Pennsylvania

599=probably

612=partnership

615=port

617=Portland Street

645=pull

646=propositions

740=soon

749=speech

754=stop

755=Ld Stormont

757=stock

758=start

759=British stock

761=submit

760=Ld Suffolk

772=suspend

785=tell

790=this

790=the

792=then

793=them

794=there

796=they

812=treaty

820=Versailles

836=Walpole

838=war

840=was

804=to

854=where

860=will

862=with

865=write

869=yours

841=watch

843=week

846=wise

853=what

Appendix K

Description of counterfeit bills, which were done in
imitation of the true ones ordered by the Honorable the
Continental Congress, bearing date 20th May, 1777,
and 11th April, 1778.*

EIGHT Dollar Bill, dated May 20, 1777, signed Jn. Taylor and Aq. Norris, is done from a copperplate, the letters of which are not only irregular, but by having been engraved, appear more delicate than in the true bills, which are done with type, have a smaller aspect, especially in the Words "*Spanish milled, Silver, Philadelphia,*" &c.—-The figures 1777, as well on the back as the front, appear less than in the true bills.—-In the border at the top of the bill over the words "United States," the two l's in the word "Dollars" are more irregular and more from a straight Line than in the true Bills.

Six Dollar Bills, dated May 20, 1777, signed Jn. Taylor and Aq. Norris, or R. Smith and A. McCallister, or G. Young and C. Lewis, are also done from a copperplate, the letters of which appear for the same reason more delicate than in the true bills, and are also more irregular, particularly the word "entitles," which stands higher than the rest of the line, and the V in the Word "Value"; is placed too high and not on a line with the rest of the word.—-After the words "Six Dollars" under the device in the true bills there is a full stop, in the counterfeits there is none—-On the back of the bill the leaf is much plainer in the counterfeits than in the true bills, the letters there being also more delicate, and the figures "1777" have a smaller appearance than in the genuine bills.

Forty Dollar Bill, dated April 11, 1778, signed D. Reintzel and S. Bryson, or D. Reintzel and J. Snowden, done from a copperplate, of which the same remark may be made as to the delicacy or neatness of the letters as in the preceding descriptions.—-Yet the whole of the letters in the words "THE UNITED STATES," in the top border of the bill, appear stronger, tho' not so uniform or so well shaped as those in the true bills.—In the border at the right hand (or end) of the counterfeit bill the words "*FORTY DOLLARS*" (which are in white letters) are ill done, besides having an E instead of an F in the same.—The larger leaf on the

*Library of Congress, Rare Book and Special Collections Division, Continental Congress and Constitutional Convention Broadsides Collection, no. 55. Printed by John Dunlap at Philadelphia, January 2, 1779.

back of the true bills having beside the branch at the upper end, five branches on each side of the stem, the lowermost of which are not very plain and smaller than the rest; the two last mentioned are entirely omitted in these counterfeits.

Another species of the Forty Dollar Bills of the same date, signed D. Reintzel and J. Snowden, also done from a copperplate, of which the same Remark may be made at to the delicacy or neatness of the letters as in the former descriptions. The letters however in the whole of the bill are very irregular, several being larger than the adjoining ones, and almost all the lines crooked, some being placed too high and others too low. In the Border at the right hand of the counterfeit bill the white letters [missing part of the broadside]

Another counterfeit Forty Dollar Bill, dated 11th April, 1778, is signed J. Duncan and R. Davis, (who by the bye were never signers of continental money) the back of which appears as if done from a copperplate, and the words in the front as if done with types; the borders and devices as if cut in metal. I am sorry to say that this bill is rather so good an imitation that it is really dangerous to most People. I will however point out a few other marks, viz. The first N in the word *Confederation* (in the device) is not placed so square as in the true bills, the last stroke of the said letter leaning more than it should do; indeed the whole of the letters of the word Confederation are not quite so bold as those in the genuine bills. The Stars in the device appear more open in the center of each of them than those in the true bills, which appear mostly closed. In the word Forty at the top of the bill the tail of the y in the counterfeits comes nearer to the bottom of the t than in the true bills; the o in the same word appears on a level with the rest of the word, whilst in the true bills it is placed rather lower than the r which follows it. In this counterfeit (like one of the others) the larger leaf on the back (exclusive of the top branch) has but four branches on each Side thereof, while the true bills have five branches on each side, of which the two lowermost are the most faint, as is already mentioned.

Note: In some of the bills of different denominations D. Remzell is signed for D. Reintzell. It may be further necessary to observe that it is very probable there may be other names affixed as signers to some or all of the different denominations than are noticed in the preceding descriptions, having mentioned in the foregoing only such as I have seen.

Some Persons in the United States having been much alarmed on comparing of bills of credit, by finding bills of the same denomination and date to differ from each other in respect to the letters, some having broken letters and others not, and frequent conclusions having been drawn that the former were true bills, and the broken letters were originally made as private or secret marks: It is therefore become necessary to inform, that those were not intended as marks, but that at the first beginning of printing an emission the letters were whole, and that during printing the emission, from hard lumps or gravel or sand in the paper, with the force of the press, those letters at different times were accidentally and unobservedly broken.

It is signed by John Gibson and the following handwritten note has been affixed to the broadside" Permit no copy of these descriptions to be taken, unless at the request of the Executive Authority of the state to be place in Confidential Hands."

Appendix L

1	and (is)†	122	may	291	your
10	army	128	must	297	Camden
13	beat	141	night	298	Ninety Six
53	for	160	on	299	Santee
61	force	162	other	300	Peedee
63	us	170	over	303	Charles Town
68	go	230	scheme	304	Wilmington
77	horse	240	to	306	Cornwallis
85	in	243	the	310	Nathanael Greene
91	immediately	244	that	311	General Sumter
94	join	263	us	312	General Marion
96	junction	272	we		
121	march	287	with		

Nathanael Greene Papers, Volume 8: 85 and 227 and NGP 27:28

†*Nathanael Greene Papers* reports 1 as "is" but NGP transcriber has it as "and".

Appendix M

Major General Edward Braddock's Cipher[*]

*William L. Clements Library, University of Michigan.

MAPS

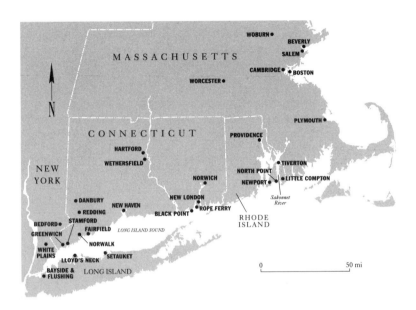

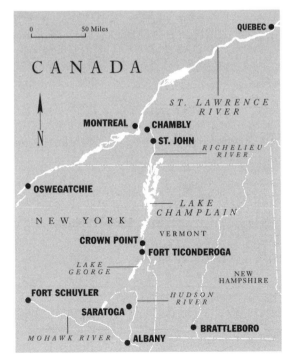

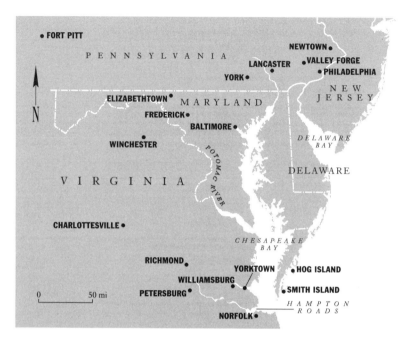

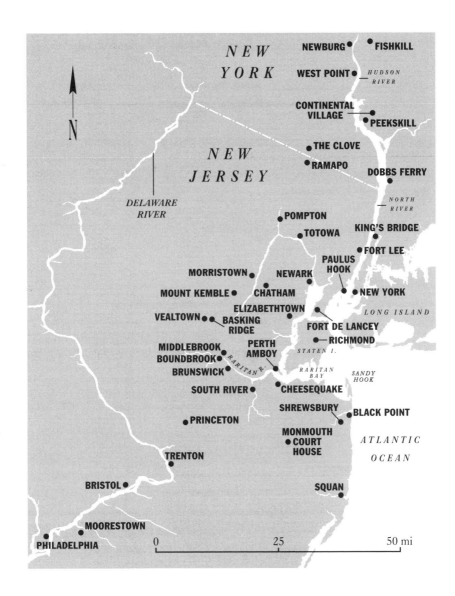

NEW YORK

NEWBURG • • FISHKILL

WEST POINT • — *HUDSON RIVER*

CONTINENTAL VILLAGE — • PEEKSKILL

• THE CLOVE

NEW JERSEY

• RAMAPO

DOBBS FERRY •

DELAWARE RIVER

NORTH RIVER

• POMPTON

• TOTOWA

KING'S BRIDGE •

• FORT LEE

MORRISTOWN •

NEWARK •

PAULUS HOOK

MOUNT KEMBLE •   • CHATHAM

• NEW YORK

ELIZABETHTOWN •

VEALTOWN • • BASKING RIDGE

LONG ISLAND

FORT DE LANCEY •

MIDDLEBROOK •   PERTH AMBOY •

• RICHMOND

BOUNDBROOK •

RARITAN R.

STATEN I.

BRUNSWICK •

RARITAN BAY   *SANDY HOOK*

SOUTH RIVER •

• CHEESEQUAKE

SHREWSBURY •

• PRINCETON

• BLACK POINT

MONMOUTH • COURT HOUSE

ATLANTIC OCEAN

TRENTON •

BRISTOL •

SQUAN •

MOORESTOWN •

PHILADELPHIA •

0   25   50 mi

NOTES

The following abbreviations appear in the notes.

CP	Sir Henry Clinton Papers at the William L. Clements Library
NGP	Nathanael Greene Papers at the William L. Clements Library
GWP	George Washington Papers at the Library of Congress
HMC	Historical Manuscript Commission
JCC	Journals of the Continental Congress
MPAED	Mississippi Provincial Archives, English Dominion
MPASD	Mississippi Provincial Archives, Spanish Dominion
NAVAL	*Naval Documents of the American Revolution* Series
NEHGR	*New England Historical and Genealogical Register*
PBF	Papers of Benjamin Franklin Series
PCC	Papers of the Continental Congress

INTRODUCTION

Note to epigraph: Mei Yao-ch`en was born in 1002 in Hsuan-ch'eng, China, but apparently lived in Wan-ling, Auhui, and died in 1060 in Kaifeng, China. His name also appears as Mei Yaochen. He inherited an official rank. Because of his poetic ability he was summoned to the Imperial Academy and rose to be a second-class secretary. He was assigned to a committee to prepare a new history of the Tang dynasty but died before completing it. Giles, *A Chinese Biographical Dictionary*: Gu Jin Xing Shi Zu Pu: 579 and Giles, *The Art of War*: Chapter 13: #6 note.

1 Sun Tzu lived circa 544 BC to 496 B.C. Giles, *The Art of War*: Chapter 13: #2 and 3.

2 Giles, *The Art of War*: Chapter 13: #4, 5, and 6.

3 Chia Lin lived during the Tang dynasty which lasted from 618 to 907. Giles, *The Art of War*: Chapter 13: #27. Note that the printed copy is in error. It says "with ears or eyes" but should be "without ears or eyes."

4 Tu Mu lived from 803 to 852 A.D. under the Tang dynasty. He was a native of Lo-yang and rose to be secretary of the Grand Council. He was an acclaimed poet and was know as the younger Tu to distinguish him from Tu Fu. He was very knowledgeable in the military history of the Ch'un Ch'iu and Chan Kuo eras. Giles, *A Chinese Biographical Dictionary*: Gu Jin Xing Shi Zu Pu: 783 and Giles, *The Art of War*: Chapter 13: #7. 8, 9, and 10.

5 Sackville Germain Papers, Volume 20, Guy Carleton to Lord George Germain, May 20, 1777.

6 Henri de La Tour d'Auvergne (1611-1675) was known for his siege technique. He was born September 11, 1611 at Sedan, France. Beginning his military career

in 1625 during the Thirty Years' War, he commanded the royal armies in the civil war of the Fronde (1648–1653), in the French invasion of the Spanish Netherlands (1667), and in the third Dutch War. He died July 27, 1675 at Sasbach, Baden-Baden.

7 Longueville, *Marshall Turenne:* 311.

8 *Joseph Reed Papers,* Volume III, New-York Historical Society quoted from Proceedings of the New Jersey Historical Society, New Series XII: 216ff.

9 Tu Yu died in 812 A.D. Giles, *The Art of War:* Chapter 13: #11 and 12. The king of Ch'i did boil a spy alive. Ch'i was an ancient state [771-221 BC] of China and is now in present day Shantung Province, in northeastern China.

10 Rankin, *North Carolina Continentals:* 43-44.

11 Daniel Brodhead Order Book, Colonel Daniel Brodhead to Lieutenant J. Robinson, May 17, 1780.

12 Miamia is the mouth of the Miami River in Ohio. Kellogg, *Frontier Retreat:* 304.

13 Pennsylvania Archives, Volume 7: 589-590, Francis Allison Jr. at Sunbury, Pennsylvania to Joseph Reed, July 28, 1779.

14 Virginia Magazine of History and Biography, Volume VII: 176-177, George Washington to Henry Lee, July 12, 1779 and Henry Lee to George Washington, October 7, 1779.

15 Pennsylvania Archives, Volume 7: 360, Petition of Inhabitants of Northampton Co[unty, Pennsylvania], May 1, 1779 to Governor and Council of the State of Pennsylvania.

16 CP 170:27, Murphy Steel's (or Stiel) report of August 16, 1781.

17 Captain Elijah Wadsworth was from Litchfield, Connecticut. George James is not listed as a man at arms nor is he listed in the recruits. CP 164:31, George James' report, July 14, 1781.

18 Parole is a shortened form of the French *parole d'honneur* which when translated means "word of honor." Lederer, *Colonial American English:* 166.

19 CP 228:2, James Gambier took Captain Hankes's deposition, February 1779.

20 Joshua Loring, British Commissary General of Prisoners, report of November 1, 1778, rebel officers who were British prisoners indicated that of 327 officers: 191 were on parole on Long Island, 51 on parole at home, 80 had broken their parole, and 5 were confined in the Provost. CP 178:15, Alex Jos. Phillips at New York to Sir Henry Clinton, October 3, 1781 and CP 45:3, Great Britain, Army in America, Return of November 1, 1778.

21 CP 146:3, Cortland Skinner to Oliver De Lancey, February 11, 1781.

22 CP 33:30, Richard Howe from on board the ship *Eagle* off of Sandy Hook, New Jersey, to Sir Henry Clinton, April 13, 1778 and CP 34:7, Lord George Germain at Whitehall to Sir Henry Clinton, February 19, 1778.

23 King's American Regiment Order Book, June 7, 1777.

24 Kelby, *Orderly Book of the Three Battalions of Loyalists:* 30 and King's American Regiment Orderly Book: August 20, 1777.

25 In the movie they used lemon juice to make invisible writing appear. Lemon juice would have been used to write the invisible message and not as a reagent to make it appear. Lemon juice turns brown when heated; it does not fade away again as it cools.

26 For an excellent study on American diplomatic codes and ciphers, I suggest Ralph E. Weber's 600-page work *United States Diplomatic Codes and Ciphers 1775-1938*.

Chapter 1

1 Haswell, *Secret Writing in the Century Magazine*: 83.

2 Plat, *The Jewel House of Art and Nature*: 13.

3 Baring-Gould, *Curiosities of Olden Times*: 20.

4 National Security Administration, United States Cryptologic History, Lecture by William F. Friedman: 33–34.

5 Readers may recognize this cipher disk as the prized collector premium known as the Captain Midnight Decoder Badge from the early 1940s. Mendelsohn Collections, Miscellaneous Manuscripts, Photocopy of pages 200–201 of *Opuscoli Morali* published in Venice in 1568.

6 Copies of *Polygraphiae*, *Opus Novum*, and *Subtilitas de Subtilitate Rerum* (The Subtlety of Matter) are in the rare book collection of the National Security Agency, Fort Meade, Maryland.

7 Wilkins, *Mercury, or the Secret and Swift Messenger*: 2–5.

8 Wilkins, *Mercury, or the Secret and Swift Messenger*: 24–25.

9 Kahn, *The Codebreakers*: 170–171, supra note 52.

10 The only known copy of Bright's book is at the Bodleian Library, Oxford, England. Westby-Gibson, *The Bibliography of Shorthand*: 29.

11 The Marquis of Worcester's book was printed in 1663, 1746, 1748, 1763, 1767, and twice in 1778.

12 CP 19:34, Sir Henry Clinton Memorandum, 1776 with a handwritten copy of Clinton's personal shorthand written on a typed translation.

13 Wilkins, *Mercury, or the Secret and Swift Messenger*: 13.

14 Baring-Gould, *Curiosities of Olden Times*: 19.

15 Ibid.: 28–29. Sir Trevanion would end up being killed at the seige of Bristol in 1643.

16 Thicknesse, *A Treatise on the Art of Decyphering*: 31–34.

17 Fraser, "The Use of Encrypted, Coded and Secret Communications Is an 'Ancient Liberty' Protected by the United States Constitution," *Virginia Journal of Law and Technology*, 2 (Fall 1997).

18 Ford, *Writings of Thomas Jefferson*, Volume I: 355–357, Thomas Jefferson to John Page, January 23, 1764.

19 John Jay Papers, Jay ID 08090, Catherine W. Livingston to Sarah Livingston Jay, July 10, 1780.

20 Bidwell, *History of Military Intelligence Division, Department of the Army General Staff 1775-1941*: 2. Most of Washington's outgoing intelligence corre-

spondence was handled by either Lieutenant Colonel Robert Hanson Harrison or Lieutenant Colonel Tench Tilghman.

21 William L. Clements Library, Broadsides Small, W. Roy Stephenson, Winchester.

22 Kitman, *George Washington's Expense Account*: 90; Journal: 51 and 275.

CHAPTER 2

1 CP 105:5, MD (Daniel Martin) to Baron Wilhelm von Knyphausen, June 17, 1780.

2 Emmett Collection, Private Intelligence: 37 and CP 108:36, DM (Daniel Martin) at Paramus to Sir Henry Clinton, July 3, 1780.

3 GWP, General Correspondence, American Intelligence to John Mercereau, July 1780, Signed, Amicus Republicae. It is one of ten reports from Amicus Republicae addressed to John Mercereau or George Washington in the George Washington Papers at the Library of Congress.

4 Monk served Cromwell with unwavering loyalty, though courted by the King in exile. He proclaimed his support for Richard as the Protector in 1658. He secretly responded to the advances of the Royalists. He took his army across the borders on January 1, 1660, and secured the return of Parliamentary Government and the restoration of the Stuart dynasty and Charles II. He was made the 1st Duke of Albemarle for his deeds.

5 CP 94:4, Mr. Turner (Nisbet Balfour) to Uncle (Sir Henry Clinton), April 22, 1780.

6 Margaret stayed with Frederick Jay, a member of the New York Assembly for all its wartime sessions from September 1, 1777, to March 23, 1783, and the brother of her second stepmother. She stayed at the Jays' for several months and then she was sent to stay with the family of an American colonel, by the name of Banker, in Elizabeth Town, New Jersey. When Howe landed on Staten Island, Margaret Moncrieffe and Mrs. Banker were sent ten miles inland. While the family was at church she fled and went back to Elizabeth Town. She stayed for a short time at the home of Continental Congressman John and Mrs. Sarah De Hart. While there she was accosted by some Pennsylvania riflemen who had recently arrived in the area. She then asked for protection from Governor William Livingston. Margaret says she was treated harshly while staying at the Livingston household.

Later James Moncrieffe was promoted to Lieutenant Colonel of the Engineers and served with General Percy. Major Moncrieffe was given the credit for planning and conducting the siege of Charleston, S.C. (See CP 255, Book 3, p. 173, Sir Henry Clinton to Lord George Germain, May 13, 1780). He is not the Captain James Moncrieffe of the Queen's Rangers who never was promoted any higher. Mather, *The Refugees of 1776 from Long Island to Connecticut*: 727–729.

7 Coghlan, *Memoirs of Mrs. Coghlan*: 24.

8 The Archibald Kennedy family lived at 1 Broadway. The building was used as Putnam's and later British headquarters. General Sir Henry Clinton, commander of the British forces in North America also rented a small farm in Bowery

Lane that belonged to Cornelius Tibout. CP 171:40, Lawrence Kortright to Sir Henry Clinton, August 23, 1781. Morristown National Historical Park Manuscript Collection, Israel Putnam to Margaret Moncrieffe, July 26, 1776.

9 Coghlan, *Memoirs of Mrs. Coghlan*: 26.

10 Coghlan, *Memoirs of Mrs. Coghlan*: 30–39.

11 The earliest book that I located on the symbolism of the colors of flowers is *Del significato de colori e de mazzolli: operetta* by Fuluio Pellegrino Morato and published in *Vinegia: per Francesco de Leno, Nell'anno del Signore* in 1559.

12 Grey, *The Complete Fabulist or a Choice Collection of Moral and Entertaining Fables in Prose and Verse*: 260 and reprinted in John Cunningham, *Poems Chiefly Pastoral* [1771]: 118–119.

13 Argens, *The Jewish Spy* [1765]: 11.

14 Morris, *History of Staten Island*: 285, attributes the story about the painting to Colonel William Leete Stone, author of the *Life of Brant*. Here she says that she fell in love with Aaron Burr and wrote to General Putnam that she wanted to accept Burr's proposal. Putnam was opposed to the union and wrote to her "that I surely most not unite with a man who would not hesitate to drench his sword in the blood of my nearest relation, should he be opposed to him in battle." General Putnam was able to get permission for her to go to her father on Staten Island. Major Aaron Burr was to escort her in the barge that belonged to the Continental Congress to General Howe's headquarters at New Dorp, Staten Island. As they came near the British man-of-war *Eagle*, the barge was stopped and Lieutenant Brown prohibited them from going any further and took Miss Margaret Moncrieffe to General Howe. Coghlan, *Memoirs of Mrs. Coghlan*: 39–48.

15 The waterway was the Charles River estuary, also known as the Back Bay. *Boston Gazette* of December 5, 1774, p2,c2. Massachusetts Historical Society, Manuscript Collection, Paul Revere to Jeremy Belknap, 1798.

16 Many years later the decendants of Captain John Pulling and Robert Newman made the claim that they hung the lanthorns.

17 Willard, *Letters on the American Revolution 1774–1776*: 174, letter from Boston dated July 25, 1775, in *Morning Chronicle* and *London Advertiser*, September 11, 1775. General Thomas Gage on July 17, 1775 ordered a Garrison Court of Enquiry, at Concert Hall. Concert Hall was a large building owned by the Deblois brothers who were Loyalists. It was used for private concerts and balls. "The prisoners were [John] Leach, James Lovell, John Hunt, Peter Edes, William Starr, a man named "Dorrington, his son, and maid, for blowing up flies." John Leach also called them "the Fly Blowers." Dorrington, his son and the maid were released on July 26th. The prisoners were taken from the stone jail on Queen Street in Boston and brought before the Court of Enquiry were thought to be spies. The stone jail in Boston was where the soldiers had been confined after the Boston Massacre. It was the only jail in the city and the provincial prisoners captured at Bunker Hill were also confined there. *New England Historical and Genealogical Register* (NEHGR), Volume 19: 256–257, "A Journal Kept by John Leach, During His Confinement by the British, in Boston Gaol [Jail]."

18 William Dorrington took care of the smallpox hospital at the west end of Boston. In the 1790s there is documentation of gunpowder explosions being used to kill flies. In 1794 an accident happened when a boy was attempting to blow up flies with gunpowder. *Annual Register of 1794:* 33.

19 Norman, *Secret Warfare, the Battle of Codes and Ciphers:* 20–24.

20 CP 234:3 and 234:4.

21 CP 13:27, William Phillips at Bath, England to Sir Henry Clinton, January 1776.

22 Gold Star Box, Sir Henry Clinton to John Burgoyne, August 10, 1777.

23 CP 24:12, Burgoyne to Sir Henry Clinton, September 21, 1777 and CP 24:14a, Burgoyne to Sir Henry Clinton, September 23, 1777.

24 CP 54:25, Sir Henry Clinton to Sir John Jervis, March 28, 1779.

25 CP 234:11, undated. Letter is marked with an "L," which was used for Charles Lee (CP 17:20, July 3, 1776) and for Lothario, which was a code name of John André, who was hung October 2, 1780.

26 General James Pattison was appointed Commandant of the City and Garrison of New York on July 5, 1779 and remained in the post until August 13, 1780. New-York Historical Society Collections, 1875 Official Letters of Major General James Pattison: 275–276, Major General James Pattison in New York City to Brigadier General Patterson, commanding on Staten Island, October 6, 1780.

27 Lewis J. Costigan reported to Colonel Matthias Ogden of the 1st New Jersey Regiment and Major General Lord Sterling.

28 GWP, General Correspondence, Lewis J. Costigan to George Washington, December 7, 1778, Intelligence Report; Signed "Z." Costigan's handwriting sometimes looks like a fancy "L," but original period annotations indicates that he used "Z."

29 Lloyd W. Smith Collection #4285, microfilm reel 8, frames 13–18.

30 Lloyd W. Smith Collection, microfilm reel 11, frame 437.

31 Black Point is now Rumson, Monmouth County, New Jersey.

32 GWP, Varick Transcripts, Letterbook 6, 358–359, George Washington to William Alexander, Lord Stirling, October 21, 1778.

33 CP 83:8 Commission Sir Henry Clinton to Thomas Ward, September 8, 1780, and CP 146:3, Cortland Skinner to Oliver De Lancey, February 11, 1781.

34 Walter Bates born March 14, 1760, to John and Sarah (Bostwick) Bates in what is now Darien, Connecticut. He went in the *Union* to St. John, New Brunswick, and became sheriff of King's County. He died in Kingston in 1842.

35 *The North American and West Indian Gazetteer,* published in 1778, does not list a Milford Bay. Milford Bay is probably Milford Harbor, Milford, Connecticut. East, *Connecticut's Loyalist:* 24.

36 Fairfield was the only place in Connecticut that the Americans would accept a flag of truce from the British. The Americans had stated that they would send no flags to Long Island. CP 30:2, January 4, 1778, Philip Browne to Commodore William Hotham. GWP, General Correspondence, Caleb Brewster to George Washington, February 14, 1781, with prisoner list.

37 CP 31:6, William Howe to Major General Robert Pigot, February 5, 1778.

38 CP 192: and Stevens, *Report on American Manuscripts in the Royal Institution of Great Britain*, Volume 2: 418, Lieutenant General Alexander Leslie to Sir Henry Clinton, March 12, 1782.

39 Barnwell, "Correspondence of the Hon. Arthur Middleton," *South Carolina Historical and Genealogical Magazine*, volume 26: 191–192, Aedanus Burke to Arthur Middleton, January 25, 1782.

40 The rest of the story on Pompey Lamb is not supported by original documentation but on the recollections of an octogenarian. The story is that Captain Lamb had Pompey obtain a pass which he could use to bring his vegetables at night. The British, needing the vegetables, gave him the countersign of "The fort is our own." On the night of the attack on the fort, July 15, 1779, Pompey approached the fort with two soldiers disguised as farmers. The soldiers overpowered the guards, which left the road leading to the fort unprotected. Wayne and his 1,200 troops using bayonets captured the fort. Pompey was given his freedom and a horse for his spying activities. Pompey Lamb did serve in the Orange County militia and possibly the 2nd New York Regiment in 1780. Loprieno, *Pompey Lamb Revisited: Black Soldiers in the American Revolution* at http://www2.lhric.org/spbattle/P0omp.html and Winslow, *Afro-Americans '76*: 52, taken from Katz, *The Negro Soldier*. Lamb was not the only American spy at the fort. Captain Allen McLane, disguised as a country bumpkin, accompanied Mrs. Smith to see her son at the British Fort at Stony Point. Captain McLane stayed at the fort for two weeks collecting information. *Nathan Hale Institute*: 13–14.

41 Letters of Delegates to Congress, 1774–1789, Volume 18: 526–527, Abraham Clark to Caleb Camp, May 22, 1782.

42 JCC, Volume XXIII, 1782: 697.

43 Washington was writing about New Jersey and New York. Raritan Bay was also known as the Amboy or Raritan Sound. The North River is also known as the Hudson River. Fitzpatrick, *Writings of Washington*, Volume 25: 322.

44 GWP, Varick Transcripts, Letterbook 4: 379, George Washington to William Livingston, November 13, 1782.

45 GWP, Varick Transcripts, Letterbook 6: 351–354, George Washington to Benjamin Lincoln, November 6, 1782.

46 Pennypacker, *General Washington's Spies*: 264.

47 Fortescue, *The Correspondence of King George the Third, from 1760 to December 1783*, Volume VI: 340, Oct. 23, 1782, Clarke was reimbursed £27,14,6 for what he paid Captain Killick.

48 Shelburne Papers, Volume 78, Shelburne at London to Unknown, April 22, 1782: 29–32.

49 Vergennes was born at Dijon, France, on December 10, 1717.

50 Baring-Gould, *Curiosities of Olden Times*: 27–28.

Chapter 3

1 Todd was the Foreign Secretary from 1752 to 1787.

2 Historical Manuscript Commission, Manuscripts of the Earl of Dartmouth, American Papers, Volume II: 371, Gilbert Barkly at Philadelphia to William Strahan, September 5, 1775, intercepted by the Post Office.

3 Stevens Facsimiles: 32, Auckland Manuscripts, Anthony Todd to William Eden, February 21, 1777.

4 Stevens Facsimiles: 209, Auckland Manuscripts, Anthony Todd to William Eden, October 27, 1777.

5 *The Cumberland Chronicle: or Whitehaven Intelligencer* [London, England] changed its name in 1777 to the *Cumberland Chronicle* or *Whitehaven Public Advertiser*. Stevens Facsimiles: 209, Auckland Manuscripts, Anthony Todd to William Eden, October 27, 1777.

6 HMC, Manuscripts of the Earl of Dartmouth, American Papers, Volume II: 373, William Donaldson at London to Peter N. B. Livingston at New York intercepted by Mr. Todd, Secretary to the Post Office.

7 Bolton, *Letters of Hugh, Earl Percy, from Boston and New York, 1774–1776:* 37, Hugh Earl Percy at Boston to Lord Northumberland [his father], September 12, 1774.

8 The Colony of Connecticut paid its citizens for guiding troops responding to the Lexington Alarm moving northward through the colony.

9 Gage Papers, Volume 128, Cadwallader Colden at New York City to Thomas Gage, April 25, 1775 and John Foxcroft, Deputy Post Master at New York City, to Thomas Gage, April 26, 1775.

10 CP 10:15, John Stuart to Thomas Gage, July 9, 1775.

11 The committee of seven was selected on the 17th, JCC Volume 3: 357–359, November 17, 1775 and JCC Volume 3: 360–361, November 20, 1775.

12 The items selected were printed in the *Pennsylvania Packet*, November 27, 1775. JCC Volume 3: 368, November 24, 1775.

13 Cortland Skinner spelled his name both Cortland and Cortlandt. Force, American Archives, Series 4, Volume 4: 363–364, Cortlandt Skinner to Lieutenant Colonel William Skinner at Westbury, Hants[, England], December 1775.

14 JCC 4: 41–42, January 9, 1776.

15 The *Asia* was built in Portsmouth, England, in 1764 with a gun deck of 158 feet, keel of 129 feet 6 1/2 inches and weighted 1,364 tons. She carried 64 guns. She was decommissioned in 1803 and broken up in 1804. While in American waters, George Vandeput was her commander.

16 JCC Volume 4: 285–286, April 16, 1776.

17 Nexsen, who was born in 1740, was a substantial citizen. He had a shop in a wooden building at Burling Slip and owned the next two brick houses at 18 and 20. (Burling Slip is the east end of the present John Street. The slip was filled in 1835.) Nexsen maintained a set of scales at his shop capable of weighing hemp, iron, logs, sugar, and tobacco. He traded with the West Indies bringing back rum, lime juice, Madeira, wines in pipes, hogsheads, and quarter casks and was also known to import and sell a slave. His sloop was the *Charity* under command of

Captain Drugal and was docked at Cruger's Wharf. Nexsen was the father of twenty-one children with three wives.

18 The Battle of Long Island was on August 27, 1776. Scoville, *The Old Merchants of New York City* (1866): 159–163, says General Clinton was commander, but it was General Howe.

19 The Rope Ferry was over the Niantic River in Waterford Township, near New London, Connecticut.

20 Oyster Pond Point is in the town of Southold, Suffolk County, Long Island, New York.

21 Gray, *Gray's Narrative*: 1–8.

22 Clinton, *Public Papers of George Clinton*, Volume VI: 771–772 and GWP Varick Transcripts, Letterbook 4: 119–120, George Washington at New Windsor, New York, to Governor George Clinton, April 15, 1781.

23 Clinton, *Public Papers of George Clinton*, Volume VI: 771–772, Governor George Clinton at Poughkeepsie, New York, to General Philip Schuyler, April 16, 1781.

CHAPTER 4

1 Captain William Kidd (1645–May 23, 1701) was tried, found guilty, and hanged for murder and piracy. The hanging took place at the "execution dock" in the Wapping area of London. Poe, *The Gold Bug* (1894 edition): 86–112.

2 Poe says that zaffre dissolved in aqua regia and diluted with four times its weight in water is sometimes used for invisible writing. Zaffre is the residue of cobalt, after the sulfur, arsenic, and other volatile components of this mineral have been expelled by calcination. Aqua regia is a compound of the nitrous and marine acids, in different proportions, according to its purpose, and usually made by dissolving common salt in nitrous acid. Aqua regia is used as a menstruum for gold; it likewise dissolves almost all other metals, except silver.

Poe also says that regulus of cobalt dissolved in spirits of nitre produces red. Regulus was a term given to metallic matters when separated from their ores by fusion (application of heat). Spirits of nitre is an alcoholic solution of nitrous (hyponitrous) ether, formerly called nitric ether, which is a compound of nitrous (hyponitrous) acid and ether. It is produced by the reaction between nitric acid and alcohol, aided by heat. Poe, *The Gold Bug* (1894 edition): 84–86.

3 Fair water meant clear, pure, and not cloudy water. Oxford English Dictionary, 1933 edition, Volume 4:27 definition III.8.b. "Coppress" is an old alternate spelling of copperas (ferrous sulfate). Plat, *The Jewel House of Art and Nature*: 11–12, #8.

4 Tragacanth is a gummy exudation from the leguminous shrub *Astragalus gummifer* of southeastern Europe and western Asia. It is obtained through incisions in the stem of the plant. Tragacanth is almost insoluble in water but swells in it to form a stiff gel. It is used in pills as an emulsifying agent.

5 F. [Falconer], *Rules for Explaining and Deciphering All Manner of Secret Writing, Plain and Demonstrative*: 98–101.

6 GWP, General Correspondence, Bezaleel Kerr to Mrs. Kerr, May 22, 1779, [Lighter text originally in invisible ink], Anonymous to Fred Kisselman, May 22, 1779, [Contains letter written in invisible ink from Bezaleel Kerr to his Wife], G. Ross to Aneas Urquhart, May 22, 1779, [Contains letter written in invisible ink from Bezaleel Kerr to Aneas Urquhart] Bezaleel, and Kerr to Aneas Urquhart, May 22, 1779, [Reverse orientation text written in invisible ink between lines of "fake" letter].

7 GWP, Varick Transcripts, Letterbook 9: 247–249, George Washington to Benjamin Tallmadge, July 25, 1779.

8 Gold Star Box, Benjamin Thompson at Woburn, Massachusetts, to Unknown at Boston, May 6, 1775.

9 French, *General Gage's Informers*: 131–132.

10 GWP, Varick Transcripts, Letterbook 9: 247–249, George Washington to Benjamin Tallmadge, July 25, 1779, and Clements Library, Gold Star Box, Benjamin Thompson at Woburn, Massachusetts, to Unknown at Boston, May 6, 1775.

11 Force, American Archives, Series 4, Volume 4: 531, Petition of Benjamin Church at the Norwich jail to the Continental Congress, January 1, 1776. He states that he was arrested on Wednesday September 27 however a general order issued on the 28th would indicate that he was unfettered. He was arrested by September 30, 1775.

12 Wilmington, Middlesex County, Massachusetts, is sixteen miles north of Boston.

13 George E. Ellis (*Memoir*: 94) quoted in French, *General Gage's Informers*: 161.

14 Ibid., 94.

15 Sanborn C. Brown and Elbridge W. Stein did a study of Thompson's original document, which is at the William L. Clements Library at the University of Michigan. A 7 kilovolt X-ray of the document ruled out both bismuth and lead inks. Both bismuth and lead inks would show on the X-ray if they were present and no trace was found. The reagent wash did show on the X-ray which is consistent with the use of gallo-tannic ink. The reagent wash of ammonia and hydrogen sulfide would not have shown on the X-ray. A test batch of gallo-tannic ink was prepared and developed with iron sulfate and it produced the same results as the document. Under visible light both the document and the test batch looked the same. Under ultraviolet light the iron sulfate shows dark purple and both the document and the test batch were the same. Although the developer was initially colorless, with moisture and time, ferrous salts oxidize to the ferric state giving the document its brown color. Under infrared light the sympathetic inks disappear but the carbon ink used to write the visible part of the letter remain. They also studied the sealing wax used on the invisible ink letter with known letters from Benjamin Thompson of the period and found them to be identical in composition. They also did a handwriting comparison and found the peculiarities of Thompson's writing matched the invisible ink letter. Brown and Stein, *Journal of Criminal Law and Criminology*, Volume 40, Number 5 (January–February 1950):

627–636, *Benjamin Thompson and the First Secret-Ink Letter of the American Revolution* and Bendikson, *Franco American Review*, Volume 1 Number 3 (December 1936), *The Restoration of Obliterated Passages and of Secret Writing in Diplomatic Missives*: 253–255.

16 Collections of the New-York Historical Society for the Year 1878: 401, John Jay at Fishkill to Robert Morris, October 6, 1776.

17 Papers of John Jay #01018 (New York Public Library), John Jay to Robert Morris, September 15, 1776.

18 Letters of Delegates to Congress, Volume 5: 225 #6992 and Force, *American Archives*, Series 5, Volume 2: 459, Robert Morris to John Jay, September 23, 1776.

19 George D. van Arsdale of Pasadena, California, was the chemical engineer who performed the chemical analysis on a Silas Deane document in the 1930's. Bendikson, *Franco American Review*, Volume 1 Number 3 (December 1936), *The Restoration of Obliterated Passages and of Secret Writing in Diplomatic Missives*: 253–255.

20 Tilghman does not provide the source of the letter. There are several Philadelphians who are possible sources of the letter, such as Andrew, John, and William Allen. They were seen at Trenton by Captain Francis Murray. Andrew Allen was also seen by someone named McPherson. Tilghman, Oswald, *Memoir of Lieutenant Colonel Tench Tilghman Secretary and Aid to Washington*: 147–148, Tench Tilghman at Coryell's Ferry to James Tilghman, December 16, 1776. When Howe arrived at Trenton in 1776, Joseph Galloway had constant communication with his friends in Pennsylvania. Examination of Joseph Galloway: 14. Although other Philadelphians were at Trenton, Galloway was known to be in contact with his friends in Pennsylvania and may be a slightly more probable source of the letter. Later he carried on a clandestine correspondence from New York with his wife in Philadelphia.

21 Tilghman, *Memoir of Lieutenant Colonel Tench Tilghman*: 151–153, Tench Tilghman to James Tilghman, February 22, 1777.

22 Upton, *The Loyal Whig: William Smith*: 225.

23 GWP, General Correspondence, G. Ross to Aneas Urquhart, May 22, 1779, [Contains letter written in invisible ink from Bezaleel Kerr to Aneas Urquhart] and Bezaleel Kerr to Aneas Urquhart, May 22, 1779, [Reverse orientation text written in invisible ink between lines of "fake" letter]; Bezaleel Kerr to Mrs. Kerr, May 22, 1779, [Lighter text originally in invisible ink] Anonymous to Fred Kisselman, May 22, 1779, [Contains letter written in invisible ink from Bezaleel Kerr to his Wife]; and G. Ross to Aneas Urquhart, May 22, 1779, [Contains letter written in invisible ink from Bezaleel Kerr to Aneas Urquhart] Bezaleel Kerr to Aneas Urquhart, May 22, 1779, [Reverse orientation text written in invisible ink between lines of "fake" letter].

24 Sir Henry Clinton after the war marked his documents with a shorthand filing code usually placed on the last page. Any letter followed by a plus or minus sign is his filing code and not an indication of a secret message.

25 CP 47:36 (two versions), William Phillips to Sir Henry Clinton, December 1778, marked ABC.

26 CP 59:27, Jonathan Odell to John André, May 31, 1779.

27 Ibid.

28 Abraham Woodhull (Culper and later known as Culper, Sr.) began spy operations in 1778. Despite some claims by historians, the Culpers were not the first American spy ring. The Mercereau spy ring was in operation in 1776.

29 GWP, Varick Transcripts, Letterbook 8: 323, George Washington to Major Benjamin Tallmadge, April 30, 1779.

30 GWP, Varick Transcripts, Letterbook 8: 323, George Washington to Benjamin Tallmadge, April 30, 1779 and GWP, Varick Transcripts, Letterbook 9: 90–91, George Washington at Smith's Tavern in the Clove to Benjamin Tallmadge, June 13, 1779.

31 GWP, Varick Transcripts, Letterbook 1: 268–269 and General Correspondence, George Washington to Elias Boudinot, May 3, 1779.

32 Bedford is in eastern Westchester County, New York but is twelve miles north of Stamford, Connecticut. Pound Ridge is situated between Bedford and the Connecticut state line.

33 Heath, *Memoirs of the American War*: 220–221.

34 Washington replaced the lost secret service funds with fifty guineas on July 21. GWP, Financial Papers, Benjamin Tallmadge to George Washington, July 21, 1779, Revolutionary War Accounts, Vouchers, and Receipted Accounts 2.

35 GWP, Varick Transcripts, Letterbook 9: 163–164, George Washington to Benjamin Tallmadge, July 5, 1779.

36 CP 119:14, Provost Report for New York City, August 28, 1780. Higday wrote a desperate letter with bad spelling to General Sir Henry Clinton that about three or four weeks prior he had taken three American officers across the Hudson River to New Jersey. "On going over thire Decourse wass what a fine thing it might be for me to fech Information over for Washenton that he would make me rich in so doing A Cordingly i being left by God and his Devine purtecktion to my Self (appently but illegibly yielded to the temptation. He went with the American officers to General George Washington) and ofered the Above purposals but he wass afreaid to venter but said he would consither on it. And did not countence me much & had sum Congress munney & thought to buy A Cow on time with it—the Money wass So bad I could not by one So I returned home for which Reson I suppose he hath sent this Letter that now is taken—Now I did not think Even they would write to me for Washington Said my name was in the black book for being A friend to Goivernment and would not trust me." CP 63:9, George Higday to Sir Henry Clinton, July 13, 1779.

37 GWP, Varick Transcripts, Letterbook 9: 247–249, George Washington to Benjamin Tallmadge, July 25, 1779.

38 GWP, Varick Transcripts, Letterbook 10: 48–50 and General Correspondence, George Washington to Benjamin Tallmadge, September 24, 1779.

39 GWP, Varick Transcripts, Letterbook 2: 41–42, George Washington to James Jay, April 9, 1780.

40 GWP, General Correspondence, James Jay at Fishkill to George Washington, April 13 and 20, 1780.

41 GWP, Varick Transcripts, Letterbook 3: 264–265, George Washington to James Jay, May 12, 1780, and Varick Transcripts, Letterbook 11: 313–314, George Washington to Udny Hay, May 13, 1780.

42 GWP, General Correspondence, James Jay to George Washington, September 19, 1780.

43 Dictionary of Canadian Biography Online: Volume V, Thomas Carleton.

44 Canada, Department of Militia and Defense, A *History of the Organization . . . Volume III, The War of the American Revolution, The Province of Quebec under the administration of Governor Frederic Haldimand, 1778–1784* (hereafter cited as Canada III, Haldimand): 20.

45 Canada III, Haldimand: 164–165 #180 and 182, Public Archives of Canada, Haldimand Papers, Series B, Volume 133: 210–211, Chr. Carleton at Chambly to General Haldimand, July 23, 1780 and Haldimand Papers, Series B, Volume 135: 122–123, Frederick Haldimand at Quebec to Major Carleton, July 24, 1780. Frederick Haldimand was born in Neuchatel, Switzerland in October 1718.

46 Canada III, Haldimand: 164–165 #182, Public Archives of Canada, Haldimand Papers, Series B, Volume 135: 122–123, Frederick Haldimand at Quebec to Major Carleton, July 24, 1780.

47 Dictionary of Canadian Biography Online: Volume V, Sir Frederick Haldimand.

48 Canada III, Haldimand: 165, #183, Public Archives of Canada, Haldimand Papers, Series B, Volume 135: 124–125, Frederick Haldimand at Quebec to Major Carleton, July 27, 1780.

49 Pierre Du Calvet's stone house built in 1725 still stands at 405 rue Bonsecours, Vieux-Montréal, Montréal. It houses an upscale bed and breakfast and a restaurant. Dictionary of Canadian Biography Online: Volume IV, Pierre Du Calvet. He also owned a country estate called the Seigniolry of the River David, near Sorel. Du Calvet, *The Case of Peter Calvet, Esq.*

50 Canada III, Haldimand: 165 #184, Public Archives of Canada, Colonial Office Records, Series Q, Volume 20: 165, Chr. Carleton at Chambly to Frederick Haldimand, July 30, 1780.

51 Canada III, Haldimand. 169 #192, Public Archives of Canada, Haldimand Papers, Series B, Volume 205: 70–72, Boyer [Pillon] at Montreal to General George Washington and Marquis de La Fayette, September 7, 1780.

52 Canada III, Haldimand: 175–178 #205, Public Archives of Canada, Colonial Office Records, Series Q, Volume 17-1: 270–298, Frederick Haldimand at Quebec to Lord George Germain, October 25, 1780.

53 Canada III, Haldimand: 172 #200, Public Archives of Canada, Haldimand Papers, Series Q, Volume 20: 44–45, Chr. Carleton at St. John's to Captain Mathews, September 24, 1780.

54 Canada III, Haldimand: 173 #201, Public Archives of Canada, Haldimand Papers, Series B, Volume 131: 78–79, Frederick Haldimand at Quebec to Brigadier General Maclean, September 28, 1780.

55 Canada III, Haldimand: 188 #215, Public Archives of Canada, Haldimand Papers, Series B, Volume 135: 156, Frederick Haldimand at Quebec to Major Carleton, November 6, 1780.

56 Canada III, Haldimand: 189 #217, Public Archives of Canada, Haldimand Papers, Series B, Volume 147: 278–280, Frederick Haldimand to Henry Clinton, November 16, 1780.

57 Canada III, Haldimand: 169 #192, Public Archives of Canada, Haldimand Papers, Series B, Volume 205: 70–72, Boyer [Pillon] at Montreal to General George Washington and Marquis de La Fayette, September 7, 1780.

58 Du Calvet, The Case of Peter du Calvet, Esq. of Montreal.

59 John Jay Papers #12326, Governor Haldimand to Unknown, July 16, 1782. The original is on file at the Great Britain Public Records Office (hereafter PRO), Image Library.

60 Shelburne Papers, Volume 35, Mr. Fraser at St. James to Lord Shelburne, August 7, 1782 enclosing a letter in white ink (The letter was not found so its source remains unknown). PRO T 1/563/358–359, Secretary of State's Office, W. Fraser asks for a payment of a sum for secret service, March 23, 1780 and T 1/567/319–322, Secretary of State's Office, W. Fraser; two letters, one of which is for secret service, April 16, 1781.

CHAPTER 5

1 Thomas Gage Papers, Volume 126, Carleton to Thomas Gage, February 4, 1775 and Gage at Boston to Carleton, March 11, 1775.

2 Thomas Gage Papers, Earl of Dartmouth at Whitehall to General Thomas Gage at Boston, April 15, 1775, received May 25, 1775.

3 Collections of the Massachusetts Historical Society, Volume V, 1st Series: 106 ff and Proceedings of the Massachusetts Historical Society, Volume 16: 371 ff. Paul Revere to Jeremy Belknap (1798). Dr. Savage lived with Dr. Church in 1775 and took care of his business and books. He knew Dr. Church was hurting for money, but a short time before the Battles of Concord and Lexington, Dr. Church came into several hundred new British guineas and he suspected that Church received the money from the British.

4 Carter, ed., Gage Correspondence, I: 172, Lord Dartmouth to Gage, August 23, 1774.

5 Public Record Office, Audit Office 12:10.97, Mrs. Church's pension request, William Warden's statement that in 1775 he was sent by General Gage to pick up Dr. Church's reports at Marblehead and Salem.

6 The committee met at the Green Dragon Tavern, built circa 1712, on Union Street just north of Hanover Street in Boston. A drawing of this brick building was made in 1773 by John Johnson and is in the collection of the American Antiquarian Society. See Fischer, Paul Revere's Ride: 53 for an illustration of this drawing.

7 HMC, Manuscripts of the Earl of Dartmouth, American Papers, Volume II: 278, Thomas Gage to Lord Dartmouth # 25, March 4, 1775. Gage stated that he would tell Lord Dartmouth the source of the information later.

8 It was on Friday April 21, 1775. Jonathan Hastings was the Harvard College steward.

9 Revere's 1798 account identifies Cane as a major. As Lt. Col. Maurice Cane was in the West Indies at the time and Captain Edward Cane became a major on July 12, 1775, this officer was probably Edward. French, *General Gage's Informers*: 166–167. Revere's account was printed by the Massachusetts Historical Society in the 5th Volume of the Society's *Collections*, 1st Series: 106 ff. and in the 16th volume of the *Proceedings*: 371 ff. Events in the city of Boston were told to Paul Revere by Deacon Caleb Davis.

10 Gage Papers, Dr. Church to Gage, undated letter but written sometime between May 1 and May 7, 1775 and French, *General Gage's Informers*: 151–154.

11 She was the widow of Major Henry Vassall. Washington's headquarters was at the home of John Vassall, Jr. (now the Longfellow National Historic Site). Henry was John's uncle. Gilman, *Cambridge of 1776, Extracts from the Diary of Dorothy Dudley*: 34, 39, and 101 which states that "B. Church, Jr." had been carved into one of the doors of the house.

12 Dr. Warren had died in the Battle at Bunker Hill on June 17, 1775.

13 John Fleming with John Mein had published the *Boston Chronicle* from December 21, 1767 to June 25, 1770 in Newberry Street opposite the White Horse Tavern. Fleming then opened a printing shop in King Street. Thomas, *The History of Printing in America*: 149–151 and 263–265. John Fleming's cipher was the same one used by Dr. Church when he wrote to Major Cane a week later.

14 Collections of the Massachusetts Historical Society, 1st Series, Volume 1 (1792): 88–89, John Fleming's letter is undated.

15 This is probably Edward Cane of the 43rd Regiment of Foot who was promoted from Captain to Major on July 12, 1775. He was routinely assigned to either the lines or the pickets (July 16, 23, 25, 31; Aug 2, 8, 11, 16, 21; and Sept. 23 and 26) until his retirement on October 8, 1775. Stevens, *General Sir William Howe's Orderly Book*: 41–42, 48, 50, 56, 62, 65, 70, 73, 94, 96, and 108. See note 9 on Edward Cane being confused with Lieutenant Colonel Maurice Cane of the 6th Regiment of Foot.

16 "Letters of Ebenezer Huntington," *American Historical Review*, Vol. V, # 4 (July 1900), 705–706, Ebenezer Huntington at Roxbury Camp to Andrew Huntington (brother), merchant at Norwich, Connecticut, October 3, 1775. Ebenezer Huntington wrote that the woman "is now with child by him [Dr. Church] and he owns himself the father (for he has dismissed his wife)." Ezra Stiles in his diary wrote she was a "girl of pleasure." Dexter, *Diary of Ezra Stiles*, Volume 1: 619. The frigate HMS *Rose* (1757–1779) was launched from the yard of Hugh Blades in Hull, England. Copies of the ship's plan are available at the National Maritime Museum in Greenwich, England. A replica of the *Rose* was

built in Lunenburg, Nova Scotia, in 1970 using the original construction draw-ings. The Island of Rhode Island includes the towns of Newport and Portsmouth.

17 Wenwood's famous bakery and bread shop was located on the waterfront at Bannister's Wharf in Newport. Dexter, *Diary of Ezra Stiles*, Volume 1: 618–619 and 628.

18 GWP, Series 2, Letterbook 7: 87, and Force, American Archives, Series 4, Volume 3: 956–958, George Washington at Cambridge to Continental Congress, October 5, 1775.

19 The letter is addressed "to Major Cane in Boston on his majesty's service" in very good penmanship. *The Papers of George Washington, Revolutionary War Series*, Volume 2: 102 footnote 3, quotes Ezra Stiles that she addressed the letter. However when comparing the aforementioned address to a letter she wrote, (GWP, General Correspondence, Unknown to Godfrey Wenwood, Baker in Newport, September 1775), it is not her poor handwriting on the letter to Major Cane.

20 GWP, General Correspondence, attributes letter to Joseph Reed and Force, American Archives, Series 4, Volume 3: 780 attributes the letter to General Horatio Gates; _[Uncertain] at Cambridge to Dr. Church, September 24, 1775.

21 GWP, General Correspondence, Unknown (Dr. Church's mistress) to Godfrey Wenwood, Baker in Newport, Sept. 1775. She stated the letter should be addressed to "Mr. Ewerd Harton living on Mr. Tapthorps farm." Little Cambridge, Massachusetts had about 300 residents at the time of the revolution and was the only part of Cambridge that was south of the Charles River. It became the town of Brighton in 1807.

22 GWP, General Correspondence, Henry Ward at Providence, R.I. to Nathanael Greene, September 26, 1775.

23 GWP, Varick Transcripts, Letterbook 1: 53–54 and Series 2, Letterbook 7; 101–104, George Washington to Congress, October 5, 1775; Van Doren, *Secret History*: 21–22; and "Letters of Ebenezer Huntington," *American Historical Review*, Volume V, # 4 (July 1900): 705–706, Ebenezer Huntington at Roxbury Camp to Andrew Huntington (brother), merchant at Norwich, Connecticut, October 3, 1775.

24 "Letters of Ebenezer Huntington," *American Historical Review*, Volume V, # 4 (July 1900): 705–706, Ebenezer Huntington at Roxbury Camp to Andrew Huntington (brother), merchant at Norwich, Connecticut, October 3, 1775. Gilman, *Cambridge of 1776, Extracts from the Diary of Dorothy Dudley*: 39. Force, American Archives, Series 4, Volume 4: 531, Petition of Benjamin Church at the Norwich jail to the Continental Congress, January 1, 1776. He states that he was arrested on Wednesday September 27, however a general order issued on the 28th would indicate that he was unfettered. He was arrested by the 30th.

25 Silas Downer (1729–1785) graduated from Harvard and practiced law in Providence. He denied the authority of Parliament over the colonies in his famous "Liberty Tree" speech of July 25, 1768.

26 *Papers of General Nathanael Greene*, Volume I: 127, Nathanael Greene at Prospect Hill, Massachusetts, to Secretary Henry Ward of Rhode Island, September 30, 1776.

27 United States National Archives, Revolutionary War Pension Application, Abel Mann's pension deposition of July 27, 1832, at the age of 79. He was a soldier in the Rhode Island militia stationed at Prospect Hill outside Boston.

28 Carl Van Doren in *Secret History of the American Revolution* believed that it was Benjamin Thompson (aka Count Rumford). Van Doren says that Thompson helped aid Dr. Church in getting information to General Gage.

29 Gilman, *Cambridge of 1776, Extracts from the Diary of Dorothy Dudley*: 34.

30 Elbridge Gerry was born in Marblehead, Massachusetts on June 17, 1744, and had graduated from Harvard in 1762. He became Vice President of the United States in 1812 and held the position until his death in 1814. Gerry had been a member of the Massachusetts General Assembly from 1772 to 1775, the Massachusetts Provincial Congress from 1774 to 1775, and the Committee of Correspondence in 1773. The term *gerrymander* is named for him.

31 GWP, General Correspondence, Elbridge Gerry at Watertown, Massachusetts, to Joseph Reed at Cambridge, October 5, 1775. Gerry had made a copy and sent it to Col. Mifflin to forward it to General Wayne at Congress. Washington through Reed had objected to Gerry getting involved in deciphering and also making a copy of the letter.

32 Samuel West was born in Yarmouth, Massachusetts, on February 21, 1731. He graduated from Harvard in 1754 and was a classmate of Dr. Church. He was pastor of the Congregational Church in Dartmouth, Massachusetts (later renamed New Bedford) from 1761 to 1803.

33 Dr. James McHenry (1753–1816) of Baltimore was captured at Fort Washington in November 1776 and exchanged in March 1778. Served as assistant secretary on Washington's staff from May 1778 to August 1780 as an aide to Gen. Lafayette until December 1781. He was a member of the Continental Congress (1783–1786) and Secretary of War (1796–1800). Fort McHenry in Baltimore is named after him. Dr. Charles McKnight (1750–1791) of Cranbury, New Jersey, served in the army medical department until 1782. GWP, General Correspondence, Benjamin Church Jr. to George Washington, October (probably the 3rd), 1775.

34 GWP, General Correspondence, Benjamin Church Jr. to Major Cane in Boston, October 3, 1775, translation of Cryptogram.

35 GWP, General Correspondence, Benjamin Church Jr. to Major Cane in Boston, October 3, 1775, translation of Cryptogram and Force, American Archives, Series 4, Volume 3: 958–959, Number 2, Doctor Church's Intercepted Letter.

36 GWP, General Correspondence, Benjamin Church Jr. to Major Cane in Boston, October 3, 1775, translation of Cryptogram and Force, American Archives, Series 4, Volume 3: 958–959, Number 2, Doctor Church's Intercepted Letter.

37 GWP, General Correspondence, Benjamin Church Jr. to George Washington. Docketed by Thomas Mifflin as October 1775. Most likely written on the 3rd.

38 Thomas Hutchinson in 1754 had agreed with Benjamin Franklin's call for a union of the colonies. In 1771 he was appointed Royal Governor of Massachusetts and wanted to faithfully follow the instructions of the Crown and ordered troops against civilians. Franklin sent intercepted letters of his back to America and they were interpreted as a call for more stringent authority over the colony. JCC, Volume 2: 111–122.

39 Massachusetts Historical Society, 2002, John Adams to Abigail Adams, October 28, 1775 [electronic edition]. Adams Family Papers: An Electronic Archive. Boston, Massachusetts: http://www.masshist.org/digitaladams/.

40 JCC, Volume 3: 334.

41 JCC, Volume 4: 352, May 14, 1776.

42 Force, *American Archives*, Series 5, Volume 1: 683, Connecticut Council of Safety, July 30, 1776. The Connecticut Council of Safety approved payment to Prosper Wetmore, Sheriff of New London County for transporting Dr. Church and payment was made for expenses while his prisoner from November 1775 to May 27, 1776, and expenses for waiting on Dr. Church for health as ordered by Congress. Expenses: transporting £11,4s; prisoner £9,5s; and waiting in the whole totaling £32,11s,10d.

43 Church, *Descendants of Richard Church of Plymouth*: 97–98. John Church proposes the theory that he was thrown overboard.

44 Shelburne Papers, Volume 67: 374, June 3, 1782.

45 CP 10:2, Sir Henry Clinton to Martha and Elizabeth Carter (his sisters), June 9, 1775.

46 Luc Urbain de Bouëxic, comte de Guichen (June 21, 1712–January 13, 1790), Lieutenant General and Commander in Chief of the French Navy in the West Indies. Famous for successfully escorting back to Europe a large convoy past a poorly managed British blockade in September 1780.

47 GWP, Varick Transcripts, Letterbook 1: 152–153, George Washington to Anne-César, Chevalier de la Luzerne, September 12, 1780, and GWP, Varick Transcripts, Letterbook 1: 154–159, George Washington in Bergen Co., N.J. to Louis Urbain du Bouëxic, Comte de Guichen, September 12, 1780 .

48 CP 157:10A, George Washington to Marquis de Lafayette, May 31, 1781.

49 CP 146:36, Samuel Wallis' letter from Philadelphia on February 27, 1781.

50 Pennypacker, *George Washington's Spies*: 215–216.

51 CP 104:27, George Washington's proclamation in code, June 7, 1780.

52 CP 113:35, Benedict Arnold to Margaret Arnold, August 14, 1780.

53 CP 234:2, Jonathan Odell notes on cipher that it was for Mr. L., who is not identified. However, in CP 60:48, Jonathan Odell to Joseph Stansbury, June 9, 1779 Odell says Lothario is impatient." He was referring to John André, therefore Mr. L—Lothario—is John André.

54 There is no explanation in any of the documents either in the *Clinton Papers* at the William L. Clements Library at the University of Michigan or in the

Emmett Collection at the New York Public Library as to why the writer would restart after reaching line "O." It may have stopped with "O" because John André thought it provided sufficient protection and would be less burdensome than constructing an entire chart to "Z" for the spy in the field.

55 GWP, General Correspondence, Charles Hector, Comte d'Estaing, Key to Letter Code; in French and English.

56 Bardeleben used two different ciphers in his diary. The second has not be determined. Burgoyne, *The Diary of Lieutenant von Bardeleben and Other von Donop Regiment*: unnumbered page 5 and These Were the Hessians: 11

57 Heitman, *Historical Register*: 258–259 and 550.

58 Littell, *Memoirs of his own Time*: 271–272.

59 When I found a document in this cipher, I reconstructed the complete cipher. Later I found the complete cipher transcribed among other Clinton documents, and it matched mine. CP 131:1, December 8, 1780 in cipher 133:5, and 234:44.

60 CP 234:10, George Beckwith to John André, July 13, 1780.

61 Gilder Lehrman Collection, GLC-00609, Nisbet Balfour at Charleston to Captain Saunders at Georgetown in code, April 24, 1781.

62 *Papers of General Nathanael Greene*, Volume 8: 85 and 227 and NGP 27:28

63 CP 234:5 and 234:8.

64 Pennypacker, *General Washington's Spies*: 219.

65 Stevens, *Facsimiles*, Volume 1, # 1. See below, Chapter 15, "Deceptions in Europe," for more on his system and its operation.

66 CP 171:27, Andrew Gautier [?], August 22, 1781. There is some doubt as to the author, as the systems used by Andrew Gautier and Ogden are so close.

67 This code was also used in the private communications between James Madison and Edmund Randolph. Copies are in the Continental Congress Papers and in the Virginia State Library. *American Historical Review*, Volume XXII, Edmund C. Burnett, *Ciphers of the Revolutionary Period*: 330–332 and Weber, *United States Diplomatic Codes and Ciphers*, WE015: 357–362.

68 Ford, *Letters of William Lee* Volume 2: 663–667, June 17, 1779.

69 England declared war on the Netherlands on December 20, 1780.

70 Sackville-Germain Papers, Volume 17.

71 British Museum, Additional Manuscripts, Haldimand Papers 21807, Frederick Haldimand to Sir Henry Clinton, November 23, 1778 in French.

72 HMC, *Report on American Manuscripts in the Royal Institution of Great Britain*, Volume 1, Sir Guy Carleton Papers, frame 2017 and 2018 (1 & 2) Number 38 , proposed cipher and see HMC, *Report on American Manuscripts in the Royal Institution of Great Britain*, Volume 3: 301, Addition to Cipher "K."

73 CP 168:8, Report #5, Haldimand to Clinton, August 1, 1781.

74 GWP, General Correspondence, James Lovell to George Washington, March 11, 1782 Concerning Vermont and enclosed Jacob Bayley to James Lovell, March 7, 1782 and Varick Transcripts Letterbook 4: 393–394, George Washington at Newburgh to James Lovell, April 1, 1782.

75 GWP, Varick Transcripts, Letterbook 1: 152–153; Letterbook 2: 219–222, George Washington to Anne Césare, Chevalier de la Luzerne, September 12, 1780; and Letterbook 1: 154–159, George Washington to Louis Urbain du B., Comte de Guichen, September 12, 1780 sent in cipher.

76 GWP, General Correspondence, 1783, Alphabet and Dictionary.

77 Documents Relating to the Colonial History of the State of New York: 802–808, Governor James Robertson to Secretary William Knox, September 21, 1780.

78 CP 125:2, H (William Heron) to Oliver De Lancey, October 1, 1780.

79 CP 127:12, Oliver De Lancey to William Heron, October 29, 1780.

80 CP 159:28, William Heron to Oliver De Lancey, June 17, 1781.

81 CP 234:5, possibly 1780. "Wallace's House" was the home of Samuel Wallis at Muncy, Pennsylvania.

82 Goodwin, *The Man in the Moone*.

83 Thicknesse, *A Treatise on the Art of Deciphering*: 43–45.

84 Sumner Papers Volume 2, Jethro Sumner at Camp Yadkin Ford to William Davidson, October 11, 1780.

85 CP 256, Book 4, Sir Henry Clinton to Lord George Germain, June 9, 1781: 224.

86 Stevens Facsimiles, 139, Auckland Manuscripts, Key of Walpole Cypher in the hand of William Eden, 1777 and Stevens Facsimiles, 237, Auckland Manuscripts, Cypher with Key of Walpole in the hand of William Eden, 1777.

87 Smith, *A Natural History of Nevis*, William Smith to Reverend Mr. Mason, Letter x: 254.

88 Smith, *A Natural History of Nevis*, William Smith to Reverend Mr. Mason, Letter x: 254: 44.

CHAPTER 6

1 Davis, *An Essay on the Art of Decyphering in which is inserted a Discourse of Dr. Wallis*: 10.

2 *Papers of Thomas Jefferson*, Volume 1: 13–14, Thomas Jefferson to John Page, January 23, 1764.

3 *Virginia Magazine of History and Biography*, Volume 10 Number 1 (July 1902): 177 footnote, Rebecca Burwell was born May 29, 1746. Her father, Lewis Burwell, had been acting governor of Virginia from November 14, 1750, to November 20, 1751. Tyler, *Encyclopedia of Virginia Biography*, Volume I: 64.

4 "Campana in die," Latin for "Bell in day," would be a bell that sounds its alarm in the day. It means that nothing else matters when the bell is rung, sounding its alarm; similarly, nothing else matters when she is around and he gives her his complete attention.

5 Shelton's *TachyGraphy, The Most Exact and Compendious Methode of Short and Swift Writing that Ever Beene Published by Any* was first printed by Samuel Cartwright in 1641. A copy is in the British Museum. Ford, *The Writings of Thomas Jefferson*, Volume I: 356-357, Thomas Jefferson to John Page, January 23, 1764.

6 Papers of Thomas Jefferson, Volume 1: 15-17, Thomas Jefferson to William Fleming, March 20, 1764 and *Virginia Magazine of History and Biography*, Volume 10 Number 1 (July 1902): 177 footnote, Rebecca Burwell married Jacqueline Ambler on May 24, 1764.

7 JCC, Volume 5: 827, September 26, 1776, Silas Deane, Benjamin Franklin, and Thomas Jefferson were appointed as commissioners to France [Jefferson was unable to accept the position because of the state of his wife's health.] and JCC, Volume 6: 897, October 22, 1776, Arthur Lee appointed a commissioner to France.

8 PCC, Record Group 360, Microfilm 247, Roll 110, p 21. Arthur Lee to the Secret Committee, June 3, 1776.

9 John Jay was born on December 12, 1745, in New York City, graduated from King's College (now Columbia University) in 1764, and was admitted to the bar in 1768.

10 Robert Bell had a major book store in Philadelphia from 1768 until his death in 1784. John Jay Papers, Jay ID 08397, John Jay to Robert Bell, March 13, 1776.

11 JCC, Volume 15: 1113, September 27, 1779.

12 Abel Boyer's French Dictionary was originally published in 1699 for the use of Queen Anne's eldest son, the Duke of Gloucester.

13 John Jay Papers, Jay ID 00804 and 07953, John Jay to Robert Livingston, February 19, 1780.

14 John Jay Papers, Jay ID 07590, Memoranda of Codes Used by John Jay, February 19, 1780 to March 2, 1780.

15 Weber, *Masked Dispatches*: 54.

16 John Jay Papers, Jay ID 07590: 16-17, Memoranda of Codes Used by John Jay, February 19, 1780 to March 2, 1780. Thomson was the first tutor hired by the Academy of Philadelphia (the forerunner of the University of Pennsylvania). He served as a Latin School tutor from 1750 until 1755.

17 New-York Historical Society, Collections of the New-York Historical Society for the Year 1878, Letters to Robert Morris and John Jay Papers, Jay ID 90299, John Jay at Madrid to Robert Morris, November 19, 1780.

18 John Jay mentioned *Entick's New Spelling Dictionary*, printed at London in 1775, which he had bought at Bell's bookstore in Philadelphia.

19 Johnston, *The Correspondence and Public Papers of John Jay*, Volume 2: 66–69, John Jay to William Bingham at St. Ildefonso, September 8, 1781.

20 Ford, *Letters of William Lee*, Volume 3: 281–284, William Lee at Paris to Charles Thomson, November 24, 1777.

21 Lee, *Life of Arthur Lee*, Volume 2: 117, Arthur Lee to Richard Henry Lee, November 25, 1777.

22 Ford, *Letters of William Lee*, Volume 2: 417 footnote.

23 Gold Star Box, Moore [Benedict Arnold] in code to Mr. Anderson [John André], July 15, 1780.

24 CP 60:48, Joseph Stansbury to Jonathan Odell, June 9, 1779.

25 CP 113:35, Benedict Arnold to Mrs. Arnold, July 29, 1780.

26 CP 85:56, Patrick Ferguson at Savannah to General Sir Henry Clinton, February 19, 1780.

27 CP 92:35, General Sir Henry Clinton to Colonel James Webster, April 14, 1780.

28 CP 94:8, Patrick Ferguson to General Sir Henry Clinton in cipher and deciphered, April 22, 1780.

29 CP 94:28, General Sir Henry Clinton to Colonel James Webster, April 14, 1780 in code.

CHAPTER 7

1 Benjamin Franklin at Philadelphia to Charles Dumas, December 9, 1775. Reprinted from The Port Folio, II (1802), 236–237; extracts: American Philosophical Society; Archives du Ministère des affaires étrangères, Paris; Algemeen Rijksarchief, the Hague. Dumas was born in Kloster Heilborn, Ansbach, and lived in Switzerland before settling in The Hague, Netherlands, circa 1750.

2 A louis d'or was a French gold coin. Ingraham, *Papers in Relation to the Case of Silas Deane:* 114. One of the couriers used to carry letters from Paris was Thomas Story of Philadelphia. PBF Volume 22: 403–412, Charles Dumas to Committee of Secret Correspondence.

3 Dumas' correspondence can be found at the American Philosophical Society, in the Papers of the Continental Congress, and the published and unpublished papers of Benjamin Franklin.

4 Beaumarchais was born Pierre Caron on January 24, 1732. Lossing, *The Pictorial Field-book of the Revolution,* Volume 2: 853. Beaumarchais set up the company Rodriguez Hortalez & Cie to handle covert shipments to America. It operated out of the Hôtel des Ambassadeurs de Hollande, 47 rue Vieille du Temple, Paris.

5 *PBF,* Volume 22: 403–412, Charles Dumas at Utrecht to Committee of Secret Correspondence, April 30, 1776.

6 St. Eustatius, also known as Statia and Saint Eustace, is one of the Leeward Islands in the Caribbean. Benjamin Franklin at Philadelphia to Charles Dumas, December 9, 1775. Reprinted from *The Port Folio,* II (1802), 236–237; extracts: American Philosophical Society; Archives du Ministère des affaires étrangères, Paris; Algemeen Rijksarchief, the Hague.

7 *PBF,* Volume 22: 403–412, Charles Dumas at Utrecht to Committee of Secret Correspondence, April 30, 1776.

8 Originally published in 1758. Dumas says it was the new edition of the book which he edited that he sent to Franklin. It was published by Harrevelt in Amsterdam. PBF, Volume 22: 74–77, Charles Dumas to Benjamin Franklin, June 30, 1775.

9 *PBF,* Volume 31: 460, Charles Dumas to Benjamin Franklin, February 8, 1780, American Philosophical Society.

10 PBF, Volume 35: 366, Benjamin Franklin to Charles Dumas, August 16, 1781.

11 *Letters of Delegates to Congress, 1774–1789*: 320–321, Minutes of Proceedings, March 2, 1776.

12 Dr. Jacques Barbeu-Dubourg was born in Mayenne in 1709 and died 1779. Franklin in 1768 had Barbeu-Dubourg's *Petit code de la raison humaine* translated into English and printed by William Strahan. Barbeu-Dubourg published a French translation of Franklin's examination before the British House of Commons in the Ephémérides du citoyen. Barbeu-Dubourg wrote *Lettre d'un Philadelphien à un ami de Paris* (Letter of a Philadelphian to a Parisian friend) and prepared a French edition of Franklin's works, *Oeuvres de M. Franklin.* Franklin helped arrange Barbeu-Dubourg's election to the American Philosophical Society (1775). PBF, Jacques Barbeu-Dubourg at Paris to Benjamin Franklin, June 10–July 2, 1776.

13 Weber, *United States Diplomatic Codes and Ciphers 1775–1938*: 26.

14 The South Latin School was one of two Latin schools that would later become the famous Boston Latin School. The date of the closing comes from Harrison Gray Otis. Information provided by John L. Bell.

15 *New England Historical and Genealogical Register* (NEHGR), Volume 19: 256, A *Journal Kept by John Leach, During His Confinement by the British, in Boston Gaol [Jail]*. It is the same Joshua Loring Jr. who later would be the commissary of prisons and husband of General Howe's mistress.

16 NEHGR, Volume 19: 257.

17 GWP, General Correspondence, James Lovell at Boston Prison to George Washington, December 6, 1775.

18 PCC, R65, item 51, unknown and undated letter.

19 Lovell used five other three-key-letter ciphers with Benjamin Franklin.

20 Adams Family Papers, John Adams to Abigail Adams, February 2, 1777.

21 John Adams Diary, Volume 3, Spring and Summer 1759.

22 *Adams Family Correspondence*, Volume 4: 36, James Lovell to Abigail Adams, December 19, 1780.

23 *Adams Family Correspondence*, Volume 4: 393–399, Appendix, The Cypher and Its Derivative.

24 *Adams Family Correspondence*, Volume 3: 363, Abigail Adams to James Lovell, June 11, 1780.

25 Wharton, *The Revolutionary Diplomatic Correspondence of the United States*, Volume 5: 192–193, John Adams to Robert Livingston, February 12, 1782.

26 Charles Francis Adams, *The Works of John Adams*, Volume 7: 629, John Adams at The Hague to Robert Livingston, September 6, 1782.

27 Sparks, *The Diplomatic Correspondence of the American Revolution*, Volume 6: 398.

28 *Adams Family Papers*, Abigail Adams to John Adams, June 17, 1782.

29 Wharton, *The Revolutionary Diplomatic Correspondence of the United States*, Volume 4: 284, John Adams to Francis Dana, March 12, 1781.

30 *PBF*, Volume 31: 520, James Lovell to Benjamin Franklin, February 24, 1780.

31 *PBF,* Volume 33: 169, Benjamin Franklin to James Lovell, August 10, 1780.

32 Fisher, *The American Instructor:* 54–55.

33 *PBF,* Volume 34: 412, Benjamin Franklin to Francis Dana, March 2, 1781.

34 *Adams Papers,* R 354, Francis Dana to John Adams, March 6, 1781.

35 John Adams in a letter to Robert Livingston was adamant that he did remember his brother-in-law's name. His problem was he could not operate the cipher. Wharton, *The Revolutionary Diplomatic Correspondence of the United States,* Volume 5: 192, John Adams to Robert Livingston, February 12, 1782.

36 *Adams Papers,* R 354, James Lovell to Francis Dana, January 6, 1781.

37 *Adams Papers,* R 354, Francis Dana to John Adams, March 16, 1781.

38 *PBF,* Volume 35: 262, Robert Morris to Benjamin Franklin, July 13, 1781.

39 *PBF,* Volume 35: 268, Robert Morris to Benjamin Franklin, July 14, 1781.

40 *PBF,* Volume 36: 19, Benjamin Franklin to Robert Morris, November 5, 1781.

41 Lossing, *The Pictorial Field-book of the American Revolution,* Volume 1: 320.

42 *PBF,* Volume 30: 141, John Paul Jones at L'Orient to Benjamin Franklin, July 25, 1779.

CHAPTER 8

1 Haldimand had been the second in command to General Thomas Gage in Boston and they frequently carried on a written communication in French. French, *General Gage's Informers:* 14, footnote 1.

2 CP 228:16, General Sir Frederick Haldimand to Sir Henry Clinton, undated.

3 CP 110:5, General Sir Frederick Haldimand to General Wilhelm von Knyphausen, July 6, 1780 in cipher, CP 129:23, General Sir Frederick Haldimand to Sir Henry Clinton, August 28, 1780, and CP 129:21, General Sir Frederick Haldimand to Sir Henry Clinton, September 8, 1780, deciphered.

4 CP 111:7, General Sir Frederick Haldimand to General Wilhelm von Knyphausen, July 11 1780. Wilhelm von Knyphausen was born November 4, 1716 in Luxembourg.

5 CP 130:21, Sir Frederick Haldimand to Sir Henry Clinton, November 15, 1780 and is marked received by Ensign Prentice of the 84th Regiment of Foot on August 19, 1781.

6 CP 130:23, General Sir Frederick Haldimand to Sir Henry Clinton, November 15, 1780.

7 CP 131:8, General Sir Frederick Haldimand to Sir Henry Clinton, undated [November 22, 1780], brought by two men from Albany who say they received it the third instant from a man who left Quebec November 22.

8 G. D. Skull, "General Sir Frederick Haldimand in Pennsylvania," *Pennsylvania Magazine of History and Biography,* Volume VIII: 309. Fort Niagara was built by the French. It is located near Youngstown, New York on the east side of the mouth of the Niagara River on Lake Ontario. Buck or Deer Island was renamed Carleton Island by General Haldimand in honor of Sir Guy Carleton. The island was the site of Fort Carleton which was renamed Fort Haldimand in

1778. During the American Revolution, it was the supply post in the Saint Lawrence River near the east end of Lake Ontario. Despite the Jay Treaty of 1794, the British occupied the fort till 1812 when it was destroyed by the Americans during the war. It was formally ceded to the United States in 1817. It is northeast of the town of Cape Vincent, Jefferson County, New York. The island today is privately owned.

9 Uhlendorf, *Revolution in America*: 414, General Haldimand at Quebec to Sir Henry Clinton, received on February 2, 1781.

10 CP 153:29, Hudibras [Dr. George Smith] at Albany, New York to Sir Henry Clinton, April 26, 1781.

11 Paltsists, *Minutes of the Commissioners for Detecting and Defeating Conspiracies in the State of New York*. Volume II 1780–1781 (1909): 728, June 1, 1781, Joseph Fay to Commissioners, May 30, 1781.

12 CP 160:6, Report from Frederick Haldimand, June 21, 1781.

13 CP 160:13, William Smith at New York to Sir Henry Clinton, June 22, 1781. Mentions the recent escape of his brother and that two of his nephews have also come into the city. See CP 160:14 William Smith notes, June 21, 1781. The nephews were the sons of Thomas Smith, Esq.

14 Louis Necker de Germany (1730–1804) and Jean Girardot de Marigny (Swiss d. 1796) were partners in the firm of Germany, Girardot & Cie. The firm was reorganized in August 1777 as Girardot, Haller & Cie. under the partnership of Jean Girardot de Marigny and Rodolphe-Emmanuel Haller (1747–1833?). Haller was born in Bern and was a merchant in Amsterdam. He was also a longtime associate of Thomas Walpole.

15 Bancroft's Memorial in 1784 to then Secretary of State Lord Carmarthen tells how he became a spy and of Lords North and Suffolk's promises.

16 Ford, *Winnowings* Number IV: 8–11.

17 Van Doren, *Franklin:* 580.

18 Stevens, *Facsimiles*, # 218.

19 The Austin Roe tavern today is a private home on Millie Lane in East Setauket, Long Island. George Washington stayed at Roe's tavern on April 22, 1790. Jackson and Twohig, *The Diaries of George Washington.* Volume VI, January 1790–December 1799: 65.

20 Pennypacker, *General Washington's Spies*: 14.

21 Although the Sakonnet is called a river, it is actually a saltwater strait that separates Rhode Island from the mainland to the east.

22 Shelburne's Additional Continental Regiment was created on January 12,1777. It included three companies from Connecticut and a number of men from Maryland. Disbanded May 1, 1780 with many of the men going to Samuel B. Webb's Regiment which became the 9th Connecticut Regiment. Berg, *Encyclopedia of Continental Army Units*: 108 and 136.

23 There still is a street to the Sakonnet River called Taggart's Ferry Road.

24 Only Wilkinson and General Cornell knew of Lieutenant Seth Chapin's mission. Wilkinson did not learn who was the source of the information brought

by Lieutenant Chapin until after the war was over. Arthur A. Ross, pastor of the First Baptist Church in Newport, *Discourse*: 48 quoted from Pennypacker, *George Washington's Spies*: 15, and Thompson, *Secret New England*: 199–203 and Turner, editor, *Rhode Island Historical Magazine*, Volume 1 Number 1: 46–48.

25 The Marquis of Granby Tavern in Newport was owned by John Fry in 1769 and had a portrait of the Marquis of Granby as a sign. The portrait showed the Marquis with a deficiency of hair. Turner, editor, Rhode Island Historical Magazine, Volume 1 Number 2: 122.

26 Bakeless, *Turncoats, Traitors, and Heroes*: 280 and Thompson, *Secret New England*: 283–284.

27 Peckham, *The Toll of Independence*: 62–63.

28 A rock on the east side of a creek just below Kitchen's Lane in Fairmount Park is called Mom Rinker's Rock. The location of Mom Rinker's Rock was documented on an 1871 map of Fairmount Park on the east side of the Wissahickon Valley. Today a statue of a Quaker bearing the inscription "Toleration" sits atop the rock. The Wissahickon Valley is located in the northwest section of the city of Philadelphia. A seven-mile long section of the valley containing 1,400 acres is preserved as part of Fairmount Park.

29 Bicknell, *The Wissahickon in History, Story, and Song in Philadelphia History: Consisting of Papers Read Before the City History Society of Philadelphia*, Volume 1: 15–17.

30 Simon Girty was born the second of four sons at Chamber's Mill at Fishing Creek, north of Harrisburg, Pennsylvania, in 1741. Simon's stepfather was burned at the stake. He along with his mother and brothers had been held captive for three years (1756–1759) by the Seneca Indians. His mother and three of her sons (Simon, James born 1743, and George born 1745) moved to Pittsburgh in 1759. In 1769 he applied for 300 acres on a branch of Four Mile Run off the Monongahela River about five miles from Fort Pitt. Historical Society of Western Pennsylvania, biographical file on Simon Girty. Application for land dated Nov. 27, 1769 at Fort Pitt.

31 HSP, Dreer Collection, Alphabetical Series, George Morgan at Pittsburgh to Simon Girty, May 1, 1776.

32 Haldimand Papers, B 122, p. 144, Henry Hamilton's Report, List of officers: Indian Department District of Detroit, September 5, 1778. Enclosed in Lieutenant Governor's Hamilton's letter without date but supposed to be the beginning of September and received the 27th at Sorel; marked Detroit Number 13.

33 Kellogg, *Frontier Advance on the Upper Ohio*: 218. Fort Laurens was built in late November 1778, on the banks of the Tuscarawas River near what is now Bolivar, Ohio. General Lachlan McIntosh named the fort in honor of the President of the Continental Congress, Henry Laurens.

34 Daniel Brodhead used the code name of "Rusticus" to hide his identity, Historical Society of Pennsylvania, Rusticus (Daniel Brodhead) to Walter Jenifer Stone, December 30, 1782. Kellogg, *Frontier Advance on the Upper Ohio*: 384, Colonel Daniel Brodhead at Pittsburgh, to Colonel Stephen Bayard, July 1, 1779

and Colonel George Woods of the Bedford County militia at Bedford to Thomas Urie of East Pennsboro Township, Cumberland County, Pennsylvania, July 4, 1779.

35 Coshocton was the town of the Turtle tribe of the Delaware Indians. It was destroyed in 1781. It was at the present site of Coshocton, Coshocton County, Ohio which was founded in 1810. Kellogg, *Frontier Advance on the Upper Ohio*, 385–386.

36 Kellogg, *Frontier Advance on the Upper Ohio*: 246.

37 Kellogg, *Frontier Advance on the Upper Ohio*: 382–383, Coochocking, Alexander McCormick to Daniel Broadhead, June 29, 1779.

CHAPTER 9

1 Some consider the story apocryphal. Wilkins, *Mercury, or the Secret and Swift Messenger*: 27–28.

2 GWP, General Correspondence, Benjamin Church. Jr. to Maurice Cone, July 1775, in Code, and Benjamin Church, Jr. to Maurice Cone, October 3, 1775, Translation of Cryptogram.

3 *Virginia History and Biography*, Volume VIII: 119–121.

4 Cedar Point is twelve miles south of Port Tobacco, Charles County, Maryland, on the east side of the Potomac River.

5 Elizabethtown, Maryland, is now known as Hagerstown.

6 Pillion is the underpad or cushion of a saddle; especially, a pad or cushion put on behind a man's saddle, on which a woman may ride. *Pennsylvania Magazine of History and Biography*, Volume XII (1888): 410–417, "A Narrative of the Transactions, Imprisonment, and Sufferings of John Connelly, an American Loyalist and Lieutenant Colonel in His Majesty's Service."

7 Spithead is the body of water between Gosport and Portsmouth, England and the Isle of Wight.

8 John Horne, also known as Horne Tooke, was put on trial on July 4, 1777, for libeling the King's government and the employment of his troops on June 8 and July 14, 1775. He was found guilty. See John (Tooke) Horne, *The Trial of John Horne* (London: S. Blandon, 1777) and also *The Trial of John Horne* (London: G. Hearsly, 1777). He would be arrested again on May 16, 1794 as a traitor, interrogated by the Privy Council and put in the Tower of London. Great Britain PRO Privy Council, PC 1/21/A35(a) and PC 1/22/A36(a) quoted from Sparrow, Secret Service: 27. I believe the town of Brintford is Brentford. John Horne was a minister in Brentford, which is on the left bank of the Thames River and a short distance downstream from Richmond. This puts it somewhat to the west of London. Brentford is located almost exactly 20 miles east of White Waltham. White Waltham is in Berkshire located a short distance west of Windsor.

9 The letter is endorsed "Israel Potters, pretended Letter from some Gent[le]m[an]. in England." However Potter performed several spy assignments from Franklin to England. American Philosophical Society, CWK and JH (John Horne) to Benjamin Franklin at Paris, Feb. 14, 1777. A copy appears in William B. Willcox's *Papers of Benjamin Franklin*, Volume 23: 332–334.

10 Trumbull, *Life and Remarkable Adventures of Israel R. Potter*: 46–52.

11 Watson, *Men and Times of the Revolution: or Memoirs of Elkanah Watson*: 29.

12 "Autobiography of Philip Van Cortlandt, Brigadier General in the Continental Army [1775–1783]" in *Magazine of American History*, Volume II, Part I, (1878): 284; GWP, General Correspondence: William Howe at New York to John Burgoyne, July 20, 1777; Henry Williams' Deposition July 24, 1777; Israel Putnam at Peekskill to George Washington, July 24, 1777; and George Washington at Ramapo to Israel Putnam, July 25, 1777 (which is also in Varick Transcripts, Letterbook 3: 398–399).

13 Livius became acting chief justice of Quebec in November 1775 and appointed to the position in August 1776.

14 Sullivan was captured on August 27, 1776, during the Battle of Long Island.

15 It appears that Amsbury's traveling companion Adams did not know of Amsbury's secret mission.

16 GWP, General Correspondence, Philip J. Schuyler, June 15, 1777 at 4 p.m., American Intelligence Report.

17 The Onion River today is known by its old Indian name, the Winooski River. At some time prior to the American Revolution it had also been known as the French River. It is in the general area of Burlington, Vermont.

18 Major General Arthur St. Clair was born in Thurso, Scotland, in 1736. He had fought in the French and Indian War. He resigned from the British Army after his marriage in 1760. In 1762 he purchased an estate in western Pennsylvania and was the largest resident property owner west of the Allegheny Mountains in Pennsylvania at the time of the American Revolution.

19 Smith, *The St. Clair Papers*: 396–400, General Arthur St. Clair at Ticonderoga to General Schuyler, June 13, 1777.

20 GWP, General Correspondence, Philip J. Schuyler, June 15, 1777 at 4 p.m., American Intelligence Report. Major General Philip Schuyler was his commanding officer and in command of the northern department of the Continental Army. Philip Schuyler was born on November 11, 1733 at Albany, New York. He had served as a commissary in the British Army during the French and Indian War. His home at Albany was built in 1765 while he was in Europe. Until the American Revolution, he lived the life of a country gentleman at his country home on Fish Creek in Schuylerville (sometimes called Schuyler's Town), New York. Schuylerville is located between Fort Edward and Saratoga. Schuyler owned over 9,000 acres of land and was a boat builder, farmer, grain and lumber merchant, military agent of government, and real estate expert.

21 PCC, Microfilm, r173, i153, v3: 170 M. Kirkman at Saint John to Commanding Officer at Isle aux Noix, June 1777. Isle aux Noix is on the present Richelieu River north of Lake Champlain.

22 Fitzpatrick, *Writings of George Washington*, Volume 8: footnote 93.

23 The name is sometimes spelled Tierce. GWP, General Correspondence, Philip J. Schuyler, June 15, 1777 at 4 p.m., American Intelligence Report and Heitman, *Historical Register*: 535 and 543.

24 Heitman, *Historical Register:* 557, identifies Lieutenant Van Valkenburgh as Second Lieutenant Bartholomew Jacob Van Valkenburgh of the 1st New York.

25 GWP, General Correspondence, Philip J. Schuyler, June 15, 1777 at 4 p.m., American Intelligence Report which has addendum of June 16, 1777 at 10 a.m.

26 GWP, General Correspondence, Philip J. Schuyler at Fort Edward to George Washington, June 16, 1777.

27 PCC, No. 153, III, folio 172, Philip J. Schuyler to Continental Congress, June 25, 1777. It was received at Congress on July 3, 1777. JCC, Volume 8: 527.

28 GWP, General Correspondence, John Sullivan to George Washington, June 21, 1777.

29 Gold Star Box, William Howe to John Burgoyne, July 17, 1777.

30 Caleb Stark, *Memoir and Official Correspondence of General John Stark*: 72.

31 Gold Star Box, William Howe to John Burgoyne, July 17, 1777.

32 Canada, Department of Militia and Defense. A *History of the Organization* . . . Volume III, *The War of the American Revolution*, The province of Quebec under the administration of Governor Frederic Haldimand, 1778–1784 (Canada III, Haldimand): 20.

33 Canada III, Haldimand: 172 # 200, Public Archives of Canada, Haldimand Papers, Series Q, Volume 20: 44–45, Chr. Carleton at St. John's to Captain Mathews, September 24, 1780.

34 *Public Papers of George Clinton*, Volume II: 398–399 [October 7, 1777].

35 CP 34:23, John Paterson at New York to Sir Henry Clinton, May 1, 1778.

36 *Public Papers of George Clinton*, Volume VII: 339, Albany Commissioners to Governor George Clinton, September 19, 1781.

37 Lossing, *Pictorial Field Book of the Revolution*, Volume 1: 79.

38 Fonblanque, *Political and Military Episodes . . . Burgoyne*: 287–290.

39 *Public Papers of George Clinton*, Volume II: 398–399 and 443.

40 Phineas Shepard born (June 19, 1757) and resided in New Hartford, Litchfield County, Connecticut and in 1832 at Brooklyn Township, Cuyahoga County, Ohio. His wife's name was Deliverance. Colonel Samuel B. Webb's Additional Continental Regiment was created January 1, 1777. In mid-May 1780 the regiment was taken into Connecticut's quota and was numbered the 9th Connecticut Regiment.

41 Richards, *Diary of Samuel Richards*: 51, October 1777.

42 Force, *American Archives*, Series 5, Volume 3: 660, Captain John Paul Jones on the Alfred off the coast of Cape Breton to Robert Smith, November 12, 1776.

43 James Van Fleet also said it was the "American Red Coat Regiment" that captured Taylor. U.S. National Archives, Revolutionary War Pension Application, James Van Fleet's deposition of October 1, 1832. Most books only mention one spy, Taylor. However two spies were captured. Daniel Roberdeau writing from York, Pennsylvania to Wharton mentions the silver ball incident and confirms that two spies were involved. It is in the Pennsylvania Archives, Volume V: 639–640. Elisha Hopkins, adjutant's report of prisoners and crimes in the provost lists Daniel Taylor and Isaac Van Vleek as both having been taken and confined as

spies. The report is in the *Public Papers of George Clinton*, Volume II: 415–416. Most importantly, Phineas Shepard, a participant in the capture, says there were two spies taken. U.S. National Archives, Revolutionary War Pension Application, Phineas Shepard's deposition of May 1, 1820.

44 U.S. National Archives, Revolutionary War Pension Application, Phineas Shepard's deposition of May 1, 1820.

45 Ephraim was also a witness to Taylor's hanging. U. S. National Archives, Revolutionary War Pension Application, Lewis Ephraim's deposition of June 16, 1840.

46 This silver bullet was in the possession of General James Tallmadge when he displayed it at the January 2, 1844, meeting of the New-York Historical Society. *New-York Historical Society Proceedings of 1843*: 11. The silver bullet was supposedly subsequently given to the New York Historical Society and lost. Benson J. Lossing writes in the *Life and Times of Philip Schuyler*, Volume 2 (1873), "I saw the bullet and its inclosed dispatch a few years ago in the possession of Charles Clinton, a grandson of General James Clinton" (p. 360).

47 *Public Papers of George Clinton*, Volume II: 412–413, George Clinton to Council of Safety, October 11, 1777; Lossing, Pictorial Field Book of the Revolution, Volume 2: 116; and U. S. National Archives, Revolutionary War Pension Application, Deliverance Smith's deposition.

48 C.C. is Captain Alexander Campbell of the 62nd Regiment of Foot. Campbell was sent back to General Burgoyne on the morning of the October 7, 1777, which was the day after the capture of Forts Clinton and Montgomery by the British. *Public Papers of George Clinton*, Volume II: 398–399.

49 Sackville Germain Papers, Volume 6, copy of letter from Sir Henry Clinton to Lieutenant General John Burgoyne, October 8, 1777, enclosed in Sir William Howe to Lord George Germain, October 21, 1777 and the same message with minor variations can be found in Lossing, Pictorial Field Book of the Revolution, Volume 2: 116.

50 U.S. National Archives, Revolutionary War Pension Application, Medad Shelly's deposition of May 7, 1845.

51 Public Papers of George Clinton, Volume II: 443–444.

52 U. S. National Archives, Revolutionary War Pension Application, Daniel Woolsey's deposition of 1832.

53 U. S. National Archives, Revolutionary War Pension Application, Phineas Shepard's deposition of May 1, 1820.

54 U. S. National Archives, Revolutionary War Pension Application, Martiness Decker's deposition. Martiness Decker married Mary Penneton on Aug. 27, 1768, died April 1802, and is buried in Dutch burying ground near Port Jervis, New York.

55 Lossing, *Pictorial Field Book of the Revolution*, Volume 2: 116. The *Virginia Gazette of Dixon & Hunter* of November 28, 1777 reported a story from Fishkill, New York dated October 23 that last Thursday (the 16th) Taylor was hanged at Harley.

56 U. S. National Archives, Revolutionary War Pension Application, Daniel Woolsey's deposition of 1832.

57 CP 172:32, Isaac Ogden to Oliver De Lancey Jr., August 29, 1781.

58 Darragh's residence (known as the Loxley House) was at 177 Second Street (old style), Philadelphia , on the east side of the street at the southeast corner with Little Dock Street below Spruce Street.

59 The Free Quaker Meeting is still standing opposite the visitors' center on Independence Mall. William and Lydia Darragh were buried in the old burying ground of the old Arch Street Meeting in what is now the parking lot behind the present Meetinghouse at 4th and Arch Streets.

60 Uhlendorf, *Revolution in America:* 150. Adjutant General Major Baurmeister's Journal, January 20, 1778. The supply situation had changed, "The city market is full of fresh meat, all kinds of fowl, and root vegetables. The residents of the city lack nothing except flour and firewood." Still, living in occupied Philadelphia had gotten extremely expensive and had reduced many people to beggary and ruin. Historical Society of Pennsylvania, Robert Proud at Philadelphia to John Proud, January 10, 1778.

61 *Pennsylvania Magazine of History and Biography*, Volume XLV, #4 (1921), W. A. Newman Dorland, *Second Troop Philadelphia City Cavalry:* 381.

62 Captains Johann Ewald and John Peebles refer to a large number of skirmishes but with little damage.

63 *Historical Magazine*, Volume III, Number 2: 34, Colonel John Jameson at Wright's Tavern to George Washington, February 2, 1778.

64 A vedette is a sentinel on horseback.

65 Uhlendorf, *Revolution in America*: 134. Adjutant General Major Baurmeister statement of December 16, 1777.

66 The text says it was an officer of the light horse and the name was Craig. A match is Captain (not Lieutenant Colonel) Charles Craig. Charles Craig wrote a letter on the day in question from Frankford where the meeting would have occurred. GWP, General Correspondence, Charles Craig at Frankford to George Washington, December 3, 1777.

67 *American Quarterly Review*, Volume 1 Number 1 (March 1827): 32–33.

68 Bourquin, *Journal of Events in the Revolution* by Elias Boudinot: 50.

69 Robert Walsh published the Darragh story in the *American Quarterly Review* in 1827 based upon information given him. Could the tale be true? The degree of certainty you want will determine your answer. There is no document from 1777 that states that Lydia was the source of the information received by Boudinot. Could the friends of the Darraghs have not gotten all their facts straight in recalling something that happened over forty years earlier? Most likely they did make some errors but would have gotten the protagonist correct. Henry Darrach's (no relation to Lydia) article *Lydia Darragh One of the Heroines of the Revolution* read before the City History Society of Philadelphia on November 10, 1915 is often overlooked. He makes a strong case that she could and most probably did do this deed.

70 Philadelphia Monthly Meeting Book for 1782–1789: 47 and 101–102.

71 Black Point is now Rumson, New Jersey. Squan was at the entrance of the Manasquan River and could be either Brielle or Point Pleasant, New Jersey.

72 Egle, *An Illustrated History of the Commonwealth of Pennsylvania*: 199, reports that it was folded as a square.

73 The complete journal was published in Nagy, *Rebellion in the Ranks: Mutinies of the American Revolution*, Appendix C. CP 144:12, Oliver De Lancey's Journal (ten-page copy).

74 Oliver De Lancey's Journal of the Pennsylvania Mutiny states that the two proposals went by way of Elizabeth Town and Newark.

75 The only documentation is from De Lancey's Journal and he does not identify the courier.

76 The English-born Playter had been living in Nottingham Township (now Hamilton Township in Mercer County), New Jersey, and practicing the trade of a cabinetmaker. Great Britain, PRO, AO 13/111/109 Memorial of George Playter. When the British occupied Philadelphia in 1777, Playter went into the city. After British General Howe took command of Philadelphia, he discontinued the services of Brigadier General Cortland Skinner's New Jersey spy network. With the recommendation of Joseph Galloway, Playter procured intelligence for General Howe and subsequently Sir Henry Clinton (Great Britain, PRO, AO 13/111/110(right) Memorial of George Playter).

77 In August 1776, Bruen was a captain in the Essex County New Jersey Militia ordinance company. GWP, Letterbook 8: 182, George Washington at New York to Colonel James Clinton at Fort Constitution, June 25, 1776.

Following the Americans losses of Fort Washington and Fort Lee, in the fall of 1776 the British army was pursuing the American army across New Jersey. After the British army had passed through Newark, Bruen and his family moved back to their Newark home, thinking the British had left and it was safe. It was a decision that started him on the slippery slope to becoming a spy. However, that night a Scottish regiment took possession of the city. In order to save his family and property, Caleb Bruen took protection from the British.

After the American victories at Trenton and Princeton, George Washington took the Continental army into winter quarters at Morristown in the Watchung Mountains. The British army in January 1777 was forced to consolidate their advance positions in New Jersey at Perth Amboy and New Brunswick. After the Scottish troops evacuated Newark, Bruen was free to move about and tried to rejoin his unit at Morristown and was unwelcome as he had resigned and taken the oath of loyalty to the King. PCC, Microfilm, r53, i42, v1, p.367–372, Alexander McWhorter's statement at Newark on Caleb Bruen to Gen. Knox, March 27, 1786.

A few months later, about April 1777, Bruen was captured and taken prisoner by the British. He came out from New York parole about June 23 or 24. Bruen sent for Major Samuel Hayes of the 2nd Regiment of Essex County militia to come to his house in Newark. Bruen informed him that it was the practice of the

British to send their spies out on parole to gather intelligence and advised that he had been sent in such a capacity. He was tasked to get to General Washington's army and find out its size and movements. Bruen, who had been given money to bribe people, told Hayes whom he was told to pay. He wanted a pass from Hayes to freely traverse the lines and offered to procure intelligence from the British for Hayes. He also informed Reverend Dr. Alexander McWhorter, pastor of the First Presbyterian Church of Newark, and Judge Joseph Hedden, Jr., two of Newark's leading citizens, about his mission. He then brought Hayes, Hedden, and McWhorter together and the deal was set. McWhorter escorted Bruen to the American camp at Short Hills where they saw General Nathanael Greene. After hearing their story, General Greene agreed to Bruen's plan. They were sent back to McWhorter's house to await a light horseman who would arrive that evening with a letter enclosing the intelligence that Greene wanted Bruen to take back to New York. The courier delivered the letter to McWhorter who then showed it to Bruen, who copied it and took the information to New York. Bruen went back to Major Samuel Hayes and showed him his pass to go back into New York. Bruen reported that the information was so exaggerated that he was not believed by the British and was confined for some time in the Provost. PCC, Microfilm, r53, i42, v1, pp. 367–372, Alexander McWhorter's statement at Newark on Caleb Bruen to Gen. Knox, March 27, 1786.

Bruen either found some way to ingratiate himself with the British or never spent the time in the Provost as he claimed. PCC, Microfilm, r53, i42, v1, p.361, Elias Dayton pass for Caleb Bruen, Joseph Gould, and Gilbert Smyth to pass to New York and return on public business, May 1, 1780.PCC, Microfilm, r53, i42, v1, p.372, Alexander McWhorter's statement at Newark on Caleb Bruen to General Knox, March 27, 1786. PCC, Microfilm, r53, i42, v1, p.360, Tench Tilghman pass for Caleb Bruen, November 27, 1780.

78 PCC, Microfilm, r53, i42, v1, p.375, Elias Dayton at Elizabeth Town statement on Caleb Bruen's secret services, Dec. 31, 1785.

79 Ward received his mail at the Sign of the Ship, which was at the corner of Fair Street and Broadway in New York City. Fulton Street between Broadway and Pearl Street was called Fair Street until 1816. CP 146:3, Cortlandt Skinner to Oliver De Lancey, February 11, 1781 and CP 159:39 William A. Kite of the ship *Bedford* to Capt. Edward Mc Michael or Captain Thomas Ward, June 19, 1981.

80 Van Doren and other historians have guessed that McFarlan was Andrew McFarland who had been captured with Captain William Bernard Gifford. Gifford had become a spy for the British. However General Anthony Wayne gave the first name of McFarlan as "Samuel" when he wrote out a pass for the two British spies, Bruen and McFarlan. PCC, Microfilm, r53, i42, v1, p.358, General Wayne, at Trenton, pass for Caleb Bruen and Samuel McFarlin to pass to Newark, New Jersey, January 22, 1781.

81 John McDole, a resident of Albany, had assisted him in making his escape from the American confinement. Paltists, *Minutes of the Commissioners for Detecting and Defeating Conspiracies in the State of New York*, Volume II: 413.

82 GWP, General Correspondence, Daniel Brodhead at Fort Pitt to George Washington, March 27, 1781.

83 GWP, General Correspondence, Myndert Fisher but signed Thomas Girty to Simon Girty, January 21, 1781.

84 Kellogg, *Fontier Retreat:* 491, trial of Myndart Fisher presided by Colonel S. Bayard, commanding the 8th Pennsylvania Regiment, July 26, 1781.

85 John Leach was born about 1724, immigrated to Boston at age 27, and married Sarah Coffin in 1750. He died at his residence in Bennet Street, Boston, June 10, 1799, aged 75. John and Sarah Leach had 17 children between 1752 and 1774. *New England Historical & Genealogical Register,* Volume 19 (1864): 259, August 13 of *A Journal Kept by John Leach, During His Confinement by the British, in Boston Gaol.*

86 GWP, Varick Transcripts, Letterbook 1, 178–179, George Washington to Henry Clinton, September 30, 1780.

87 Mississippi Provincial Archives, English Dominion (MPAED), Volume VIII, 30–31, Memorial of John Campbell and Robert Ross to Governor Chester, September 9, 1778.

88 MPAED, Volume VIII, Spanish Process: 112.

89 Mississippi Provincial Archives, Spanish Dominion (MPASD), Volume I, 147.

90 MPASD, Volume I, 147.

91 MPAED, Volume VIII, Spanish Process: 114.

92 MPASD, Volume I: 147–148 and MPAED, Volume VIII: 31, Memorial of John Campbell and Robert Ross to Governor Chester, September 9, 1778 and Spanish Process: 113.

93 MPAED, Volume VIII, Spanish Process: 113 and Anonymous to Anthony Hutchins, May 11, 1778.

94 MPAED, Volume VIII, Spanish Process: 113–116.

95 MPAED, Volume VIII, Spanish Process: 154.

96 MPAED, Volume VIII, Spanish Process: 34–35.

97 MPAED, Volume VIII, 31, Memorial of John Campbell and Robert Ross to Governor Chester, September 9, 1778.

98 MPASD, Volume VIII, Bernardo de Gálvez to José Navarro, June 12, 1778 and Confidential Dispatches of Don Bernardo de Gálvez to José de Gálvez, New Orleans, June 12, 1778.

99 Coldham, American Loyalist Claims: 455–456.

100 He sailed for Quebec on the *Grace* on September 9, 1783. Coldham, *American Migrations:* 343 (AO12/27/154, 109/282).

101 Bryan, *The Spy in America:* 95 and Coldham, American Loyalist Claims: 456 dates the memorial as February 24, 1786 at Sorel (AO13/15/414–418).

102 CP 57:10, Peter Dubois to Sir Heny Clinton written sometime after May 1, 1779.

103 Ibid.

104 Sabine, *Historical Memoirs of William Smith 1778–1783:* 74–75, February 15 and 18, 1779.

105 Crèvecoeur, born in 1735, wrote *Letters from an American Farmer* in 1782.

106 CP 150:34, George Beckwith's report on Jabes Sayers of Newark, New Jersey, March 22, 1781.

107 Burstyn, *Past and Promise*: 41–43.

108 Sellers, *Patience Wright*: 69–73.

109 In 1781 she left London and moved to Paris to open a shop. After a year she returned to London and was preparing to return to America when she died on March 23, 1786. Burstyn, *Past and Promise*: 41–43.

CHAPTER 10

1 Jane Emott married Thomas Bradbury Chandler (1726–1790) in 1750 or 1752. Burr, *Anglican Church in New Jersey*: 595. Thomas Chandler had been ordained in London, England in 1751 and was the rector at Saint John's Church in Elizabeth Town. He was granted a Doctor of Divinity degree from Oxford in 1766 and Columbia in 1767. He was the author of "An Appeal to the Public in Behalf of the Church of England in America" which was published in 1767, and in 1771 "A Sermon Preached before the Corporation For the Relief of the Widows and Children of Clergymen, in the Connection of the Church of England in America, at their Anniversary meeting on the 2d of October, 1771 at Perth Amboy."

2 Chandler returned to the United States in 1785. Kail, *Who Was Who During the American Revolution*: 196.

3 William Skinner had been the clergyman at Perth Amboy from November 1722 to his death in 1758.

4 Lundin, *Cockpit of the Revolution: The War for Independence in New Jersey*: 379.

5 Prince, *Papers of William Livingston*, Volume 2: 212, William Livingston at Trenton to Mary Martin, February 16, 1778.

6 Stanley, *Canada Invaded*: 87.

7 Parole is a shortened form of the French *parole d'honneur*, that is, your word of honor. Lederer, *Colonial American English*: 166.

8 CP 228:2, James Gambier, February 1779.

9 Joshua Loring, British Commissary General of Prisoners, report of November 1, 1778, indicates that of 327 rebel officers who were British prisoners, 191 were on parole on Long Island, 51 on parole at home, 80 had broken their parole, and 5 were confined in the Provost. CP 45:3, Great Britain, Army in America Return of November 1, 1778 and CP 178:15, October 3, 1781 at New York, Alex Jos. Phillips to Sir Henry Clinton.

10 CP 33:30, Richard Howe from on board the ship *Eagle* off of Sandy Hook, New Jersey, to Sir Henry Clinton, April 13, 1778 and CP 34:7, Lord George Germain at Whitehall to Sir Henry Clinton, February 19, 1778.

11 Letters of Colonel Armand (Marquis de la Rouerie) 1777–1791, Collections of the New York Historical Society for the Year 1878: 297, Colonel Armand to General [Charles] Scott, October 10, 1778.

12 Valentine, Manual, 1863: 637.

13 King's American Regiment Order Book, June 7, 1777.

14 Kelby, Orderly Book of the Three Battalions of Loyalists: 30 and King's American Regiment Orderly Book, August 20, 1777.

15 Valentine, Manual, 1863: 645–646 and New Jersey Archives, Second Series, Volume 1: 443.

16 Valentine, Manual, 1863: 656–657.

17 Lundin, Cockpit of the Revolution: 379.

18 CP 65:20, Leslie Alexander at Staten Island to Sir Henry Clinton, August 3, 1779.

19 CP 107:44, Stephen Payne to Major Henry Bruen, June 30, 1780.

20 Valentine, *Manual*, 1863: 678.

21 Valentine, *Manual*, 1863: 709.

22 Ward, *Maxwell:* 58, Maxwell to Washington, February 9, 1777.

23 Ward, Maxwell: 108, Maxwell to Washington, August 31, 1778.

24 GWP, General Correspondence and Varick Transcripts, Letterbook 10: 365, George Washington at Morristown to General Samuel H. Parsons, December 13, 1779.

25 Virginia War Office Book at Clements Library: 45, March 4, 1780.

26 Diary of Samuel Bixby in Isaac Bolster's Company of Sutton in Colonel Larnerd's Regiment, May 1 to December 31, 1775, in *Proceedings of the Massachusetts Historical Society*, Volume XIV (1876): 289, July 6, 1775.

27 Thomas Bradford Manuscripts, British Army Prisoners, Volume 3: 95, John Adams at Elizabeth Town to Thomas Bradford at Philadelphia, August 1, 1780.

28 Thomas Bradford Manuscripts, British Army Prisoners, Volume 3: 93, Abraham Skinner to Thomas Bradford, August 12, 1780.

29 Diary of Samuel Bixby in Isaac Bolster's Company of Sutton in Colonel Larnerd's Regiment enlisted May 1 to December 31, 1775 in *Proceedings of the Massachusetts Historical Society*, Volume XIV (1876): 286, June 6, 1775.

30 Lundin, *Cockpit of the Revolution:* 377–378.

31 Tallmadge, Memoir of Colonel Benjamin Tallmadge: 50 and CP 47:15, Convention army, November 1778 and CP 47:21, Quartermaster General's Department, Return of Vessels in and about New York, December 1, 1778.

32 Frederick Mackenzie Papers, Quartermaster General's Report, April 1, 1781.

33 Prince, *Papers of William Livingston*, Volume 2: 280–281, William Livingston to George Washington, April 4, 1778.

34 Robertson, *Francisco de Miranda and the Revolutionizing of Spanish America*: 235–237 .

35 GWP, Varick Letterbook 3: 23–24, George Washington to Joseph Reed and John Cox, April 7, 1777.

36 Scott, "A British Counterfeiting Press in New York Harbor," *New-York Historical Society Quarterly*, 1955: 117–120.

37 Q.E.D. is Latin for *quod erat demonstrandum* which means that which was to be demonstrated. Parker, *Connecticut's Colonial and Continental Money*: 38.

38 Pennsylvania Colonial Records, Series 2, Volume XI: 375, Col. James Chambers' 1st Pennsylvania Orderly Book and Parker, *Connecticut's Colonial and Continental Money*: 40.

39 Love, *The Colonial History of Hartford*: 291.

40 Parker, *Connecticut's Colonial and Continental Money*: 40.

41 Pennypacker, *General Washington's Spies*: 71.

42 Thomas Bradford Manuscripts, British army prisoners, Volume 1: 53, July 3, 1778; Stephen McPherson to Thomas Bradford.

43 New Jersey Archives Series 2, Volume IV, Extracts from American Newspapers: 551.

44 New Jersey Historical Society Proceedings, Third Series, Volume III: 87.

45 New Jersey Historical Society Proceedings, New Series, Volume VII, Number 1: 29.

46 Prince, *Papers of William Livingston*, Volume 4: 254, Asher [Fitz]Randolph at Woodbridge to William Livingston, August 18, 1781.

47 William Armistead's James would in 1781 become a spy for General Lafayette sending back intelligence from British General Cornwallis' camp at Yorktown.

48 Naval Chronicle for 1814, Biographical Memoir of Sir George Collier: 365–366.

49 Lafayette in Virginia, Unpublished Letters: 16, Lafayette at Rawson's Ordinary to [Thomas Jefferson?], June 26, 1781, 6 a.m.

50 Virginia State Papers, III: 238, Colonel John Newton at Norfolk to Colonel Davies, July 30, 1782.

51 GWP, Varick Transcripts, Letterbook 4, 274–275, George Washington to William Livingston, January 12, 1782.

52 Washington was referring to the communications between Staten Island and Elizabeth Town.

53 The draft is in the hand of Tench Tilghman. GWP, Varick Transcripts, Letterbook 14: 368–369, George Washington to Elias Dayton, January 26, 1782.

54 GWP, Varick Transcripts, Letterbook 4: 321–322, George Washington to Jonathan Trumbull, May 10, 1782 (also to William Livingston).

55 GWP, Varick Transcripts, Letterbook 5: 12–13, George Washington to Jonathan Trumbull, March 5, 1783.

56 The translation and the distribution of this proclamation were given to Daniel Coxe. Smith, *William Smith's Historical Memoirs 1778–1783*: 370.

57 Putnam, *Memoirs*: 80.

58 CP 129:18, William Bernard Gifford at New Utrect to Oliver De Lancey, November 10, 1780.

59 CP 131:35, William Bernard Gifford to Oliver De Lancey, November 28, 1780.

60 The tavern in Elizabeth Town was owned by a physician who had plenty of books. CP 132:44, William Bernard Gifford to Oliver De Lancey, December 7, 1780, and Hughes, *A Journal by Thos: Hughes*: 101–102.

61 Valentine, *Manual*, 1863: 727.

CHAPTER 11

1 Setauket is on the north shore of Suffolk County, Long Island, between Drowned Meadow (now known as Port Jefferson) and Stony Brook.

2 CP 23:31, September 3, 1777, Richard Hewlett to William Tryon.

3 GWP, Varick Transcripts, Letterbook 6: 144, George Washington to Alexander Clough, August 25, 1778.

4 Heitman, *Historical Register*: 161.

5 Tallmadge did not have responsibility or knowledge of the spies operating from New Jersey into New York City and Staten Island.

6 Benjamin Tallmadge was born February 25, 1754, at Brookhaven, Suffolk County, Long Island. He was in the 2nd Regiment Continental Light Dragoons.

7 Pennypacker, *General Washington's Spies*: 31–32.

8 Fitzpatrick, *Writings of George Washington*, XIII: 476. Draft was written in the hand of Tench Tilghman.

9 Simcoe Papers, P. Alliard to Simcoe, January 29, 1779.

10 GWP, General Correspondence, Samuel Culper to Benjamin Tallmadge, February 26, 1779: 7.

11 Pennypacker, *General Washington's Spies*: 259–260.

12 CP 52:34, Samuel Blackdon to [Benjamin Tallmadge], February 15, 1779 with note Silvester Deering to Benjamin Tallmadge, June 12, 1779.

13 GWP, General Correspondence, Samuel Culper to Benjamin Tallmadge, February 26, 1779 and Pennypacker, ibid.: 37. He was in Boston by February 15, 1779 see CP 52:34, Samuel Blackdon to [Benjamin Tallmadge], February 15, 1779 with note Silvester Deering to Benjamin Tallmadge, June 12, 1779.

14 Middlebrook is today known as Bound Brook, New Jersey.

15 GWP, Varick Transcripts Letterbook 8: 207–209, George Washington to Benjamin Tallmadge, March 21, 1779.

16 The Kennedy family lived at 1 Broadway, the Watts family at #3, and Chief Justice Robert Livingston was at #5. John and Elizabeth Stevens (also residents of Perth Amboy, N.J.) in 1761 bought and lived at #7, and the Van Cortlandt family at #9. Henry Clinton, commander of the British forces in North America was living at the Archibald Kennedy house at 1 Broadway, New York City. Clinton also rented a small farm in Bowery Lane that belonged to Cornelius Tibout. CP 171:40, Lawrence Kortright to Sir Henry Clinton, August 23, 1781. Lawrence Kortright was still a merchant in New York City in 1789 per p. 50 of *The New-York Directory and Register* for the year 1789.

17 Victualling is the eighteenth-century military term for feeding people. GWP, Varick Transcripts Letterbook 8: 207–209, George Washington to Benjamin Tallmadge, March 21, 1779.

18 GWP, General Correspondence, Samuel Culper to Benjamin Tallmadge, April 10, 1779, Intelligence Report.

19 GWP, General Correspondence, Samuel Culper to Benjamin Tallmadge, April 12, 1779.

20 GWP, General Correspondence, James Jay at Fishkill to George Washington, April 13 and 20, 1780; GWP, Varick Transcripts, Letterbook 3:

264–265, George Washington to James Jay, May 12, 1780, and Varick Transcripts, Letterbook 11: 313–314, George Washington to Udny Hay, May 13, 1780; and GWP, General Correspondence, James Jay to George Washington, September 19, 1780.

21 Pennypacker, *General Washington's Spies*: 42–43.

22 CP 60:49, George Washington to Benjamin Tallmadge, June 13, 1779 and GWP, Varick Transcript, Letterbook 9: 90–91, George Washington to Benjamin Tallmadge, June 13, 1779.

23 Anna Smith Strong was called Nancy. Currie, *Anna Smith Strong and the Setauket Spy Ring*: 6 and CP 61:30, Caleb Brewster to Benjamin Tallmadge, June 21, 1779.

24 Robert Townsend was born on November 25, 1753, and died at age eighty-four on March 7, 1838, at Oyster Bay, Long Island. GWP, General Correspondence, Samuel Culper to John Bolton, June 5, 1779, two letters the same day.

25 Pennypacker, *General Washington's Spies*: 8.

26 Pennypacker, *General Washington's Spies*: 10–11.

27 GWP, General Correspondence, Samuel Culper to Benjamin Tallmadge, June 20, 1779.

28 GWP, General Correspondence, Samuel Culper to Benjamin Tallmadge, June 29, 1779.

29 Pennypacker, *General Washington's Spies*: 54.

30 GWP, General Correspondence, Samuel Culper to John Bolton, August 15, 1779, in code with translation. It is also in Pennypacker, *General Washington's Spies*: 252–253 (still in cipher).

31 GWP, Varick Transcripts, Letterbook 10: 48–50, George Washington to Benjamin Tallmadge, September 24, 1779.

32 GWP, Varick Transcripts, Letterbook 10: 48–50, George Washington to Benjamin Tallmadge, September 24, 1779.

33 GWP, Varick Transcripts, Letterbook 10: 123, George Washington to Benjamin Tallmadge, October 9, 1779.

34 GWP, General Correspondence, Samuel Culper to John Bolton, October 9, 1779.

35 GWP, General Correspondence, Samuel Culper Jr. to Benjamin Tallmadge, October 21, 1779.

36 GWP, General Correspondence, Samuel Culper Jr. to John Bolton, October 10, 1779.

37 Possibly Ephraim Blaine, Commissary General of Purchases.

38 GWP, Varick Transcripts, Letterbook 11: George Washington to Benjamin Tallmadge, February 5, 1780.

39 GWP, Varick Transcripts, Letterbook 11: George Washington to Benjamin Tallmadge, February 5, 1780.

40 Pennypacker, *General Washington's Spies*: 76–77. The message was written in invisible ink between the lines of a poem titled "The Lady's Dress."

Washington's Papers, March 23, 1780, No. 17458 and GWP, General Correspondence, Samuel Culper Jr. to Benjamin Tallmadge, March 23, 1780 (damaged and partially illegible).

41 GWP, General Correspondence, Samuel Culper to George Washington, May 4, 1780.

42 GWP, Varick Transcripts, Letterbook 11: 340, George Washington to Benjamin Tallmadge, May 19, 1780. Draft written by Tench Tilghman and brackets added by George Washington.

43 GWP, General Correspondence, Samuel Culper to John Bolton, June 10, 1780.

44 GWP, Varick Transcripts, Letterbook 12: 48–49, George Washington to Benjamin Tallmadge, July 11, 1780.

45 GWP, General Correspondence, Benjamin Tallmadge to George Washington, July 14, 1780.

46 The reagent covered the reverse side of the letter. One can tell there is writing there but it is illegible. GWP, General Correspondence, Samuel Culper to Richard Floyd, July 20, 1780.

47 Pennypacker, *General Washington's Spies:* 14.

48 Pennypacker, *General Washington's Spies:* 14–15.

49 GWP, General Correspondence, Samuel Culper to Caleb Brewster, July 20, 1780.

50 GWP, General Correspondence, Samuel Culper to John Bolton, July 20, 1780, partially in cipher.

51 GWP, General Correspondence, Benjamin Tallmadge to George Washington, July 22, 1780 [Date on letter is wrong as it was received by Alexander Hamilton on the 21st], GWP, Varick Transcripts, Letterbook 13: 1–2, Alexander Hamilton to Marquis de Lafayette, July 21, 1780.

52 GWP, Varick Transcripts, Letterbook 13: 1–2, Alexander Hamilton to Marquis de Lafayette, July 21, 1780, and Letterbook 13: 2–4, George Washington to Marquis de Lafayette, July 22, 1780, two same date (mentions that Hamilton informed Lafayette previous day).

53 The Long Island signal fires were at Norwich Hill, which is two miles south of Oyster Bay; Sutton's Hill, which is now known as Beacon Hill and is three miles from Cowneck Point; and Flushing Heights.

54 Pennypacker, *General Washington's Spies:* 83.

55 East Chester is eight miles southwest of Rye. Morse, *The American Gazetteer.*

56 GWP, General Correspondence, American Intelligence to George Washington, July 21, 1780, Signed, L D (annotated through the 26th).

57 George Smith had served as a lieutenant in a Suffolk County militia regiment.

58 Nissequogue and Smithtown, Long Island are near each other on the Nissequogue River.

59 Ford, *Peculiar Service:* 279.

60 GWP, Varick Transcripts, Letterbook 12: 116–117, George Washington to Elisha Sheldon, July 31, 1780.

61 Pennypacker, *General Washington's Spies:* 91–92.

62 If you are counting letters, please remember that a double letter "LL" would be transcribed once, such as Bqyim, which is Howell.

63 He was Joseph Easton Trowbridge of New Haven, Connecticut.

64 GWP, General Correspondence, Samuel Culper to John Bolton, September 1, 1780.

65 GWP, General Correspondence, Samuel Culper to John Bolton, September 18, 1780, two the same day.

66 GWP, General Correspondence, Samuel Culper to Benjamin Tallmadge, October 14, 1780.

67 GWP, General Correspondence, Benjamin Tallmadge to George Washington, October 17, 1780.

68 GWP, General Correspondence, Samuel Culper to John Bolton [Benjamin Tallmadge], February 8, 1781.

69 CP 131:31, Henry Vandyke's report, November 26, 1780.

70 CP 134:26, Nehemiah Marks to Oliver De Lancey, December 21, 1780.

71 CP 138:40, also numbered 41, Nehemiah Marks to Oliver De Lancey, January 3, 1781.

72 CP 145:1, Hiram in cipher to Oliver De Lancey, February 1, 1781.

73 William L. Clements Library, Map Division, Clinton Map 129, Plan of Brookhaven, or Setalket on Long Island and Clinton Map 130, "A plan of Brookhaven or Setalket Harbour with its environs / surveyed by Major Holland." Both maps have locations of homes and public buildings have been indicated and property lines defined. Map 130 also has an encampment of British troops, the location of a redoubt, and General William Tryon's headquarters.

74 GWP, General Correspondence, Samuel Culper to Benjamin Tallmadge, May 19, 1781.

75 GWP, General Correspondence, Samuel Culper to John Bolton, May 27, 1781.

76 GWP, General Correspondence, Samuel Culper to John Bolton, June 4, 1781.

77 GWP, General Correspondence, Benjamin Tallmadge at Litchfield, Connecticut to George Washington, August 16, 1783 and Tallmadge, Memoir of Colonel Benjamin Tallmadge: 61.

78 GWP, General Correspondence, Samuel Culper to Benjamin Tallmadge, July 5, 1783.

79 GWP, General Correspondence, Benjamin Tallmadge to George Washington, August 16, 1783.

80 GWP, Varick Transcripts, Letterbook 3: 184–186, George Washington to Benjamin Tallmadge, September 11, 1783.

81 GWP, General Correspondence, Benjamin Tallmadge to George Washington, August 16, 1783.

CHAPTER 12

1 GWP, Varick Transcripts, Letterbook 5: 176–177, Nathanael Greene, September 26, 1780, General Orders.

2 PCC, Volume 7: 132–133, February 19, 1777.

3 GWP, Varick Transcripts, Letterbook 2, 335–336, George Washington to Benedict Arnold, March 3, 1777.

4 GWP, Varick Transcripts, Letterbook 3, 6–7, George Washington to Benedict Arnold, April 3, 1777.

5 GWP, Varick Transcripts, Letterbook 3, 220–222, General Orders May 28, 1778.

6 GWP, General Correspondence, George Washington to Benedict Arnold, June 19, 1778.

7 JCC Volume 11: 571, June 4, 1778.

8 JCC Volume 12: 1071, October 28, 1778.

9 JCC Volume 13: 184, February 15, 1779.

10 JCC Volume 13: 324, March 17, 1779.

11 JCC Volume 13: 337, March 18, 1779 and original in PCC No. 162, folio 169.

12 GWP, General Correspondence, George Washington to Pennsylvania Council, April 20, 1779.

13 GWP, General Correspondence, Benedict Arnold to George Washington, May 5, 1779.

14 In Shakespeare's *Othello*, Iago is a soldier who has fought beside Othello for several years and has become his trusted advisor. At the beginning of the play, Iago claims to have been unfairly passed over for a promotion to the rank of Othello's lieutenant in favor of Michael Cassio. Van Doren Papers, manuscript notes and correspondence, Carl Van Doren to Howard Peckham, January 20, 1941.

15 CP 241:6, Sir Henry Clinton's memorandum on Arnold, undated but after the war.

16 CP 241:5, Sir Henry Clinton note on Arnold, undated but suspected 1780.

17 CP 125:9, Sir Henry Clinton to Martha and Elizabeth Carter, October 4, 1780.

18 HMC, *Report on American Manuscripts in the Royal Institution of Great Britain*, Volume IV: 266, (Volume 49, No. 112), Memorial of Joseph Stansbury to Sir Guy Carleton, August 6, 1783.

19 Van Doren says that he believed that the reason Benedict Arnold used the name of Monk was a reference to the Scottish general who in 1660 turned against Parliament to restore the monarchy and was handsomely rewarded. Arnold's analogy was that he would turn on Congress and be handsomely rewarded by the grateful monarch who would be restored.

20 CP 57:30, John André to Joseph Stansbury, May 10, 1779 and Van Doren, *Secret History*: 198–199.

21 CP 59:27A, John André to Margaret Chew, May 1779.

22 CP 59:30, Benedict Arnold through Joseph Stansbury to John André, Pre May 23, 1779.

23 Heitman, *Historical Register of Officers of the Continental Army*: 72.

24 CP 59:1, Benedict Arnold to John André, May 23, 1779. Van Doren, *Secret History*: 442 gives the addressee as M— JA— but the envelope is actually addressed to M— J— An [Major John André].

25 In Act 5, Scene 1 of Shakespeare's *Hamlet*, Yorick was the deceased court jester whose skull is exhumed by the gravedigger.

26 CP 59:7, Joseph Stansbury to Jonathan Odell, May 26, 1779.

27 CP 59:27, Jonathan Odell to John André, May 31, 1779.

28 CP 60:48, Jonathan Odell to Joseph Stansbury, June 9, 1779 copy provided to John André.

29 CP 59:27 Jonathan Odell to John André, May 31, 1779.

30 Clinton Papers 234:2. Jonathan Odell notes on cipher that it was for Mr. L., who is not identified. However in CP 60:48, Jonathan Odell to Joseph Stansbury, June 9, 1779, Odell says "Lothario is impatient," referring to John André.

31 Rattoon's tavern was located at the end of the old road to Bordentown now known as Main Street in South Amboy. Rattoon's tavern is identified as the "Railroad House Hotel (A. D. Vanpelt, Proprietor)" on the Map of the County of Middlesex, New Jersey, by Smith Gallop & Co. published in 1861. The building was laid out in an east and west direction nearly parallel with the shoreline. The west side of the building was the original portion of the tavern and it was two stories high. It was forty feet long and thirty feet deep. On the east side was a story and half addition that was fifty feet wide and twenty-five feet deep. The tavern had a dock that was located about a half mile away across the salt marsh. The marsh provided ample coverage for anyone traversing from the bay to the tavern or vice versa who did not want to be seen. Clayton, *History of Union and Middlesex Counties*: 824.

32 The armed vessel that was sometimes at Sandy Hook would have been referred to being "at the Hook." The vessel referred to in Beckwith's document was off the southeast end of Staten Island at Princess Bay.

33 CP 157:7, Captain Beckwith's memo, May 31, 1781.

34 John Rattoon brought Joseph Stansbury's letters of June 4 and 9, 1779. CP 60:47, Jonathan Odell to John André, June 13, 1779.

35 CP 60:48, S___ [Joseph Stansbury] to Jonathan Odell, [June] 9, [1779].

36 CP 60:47, Jonathan Odell to John André, June 13, 1779.

37 CP 62:35, John André to Benedict Arnold to be enciphered, Middle of June [1779].

38 CP 59:1, Benedict Arnold to John André, June 18, 1779.

39 CP 63:19, Jonathan Odell to John André, July 18, 1779 enclosing CP 63:3. Jonathan Stevens (Joseph Stansbury) to John Anderson (John André), July 11, 1779.

40 CP 63:26, Jonathan Odell to John André, July 21, 1779.

41 "Wyoming" refers to the Wyoming Valley, in the general area of Wilkes-Barre.

42 CP 63:3, Jonathan Stevens (Joseph Stansbury) to John Anderson (John André), July 11, 1779.

43 CP 63:19, Jonathan Odell to John André, July 18, 1779 enclosing CP 63:3. Jonathan Stevens (Joseph Stansbury) to John Anderson (John André), July 11, 1779.

44 CP 63:26, Jonathan Odell to John André, July 21, 1779.

45 CP 81:24, Jonathan Odell to John André, December 21, 1779. See endorsement of December 24, 1779.

46 CP 60:40, Joseph Stansbury to Jonathan Odell, December 3, 1779.

47 Martin, *Private Yankee Doodle*: 149–150.

48 American General Benjamin Lincoln surrendered Charleston, South Carolina to General Sir Henry Clinton on May 12, 1780. CP 111:12, J. O. [Jonathan Odell] to M[ajo]r A[ndre], July 29, 1780.

49 CP 102:37, Knyphausen's Notes, Draft, Answer, and Memo, May, 1780.

50 CP 104:26, Benedict Arnold to the executor of John Anderson (John André) which was George Beckwith, June 7, 1780.

51 CP 104:27, George Washington and Marquis de Lafayette, [June 1780].

52 A translation of the proclamation was forwarded by General Sir Henry Clinton to Lord George Germain in his dispatch of August 31, 1780. A copy of it is in the British Transcripts, C. O. 5, Volume 100, folio 243, Library of Congress. GWP, Varick Transcripts, Letterbook 11, George Washington to Marquis de Lafayette, May 19, 1780 and GWP, General Correspondence, George Washington at Morristown to Benedict Arnold in Philadelphia, June 4, 1780.

53 CP 110:23, Joseph Stansbury to George Beckwith or John André, July 7, 1780.

54 CP 111:12, J. Moore to John Anderson [John André] merchant to the care of James Osborn [Jonathan Odell] and to be left at Mr. [Jonathan] Odell's, July 11, 1780. Odell lived on Wall Street.

55 GWP, General Correspondence, Gustavus to John Anderson [John André] merchant to the care of James Osborn [Jonathan Odell] and to be left at Reverend [Jonathan] Odell's, August 30, 1780.

56 CP 111:12, J. [Jonathan] O. [Odell] to M[ajo]r A[ndre], July 29, 1780.

57 CP 111:12, J. Moore to John Anderson [John André] merchant to the care of James Osborn [Jonathan Odell] and to be left at Mr. [Jonathan] Odell's, July 12, 1780. [Filed in same folder with item of July 11, 1780.]

58 Gold Star Box, Moore [Benedict Arnold] to Captain John Anderson [John André] to be left at Mr. Odell's, Baltimore, July 15, 1780.

59 CP 113:11, James Osborne [Reverend Jonathan Odell] to Mr. Stevens [Joseph Stansbury], July 24, 1780.

60 CP 113:11, [John André to Benedict Arnold] accompanied with James Osborne [Reverend Jonathan Odell] to Mr. Stevens [Joseph Stansbury].

61 CP 111:12 George Beckwith, ADC at Head Quarters Morris House, July 30 [1780], twelve at night and endorsed [in John André's handwriting] Captain Beckwith.

62 CP 111:12 J. [Jonathan] O. [Odell] to M[ajo]r A[ndre], July 29, 1780.

63 CP 118:31, Mr. Stevens [Joseph Stansbury] to Jasper Overhill [Jonathan Odell], August 14, 1780 and received in New York City on August 23, 1780 via John Rattoon.

64 CP 119:1 or 2 and Van Doren, *Secret History*: 469–470, George Beckwith, ADC Morris House to Major André, August 27, 1780.

65 CP 122:17, Jonathan Odell to John André, September 7, 1780 enclosing Thomas Charlton [Joseph Stansbury] to Jasper Overhill [Jonathan Odell], August 25, 1780.

66 CP 123:19, Benedict Arnold to ____ [John André], September 15, 1780, transcribed by Jonathan Odell.

67 Van Doren, *Secret History*: 340.

68 GWP, General Correspondence, Continental Army, September 29, 1780, Proceedings against John L. André as a Spy, by Continental Army Board of General Officers.

69 Van Doren, *Secret History*: opposite 366, photographic reproduction.

70 GWP, Varick Transcripts, Letterbook 5: 180–181, George Washington, October 1, 1780, General Orders.

CHAPTER 13

1 GWP, General Correspondence, Landon Carter to George Washington, October 7, 1755.

2 GWP, Varick Transcripts, Letterbook 1: 129–133, George Washington at White Plains, New York to Lund Washington at Mount Vernon, Virginia, August 15, 1778.

3 GWP, Varick Transcripts, Letterbook 2: 153–155, George Washington to William Alexander, Lord Stirling, December 14, 1776.

4 GWP, Varick Transcripts, Letterbook 2: 145–146, George Washington to John Cadwalader, December 12, 1776.

5 GWP, Varick Transcripts, Letterbook 1: 320–321, George Washington to John Cochran, August 16, 1779.

6 Watson, *Men and Times of the Revolution: or Memoirs of Elkanah Watson*: 9, 20, and 25–26.

7 John Greenwood remembered "the person who kept the [Charlestown] ferry" as "Mr. Enoch Hopkins, whose son used to go to school with me." This Hopkins died on December 27, 1778, at the age of fifty-five. Greenwood, *A Young Patriot in the American Revolution*: 44.

8 Force, American Archives, Series 4, Volume 2: 1003–1004.

9 Osnaburg was a heavy coarse cotton in a plain weave used for grain sacks. Force, American Archives, Series 4 Volume 2: 1003–1004, William Stoddard, Boston, to Captain James Littlefield, Watertown, June 15, 1775.

10 Callender, *Selections from the Economic History of the United States, 1765–1860*: 54.

11 McClellan, *Smuggling in the American Colonies at the Outbreak of the Revolution…*: 88.

12 New Jersey Archives, First Series, Volume 9: 402–404, William Franklin to Lords of Trade, February 8, 1764.

13 The Battle of Bunker's Hill was on June 17, 1775.

14 For a facsimile of the document see Bolton, *The Private Soldier Under Washington:* 90 [Original in the Massachusetts Historical Society] and Dandridge, Historic Shepherdstown, Sergeant Henry Bedinger Journal: 107, August 24, 1775.

15 GWP, Varick Transcripts, Letterbook 2: 142–146, George Washington to Continental Congress, January 5, 1777.

16 GWP, Varick Transcripts, Letterbook 2: 146–147, George Washington to Continental Congress, January 7, 1777.

17 New Jersey was originally two colonies. There was the colony of East Jersey with its capital at Perth Amboy and the colony of West Jersey with its capital at Burlington. The proprietors had surrendered power to govern back to the crown and the colony of New Jersey was created in 1702 with alternating the legislative sessions between Burlington and Perth Amboy.

18 GWP, Varick Transcripts, Letterbook 2: 198–199, George Washington at Pluckemin to William Heath, January 5, 1777.

19 Bourquin, *Journal of Events in the Revolution by Elias Boudinot:* 54–55, 199.

20 Bourquin, *Journal of Events in the Revolution by Elias Boudinot:* 54–55, 199.

21 Bourquin, *Journal of Events in the Revolution by Elias Boudinot:* 55.

22 Graydon, *Memoirs of His Own Time:* 212, quote of Alexander Hamilton from a 1786 eulogy of General Nathanael Greene before the Society of the Cincinnati at New York City.

23 Nassau Hall was built in 1756 and named for King William III, Prince of Orange-Nassau. The building was 177 feet by 54 feet. Nassau Hall was planned by Robert Smith and Dr. William Shippen of Philadelphia. It contained a dining room, lecture rooms, library room, prayer hall, and living quarters for the faculty as well as forty-nine dormitory rooms. The stone building was in deteriorating condition after having been used by the British in December 1776 as a barracks and a stable.

24 McPherson is listed as belonging to the 17th Regiment of Foot in "Losses of the Military and Naval Forces Engaged in the War of the American Revolution," *Pennsylvania Magazine of History and Biography*, Volume XXVII (1903): 183 which quoted from *Pennsylvania Magazine*, Volume VII: 237, which is a list compiled by Lieutenant George Inman, 26th Regiment of Foot in 1784. McPherson is listed as being in the 19th Regiment of Foot in Putnam, *Memoirs of Israel Putnam:* 69–70.

25 Hubert S. Smith Naval Collection and in NAVAL, Volume 8, 245–246, Governor Thomas Johnson Jr. at Annapolis to Robert Morris, April 1, 1777.

26. GWP, Varick Transcripts, Letterbook 5: 311–313, George Washington to Marquis de Lafayette, May 18, 1778.

27 CP 82:39, Henry Clinton to Campbell, undated; Port Royal is an island on the southern coast of South Carolina. It is separated from the mainland on the West by the Broad River. It is eleven miles long and about one mile wide. The town of Beaufort is located on the island, which has an excellent harbor, sufficient to contain the largest fleet in the world.

28 American Philosophical Society, Dr. De Laville at Cherbourg to Benjamin Franklin, June 16, 1777.

29 *PBF*, Volume 24: 222, American Commissioners to Vergennes, June 26, 1777.

30 Library of Congress, Benjamin Franklin at Paris to Messrs. Du Longprey Coney & Son, [Cherbourg merchant] June 23, 1777.

31 George Johnstone was born in Dumfries, Scotland, as the third son of Sir James Johnstone. After serving in the navy, he became the first governor of West Florida in 1763 and served until 1767 when he was recalled by King George III. He represented Appleby and Cockermouth in Parliament. In 1778 he was sent as a commissioner with Lord Carlisle to the United States to deal with Congress.

32 GWP, General Correspondence, Henry Laurens to George Washington, September 23, 1778 and GWP, Varick Transcripts, Letterbook 1: 154–156, George Washington to Henry Laurens, October 3, 1778.

33 This was the start of what would develop into the Culper spy ring. GWP, Varick Transcripts, Letterbook 8: 207–209, George Washington to Benjamin Tallmadge, March 21, 1779.

34 GWP, Varick Transcripts, Letterbook 9: 328–329, George Washington to Robert Howe, August 17, 1779.

35 CP 55:31, Elijah Hunter's report, April 2, 1777. It is annotated "intelligence from Governor Tryon's friend."

36 Sabine, *Historical Memoirs of William Smith 1778–1783*: 85, Governor William Tryon through William Smith to General Sir Henry Clinton, March 6, 1779.

37 GWP, General Correspondence for draft and Varick Transcripts, Letterbook 9: 310–313, George Washington to Elijah Hunter, August 12, 1779, and report.

38 Mr. Naigts is Mr. John Naight.

39. GWP, Letterbook 22: 279, George Washington to Elijah Hunter, February 25, 1790.

40 GWP, Varick Transcripts, Letterbook 16: 229–230, George Washington to Elijah Hunter at Bedford, June 11, 1783.

41 GWP, Varick Transcripts, Letterbook 10: 63–67, George Washington to Benjamin Lincoln, September 28, 1779.

42 GWP, General Correspondence and Varick Transcripts, Letterbook 11: 336–338, George Washington to Marie Joseph Paul Yves Roche Gilbert du Motier, Marquis de Lafayette, May 19, 1780.

43 GWP, Varick Transcripts, Letterbook 11: 386, George Washington at Morristown to Benedict Arnold at Philadelphia, June 4, 1780.

44 CP 104:26. Mr. Moore [Benedict Arnold] to Executor of John Anderson [Captain George Beckwith] June 7, 1780.

45 Library of Congress, British Transcripts, C. O. 5, Volume 100, folio 243, Sir Henry Clinton to Lord George Germain, August 31, 1780.

46 Historical Society of Pennsylvania, Benedict Arnold to George Washington, June 7, 1780.

47 Sometimes his name is spelled Ottendorff.

48 Smith, William, St. Clair Papers, General St. Clair at Morristown to James Wilson, February 10, 1777: 382.

49 Scott, *Rivington's New York Newspaper Extracts:* 217, April 5, 1780. Ottendorf had gone over to the British by April 5, 1780 when he stated that Captain James Willing, an American officer on parole on Long Island had insulted him and refused him satisfaction in a duel. Note many sources say Ottendorf left the Continental army to join Benedict Arnold's Legion. This is not correct as Ottendorf was in New York several months prior to Arnold's defection to the British. Lord George had instructed that Ottendorf be appointed a captain in the 60th (Royal American) Regiment of Foot; CP 196:6, Thomas Townsend (1st Viscount Sydney) to Sir Henry Clinton, September 13, 1782. Captain John Smith had arranged for Ottendorf to be paid ten shillings per day as a captain from June 17, 1780 to February 28, 1782 as per a letter from Lord George dated June 7, 1780. CP 191:38, John Smith, after February 26, 1782.

50 CP 140:40, Joshua Loring to Oliver De Lancey, January 14, 1781.

51 Schoff Revolutionary War Collection, M-636, ALS to Mrs. Kempe (possibly Grace Coxe Kempe), October 2, [1778].

52 Her diary was published in the *Pennsylvania Magazine of History and Biography*, Volume LV: 35–94 and Volume LVIII: 152–189. A painting of her done in 1750 by Stokes is opposite of page 32 of Volume LV.

53 Pennsylvania Historical Society, G. Galloway at Philadelphia to child, February 12, 1779.

54 John Cunningham was a New Jersey resident for the last four years and had been in the New Jersey militia up until December 15, 1779 when he was discharged. He had served mostly at Trenton and Elizabeth Town. His visit to Morristown was prior to his leaving Elizabeth Town on the night of February 25. CP 87:1, John Cunningham's deposition, February 26, 1780.

55 Morristown National Historical Park Manuscript Collection, Aaron Burr at White Plains to General Malcolm, January 21, 1779.

56 Morris, *History of Staten Island*, Volume 1: 337–338. Washington, October 7, 1755.

57 GWP, Varick Transcripts, Letterbook 1: 129–133, George Washington at White Plains, New York to Lund Washington at Mount Vernon, Virginia, August 15, 1778.

58 GWP, Varick Transcripts, Letterbook 2: 153–155, George Washington to William Alexander, Lord Stirling, December 14, 1776.

59 Bernardo de Gálvez was born in Macharaviaya, among the mountains of Málaga, Spain on July 23, 1746.

60 Mississippi Provincial Archives, Spanish Dominion (MPASD) Volume I, John Stephenson to "Irish friend," April 2, 1778.

61 Rial is both an old English gold coin with the value of 15 shillings during the reign of Elizabeth I (1558–1603) and variant English spelling for "Real" which was a small Spanish coin that circulated in the United States until approx-

imately 1850. MPASD Volume I: 229, Alexander Ross to Dumbandt (W54. lliam Dunbar), April 10, 1778.

62 National Archives of Cuba, Dispatches of Bernardo de Gálvez 55, to José Navarro, July 28, 1778.

63 GWP, Varick Transcripts, Letterbook 4, 274–275, George Washington to William Livingston, January 12, 1782.

64 Valentine, *Manual*, 1863: 645–646 and New Jersey Archives, Second Series, Volume 1: 443.

65 Valentine, Manual, 1863: 656–657.

66 Virginia War Office Book: 45, March 4, 1780.

67 Calendar of Virginia State Papers, Volume III: 238.

68 Fort Dayton was constructed in 1776 by the 4th New Jersey Regiment under the command of Colonel Elias Dayton. The fort was named in Dayton's honor. It previously was the site of Fort Herkimer which was a wooden blockhouse from the French and Indian War. The newer Fort Herkimer was two miles east. A house was erected on the site in 1884.

69 Lossing, *Pictorial Field Book of the Revolution*, Volume 1: 251.

70 Lossing, *Pictorial Field Book of the Revolution*, Volume 1: 251–252 and Lamb, *An Original and Authentic Journal of Occurrences*: 149–151.

71 Killion and Waller, *Georgia in the Revolution*, 77–79.

72 A neighbor of Nancy Hart was Colonel John Dooly, commander of the Wilkes County militia. He certified a report April 17, 1780 from Fort Dooly, Wilkes County, Georgia from Captain John Hill who reported that he had two spies on his payroll. It is unknown if these were spies or scouts and if one was Nancy Hart. Force, *American Archives*, Series 5 Volume I: 1193 also in PBF, Volume 22: 583 JCC: 653–655, Congress on August 27, 1776, adjusted the offer of land according to rank (see pp. 705–709).

73 Collections of the New York Historical Society, 1881: 451, Journal of Captain John Montresor, September 11, 1777.

74 GWP, General Correspondence and Varick Transcripts, Letterbook 4: 277–278, George Washington to John Clark, November 4, 1777.

75 GWP, General Correspondence, John Clark Jr. to George Washington, November 4, 1777.

76 Fitzpatrick, *Writings of Washington*, Vol. XI, General Order May 6, 1778.

77 CP 21:49, Burgoyne to Sir William Howe, May 14, 1777.

78 Henry Williams was the son of Erasmus Williams, a member of the New York State Convention.

79 Preble, *Preble Family in America*: 83.

80 CP 22:4, Sir William Howe to John Burgoyne, July 20, 1777.

81 Wyck, "Autobiography of Philip Van Cortlandt, Brigadier General in the Continental Army [1775–1783]" in *Magazine of American History*, Vol. II, Part I, (1878): 284; and Washington Papers at LOC, General Correspondence: William Howe at New York to John Burgoyne, July 20, 1777, Henry Williams' Deposition July 24, 1777, Israel Putman at Peekskill to George Washington, July 24, 1777 and

George Washington at Ramapo to Israel Putnam, July 25, 1777 (which is also in Varick Transcripts, Letterbook 3: 398–399).

82 GWP, Varick Transcripts, Letterbook 12: 7–12, George Washington to Marie Joseph Paul Yves Roch Gilbert du Motier, Marquis de Lafayette, February 15, 1785 which was in response to Lafayette, dated on board the frigate *Nymph* in the harbor of New York, to George Washington, December 21, 1784, and GWP, Varick Transcripts, Letterbook 12: 41, George Washington to Mathew Carey, March 15, 1785. The text of the original, said to be in Worcester College, Ohio, varies somewhat from this letter, the last sentence being "It has sometimes occurred to me, that there are persons who wishing to read News Papers, without being at the expense of paying for them, make free with those which are addressed to others. Under the garb of a letter, it is not presumable this liberty would be taken." Worcester College, Ohio, states they do not have such a letter.

CHAPTER 14

1 Force, American Archives, Fourth Series Volume 1: 1263–1268.

2 Force, American Archives, Fourth Series Volume 2: 243–245, John Brown to Boston, Massachusetts Committee of Correspondence.

3 Force, American Archives, Fourth Series Volume 3: 67–68, General Montgomery at Albany, New York to the New York Congress, August 8, 1775.

4 Force, American Archives, Fourth Series Volume 3: 1681–1682, Major General Philip Schuyler at Fort Ticonderoga to the President of Congress, John Hancock, November 27, 1775.

5 In Capt. Edward Mott's Journal he says that a Captain Elisha Phelps, brother of Captain Noah Phelps, wrote in a letter to the General Assembly that the other spy was Mr. Hickok. Mott says that Captain Ezra Hichock was on the trip. Mott wrote that the spies were Mr. Noah Phelps and Mr. Heacock. There is also an Ezra Hecock of Sheffield (there are two Sheffields, one in Massachusetts and the other in the New Hampshire Grants, i.e., Vermont) who spent twenty-two days in military service. Since Mott referred to the Hicock/Heacock as "Mr." the same significance as "Mr." Phelps who was a Captain, my guess is that the other spy was Captain Ezra Hicock rather than non-officer Ezra Hecock. For Mott's Journal see *Connecticut Historical Society Collections*, Volume 1 (1860): 167, 169, and 174–175.

6 Johnston, *Connecticut Military Record 1775–1848*: 29, 81.

7 Force, American Archives, Fifth Series Volume 1: 1193 also in PBF, Volume 22: 583.

8 JCC, Volume 5: 654–655, August 14, 1776.

9 Force, American Archives, Series 4 Volume 1: 1297, Speech of Mr. Wilkins, of Westchester County.

10 PBF, Volume 26: 624, Rudolphe Ernest Hartman at Amsterdam, Holland to Benjamin Franklin, June 15, 1778.

11 Internet edition of the Papers of Benjamin Franklin at http://www.franklin-papers.org/franklin/. Unpublished letters: Rudolph Ernest Hartmann to Benjamin Franklin, June 25, 1778; Rudolphe Ernest Hartmann to Benjamin

Franklin, February 8, 1779; and Rudolphe Ernest Hartmann with Benjamin Franklin's Draft of a Reply, March 6, 1779.

12 HMC, Manuscripts of the Earl of Dartmouth, American Papers, Volume II: 371, J. Robertson to Isaac Wilkins, September 4, 1775.

13 JCC, Volume IV: 190, March 8, 1776.

14 The Committee of Claims of Congress determined that he was due $255.60 for his expenses in caring for his wound from the fall till his arrival in Philadelphia. JCC, Volume IV: 270–271, April 11, 1776, Committee of Claims' report, and JCC, Volume IV: 263, April 9, 1776, Return of prisoners Zedwitz brought back from Canada.

15 Herman Zedwitz's first name sometimes appears as Harman and his last name was sometimes spelled Zedtwitz and sometimes misspelled as Sedwitz. He claimed to be a baron and was said to have been an officer in the Swiss army (Willett, *Narrative of the Military Actions of Colonel Marinus Willett*: 34). He was a violin teacher who had studied in London and Germany. In 1773 he was residing at Mrs. Buskirk's opposite the Old Presbyterian Meeting in New York City. Scott, *Rivington's New York Newspaper Extracts*, April 29, 1773: 31.

16 Captain Hamilton is most likely Alexander Hamilton and the general is probably George Washington. GWP, General Correspondence, Augustus Stein, August 25, 1776, Record of Testimony at Zedwitz Court Martial.

17 GWP, General Correspondence, Herman Zedwitz to William Tryon, August 24, 1776. Zedwitz's letter is published in facsimile in Force's American Archives, Fifth Series, Volume 1.

18 Peter Kinnan was born at Perth Amboy, New Jersey, in May 1751. He was the son of Thomas Kinnan and Mary Savery. He enlisted in the New Jersey militia at the beginning of the American Revolution and served until the end of the war.

19 Kinnan, Order Book Kept by Peter Kinnan: 86 and Force, American Archives, Series 5 Volume 2: 1012, Letter from Colonel Smallwood to Maryland Convention, October 12, 1776. (Members of the court-martial board were Colonel Haslet and his Lieutenant Colonel, Bedford, of the Delaware Battalion, with Lieutenant Colonel Hare and Colonel Smallwood.)

20 GWP, General Correspondence, Herman Zedwitz, August 25, 1776, Military Service.

21 GWP, General Correspondence, Augustus Stein, August 25, 1776, Record of Testimony at Zedwitz Court-Martial.

22 JCC, Volume VI: 971–972, Resolve of November 22, 1776.

23 Prince, *Papers of William Livingston*, Volume 1: 190–191, William Livingston at Burlington to David Rittenhouse, November 30, 1776.

24 JCC, Volume VI: 958 and 971–972, Petition of Juliana Zedwitz and Resolve of November 22, 1776.

25 Virginia Gazette of Dixon & Nicolson, June 5, 1779: p. 2, c. 1, an article dated May 19 from Trenton, New Jersey.

26 Whisenhunt, *Delegate from New Jersey–The Journal of John Fell*: 34, 66, 203, January 20, April 1, and July 14, 1779.

27 PBF, Volume 22: 583, Benjamin Franklin to Horatio Gates, August 28, 1776.

28 GWP, Letterbook 10: 132–133, George Washington to Continental Congress, August 18, 1776.

29 Christopher Ludwick was born in Geissen, Germany, on October 17, 1720. He became a baker just like his father. He was in the military from 1737 to 1741. He went to sea circa 1746 and after seven years as a sailor, in 1754, he immigrated to Philadelphia where he made a living as a baker. Congress in May 1777 appointed him superintendent of bakers. He died on June 17, 1801, in Philadelphia.

30 Prince, *Papers of William Livingston*, Volume 1: 119, Joseph Reed at New York to William Livingston, August 19, 1776.

31 Hugh Mercer had secretly sent Captain John Mercereau to his brother's place on Staten Island. GWP, General Correspondence, Hugh Mercer to George Washington, July 16, 1776.

32 Prince, *Papers of William Livingston*, Volume 1: 124, William Livingston at Elizabeth Town to Hugh Mercer, August 23, 1776.

33 GWP, letterbook 10: 159–161 and Varick Transcripts, letterbook 1: 388–390, George Washington to Continental Congress, August 26, 1776.

34 GWP, Financial Papers, Warrant Book: Lawrence Mascoll paid for going into enemy lines for intelligence, August 23, 1776.

35 Fitzpatrick, *Writings of Washington*, Volume 5: 496, George Washington at Long Island to the President of Congress, August 29, 1776.

36 Uhlendorf, *Revolution in America*, p. 41.

37 Colonel Stephen J. Schuyler was a brother of General Philip Schuyler, and having the oldest commission among the colonels on that station, he acted as brigadier general in the latter part of the campaign.

38 Christopher Fisher was a native of Schoharie County, New York and was of German origin. He moved to Rensselaer County just before the war. Simms, History of Schoharie County (1845): 257–259.

39 Jacob van Alstyne died in May 1844, aged nearly ninety-five years. Simms, *History of Schoharie County* (1845): 259. It probably was not gold that Fischer showed van Alstyne, but a hard currency such as silver coins instead of Continental dollars.

40 Longstreet, *Fourth of July—1776*: 24.

41 *Pennsylvania Evening Post*, November 25, 1777.

42 Nathan Hale Institute: 13.

43 Potter, *Military History of New Hampshire*, Volume 1: 289–290.

44 How accurate is the story? The part of the story of his partying with British officers certainly sounds like an embellishment to the basic deed. Do not confuse Joseph Badger, father, with Joseph Badger, the son. This story is about the son but usually incorrectly attributed to the father. The father was in New Hampshire at the time and was a Brigadier General. The father was born at Haverhill, Massachusetts, on January 11, 1722; son of Joseph and Hannah (Peaslee) Badger. He was a farmer, served in the militia, and held the ranks of ensign, lieutenant,

and captain, successively. At the age of twenty-three he was made a deputy sheriff, and afterward justice of the peace. On January 31, 1740, he was married to Hannah Pearson, and their son Joseph Badger married Elizabeth, daughter of William Parsons of South Hampton. In July 1763, the father removed to Gilmanton, New Hampshire, where he was the first magistrate, and on July 10, 1771, received the appointment of colonel of the 10th New Hampshire Regiment. In 1771 he acted as a muster-master for the state, was elected a delegate to the provincial congress, and was made brigadier general in the state militia, June 27, 1780. He served on the governor's council from 1784 to 1791. Badger later became a general and died April 4, 1803, at Gilmanton. Stark, *Memoir and Official Correspondence of General John Stark*: 36 footnote.

45 GWP, Varick Transcripts Letterbook 3: 275–276, George Washington at Middle Brook, New Jersey, to Daniel Morgan, June 13, 1777.

46 Major Barnet Eichelberger was from York County, Pennsylvania. GWP, Varick Transcripts, Letterbook 8: 140–141, George Washington to Zebulon Butler, George Washington to Major Barnet Eichelberger, George Washington to Commanding Office at Fort Willis, March 1, 1779.

47 GWP, General Correspondence, William Patterson to George Washington, April 3, 1779.

48 Gibbes, *Documentary History of the American Revolution*, Volume 2: 265.

49 Peckham, *Sources of American Independence*, Volume 1: 255, translated from Journal of the Brunswick Corps in America under General Von Riedesel by V. C. Hubbs.

50 Hunt, *Fragments*, General Charles Lee to James Monroe, June 25, 1780.

51 General Howe also expressed his disappointment at getting 10,000 Hessians in place of the Russians. He states, "They will not act with the same willingness as your northern friends." CP 15:10, Sir William Howe to Sir Henry Clinton, April 12, 1776.

52 There is a Captain Zechariah Hawkins, farmer, listed in Orcutt, *History of the Old Town of Derby*: 202 and 238.

53 Thompson, *Secret New England*: 144.

54 Lewis J Costigan was made a First Lieutenant in the 1st New Jersey Regiment on Nov. 21, 1775. Papers of the Continental Congress, Microfilm, r82, i68, pp. 207 and 211, Samuel Tucker, President of New Jersey Provincial Congress to the Chairman of the War and Ordinance Office, August 16, 1776.

55 Lewis J. Costigan used the code name "Z" but some documents appear to be signed as coming from "L" because of Costigan's handwriting. Costigan spent money to procure information while in New York City. Lieutenant Colonel Matthias Ogden of the 1st New Jersey Regiment signed a document at Elizabeth Town on April 4, 1782 certifying Costigan's spy activities and that Costigan sent him "frequent and useful intelligence." GWP, General Correspondence, Costigan's memorial to Washington for compensation for his spy activities, April 4, 1782. Costigan's bill for his spy activities while in New York City was £65.

56 GWP, General Correspondence, Lewis J. Costigan to Samuel Holden Parsons, April 13, 1779.

57 Brooks say James Grierson was a general but he was a loyalist colonel. *Historical Magazine*, Volume III, Number 10, October 1859: 304, statement of Micajah Brooks an eyewitness.

58 Captain Alexander Campbell is usually referred to as C.C. in the dispatches. *Public Papers of George Clinton*, Volume VII: 339, Albany Commissioners to Governor George Clinton, September 19, 1781.

59 Daly, *Woodbridge and Vicinity*: 278–279.

CHAPTER 15

1 *The Morning Post* was founded in 1772 and merged with the *Daily Telegraph* in 1937.

2 Fortescue, *The Correspondence of King George the Third, from 1760 to December 1783*, Volume V: 470–471. In 1781 Bate received a lump sum payment of £3,250 in place of his pension. However, Bate was still on the active secret service payroll in 1784. Aspinall, *The Later Correspondence of George III*, Volume 1: 118.

3 Lucas, *Lord North, 1732–1792*, Volume I: 125.

4 Keppel, *Memoirs of the Marquis of Rockingham and his Contemporaries*, Volume II: 109.

5 Junius was the pseudonym of a still unknown writer of letters, from January 21, 1769 to January 21, 1772, to the *Public Advertiser*, a London newspaper. Junius wanted to inform the public of their rights and liberties as Englishmen and how government was infringing on those rights.

6 Fort Lee was originally named Fort Constitution but was renamed Fort Lee in honor of American General Charles Lee.

7 Ford, *The Spurious Letters Attributed to Washington*: 9.

8 For a copy of Jacob Duché's letter see GWP, General Correspondence, Jacob Duché to George Washington, October 8, 1777. Duché was the rector of Christ Church, the city's largest Anglican congregation located at Second and Market Streets. Soon afterward Dr. and Mrs. Duché sailed home to England. Ford, *The Spurious Letters Attributed to Washington*: 13.

9 Tilghman, *Memoir of Lieutenant Colonel Tench Tilghman*: 166, Tench Tilghman at Valley Forge to James Tilghman, April 24, 1778.

10 GWP, Varick Transcripts, Letterbook 1: 61–64, George Washington to Bryan Fairfax, March 1, 1778.

11 GWP, General Correspondence, Richard Henry Lee at York to George Washington, May 6, 1778.

12 Ford, *The Spurious Letters Attributed to Washington*: 11.

13 GWP, Varick Transcripts, Letterbook 15: 329–330, George Washington to Mathew Carey, October 27, 1788.

14 GWP, Varick Transcripts, Letterbook 24: 271–273, George Washington at Philadelphia to Benjamin Walker, January 12, 1797. These comments were

caused by a reprint of the letters in *Epistles domestic, confidential, and official, from General Washington, written about the commencement of the American contest, when he entered on the command of the Army of the United States...* Printed by G. Robinson...and J Bull and sold by James Rivington, New York, New York, 1796.

15 *Monthly Review or Literary Journal,* Volume LVI, January to June 1777: 475.

16 *Monthly Review or Literary Journal Enlarged,* Volume XXI, September to December 1796: 475–476.

17 British Museum, Additional Manuscripts, 34414, f. 28.

18 Bemis, "British Secret Service and the French-American Alliance" in *American Historical Review,* XXIX: 479.

19 Schoenbrun, *Triumph in Paris:* 126.

20 Carmichael also identifies a letter from a Colonel Campbell bitterly complaining of his cruel confinement as being a forgery. Carmichael served as a member of the Continental Congress from 1778 to 1780. Deane Papers, Volume 2: 75, William Carmichael from Paris to Charles W. F. Dumas, June 20, 1777.

21 Randolph, *Letters from General Washington, to several of his friends in the year 1776.* William L. Clements Library attributes the letters to John Randolph and John Vardill, and I concur with John Randolph. Of the seven letters attributed to Washington, five are addressed to Lund Washington, one to John Parke Custis, and one to Mrs. Washington.

22 Einstein, *Divided Loyalties:* 52–53.

23 Shelburne Papers, Volume 67: 390, June 3, 1782.

24 Heitman, *Historical Register of Officers of the Continental Army:* 458.

25 Pierre Eugène Du Simitière was born in Geneva, Switzerland, circa 1736. He went to the West Indies about 1750, then after nearly fifteen years went to New York, and in 1766 to Philadelphia. He painted numerous portraits. His heads of thirteen notables—Benedict Arnold, Silas Deane, John Dickinson, William H. Drayton, General Horatio Gates, Samuel Huntingdon, John Jay, Henry Laurens, Gouverneur Morris, Joseph Reed, Baron Steuben, Charles Thomson, and George Washington were engraved by Benjamin Reading and published in a quarto volume (London, 1783). He died in Philadelphia in October 1784. Ford, *The Spurious Letters Attributed to Washington:* 32.

26 Tilghman, *Memoir of Lieutenant Colonel Tench Tilghman:* 166.

27 PBF, Volume 32: 545, Benjamin Franklin at Passy to Samuel Wharton, June 17, 1780.

28 PBF, Volume 32: 475, Benjamin Franklin to Charles Dumas, June 5, 1780.

29 *Gazette de Haye* was published at The Hague, United Provinces (Netherlands) from 1744 to circa 1790. Barker, *Press, Politics, and the Public Sphere in Europe and North America, 1760–1820:* 24.

30 *Gazette de Leyde* was published at Leiden, United Provinces (Netherlands) from 1677 to 1811. Barker, *Press, Politics, and the Public Sphere in Europe and North America, 1760–1820:* 24.

31 *Courier du Bas-Rhin* was published at Cleves, Wesel (Prussia) from 1767 to circa 1807. Barker, *Press, Politics, and the Public Sphere in Europe and North America, 1760–1820*: 24.

32 Ford, *Letters of William Lee* Volume 3: 809–811, William Lee to John Adams, July 8, 1780 citing John Adams to William Lee, July 20, 1780 and Wharton, *The Revolutionary Diplomatic Correspondence of the United States*, Volume 3: 841.

33 PBF, Volume 24: 8, Ben Franklin to John Winthrop, May 1, 1777.

34 Thomas Townsend, Lord Sydney Papers, Government Account ledger book with Thomas Lord Sydney on secret service payments. Thomas Lord Sydney paid John Thornton £50 on August 17 as a half year's annuity. Sydney Papers, August 3, 1782, letter from John Thornton to be forwarded to Secretary Townsend.

35 Stevens, *Facsimiles*, Volume 1, #1, December 5, 1776.

36 Einstein, *Divided Loyalties*: 33.

37 Einstein, *Divided Loyalties*: 33.

38 Einstein, *Divided Loyalties*: 35–36 and Stevens, *Facsimiles*, #1818 and 1833.

CHAPTER 16

1 NEHGR Volume XXVII (1873): 411, The Chevalier de Terney by Sidney Everett.

2 Peckham, *The Toll of Independence*: 74.

3 Lord Rawdon was communicating with Lord Cornwallis in cipher. Ross, *Correspondence of Charles, First Marquis, Cornwallis*, Volume 1: 98, Lord Rawdon at Camden to Earl Cornwallis, April 25, 1781 (deciphered text). Tarleton, *A History of the Campaigns of 1780 and 1781 in the Southern Provinces of North America*: 330.

4 Tarleton, *A History of the Campaigns of 1780 and 1781*: 332.

5 GWP, Varick Transcripts, Letterbook 2: 219–221, George Washington to Marquis de Lafayette, April 22, 1781.

6 GWP, Varick Transcripts, Letterbook 13: 396–397, George Washington to Marquis de Lafayette, May 31, 1781.

7 GWP, Varick Transcripts, Letterbook 2: 208–212, George Washington to John Laurens, April 9, 1781.

8 There were 1,250 infantry and 67 artillery men discharged and 1,150 men were given a furlough. Nagy, *Rebellion in the Ranks: Mutinies of the American Revolution*: 165.

9 GWP, General Correspondence, Massachusetts 2nd Regiment to Ebenezer Sprout, January 17, 1781.

10 Nagy, *Rebellion in the Ranks: Mutinies of the American Revolution*: 167—182.

11 GWP, Varick Transcripts, Letterbook 1: 259–260, George Washington to Jean Baptiste Donatien de Vimeur, Comte de Rochambeau, May 14, 1781.

12 GWP, Varick Transcripts, Letterbook 1: 408-419, George Washington and Jean B. Donatien de Vimeur, Comte de Rochambeau, May 23, 1781, Result of Hartford [Wethersfield], Connecticut, Conference.

13 CP 158:21, George Washington to John Sullivan, May 29, 1781 [Intercepted Mail] and GWP, Varick Transcripts, Letterbook 13: 392-394, George Washington to John Sullivan, May 29, 1781.

14 CP 157:10A, George Washington to Marquis de Lafayette, May 31, 1781 [Intercepted Mail] and GWP, Varick Transcripts, Letterbook 13: 396-397, George Washington to Marquis de Lafayette, May 31, 1781.

15 GWP, Varick Transcripts, Letterbook 13: 390, George Washington to Elias Dayton, May 28, 1781.

16 Smith, *Historical Memoirs of William Smith 1778-1783*: 421, June 15, 1781.

17 Mackenzie, *Diary of Frederick Mackenzie . . .* Volume 2: 536.

18 Smith, *Historical Memoirs of William Smith 1778-1783*: 421, June 15, 1781.

19 Stevens, *The Campaign in Virginia, 1781 also known as the Clinton-Cornwallis Controversy*, Volume 1: 381.

20 Gold Star Box, George Washington at New Windsor to Dr. John Baker [at Philadelphia, Pennsylvania], May 29, 1781, intercepted mail.

21 Library of Congress, British Transcripts, C. O. 5, 102, folios 312.

22 GWP, Varick Transcripts, Letterbook 1: 276-278, George Washington to Jean B. Donatien de Vimeur, Comte de Rochambeau, June 13, 1781.

23 Private Collection, Ezra Birch's Pay Abstract for a Company of Teams, July 20, 1781 and sworn before Jabez Botsford, Justice of the Peace at New Town, August 10, 1781.

24 CP 160:44, Sir Henry Clinton to Sir George Brydges Rodney, June 28, 1781, see also CP 169:7, Rear Admiral Samuel Hood to Sir Henry Clinton, August 4, 1781.

25 Jean-Louis Aragon de Sibille was born in 1759 in Narbonne (Languedoc) to Antoine Aragon, tobacco warehouse owner, and Marguerite Louise de Sibille. The passenger list of Ternay's fleet lists de Sibille having sailed on the Duc de Bourgogne with Rochambeau and without rank but as "secretaire interprete de M le comte de Rochambeau" and eating at the officers' table. The roster of the Duc de Bourgogne (AN-Marine C6 619) lists Desibille "at the table" of the officers. GWP, General Correspondence, George Washington to [Jean-Louis Aragon] de Sibille, July 21, 1781.

26 GWP, Varick Transcripts, Letterbook 1; 307-309, George Washington to François Joseph Paul, Comte de Grasse, July 21, 1781.

27 Jackson, *Diaries of George Washington*, Volume III: 398, July 21, 1781.

28 Sneden's Landing was on the west side of the Hudson River opposite Dobbs Ferry. CP 167:17, Oliver De Lancey to Lieutenant Colonel Edmund Eyre, July 29, 1781.

29 Kings Ferry is just north of Stony Point which is at the top of Haverstraw Bay.

30 CP 167:34, Thomas Ward to Oliver De Lancey, July 31, 1781.

31 Bakeless, *Turncoats, Traitors, and Heroes*: 346-356.

32 During the time of the American Revolution it was known as Cape Francois, Cap Francois and Cap Francais. Later it was known as Cap Henry and today in French it is Cap Haitien, Haiti.

33 Gruber, *John Peebles' American War*: 465, Tuesday August 14, 1781.

34 GWP, Varick Transcripts, Letterbook 14, 134-135, George Washington to Samuel Miles, August 15, 1781.

35 Robert Greene in 33 *Strategies of War* (2007) calls it Misperception Strategies, and the series *Battle Plan* has an excellent episode on deception.

36 Smith, *Historical Memoirs of William Smith 1778-1783*: 423, June 23, 1781.

37 Hell Gate is a narrow channel of the East River between Wards Island and Astoria, Queens. It was dangerous to ships going between the East River and the Long Island Sound because of its strong tidal currents and rocks. Gruber, *John Peebles' American War*: 467.

38 CP 241:47, Sir Henry Clinton's comments after the war on Rochambeau's book.

39 Smith, *Historical Memoirs of William Smith 1778-1783*: 435, August 28, 1781.

40 CP 171:14, Beckwith's report, August 21, 1781.

41 CP 171:14, Beckwith to Oliver De Lancey, August 21, 1781.

42 Gruber, *John Peebles' American War*: 467, August 23, 1781.

43 *Collections of the New York Historical Society for the Year 1882, Von Kraft's Journal 1775-1784*: 147.

44 The 42nd Regiment of Foot was also known as the Royal Highland or Black Watch and the 57th Regiment of Foot was later known as the Lancashire Regiment. Ford, *British Officers Serving in the American Revolution*: 7.

45 The 37th Regiment of Foot would later be known as the North Hampshire Regiment and the 54th in 1783 became the East Essex Regiment. Ford, *British Officers Serving in the American Revolution*: 6-7 and Gruber, *John Peebles' American War*: 467-468, August 26-29, 1781.

46 *Collections of the New York Historical Society for the Year 1882, Von Kraft's Journal 1775-1784*: 148.

47 CP 171:41, William Sproule's report, August 23, 1781.

48 CP 172:2, Ezekiel Yeomans' report, August 24, 1781; CP 172:3, Beckwith's report on intelligence from Jersey, August 24, 1781; and 172: 4, Beckwith's report of August 24, 1781. Yeomans would go out again but was captured near the Hoboken Ferry and sent to Fishkill, New York, from which place he was exchanged and returned to the British lines on December 4, 1781. CP 185:23, Beckwith in New York to Oliver De Lancey, December 5, 1781.

49 Peckham, *The Toll of Independence*: 24, General Greene on October 14, 1776 and 39, Sullivan, August 22, 1777. Also Gruber, *John Peebles' American War*: 425, January 19, 1781.

50 Smith, *Historical Memoirs of William Smith 1778-1783*: 426, July 4, 1781.

51 GWP, Letterbook 15: 195-196, George Washington to Noah Webster, July 31, 1788.

52 Thacher, *A Military Journal During the American Revolutionary War*: 262

53 The British army had a total of thirty pontoon bridge sections each totaling a distance of ten feet. It took 118 horses to move the thirty pontoons. The pontoons were the responsibility of a captain of artillery who was also the "bridgemaster." CP 54:2, Return of Pontoons, March 13, 1779.

54 I did not find Montagnie or Montagner in William Buell Sprague's *Annals of the American Pulpit*. I have found that Sprague does list most but not all colonial ministers. Lossing appears to be the first person to tell this story in 1852. He says he received it from a Mr. Pierson who received it directly from Montagnie. Lossing says a Mrs. Elizabeth Oakes Smith also received the story from Mr. P(ierson) a person who was 87 at the time. She gives the name as Montagner in the *Salamder*. Smith, *The Salamander*: 16 and Lossing, *The Pictorial Field Book of the Revolution*, Volume 1: 213-214.

55 Hufeland, *Westchester County During the American Revolution 1775-83*: 401.

56 GWP, Varick Transcripts, Letterbook 14: 137-138, George Washington to Marquis de Lafayette, August 17, 1781.

57 GWP, George Washington's Diary, August 19, 1781.

58 Jackson, *Diaries of George Washington*, Volume III: 411, August 19, 1781 and GWP, Varick Transcripts, Letterbook 14: 145, George Washington to Elias Dayton, August 19, 1781.

59 Weelan, *Rochambeau, Father and Son*: 224-225. The ovens were completed as Baron Closen wrote in his Journal on September 11, 1782. "We re-discovered the ovens M. de Villemanzy had ordered to be constructed at Chatham last year to supply the army. They are in very good condition and are being used to provision the army until it reaches the north River." Acomb, *The Revolutionary Journal of Baron Ludwig Von Closen, 1780-1783*: 236-237, September 11, 1782.

60 Concerning the ovens near Sandy Hook, orders were issued to prepare ovens near there and contracts were issued for future supplies to be delivered after the arrival of the army. I was unable to find any further reference to these ovens. There is no indication that any were built.

61 *Proceeding of the Massachusetts Historical Society* (1876): 332, Journal of Colonel Jonathan Trumbull, August 21, 1781.

62 Baron von Ludwig Closen, *Revolutionary Journal, 1780-1783*: 104.

63 Willcox, *The American Rebellion*: 326.

64 The intelligence said that the carriages were "100 yards from the dock at Kings Ferry and 600 [yards] from the block house at Honey Point, and a string of them close to each other of 300 yards." Smith, *Historical Memoirs of William Smith 1778-1783*: 424, June 23, 1781.

65 *Proceedings of the Massachusetts Historical Society* (1876): 331, Minutes Respecting the siege and capture respecting York in Virginia, extracted from the Journal of Colonel Thomas Trumbull, Secretary to the General, 1781.

66 Jackson, *Diaries of George Washington*, Volume 3: 411, August 19, 1781.

67 Smith, *Historical Memoirs of William Smith 1778-1783*: 433, August 20, 1781.

68 Prince, *Papers of William Livingston*, Volume 4: 254-255, George Washington at King's Ferry to William Livingston, August 21, 1781.

69 GWP, Varick Transcripts Letterbook 4: 214-216, George Washington to William Livingston [New Jersey], September 3, 1781 (also to Thomas Sim Lee [Maryland] and Caesar Rodney [Delaware]).

70 The Arthur Kill was on occasion called the Raritan Sound during the eighteenth century. Connecticut Farms is located in Union Township, Union County, New Jersey. Fitzpatrick, *Writings of George Washington*: Note 63, George Washington to Benjamin Lincoln, August 24, 1781. GWP, Letterbook 14: 150-152, George Washington to Benjamin Lincoln, August 24, 1781, and General Correspondence, George Washington to Benjamin Lincoln, August 24, 1781 but the following is crossed out, "I have put Colo[nel]. Seely who Commands the Jersey Militia in the vicinity of Dobbs ferry under your orders; it will be proper therefore to direct him to march for Hackensack on the same day that you march for Acqua Kanack; and for the Connecticut Farms the day you march for Springfield where or in that Neighbourhood he is remain, keeping constant patroles on the Sound as far as [Perth] Amboy till the French Army has passed Princeton and then act under the orders he may receive from Governor Livingston."

71 GWP, Varick Transcripts Letterbook 14: 147-148, George Washington to Sylvanus Seely, August 21, 1781.

72 GWP, Varick Transcripts, Letterbook 14: 153-144, George Washington to Brigadier General William Smallwood in Maryland, August 24, 1781 and GWP, Varick Transcripts, Letterbook 14: 148-149, George Washington to Major General Arthur St. Clair at Philadelphia, August 22, 1781.

73 GWP, Varick Transcripts, Letterbook 14: 154, George Washington to David Forman, August 24, 1781.

74 GWP, Varick Transcripts, Letterbook 14: 154-155, George Washington to Elias Dayton, August 24, 1781.

75 Acquacknack, sometimes spelled Acquakinunk, is a town on the west side of the Passaic River about ten miles north of Newark. Morse, *The American Gazetteer*.

76 GWP, Varick Transcripts Letterbook 14: 157, George Washington to Sylvanus Seely, August 25 1781.

77 Jackson, *Diaries of George Washington*, Volume 3: 414, August 25, 1781.

78 Deux-Ponts, *My Campaigns in America: A Journal Kept by Count William de Deux-Ponts, 1780-81*: 125, August 27, 1781 while camped at Whippany, New Jersey.

79 GWP, Varick Transcripts, Letterbook 14: 156-157, George Washington to Philip van Cortlandt, August 25, 1781. Washington had complained to Major General Alexander McDougall about the delay in moving the thirty boats to Kings Ferry. GWP, Varick Transcripts, Letterbook 14: 139, George Washington to Alexander McDougall, August 18, 1781.

80 GWP, Varick Transcripts, Letterbook 14: 165, George Washington to Philip van Cortlandt, August 28, 1781.

81 GWP, Varick Transcripts, Letterbook 14: 166, George Washington to Colonel Timothy Pickering, August 28, 1781.

82 GWP, Varick Transcripts, Letterbook 14: 160-162, George Washington to Samuel Miles, August 27, 1781.

83 GWP, Varick Transcripts, Letterbook 6: 120-121, George Washington at Chatham to Continental Congress, August 27, 1781.

84 The distinguished French officer is believed to be Donatien-Marie-Joseph de Vimeur, vicomte de Rochambeau. His mistress did follow him from Rhode Island to New York. Burgoyne, *Journal of the Hesse-Cassel Jaeger Corps*: 161.

85 GWP, Varick Transcripts, Letterbook 1: 332-333, George Washington to Jean B. Donatien de Vimeur, Comte de Rochambeau, August 27, 1781.

86 Smith, *Historical Memoirs of William Smith 1778-1783*: 434, August 23, 1781.

87 GWP, Varick Transcripts, Letterbook 14: 169-170, George Washington to Major General William Heath, August 29, 1781.

88 Villemanzy crossed from Brest to America with Rochambeau and Ternay in the ship of the line *L'Ardent* (captured from the British in 1779 and recaptured by them in 1782), in company of six officers, including Comte Dillon and Jean-Jacques de Trentinian, both officers in Lauzun's Legion. He is sometimes referred to Comte de Villemanzy, however he was not made comte until August 15, 1809. Balch, *The French in America During the War of Independence of the United States, 1777-1783*: Volume 1, 172 and Volume 2: 248, Villemanzy.

89 Closen says the bricks were collected on the left bank of the Raritan and the men were fired on by the advance works of Paulus Hook (present Jersey City). Closen, *The Revolutionary Journal of Baron Ludwig von Closen*: 109. The Raritan River does not pass near Paulus Hook. He has made other mistakes in identifying locations in his journal. The only British battery in the area of the Raritan River was at the home of Christopher Billopp, also now known as the Conference House, on Staten Island, New York. Because of the distance the only area at the mouth of the Raritan that it could threaten would be at the general area of present day Front and Smith Streets in Perth Amboy, New Jersey. Weelan, *Rochambeau, Father and Son*: 224-225.

90 GWP, Varick Transcripts, Letterbook 1: 334, George Washington to Antoine Charles du Houx, Baron de Viomenil, August 29, 1781.

91 Jackson, Diaries of George Washington, Volume III: 411, August 19, 1781 and GWP, Varick Transcripts, Letterbook 14: 145, George Washington to Elias Dayton, August 19, 1781.

92 CP 83:9, Oliver De Lancey to Major Thomas Ward at Bergen Neck, August 21, 1781.

93 CP 172:13, Thomas Ward at New York to Oliver De Lancey, August 24, 1781. Lieutenant Colonel Andreas Emmerich reported on information from two men who were sent out last Tuesday. CP 172:38, Andreas Emmerich to Oliver De Lancey, August 30, 1781. It is unknown which of privates Abraham, John, and William Green who served in Ward's corps was sent.

94 Jackson, *Diaries of George Washington*, Volume 3: 414, August 30, 1781.

95 *Proceedings of the Massachusetts Historical Society* (1876): 332, Minutes Respecting the Siege . . . Journal of Colonel Thomas Trumbull.

96 GWP, General Correspondence, Sylvanus Seely to George Washington, September 3, 1781.

97 Sylvanus Seely Diary, original in Morristown National Historic Park Collection.

98 GWP, General Correspondence, Sylvanus Seely to George Washington, October 14, 1781.

99 GWP, General Correspondence, Sylvanus Seely to George Washington, October 18 1781.

100 Heitman, *Historical Register of Officers of the Continental Army*: 336.

101 JCC, Volume 14: 890, July 26, 1779.

102 Gilder Lehrman Collection, GLC-05224, British Spy Reports, report on George Knox, September 5, 1781.

103 CP 173:35, Nehemiah Marks to Oliver De Lancey, September 4, 1781.

104 CP 175:4, Nehemiah Marks to Oliver De Lancey, September 18, 1781.

105 CP 174:20, Intelligence and 174:29 envelope to Isaac Ogden, September 14, 1781.

106 CP 174:36, [Joseph] Gould, September 16, 1781.

107 The only place in the Clinton Papers where Gould's first name of Joseph is used is in CP 274, July 1, 1779, Andre's Intelligence Journal.

108 Papers of the Continental Congress, Microfilm, r53, i42, v1, p.361, Elias Dayton pass for (spies) Caleb Bruen, Joseph Gould, and Gilbert Smyth to pass to New York and return on public business, May 1, 1780. GWP, General Correspondence, [Joseph] Gould to Elias Dayton, February 22, 1781.

109 CP 149:39, Cortland Skinner to Sir Henry Clinton, March 15, 1781.

110 CP 174:35, Major Thomas Millidge at New York to Oliver De Lancey, September 16, 1781. Isaac Sweasy used the code name of J. S___e when he was behind American lines and sent in his reports. CP 186:25, Isaac Sweasy to Capt. John Stapleton, December 11, 1781.

111 GWP, Washington's Diary, September 5, 1781.

112 Nesmith, "Journal of Abbé Robin Chaplain of Count Rochambeau's Army, Relating to the Revolution," *Granite Monthly*, Volume 4: 424-428.

113 Willcox, *The American Rebellion*: 562, Sir Henry Clinton to Earl Cornwallis, August 27, 1781.

114 CP 173:36, Sir Edmund Affleck to Sir Henry Clinton, September 5, 1781; Stevens, *Clinton-Cornwallis Controversy*, 2:151, Cornwallis to Clinton, September 4, 1781 and Willcox, *The American Rebellion*: 330.

115 Smith, *Historical Memoirs of William Smith 1778-1783*: 42-43, July 14, 1781.

116 Morris House is the Morris-Jumel Mansion Museum at 65 Jumel Terrace, between 160th and 162nd Streets in New York City.

117 CP 175:20, Marquard to Oliver De Lancey, September 22, 1781.

118 CP 176:10, Marquard to Oliver De Lancey, September 24, 1781.

119 CP 177:1, Sir Henry Clinton's notes, September 30, 1781.

120 CP 176:1, Report from South Amboy, New Jersey, September 24, 1781.

121 CP 181:4, Report from R. [John Rattoon], October 29, 1781.

122 CP 176:46, Beckwith, September 28, 1781.

123 GWP, Varick Transcripts, Letterbook 14: 140-144, George Washington at Dobbs Ferry to William Heath, August 19, 1781.

124 CP 178:18, Accusations against Van Wagoner, October 6, 1781 and 181:7, Captain Ward's report on the activities of Jacob Van Wagoner and on page 2 are the activities of Garret Frealin, October 1781.

125 CP 256, Book 5, Sir Henry Clinton at New York City to Lord George Germain, September 26, 1781: 39-45.

126 Little Egg Harbor, New Jersey is the body of water between Long Beach Island and Tuckerton, New Jersey.

127 Thomas McKean, President of Congress, advised George Washington that Lovell's deciphering key had decoded the messages. Burnett, Letters of Members of the Continental Congress, Volume VI: 239.

128 The bar at the entrance to lower New York harbor was southeast of Staten Island and just north of Sandy Hook, New Jersey.

129 GWP, General Correspondence and Varick Transcripts, Letterbook 6: 139, George Washington to James Lovell, October 6, 1781.

130 Some of the original intercepted letters were sent by Washington to Count de Grasse. GWP, General Correspondence, Charles Cornwallis to Henry Clinton, September 8, 1781 and Mordecai Gist to George Washington, September 24, 1781.

131 Many of the deciphered messages can be seen in the book *The Campaign in Virginia, 1781: An Exact Reprint Of Six Rare Pamphlets on the Clinton Cornwallis Controversy* (1888).

132 Kahn, *Codebreakers*, 182.

133 Kahn, *Codebreakers*, 183.

134 Crary, "The Tory and the Spy: The Double Life of James Rivington," *William and Mary Quarterly*, volume 16, number 1, January 1959: 68. See Appendix G for more on the story. Robert Townsend and James Rivington had become the purveyors of the "syrup of soot and old shoes" (in seventeenth-century England, Tories described coffee as the "syrop of soot and old shoes"). Townsend and Rivington had invested in a coffeehouse in the vicinity of Wall Street opposite Rivington's printing office at the corner of Queen Street. The financially successful coffeehouse provided Rivington with the information he wanted from the soldiers for his newspaper. Townsend was also supplying good copy for Rivington's newspaper. Pennypacker, *General Washington's Spies*: 12-14. Henry Wansey wrote in his journal that on June 23, 1794 that he dined with James Rivington. Wansey states that Rivington had "opened a kind of coffee-house for the officers; his house was a great place of resort; he made a great deal of money during that time period, though many of the officers quitted at considerably in arrears to him." Pennypacker, *General Washington's Spies*: 7.

135 Porter is a heavy dark brown ale made with malt browned by drying at a high temperature.

136 United States Navy, *Dictionary of American Naval Fighting Ships* on-line, *Lee*. http://www.history.navy.mil/danfs/l5/lee-i.htm. The schooner was the former *Two Brothers* and was hired for Washington's navy in October 1775 by Colonel John Glover from Thomas Stevens of Marblehead, Massachusetts.

137 NAVAL, Volume 3: 17, William Bartlett to George Washington, December 9, 1775 and 54-56, Nicholas Brown at Providence to John Brown, December 11, 1775.

138 NAVAL, Volume 3: 45, George Washington to John Hancock, December 11, 1775.

139 United States Navy, *Dictionary of American Naval Fighting Ships* on-line, Hancock, http://www.history.navy.mil/danfs/h2/hancock-i.htm. The schooner was the former schooner *Speedwell* of 72 tons and was rented from Thomas Grant of Marblehead in October 1775.

140 Nantasket Road is a body of water in the outer Boston Harbor between Long Island and Pemberton, Massachusetts.

141 *American Historical Review*, Volume I: 500, Diary of Richard Smith in the Continental Congress 1775-1776 part II, February 9, 1776; NAVAL, Volume 3: 995, Francis Hutcheson to Major General Frederick Haldimand, January 26, 1776; 996 footnote 2 Extract of a letter from Whitehaven, June 18, 1776 from Almon, editor, *Remembrancer* (1776), III, Part II: 139-140; 1024, Extract of a letter from Cambridge from the Pennsylvania Packet, February 12, 1776; 1029 footnote 1, *Boston Gazette*, January 29, 1776; and 1185, Diary of Richard Smith and footnote.

142 NAVAL, Volume 2: 146-147, Journal of Eleazer Oswald, September 19, 1775 quoted from John Hancock Papers III: 308-310. Captain Charles Alexander's signals for the Continental navy fleet in the Delaware River can be found in NAVAL, Volume 9: 807-808, August 25, 1777.

143 Simcoe Papers, folder marked "9 Miscellaneous Items" at the Clements Library, Howe to Pownoll, December 13, 1777.

144 University of Pennsylvania, Rare Book and Manuscript Library, Signals on Staten Island, October 14–15, 1779.

145 CP 178:8 Charles Cochran to Sir Henry Clinton, Before October 3, 1781.

146 CP 181:16, October 1781 written in Arch Robertson's hand.

147 Hog Island is off the Delmarva Peninsula east of Nassawadox, Virginia.

148 CP 178:33, Charles Cochrane's report of October 9, 1781, which was received on October 12, 1781.

149 CP 181:8, Report of Mr. Cary in the Dundass Galley, October 1781.

150 CP 178:33 Major Cochrane, October 9, 1781. Smith Island is off the southeast tip of the Delmarva Peninsula east of Cape Charles, Virginia.

151 Cape Henry is the northeast corner of Virginia Beach, Virginia.

152 CP 181:16, Major Cochrane's signals, October 1781.

153 This is probably Robert B. Carre, who was paid 200 guineas by Sir Henry Clinton for services rendered during siege of York. HMC, *Report on American Manuscripts in the Royal Institution of Great Britain*, Volume IV: 357 (Volume 47, Number 47), Robert B. Carre at New York to Sir Guy Carleton, September 15, 1783.

154 CP 181:3, An intelligence report of October 24-29, 1781 enclosed in Sir Henry Clinton to Lord George Germain.

155 The word "Sufsful" in the original document was interpreted to mean successful. CP 180:16, Cornwallis to Sir Henry Clinton, October 11, 1781.

156 The fleet's departure was delayed due to repairs necessitated by storm damage and the recent battle.

157 CP 181:5, Instructions, October 1781.

158 CP 180:29, Instructions to Lieutenant Blanchard, October 24, 1781.

159 CP 181:3, An intelligence report of October 24-29 enclosed in Sir Henry Clinton to Lord George Germain.

160 The sloop *Tarleton* was owned by a Mr. Young of New York. CP 180:30, Reports of James Rider and James Robinson, African-Americans, and Robert Morsse, October 24, 1781.

161 CP 180:30, Reports of James Rider and James Robinson, African-Americans, and Robert Morsse, October 24, 1781.

162 CP 181:1, Sir Henry Clinton on the ship London off of Cape Charles, Va. to Lord George Germain, Oct. 29, 1781 and CP 256 Book 5: 27.

163 CP 181:3, An intelligence report of Mr. Caldwell of October 24-29 enclosed in Sir Henry Clinton to Lord George Germain, October 29, 1781.

164 CP 181:1, Sir Henry Clinton on the ship *London* off of Cape Charles, Virginia, to Lord George Germain, Oct. 29, 1781 and CP 256 Book 5: 27.

CONCLUSION

1 United States Department of Justice, Federal Bureau of Investigation, Famous Cases, Rudoplh Ivanovich Abel (Hollow Nickel case) at http://www.fbi.gov/libref/historic/famcases/abel/abel.htm.

2 United States Department of Justice, Federal Bureau of Investigation, Famous Cases, Robert Philip Hanssen Espionage Case, February 20, 2001 at http://www.fbi.gov/libref/historic/famcases/hanssen/hanssen.htm.

3 British Broadcasting Corporation, BBC News, January 23, 2006 http://news.bbc.co.uk/2/hi/europe/4639758.stm.

4 United States Department of Justice, Press Release, April 30, 2009 at http://www.usdoj.gov/opa/pr/2009/April/09-nsd-415.html.

BIBLIOGRAPHY

MANUSCRIPT COLLECTIONS

American Philosophical Society, Philadelphia
  Benjamin Franklin Papers
Bodleian Library, Oxford, England
  Carte Paper, Ireland
British Museum, London
  Additional Manuscripts
Columbia University Libraries, New York
  Papers of John Jay on the Internet
David Library of the American Revolution, Washington Crossing, Pennsylvania
  Feinstone Collection
  Microfilm Collections
Great Britain, National Archives [Public Record Office], Kew, Richmond, Surrey, England
  Audit Office Papers
  Colonial Office Records
  Image Library
  Records of the Privy Council
  Secretary of State's Office Papers
Haverford College, Haverford, Pennsylvania
  Philadelphia Monthly Meeting Minute Book for 1782–1789
Historical Society of Pennsylvania, Philadelphia
  Thomas Bradford Manuscripts
  Dreer Collection
  Individual Letters
Library of Congress, Washington, D.C.
  British Transcripts
  John Hancock Papers, Journal of Eleazer Oswald
  George Washington Papers
Massachusetts Historical Society, Boston
  John Adams Diary
  Adams Family Papers
  Adams Family Papers: An Electronic Archive at http://www.masshist.org/digitaladams/
  Paul Revere Letter
Morristown National Historic Park, Morristown, New Jersey
  Sylvanus Seely Diary
  Lloyd W. Smith Collection on Microfilm
National Archives of Cuba
  Dispatches of Bernardo de Gálvez
New-York Historical Society, New York
  Gilder Lehrman Collection

New York Public Library, New York
  Emmett Collection on Microfilm
United States National Archives
  Revolutionary War Pension Applications
University of Pennsylvania, Van Pelt-Dietrich Library, Rare Book and Manuscript
  Library
  Mendelsohn Collection
  Signals on Staten Island
University of Pittsburgh, Darlington Memorial Library
  Daniel Brodhead Order Book, April 13, 1779–May 6, 1781
Virginia State Library, Richmond, Virginia
  Virginia Governors Letters Received
William L. Clements Library, University of Michigan, Ann Arbor
  Broadsides, Small
  Henry Clinton Papers
  Henry Clinton Papers Map Collection
  Nathaniel Freeman Papers
  Thomas Gage Papers
  Gold Star Box
  Nathanael Greene Papers
  King's American Regiment Orderly Book
  Frederick Mackenzie Papers
  Sackville-Germain Papers
  James S. Schoff Collection
  Shelburne Papers
  Hubert S. Smith Naval Collection
  Simcoe Papers
  Thomas Townsend, Lord Sydney Papers
  Van Doren Papers
  Virginia War Office Book

PRINTED MATERIALS

Adams Family. *Adams Family Correspondence*. Massachusetts Historical Society, Boston, 1963–.

Adams, John. *The Works of John Adams, Second President of the United States: with a Life of the Author, Notes and Illustrations, by his Grandson Charles Francis Adams*, 10 volumes. Little, Brown, Boston, 1856.

Alberti, Leon Battista. *Ne'Quali si contengono Molti Ammaestramenti necessarii al viver de l'Huomo, cosi posto in dignità, come private tradotti, se parte corretti da M. Cosimo Bartoli*. Cosimo Bartoli, Venice, 1568.

— — —. *Opuscoli Morali*. Venice, 1568.

American Historical Review. Macmillan, New York, 1896–.

American Quarterly Review, Volume 1 Number 1 (March 1827). Robert Walsh, Philadelphia, 1827–1837.

Annual Register, or a View of the History, Politics, and Literature for the Year 1794. G. Auld, London, 1799.

Argens, Jean Baptiste de Boyer. *The Jewish Spy: Being a Philosophical, Historical, and Critical Correspondence by Letters, which Lately Passed Between Certain Jews in Turkey, Italy, France, Etc.* Third Edition, Volume 5. A. Miller, London, 1765.

Bacon, Donald J. *Second World War Deception Lessons Learned for Today's Joint Planner.* Air Command and Staff College Wright Flyer Paper Number 5, United States Air Force, Air Command and Staff College Air University, Maxwell Air Force Base, Alabama, 1998.

Bakeless, John. Turncoats, Traitors & Heroes. J. B. Lippincott, New York, 1959 reprinted Da Capo Press, New York, 1998.

Balch, Thomas; Balch, Edwin Swift; and Balch, Elise Willing. *The French in America During the War of Independence of the United States, 1777–1783,* Volume 1 and 2. Porter and Coates, Philadelphia, 1891 and 1895.

Baring-Gould, Sabine. *Curiosities of Olden Times.* John Grant, Edinburgh, 1896.

Barker, Hannah and Burrows, Simon, editors. *Press, Politics, and the Public Sphere in Europe and North America, 1760–1820.* Cambridge University Press, Cambridge, England, 2002.

Barnwell, James W. "Correspondence of the Hon[orable]. Arthur Middleton," *South Carolina Historical and Genealogical Magazine,* Volume 26. South Carolina Historical Society, Charleston, 1925.

Barwick, Peter and translated from Latin by Bedford, Hilkiak. *The Life of the Reverend Dr. John Barwick, D.D.* J. Bettenham, London, 1724.

Bemis, Samuel F. "British Secret Service and the French-American Alliance." *American Historical Review,* Volume XXIX.

Bendikson, Lodewyk. *Franco American Review,* Volume 1 Number 3 (December 1936), *The Restoration of Obliterated Passages and of Secret Writing in Diplomatic Missives.*

Berg, Fred Anderson. *Encyclopedia of Continental Army Units.* Stackpole Books, Harrisburg, Pennsylvania, 1972.

Bicknell, Joseph D. *The Wissahickon in History, Story, and Song in Philadelphia History: Consisting of Papers Read Before the City History Society of Philadelphia: with a History of the Society and a General Index.* By City History Society of Philadelphia, Volume 1, 1917.

Bidwell, Bruce W. *History of Military Intelligence Division, Department of the Army General Staff 1775–1941.* University Presses of America, Frederick, Maryland, 1975.

Bolton, Charles Knowles. *Letters of Hugh, Earl Percy, from Boston and New York, 1774–1776.* Charles E. Goodspeed, Boston, 1902.

———. *The Private Soldier Under Washington.* Charles Scribner's Sons, New York, 1902.

Boston Gazette, 1774.

Boston, Town of. *Short Narrative of the Horrid Massacre in Boston . . .: The Fifth Day of March, 1770, by Soldiers of the 29th Regiment . . . with Some Observations on the State of Things Prior to that Catastrophe.* Edes & Gill, and T. & J. Fleet, Boston, 1770.

Bourquinn, Frederick, editor. *Journal of Events in the Revolution by Elias Boudinot.* H. J. Bicking Printer, Philadelphia, 1894.

Breitenbach, Lieutenant Colonel Daniel L. *Operation Desert Deception, Operational Deception in the Ground Campaign.* Operations Department, Naval War College, Newport, Rhode Island, 1992.

Bright, Timothe [Timothy]. *Characterie An Arte of Shorte, Swifte, and Secrete Writing by Character.* I. Windet, London, 1588.

British Broadcasting Corporation, BBC News.

Brown, Sanborn C. and Stein, Elbridge W., *Journal of Criminal Law and Criminology,* Volume 40, Number 5 (January – February, 1950): 627–636, *Benjamin Thompson and the First Secret-Ink Letter of the American Revolution.*

Bryan, George S. *The Spy in America.* J. B. Lippincott, Philadelphia, 1943.

Burgoyne, Bruce E., translator. *The Diary of Lieutenant von Bardeleben and Other von Donop Regiment.* Heritage Books, Westminster, Maryland, 2008.

———. *Journal of the Hesse-Cassel Jaeger Corps.* Heritage Books, Bowie, Maryland, 2005.

———. *These Were the Hessians.* Heritage Books, Westminster, Maryland, 2008.

Burnett, Edmund C. *Letters of Members of the Continental Congress,* 8 Volumes. Carnegie Institution of Washington, Washington, D.C., 1921–1946.

Burstyn, Joan N., editor. *Past and Promise—Lives of New Jersey Women.* Scarecrow Press, Metuchen, New Jersey, 1990.

Calendar of Virginia State Papers and other Manuscripts Preserved in the Capitol at Richmond (1652–1869) in 11 volumes. Richmond, Virginia, 1875–1893.

Callender, Guy Stevens. *Selections from the Economic History of the United States, 1765–1860.* Ginn and Company, Boston, 1909.

Canada. Department of Militia and Defense. *A History of the Organization, development and services of the military and naval forces of Canada from the peace of Paris in 1763, to the present time: with illustrative documents/ edited by the historical section of the general staff.* Volume III, The War of the American Revolution, The Province of Quebec under the administration of Governor Frederic Haldimand, 1778–1784. Ottawa, Canada, 1920.

Carter, Clarence Edison, compiler and editor. *Correspondence of General Thomas Gage with the Secretaries of State and with the War Office and Treasury,* Volume II. Yale University Press, New Haven, Connecticut, 1933.

Church, John A. Descendants of Richard Church of Plymouth, Massachusetts. The Tuttle Company, Rutland, Vermont, 1913.

Clayton, W. Woodward, editor. *History of Union and Middlesex Counties with Biographical Sketches of Many of Their Pioneers and Prominent Men.* Everts and Peck, Philadelphia, 1882.

Clayton, W. Woodward and Nelson, William. *History of Bergen and Passaic Counties, New Jersey: With Biographical Sketches of Many of Its Pioneers and Prominent Men.* Everts and Peck, Philadelphia, 1882.

Clinton, George. *Public Papers of George Clinton, First Governor of New York, 1777–1795–1801–1804*, 10 Volumes. State of New York, Albany, New York, 1899–1914.

Closen, Baron von Ludwig. *Revolutionary Journal, 1780–1783*. Institute of Early American History and Culture, Williamsburg, Virginia, published for the Institute of Early American History and Culture at Williamsburg, Virginia by the University of North Carolina Press, Chapel Hill, 1958.

Coghlan, Margaret. *Memoirs of Mrs. Coghlan, Daughter of the Late Major Moncrieffe*. London, 1794. Reprinted T. H. Morrell, New York, 1864.

Coldham, Peter Wilson. *American Loyalist Claims, Volume 1*, Abstracted from the Public Records Office Series 13 Bundles 1–35 and 37. National Genealogical Society, Washington, D.C., 1980.

Collections of the Massachusetts Historical Society, series, 1792–1941.

Connecticut Historical Society Collections, Series starting in 1860, Connecticut Historical Society, Hartford, Connecticut.

Cortambert, Louise, Translator. *The Language of Flowers*. Fourth Edition. Saunders and Otley, London, 1835.

Crary, Catherine. "The Tory and the Spy: The Double Life of James Rivington." *William and Mary Quarterly*, volume 16, number 1, January 1959.

Cunningham, John. *Poems Chiefly Pastoral*. T. Slack, Newcastle, England, 1771.

Daly, Rev. Joseph. *Woodbridge and Vicinity*. 1873, reprinted by Hunterdon House, Lambertville, New Jersey, 1989.

Dana, Elizabeth Ellery. *The British in Boston: The Diary of Lieutenant John Barke of the King's Own Regiment from November 15, 1774 to May 31, 1776*. Harvard University Press, Cambridge, Massachusetts, 1924.

Dandridge, Danske. *Historic Shepherdstown*. Michie Company, Charlottesville, Virginia, 1910; reprinted Specialty Binding and Printing Company, Shepherdstown, West Virginia, 1985.

Davis, John. *An Essay on the Art of Decyphering [sic] in which is inserted a discourse of Dr. Willis*. L. Gilliver and J. Clarke, London, 1737.

Deux-Ponts, Guillaume, comte de. *My campaigns in America: a journal kept by Count William de Deux-Ponts, 1780–81*. Translated from the French manuscript, with an introduction and notes, by Samuel Abbott Green. J. K. Wiggin and P. Lunt, Boston, 1868.

Dexter, Franklin Bowditch. *Diary of Ezra Stiles*, Volume 1. Charles Scribner's Sons, New York, 1901.

Dictionary of Canadian Biography Online. http://www.biographi.ca/index-e.html.

Dircks, Henry and Worcester, Edward Somerset. *The Life, Times and Scientific Labours of the Second Marquis of Worcester: To which is Added, a Reprint of His Century of Inventions, 1663, with a Commentary Thereon*. Bernard Quaritch, London, 1865.

Documents Relating to the Colonial History of the State of New York Procured in Holland, England, and France . . ., Volume 8. Weed, Parson and Company. Albany, New York, 1857.

Du Calvet, Peter. *The Case of Peter du Calvet, Esq. of Montreal in the province of Quebeck Containing (amongst Other Things Worth Notice) an Account of the Long and Severe Imprisonment He Suffered in the Said Province by the Order of General Haldimand, the Present Governour of the Same, Without the Least Offence....* London, 1784.

East, Robert A. *Connecticut's Loyalists.* American Revolution Bicentennial Commission, Hartford, Connecticut, Volume VI, 1974.

Egle, William Henry. *An Illustrated History of the Commonwealth of Pennsylvania; civil, political and military, from its earliest settlement to the present time, including historical descriptions of each county in the state, their towns, and industrial resources,* 2nd Edition. E. M. Gardner, Philadelphia, 1880.

Einstein, Lewis. *Divided Loyalties: Americans in England During the War of Independence.* Houghton Mifflin, Boston, 1933, reissued by Russell & Russell, New York, 1970.

English Mechanics and the World of Science, Journal. London, 1865–1926.

The Examination of Joseph Galloway, esq.; the Late Speaker of the House of Assembly of Pennsylvania, Before the House of Commons in a Committee on the American Papers. J. Wilkie, London, 1779.

F. (Falconer), J. *Rules for Explaining and Deciphering All Manner of Secret Writing, Plain and Demonstrative.* Printed for Dan. Brown and Sam. Manship, London, 1692.

Fisher, George. *The American Instructor.* Benjamin Franklin and D[avid]. Hall, Philadelphia, 1748.

Fitzpatrick, John C., editor. *Writings of George Washington from the Original Manuscript Sources, 1745–1799.* U.S. Government Printing Office, Washington, D.C., series 39 volumes, 1931–1944.

Fonblanque, Edward Barrington de. *Political and Military Episodes in the Later Half of the Eighteenth Century derived from the Life and Correspondence of the Right Hon[orable]. John Burgoyne.* Macmillan, London, 1876.

Force, Peter. *American Archives.* Johnson Reprint Corporation, New York, 1972; reprint of 1837–1853 editions.

Ford, Paul Leicester. *The Writings of Thomas Jefferson.* G. P. Putnam's Sons, New York, 1892.

Ford, Worthington Chauncey, compiler. *British Officers Serving in the American Revolution 1774–1783.* Historical Printing Club, Brooklyn, New York, 1897.

— — —. *Letters of William Lee,* Volumes 1–3. Historical Printing Club, Brooklyn, New York, 1891.

— — —. *The Spurious Letters Attributed to Washington.* Privately Printed, Brooklyn, New York, 1889.

Fortescue, Sir John, Editor. *The Correspondence of King George the Third, from 1760 to December 1783.* Macmillan, London, 1928.

Fraser, John A. III. *The Use of Encrypted, Coded and Secret Communications is an "Ancient Liberty" Protected by the United States Constitution. Virginia Journal of Law and Technology,* University of Virginia, Charlottesville, Fall 1997.

French, Allen. *General Gage's Informers.* University of Michigan Press, Ann Arbor, 1932.

Funk, Arville, L. *Revolutionary War Era in Indiana.* ALFCO Publications, Corydon, Indiana, 1975.

Gibbes, Robert Wilson. *Documentary History of the American Revolution: 1776–1782.: Consisting of Letters and Papers Relating to the Contest for Liberty, Chiefly in South Carolina, from Originals in the Possession of the Editor, and Other Sources,* Volume 2. D. Appleton & Company, New York, 1857.

Giles, Herbert Allen. *A Chinese Biographical Dictionary: Gu Jin Xing Shi Zu Pu. Kelly and Walsh.* London, 1898.

— — —, translator. *Sun Tzu on the Art of War, the Oldest Military Treatise in the World.* Luzac and Company, London, 1910.

Gilman, Arthur, editor. *Cambridge of 1776, Extracts from the Diary of Dorothy Dudley.* Reissued Kennikat Press, Port Washington, New York, 1970.

Godwin, Francis. *The Man in the Moone: A Discourse of a Voyage Thither.* John Norton, England, 1638.

Gray, David. *Gray's Narrative.* 1825.

Graydon, Alexander and Littell, John Stockton. *Memoirs of His Own Time: With Reminiscences of the Men and Events of the Revolution.* Lindsay and Blakiston, Philadelphia, 1846.

Great Britain War Office. *By permission of the Right Honourable the Secretary at War: a list of the generals and field-officers as they rank in the Army, of the officers in the several regiments of horse, dragoons, and foot, on the British and Irish establishments: with the dates of their commissions as they rank in each corps and as they rank in the Army : the royal regiment of artillery, Irish artillery, engineers, the marines, and independent companies: governors, lieutenant-governors of His Majesty's garrisons at home and abroad, with their allowances and the officers on half pay, &c.* Printed for J. Millan, London, England, 1778. There are copies in the Library of Congress, United States Military History Institute at Carlisle, Pennsylvania, Brown University, University of Pittsburgh, and the Detroit, Michigan Public Library.

Greene, Nathanael. *Papers of General Nathanael Greene,* Volumes 1–13. University of North Carolina Press, Chapel Hill, North Carolina, 1976–2005.

Greene, Robert and Joost Elffers. *The 33 Strategies of War.* Viking Penguin, New York, 2006.

Greenwood, John. *A Young Patriot in the American Revolution, 1775 1783: The Wartime Services of John Greenwood: A Record of Events Written During the Year 1809 at Such Leisure Moments as the Arduous Duties of a Professional Life Permitted the Dentist to His Excellency George Washington.* Westvaco, 1981.

Grey, Gilbert. *The Complete Fabulist or a Choice Collection of Moral and Entertaining Fables in Prose and Verse.* Thomas Slack, Newcastle Upon Tyne, England, 1732.

Gruber, Ira D., editor. *John Peebles' American War: The Diary of a Scottish Grenadier, 1776–1782.* Stackpole Books, Mechanicsburg, Pennsylvania, 1998.

Haswell, John H. "Secret Writing." *The Century Illustrated Monthly Magazine*. Century Company, New York, Volume LXXXV, New Series Volume LXIII, November 1912–April 1913.

Heath, William. *Heath's Memoirs of the American War*. A. Wessels Company, New York, 1904, a reprint of *Memoirs of Major-General Heath*, I. Thomas and E. T. Andrews, Albany, New York and Worcester, Massachusetts, 1798.

Heitman, Francis B. *Historical Register of Officers of the Continental Army during the War of the Revolution, April, 1775 to December, 1783*. Rare Book Shop Publishing Company, Washington, D.C., 1914.

The Historical Magazine, and notes and queries concerning the antiquities, history, and biography of America. C. B. Richardson, Boston, 1857–1875.

Historical Manuscript Commission, *Manuscripts of the Earl of Dartmouth, American Papers*, Volume II, 14th Report, Appendix, Part X, 1895, reprinted Gregg Press, Boston, 1972.

———. Report on American Manuscripts in the Royal Institution of Great Britain, Volume 1, Sir Guy Carleton Papers.

———. Report on American Manuscripts in the Royal Institution of Great Britain, Volume 3, Henry Clinton, Guy Carleton Dorchester. Mackie and Company, London, 1907.

Hopkins, William. *The Flying Pen-Man or the Art of Short Writing by a more easie exact compendious and speedy way composed by William Hopkins author and teacher of the said art*, CH. printer, London, 1674. [Samuel Lee, London, England printed the 1680 edition.].

Huefeland, Otto. *Westchester County [New York] During the American Revolution 1775–1783*. Westchester County Historical Society, White Plains, New York, 1926.

Hunt, Gaillard. *Fragments of Revolutionary History*. Historical Printing Club, Brooklyn, New York, 1892.

Jackson, Donald and Twohigs, Dorothy, editors. *The Diaries of George Washington*. Volumes III and VIII. 1771–75 and 1780–81. University Press of Virginia, Charlottesville, 1978.

Johnston, Henry P. *Connecticut Military Records 1775–1848*. The Case Lockwood and Brainard Company, Hartford, Connecticut, 1889.

———. *The Correspondence and Public Papers of John Jay*. Putnam, New York, 1890.

Journals of the Continental Congress, 1774–1789, ed. Worthington C. Ford et al., Washington, D.C., 1904–1937.

Kahn, David. *The Code Breakers*. Macmillan, New York, 1967, 7th printing, 1972.

Kelby, William, compiler. *Orderly Book of the Three Battalions of Loyalists Commanded by Brigadier General Oliver De Lancey, 1776–1778*. Genealogical Publishers Company, Baltimore, 1972.

Kellogg, Louise Phelps, editor. *Frontier Retreat on the Upper Ohio, 1779–1781*. Wisconsin State Historical Society, Madison, 1917.

Keppel, George, Thomas (6th Earl of Albermarle). *Memoirs of the Marquis of Rockingham* [Charles Watson-Wentworth] *and his Contemporaries*, Volume II. Richard Bentley, London, 1852.

Kinnan, M. E. *Order Book Kept by Peter Kinnan July 7–September 4, 1776.* Privately Printed at the Princeton University Press, Princeton, New Jersey, 1931.

Kitman, Marvin. *George Washington's Expense Account.* Simon and Schuster, New York, 1970.

Lederer, Jr., Richard M. *Colonial American English.* Verbatim Book, Essex, Connecticut, 1985.

Lee, Richard Henry and Lee, Arthur. Life of Arthur Lee, LL. D.: *Joint Commissioner of the United States to the Court of France, and Sole Commissioner to the Courts of Spain and Prussia, During the Revolutionary War. With His Political and Literary Correspondence and His Papers on Diplomatic and Political Subjects, and the Affairs of the United States During the Same Period*, Volume II. Wells and Lilly, Boston, 1829.

Letters of Delegates to Congress, *1774–1789*, 25 volumes, Smith, Paul H., et al., eds. Washington, D.C.: Library of Congress, 1976–2000.

Littell, John Stockton, editor. *Memoirs of his own time with Reminiscences of the Men and Events of the Revolution by Alexander Graydon.* Lindsay and Blakiston, Philadelphia, 1846.

Longstreet, Elias S. "Fourth of July–1776." *Asbury Park Sunday Press*, Asbury Park, New Jersey, June 30, 1935.

Longueville, Thomas. *Marshall Turenne.* Longmans, Green and Company, London, 1907.

Loprieno, Don. Pompey Lamb Revisited Black Soldiers in the American Revolution at http://www2.lhric.org/spbattle/Pomp.html.

Lossing, Benson John. *The Pictorial Field-book of the Revolution ; Or, Illustrations, by Pen and Pencil, of the History, Biography, Scenery, Relics, and Traditions of the War for Independence: Or, Illustrations, by Pen and Pencil, of the History, Biography, Scenery, Relics, and Traditions of the War for Independence*, Volume 1 and 2. Harper and Brothers, New York, 1851–1860.

Love, William DeLoss. *The Colonial History of Hartford.* Connecticut Printers Inc., Hartford, Connecticut, 1935. Reprinted by Centinel Hill Press in association with the Pequot Press, Chester, Connecticut, 1974.

Lucas, Reginald. *Lord North, 1732–1792*, Volume I. Arthur L. Humphreys, London, 1913.

Lundin, Leonard. *Cockpit of the Revolution: The War for Independence in New Jersey.* Princeton University Press, Princeton, New Jersey, 1940.

Mackenzie, Frederick. *Diary of Frederick Mackenzie.* Harvard University Press, Cambridge, Massachusetts, 1930.

Magazine of American History, Volume II (1878) New York, Volumes 1–30, January 1877 to September 1893.

Martin, Joseph Plumb. *Private Yankee Doodle.* Eastern Acorn Press, Yorktown, Virginia, 1962.

Maryland State Archives Series, http://www.aomol.net/html/volumes.html. 1883 to present.

Mather, Frederic Gregory. *The Refugees of 1776 from Long Island to Connecticut.* J. B. Lyon, Albany, New York, 1913.

McClellan, William Smith. *Smuggling in the American Colonies at the Outbreak of the Revolution: With Special Reference to the West Indies Trade.* Printed for the Department of Political Science of Williams College by Moffat, Yard and Company, New York, 1912.

McCormick, Richard Patrick. *Experiment in Independence: New Jersey in the Critical Period, 1781–1789.* Rutgers University Press, New Brunswick, New Jersey, 1950.

McLean, Renwick. "Madrid Suspects Tied to E-mail Ruse." *International Herald Tribune,* April 28, 2006.

Mississippi Provincial Archives, English Dominion (MPAED) (transcripts). Mississippi Department of Archives and History, Jackson, Mississippi.

Mississippi Provincial Archives, Spanish Dominion (MPASD) (transcripts). Mississippi Department of Archives and History, Jackson, Mississippi.

Monthly Review or Literary Journal, Volume LVI. R. Griffiths, London, 1777.

Monthly Review or Literary Journal Enlarged, Volume XXI. R. Griffiths, London, 1796.

Morato, Fuluio Pellegrino. *Del significato de colori e de mazzolli: operetta.* Venice: Francesco de Leno, 1559.

Morris, Ira. *History of Staten Island,* Volume 1. Memorial Publishing Company, New York, 1898.

Morse, Jedidiah. *The American Gazetteer.* Thomas and Andrews, Boston, 1810.

Nagy, John A. *Rebellion in the Ranks: Mutinies of the American Revolution.* Westholme Publishing, Yardley, Pennsylvania, 2007.

National Security Administration. United States Cryptologic History, Sources in Cryptologic History Number 3. Center for Cryptologic History, Fort Meade, Maryland, 1992.

Naval Documents of the American Revolution. U.S. Government Printing Office, Washington, D.C. Series Volumes 1 to 11 to date.

Nelme, Lemuel Dole. *An Essay Towards an Investigation of the Origin and Elements of Language.* S. Leacroft, London, 1772.

Nelson, William, Editor. *Plain Dealer Newspaper,* Issue Number 2, January 1776 in *Plain Dealer, the First Newspaper in New Jersey.* Privately Printed, 1894.

Nesmith, George W. "Journal of Abbé Robin Chaplain of Count Rochambeau's Army, Relating to the Revolution," *The Granite Monthly,* Volume 4. John McClintock, Concord, New Hampshire, 1881.

New American Bible, Catholic Bible Publishers, Wichita, Kansas, 1988.

New England Historical and Genealogical Register, Volume 19 (1865) and 27 (1873). New England Historical & Genealogical Society, Boston, 1847 to present.

New Jersey Archives, First Series, Volume 9 and Series 2, Volume 4. Daily

Advertising Printing House, Newark, New Jersey, Series of 47 volumes, 1880–1949.

New Jersey Historical Society Proceedings, Third Series, Volume III; New Series, Volume VII, Number 1; and New Series XII, New Jersey Historical Society, Newark, New Jersey.

New-York Historical Society. *Collections of the New-York Historical Society for the Year 1875,* "Official Letters of Major General James Pattison and 1878."

———. *Collections of the New-York Historical Society for the Year 1882,* "von Kraft's Journal."

Norman, Bruce. *Secret Warfare, the Battle of Codes and Ciphers.* David and Charles, Newton Abbot, England, 1973.

North American and West Indian Gazetteer, 2nd Edition. G. Robinson, Pater Noster Row, London, 1778.

Orcutt, Samuel and Beardsley, Ambrose. *The History of the Old Town of Derby, Connecticut, 1642–1880: With Biographies and Genealogies.* Press of Springfield Printing Company, Springfield, Massachusetts, 1880.

Palmer, Frederick. *Clark of Ohio–A Life of George Rogers Clark.* Dodd, Mead and Company, New York, 1929.

Paltists, Victor Hugo, editor. *Minutes of the Commissioners for Detecting and Defeating Conspiracies in the State of New York.* State of New York, Albany, New York, Volume I 1778–1779 (1909), Volume II 1780–1781 (1909), and Volume III Analytical Index (1910).

Papers of Benjamin Franklin. Yale University Press, New Haven, Connecticut (1959–) and http://www.franklinpapers.org/franklin/.

Papers of the Continental Congress both published and microfilm.

Papers of Thomas Jefferson Series, Volume 1. Princeton University Press, Princeton, New Jersey, 1950.

Parker, Wyman W. *Connecticut's Colonial and Continental Money.* American Revolution Bicentennial Commission, Hartford, Connecticut, Volume XVIII, 1976.

Peckham, Howard Henry. *Sources of American Independence, Volumes I and II.* University of Chicago Press, Chicago, 1978.

———, editor. *Memoirs of the Life of John Adlum in the Revolutionary War.* Caxton Club, Chicago, 1968.

———. *The Toll of Independence—Engagements and Battle Casualties of the American Revolution.* University of Chicago Press, Chicago, 1974.

Pennsylvania Archives [1st series]: selected and arranged from original documents in the Office of the Secretary of the Commonwealth. J. Stevens, Philadelphia, 1852–1856.

Pennsylvania Evening Post, Philadelphia, 1777.

Pennsylvania Magazine of History and Biography. Historical Society of Pennsylvania, Philadelphia, 1877 to present.

Pennsylvania Packet Newspaper, Philadelphia, 1775 and 1776.

Pennypacker, Morton. *General Washington's Spies on Long Island and in New York.* Long Island Historical Society, Brooklyn, New York, 1939.

Plat, Sir Hugh. *The Jewel House of Art and Nature.* Elizabeth Alsop, London, 1653.

Poe, Edgar Allan. *The Gold Bug.* George Routledge and Sons, London, 1894.

Polmar, Norman and Allen, Thomas B. *Spy Book: The Encyclopedia of Espionage.* Random House, New York, 1997.

Potter, Chandler Eastman. *The Military History of the State of New Hampshire, 1623–1861* in two volumes 1866 and 1868. Reprint by Genealogical Publishing Company, Baltimore, 1972.

Prince, Carl E., editor. *The Papers of William Livingston,* 5 Volumes. New Jersey Historical Commission, Trenton, New Jersey, 1979. Also Microfilm edition for unpublished papers on the Pennsylvania Line Mutiny.

Proceedings of the Massachusetts Historical Society Series. Massachusetts Historical Society, Boston.

Randolph, John and John Vardill. *Letters from General Washington, to several of his friends in the year 1776. In which are set forth a fairer and fuller view of American politics, than ever yet transpired, or the public could be made acquainted with through any other channel.* John Bew, London, 1777.

Rankin, Hugh F. *North Carolina Continentals.* University of North Carolina Press, Chapel Hill, 1971.

Robertson, William Spence. Francisco de Miranda and the Revolutionizing of Spanish America. United State Government Printing Office, Washington, District of Columbia, 1909 Reprinted from the *Annual Report of the American Historical Association for 1907,* Volume 1: 189–540.

Rose, Alexander. *Washington's Spies: The Story of America's First Spy Ring.* Bantam Dell, New York, 2006.

Ross, Charles. *Correspondence of Charles First Marquis Cornwallis,* Volume 1. John Murray, London, 1859.

Sabine, William H. W., editor. *Historical Memoirs of William Smith 1763–1778,* Volume 2. New York Times and Arno Press, New York, 1969.

– – –. *Historical Memoirs of William Smith 1778–1783.* New York Times and Arno Press, New York, 1971.

Schoenbrun, David. *Triumph in Paris: The Exploits of Benjamin Franklin.* Harper and Row, New York, 1976.

Scott, Kenneth. "A British Counterfeiting Press in New York Harbor." *New-York Historical Society Quarterly,* 1955.

– – –, compiler. *Rivington's New York Newspaper Excerpts from a Loyalist Press 1773–1783.* New-York Historical Society, New York, 1973.

Scoville, Joseph Alfred. *The Old Merchants of New York City.* G. W. Carleton Publisher, New York, 1866.

Sellers, Charles Coleman. *Patience Wright American Artist and Spy in George III's London.* Wesleyan University Press, Middletown, Connecticut, 1976.

Shelton, Thomas. *TachyGraphy, The Most Exact and Compendious Methode of Short and Swift Writing that Ever Beene Published by Any.* Samuel Cartwright, London, 1641.

Simms, Jeptha Root. *History of Schoharie County, and Border Wars of New York: Containing Also a Sketch of the Causes which Led to the American Revolution; and Interesting Memoranda of the Mohawk Valley . . . Illustrated with More Than Thirty Engravings.* Munsell and Tanner, printers, Albany, New York, 1845.

Smith, Elizabeth Oakes Prince. *The Salamander: A Legend for Christmas, Found Amongst the Papers of the Late Ernest Helfenstein.* George P. Putnam, New York, 1848.

Smith, William. *A Natural History of Nevis and the rest of the English Leeward Charibee Islands in America with many other observations on nature and art; particularly an introduction to the art of Decyphering [sic] in eleven letters from the Reverend Mr. [William] Smith sometime rector of St. John's at Nevis and now rector of St. Mary's in Bedford, to Reverend Mr. Mason, B.D. Woodwardian professor and fellow of Trinity College in Cambridge.* J. Bentham, Cambridge, England, 1745.

Smith, William Henry, arranger and annotator. *The St. Clair Papers.* Robert Clarke and Company, Cincinnati, 1882.

South Carolina Historical and Genealogical Magazine. South Carolina Historical Society, Charleston, South Carolina, 1900 to present.

Sparks, Jared, editor. *The Diplomatic Correspondence of the American Revolution,* Volume 6. Boston: 1830.

Stark, Caleb. *Memoir and Official Correspondence of Gen[eral]. John Stark with Notices of Several Other Officers of the Revolution. Also, a Biography of Capt[ain]. Phineas Stevens, and of Col[onel]. Robert Rogers, with an Account of His Services in America During the "Seven Years' War."* G. Parker Lyon, Concord, New Hampshire, 1860. Reprinted by Gregg Press, Boston, 1972.

Stevens, Benjamin F. *The Campaign in Virginia, 1781. An exact reprint of six rare pamphlets on the Clinton-Cornwallis controversy, with very numerous important unpublished manuscript notes by Sir Henry Clinton, K.B., and the omitted and hitherto unpublished portions of the letters in their appendixes added from the original manuscripts.* London, 1888.

———. *Facsimiles of Manuscripts in European Archives Relating to America 1773–1783,* 25 Volumes, 1889–1895, reprint by Mellifont Press, Wilmington, Delaware, 1970.

———. General Sir William Howe's Orderly Book at Charlestown, Boston, and Halifax. London, 1890, reprinted Kennikat Press, Port Washington, New York, 1970.

———. *Report on American Manuscripts in the Royal Institution of Great Britain.* John Falconer, Dublin, 1906.

Striker, William Scudder. *Official Register of the Officers and Men of New Jersey in the Revolutionary War.* W. T. Nicholson and Company, Trenton, New Jersey, 1872.

Tallmadge, Benjamin. *Memoir of Colonel Benjamin Tallmadge.* Thomas Holman, Book and Job Printer, New York, 1858, Reprinted by New York Times and Arno Press, New York, 1968.

Tarleton, Lieutenant Colonel Banastre, A History of the Campaigns of 1780 and 1781 in the Southern Provinces of North America. T. Cadell, London, 1787, Reprinted by New York Times and Arno Press, New York, 1968.

Thacher, James. A military journal during the American Revolutionary war, from 1775 to 1783... by James Thacher, M.D. Late surgeon in the American Army. Cottons & Barnard, Boston, 1827.

Thicknesse, Philip. A Treatise on the Art of Decyphering, and of Writing in Cypher: With an Harmonic Alphabet. W. Brown, London, 1772.

Thomas, Isaiah. The History of Printing in America. Weathervane Books, New York, 1970.

Thompson, Edmund R., editor. Secret New England, Spies of the American Revolution. David Atlee Phillips New England Chapter, Association of Former Intelligence Officers, Kennebunk, Maine, 1991.

Tilghman, Oswald. Memoir of Lieutenant Colonel Tench Tilghman Secretary and Aide to Washington. J. Munsell, Albany, New York, 1876.

Trithemius, Johannes. Polygraphiae libri sex, Ioannis trithemii... Würzburg, 1518.

Trumbull, Henry. Life and Remarkable Adventures of Israel R. Potter. J. Howard, Providence, Rhode Island, 1824.

Tyler, Lyon Garner. Encyclopedia of Virginia Biography. Lewis Historical Publishing Company, New York, 1915.

Uhlendorf, Bernhard A., translator and annotator. Revolution in America: Confidential Letters and Journals 1776–1784 of the Adjutant General Major Baurmeister of the Hessian Forces. Rutgers University Press, New Brunswick, New Jersey, 1957. The original journal is part of the Von Jungkenn Papers in the William L. Clements Library, Ann Arbor, Michigan.

United States Army, Department of the Army General Staff. History of Military Intelligence Division, 1775–1941.

United States Department of Justice, Federal Bureau of Investigation, Famous Cases, Rudoplh Ivanovich Abel (Hollow Nickel case) at http://www.fbi.gov/libref/historic/famcases/abel/abel.htm.

—— —. Federal Bureau of Investigation, Famous Cases, Robert Philip Hanssen Espionage Case, February 20, 2001 at http://www.fbi.gov/libref/historic/famcases/hanssen/hanssen.htm.

—— —. Press Release, April 30, 2009 at http://www.usdoj.gov/opa/pr/2009/April/09-nsd-415.html.

United States Navy. Dictionary of American Naval Fighting Ships at http://www.history.navy.mil/danfs.

Upton, Leslie Francis Stokes. The Loyal Whig: William Smith of New York and Quebec. University of Toronto Press, Toronto, Canada, 1969.

Valentine, D. T. Manual of the Corporation City of New York. 1857 and 1863.

Van Doren, Carl. Benjamin Franklin. Viking Press, New York, 1938.

—— —. Secret History of the American Revolution. Viking Press, New York, 1941.

Vattel, Emer de. Le droit des gens, ou Principes de la loi naturelle, appliqués à la conduite et aux affaires des nations et des souverains. Harrevelt, Amsterdam, 1775.

Virginia Gazette of Dixon and Nicolson, Williamsburg, Virginia, 1779.

Virginia Magazine of History and Biography. Virginia Historical Society, Richmond, Virginia, 1893 to present.

Ward, Harry M. *General William Maxwell and the New Jersey Continentals.* Greenwood Press, Westport, Connecticut, 1997.

Watson, Winslow C., editor. *Men and Times of the Revolution: or Memoirs of Elkanah Watson.* Dana and Company, New York, 1856.

Weber, Ralph Edward. *Masked Dispatches: Cryptograms and Cryptology in American History, 1775–1900.* Center for Cryptologic History, National Security Agency, Fort George G. Meade, Maryland, 1993.

— — —. *United States Diplomatic Codes and Ciphers: 1775–1938.* Precedent Publishing Inc., Chicago, 1979.

Weelan, Jean Edmond. *Rochambeau, father and son; a life of the Maréchal de Rochambeau,* by Jean-Edmond Weelen and the Journal of the Vicomte de Rochambeau (hitherto unpublished) translated by Lawrence Lee with a preface by Gilbert Chinard. H. Holt and Company, New York, 1936.

Westby-Gibson, John. *The Bibliography of Shorthand.* Isaac, Pitman and Sons, Bath, England, 1887.

Wharton, Francis. *The Revolutionary Diplomatic Correspondence of the United States,* 6 Volumes. Government Printing Office, Washington, D.C., 1889.

Whisenhunt, Donald W., editor. *Delegate from New Jersey–The Journal of John Fell.* National University Publications, Kennikat Press, Port Washington, New York, 1973.

Wilkins, John. *Mercury, or the Secret and Swift Messenger.* I. Norton, London, 1641.

Willard, Margaret Wheeler, editor. *Letters on the American Revolution 1774–1776.* Houghton Mifflin, Boston, 1924; reprinted Kennikat Press, Port Washington, New York, 1968.

Willcox, William B. *The American Rebellion: Sir Henry Clinton's Narrative of his Campaigns, 1775–1782, with an Appendix of Original Documents.* Yale University Press, New Haven, Connecticut, 1954.

William and Mary Quarterly. Omohundro Institute of Early American History and Culture, Williamsburg, Virginia, 1892–present.

Winslow, Eugene. *Afro-Americans '76 : Black Americans in the Founding of Our Country.* Afro-Am Publishing Company, Chicago, 1975.

Worcester, Marquis of (Edward L. Herbert). *A Century of the Names and Scantlings of Such Inventions . . .* J. Grismond, London, 1663.

INDEX